The Complete Book of Dog Health

The Complete Book of

DOG HEALTH

THE ANIMAL MEDICAL CENTER

William J. Kay, DVM, Chief of Staff

with Elizabeth Randolph

Illustrations by Nancy Lou Makris

HOWELL
BOOK HOUSE
New York

Copyright © 1985 by The Animal Medical Center of New York and
G. S. Sharpe Communications Inc.
Illustrations by Nancy Lou Makris
Photographs by John A. Hettich (except numbers 14 and 16 as noted)
Produced by G. S. Sharpe Communications Inc.

Howell Book House
Macmillan Publishing Company
866 Third Avenue, New York, NY 10022
Collier Macmillan Canada, Inc.

Library of Congress Cataloging-in-Publication Data
The Complete book of dog health / the Animal Medical Center; [edited
  by] William J. Kay with Elizabeth Randolph; illustrations by Nancy
  Lou Makris.—1st paperback ed.
       p.   cm.
  Reprint. Originally published: New York: Macmillan, © 1985.
  Includes bibliographical references (p.).
  ISBN 0-87605-455-6
  1. Dogs—Health. 2. Dogs—Diseases. I. Kay, William J.
II. Randolph, Elizabeth.   III. Animal Medical Center (U.S.)
[SF991.C66   1990]   89-28170   CIP
636.7′089—dc20

Macmillan books are available at special discounts for bulk purchases
for sales promotions, premiums, fund-raising, or educational use. For
details, contact:
Special Sales Director
Macmillan Publishing Company
866 Third Avenue
New York, NY 10022

10 9 8 7

First Paperback Edition 1990

Designed by Jacques Chazaud

Printed in the United States of America

In memory of Otis, who gave us many years
of nonjudgmental love and affection.

Acknowledgments

Thanks to all of The Animal Medical Center veterinarians for their cooperation and care in helping me to prepare material in their areas of expertise, and especially to Dr. William J. Kay, Chief of Staff, and Dr. Michael S. Garvey, Chairman of the Departments of Medicine and Surgery, who made this project possible.

Thanks also to those on the nonmedical staff of The AMC who were helpful and encouraging: in particular Joan M. Weich, Director of Public Relations, and Christine MacMurray.

Special and very sincere thanks to Maija Jezina, without whose cheerful persistence this book would never have been completed.

For all of their efforts to make this project a success, many thanks to Genell J. Subak-Sharpe, who put the whole thing together, and Arlene Friedman, our editor at Macmillan.

Elizabeth Randolph

Contents

Photograph 1: The Animal Medical Center

The Animal Medical Center
Contributors to This Book

WILLIAM J. KAY, DVM
Diplomate, American College of Veterinary Internal Medicine
   Specialties of Internal Medicine and Neurology
Chief of Staff
Staff Neurologist

MICHAEL S. GARVEY, DVM
Diplomate, American College of Veterinary Internal Medicine
   Specialty of Internal Medicine
Chairman, Departments of Medicine and Surgery
Staff Internist/Gastroenterology

DAVID P. AUCOIN, DVM
Associate Staff Internist/Clinical Pharmacology

PETER L. BORCHELT, PH.D.
Director, Animal Behavior Clinic

JOSEPH M. CARRILLO, DVM
Diplomate, American College of Veterinary Internal Medicine
   Specialty of Internal Medicine
Staff Internist/Neurology

SUSAN PHILLIPS COHEN, CSW, ACSW
Director of Counseling
Chairperson of The AMC Institute for the Human/Companion Animal Bond

PHILIP R. FOX, DVM
Diplomate, American College of Veterinary Internal Medicine
   Specialty of Cardiology
Director of Clinics
Staff Cardiologist

STEPHEN L. GROSS, VMD
Diplomate, American College of Veterinary Ophthalmologists
Staff Ophthalmologist

KAREN A. HELTON, DVM
Resident in Dermatology

CONNIE E. LEIFER, DVM
Diplomate, American College of Veterinary Internal Medicine
Associate Staff Internist/Oncology

DAVID T. MATTHIESEN, DVM
Associate Staff Surgeon/General Surgery

ROBERT E. MATUS, DVM
Diplomate, American College of Veterinary Internal Medicine
    Specialty of Internal Medicine
Head, Donaldson-Atwood Cancer Clinic
Staff Internist/Oncology

CHERYL J. MEHLHAFF, DVM
Associate Staff Surgeon/General Surgery

KATHLEEN E. NOONE, VMD
Diplomate, American College of Veterinary Internal Medicine
    Specialty of Internal Medicine
Staff Internist/Respiratory Medicine

MARK E. PETERSON, DVM
Diplomate, American College of Veterinary Internal Medicine
    Specialty of Internal Medicine
Staff Internist/Endocrinology

RICHARD C. SCOTT, DVM
Diplomate, American College of Veterinary Internal Medicine
    Specialty of Internal Medicine
Director of Education
Staff Internist/Nephrology

DENNIS A. ZAWIE, DVM
Diplomate, American College of Veterinary Internal Medicine
    Specialty of Internal Medicine
Staff Internist/Gastroenterology

Introduction

The Purpose of This Book

The purpose of this book is to provide dog owners and potential dog owners with the information they need to enjoy a happy life with their pets. How do we propose to do this? By putting together an unparalleled collection of expert advice to help with every aspect of dog ownership. Each contributor to this book is a recognized authority in his or her particular field. Many are recognized Diplomate Veterinary Specialists, experts in their fields. By coupling the enormous diversity of these individuals' knowledge with The Animal Medical Center's seventy-five-year experience in canine veterinary medical practice, this book offers an unbeatable combination of useful information for any dog owner. The information is written in lay terms for both experienced and inexperienced dog owners. Although the problems of dog ownership and dog health are not simple, we have tried to clarify even the most complex topics, from raising newborn pups to the death of a dog. We also include sections on how to recognize symptoms of common canine diseases and disorders and how to deal with the behavior problems that may arise at various stages in a dog's life. In short, we think that this is the only book anyone who owns a pet dog will ever need.

Unfortunately, dog ownership is not always a satisfying experience. More dogs are given up because they don't fit well into their owners' lives than for any other reason. Almost always, the fault lies in unrealistic expectations about what dog ownership entails, what a particular dog is going to be like, and what role that dog is going to play in the owner's life. This is not surprising when we consider that many people choose a puppy without having the faintest idea of what the animal they choose will become and how owning a dog may change their lives. Many also fail to consider the changes that a dog will make in their life-styles. Children will grow up, families may move, and financial circumstances can be altered—potential dog owners should be aware that these things might happen in the lifetime of the average dog. By the same token, people often have no idea what they really want in a pet dog. If potential dog owners would stop to think that the decision to own a dog is one that probably will have a major influence on their lives for an average of fifteen years, they would give that choice much more serious consideration.

This book is filled with information for people who already own a dog. Here, however, I'd

1

like to touch briefly on some points to bear in mind *before* getting a dog. They may help to avoid disappointment and dissatisfaction later on. I do not want to discourage dog ownership in any way; rather, I hope to help people make intelligent choices by being realistic about what owning a dog is really like.

Should You Own a Dog?

Both prospective first-time dog owners and experienced hands at dog ownership should face a few facts before embarking on a relationship with a pet dog. Some general considerations are:

• *Economic:* The overall expense of owning a dog often comes as a rude surprise to a new owner. A dog is not a cheap pet to own. No matter what size or breed you choose, there are certain fixed costs involved in dog ownership. Spaying or neutering operations are desirable for most female and some male pet dogs, and all dogs require regular immunizations. Other kinds of veterinary care can be expensive, too. Major illnesses and injuries can run into thousands of dollars over the course of a dog's lifetime. Dog food can be expensive; it costs a thousand dollars a year to keep a large dog on a simple maintenance diet. Some dogs require professional grooming every four to six weeks; at an average cost of twenty dollars a session, this can add up to several hundred dollars a year. Yearly license fees cost around five dollars in most communities. Owners who plan to travel or take vacations will also have to take boarding or sitter costs (or the cost of transporting a dog with them) into consideration. In addition, no matter how well trained, any dog will add to the wear and tear on furnishings and floors in a home.

• *Time and Energy:* Another important factor to consider is the cost of dog ownership in terms of time and energy. Even if a dog requires a minimum of exercise, thirty minutes twice a day, every day, can add up to 365 hours a year of leisure time, which an owner might spend in other pursuits. Routine training, including housebreaking and obedience, is time-consuming. Specialized training for showing or hunting is more so. Grooming a dog regularly or taking him to a professional groomer; going to the veterinarian for checkups and immunizations—all of these necessities cut into an owner's free time.

• *Disruptions in Routine:* Dog ownership is also likely to result in some disruptions and upsets in a household and in owners' plans and routines. Dogs do get sick and need medications and special care. Accidents will happen, paws will be muddy or wet, and fur will shed. People who have difficulty dealing with any kind of disruption or lack of order in their lives should probably consider owning a different kind of pet, or no pet at all.

All of these considerations can be summarized in one question: Are the things I'll give up—time, money, tidiness, calm, freedom to come and go—worth it to me in order to have a dog? For most dog owners, these sacrifices are negligible compared to the satisfaction they gain from dog ownership.

Choosing a Dog

If your answer to the above question is "yes," the next question is: What kind of dog do I want to get? The reasons why a particular person, or family wants a dog have a great deal to do with the kind of dog they should decide on.

One of the first questions to resolve is: Do I want a purebred dog or a mixed-breed? There are advantages and disadvantages to both types of dog. Purebred dogs have arrived at today's particular point of body conformation, haircoat, temperament, and personality by means of careful genetic selection. A purebred pup raised in ideal conditions by a reliable breeder will grow into an adult dog with the temperament, size, haircoat, etc. he was intended to have. This is very important to many people who know exactly what they want in a dog's looks and performance. Unfortunately, some purebred dogs also have some faults or predispositions toward certain diseases and disorders that have been bred into them over the years. We discuss many of these problems in this book, and we urge you to research the possibilities carefully before you decide on a breed.

Mixed-breed pups are often healthier and hardier than their purebred cousins, avoiding inbred disorders. However, the specifics—adult size, coat, etc.—are highly unpredictable. Some combinations of breeds result in wonderful dogs, comprising the best of both (or many). Others don't end up as well. If a mixed-breed dog appeals to you, try to find out what its parents were. This may help to determine what it is going to grow up to be. Or choose an adult dog to avoid surprises.

It's far better to choose the right dog in the first place than to spend fruitless and frustrating time trying to adapt the wrong dog to your life-style and expectations. Whether you decide on a purebred or mixed breed animal, one of the first points you should consider is the environment you and the dog will be sharing. You don't want to get a fragile dog like a whippet if you have a house full of little boys; nor should you expect a giant dog such as a huge Newfoundland, who needs lots of vigorous exercise every day, to live happily in a studio apartment. Common sense should dictate that the dog's size and exercise requirements as well as its energy level are primary considerations. So is the energy level of the owner. If you love to jog and intend to take your dog on long runs, a short-legged dachshund or a tiny toy breed obviously would not satisfy you. At the same time, a bouncy, strong Labrador retriever would be impossible for a frail person to handle.

In addition to environmental and energy considerations, ask yourself why you and your family want a dog. Will the dog's role be primarily that of a playmate for children, or will it be a cuddly companion for a single adult? Do you want a watchdog or a dog who never barks? What about looks and care? Does your ideal dog have a beautiful long, silky coat, or would you rather have a pet with short, easy-to-care-for fur?

If you've never owned a dog before, how do you find out about all these things? By doing a lot of research. First and foremost, go to dog shows. See and touch the breed you think you might be interested in. Talk to breeders and owners. Observe the breed in action. There are good books and pamphlets about various dog breeds and about choosing dogs. Some of these are listed in the Bibliography at the back of this book. Paperback books about specific breeds are also available in most pet stores. Even more important, because breeders and people who write books about particular breeds are apt to be prejudiced in favor of "their" breed, talk to as many owners as you can, and ask a lot of questions not only about the advantages of a particular breed but also about the breed's drawbacks if any. Ask about the life expectancy of the breed and what special care is required. If you can, borrow a dog for a day or two to see if you really like having *any* dog in your house, and whether you care for that type of dog in particular.

The choice of a dog that will live in close proximity to you and your family for a number of years shouldn't be made on impulse.

Where to Get a Dog

This brings us to a very important question: What is the best source for a satisfactory dog?

There really is no hard and fast answer to this question, and there are always exceptions to any rules. I have known people who have had wonderful relationships with a pet dog they found wandering on the street and others who ended up with an unsatisfactory pet from a well-established breeder. All we can do is to use the law of averages and our years of experience to offer some suggestions.

Pet Stores

In general, pet stores rely on impulse sales made to people who know little about dogs. Pet stores can be the worst places to get a dog. Breeders unknown to them from all over the country supply the puppies they sell. Often, in order to meet seasonal demands, these puppies are taken from their mothers too early; and in many cases they have been shipped long distances in bad conditions. A buyer has no way of knowing if the pup has been bred carelessly in a so-called puppy mill—that is, by people who care only about producing the largest possible number of salable animals in the shortest amount of time, with no consideration for proper genetics and health needs. The result may be a pup who, although he looks healthy, can be incubating a contagious disease and will sicken in a week or two (see the section on immunization in Chapter 3) or one who may develop one of a number of genetic health and/or personality problems brought about by careless breeding. What's more, the "guarantee" given by many pet stores will usually expire before any of these problems surface.

There are, of course, exceptions. If the small local pet store that's been in business downtown for twenty years has a litter of pups for sale, it will usually be from a local source, and potential buyers will be able to obtain information about the puppies and firm guarantees as to their health and parentage.

Individuals

Advertisements abound in the newspapers, especially around holiday times, from individuals who have a litter of pups for sale. Buyers should beware, unless they know the individuals or have some way of judging the health and soundness of the mother and puppies. Unfortunately, irresponsible people often try to cash in on the popularity of a particular breed or type of dog and hope to lure buyers with cut-rate prices. The trouble is that these people usually know little about genetics or proper breeding and health procedures. The end result may be pups with built-in problems.

Pounds and Shelters

Most animal shelters, humane societies, and pounds have a number of dogs for adoption. A visit to several of these organizations may help a potential adopter locate a suitable pet.

Very often full-grown animals far outnumber puppies in shelters. People should realize that these dogs are often not "rejects," but are there because their owners had to give them up. A grown dog can be a good choice, especially for a first-time pet owner, as many health-care and training routines attendant on owning a puppy have already been taken care of. In addition, a grown, mixed-breed dog will already be mature as far as size and coat are concerned. Choosing a mixed-breed puppy from a shelter can be somewhat risky unless the previous owners have given some indication of its parentage, but many happy dog owners who are not fussy have taken their chances.

Occasionally, full or half-grown purebred dogs will show up in a shelter. If you have a particular breed of dog in mind and would consider adopting one, get in touch with your local shelter so that they can let you know if the breed of your choice should come in.

Breeders

Breeders and kennels usually specialize in one or two breeds of dogs. Most are serious about their work and devoted to producing sound specimens of the breed. Many are very particular about who owns their dogs and won't allow just anyone to purchase one.

The American Kennel Club (AKC) can provide a list of registered breeders of the 124 breeds of dog that it recognizes. Its address is in the Bibliography. There are some excellent dog breeds that are not yet recognized by the AKC. A list of these breed clubs is also in the Bibliography.

Once you have decided on a particular breed, try to visit several different breeders before making a selection. Different "lines," or variations of the same breed, may appeal to you because of color, size, temperament, etc., and you will be better able to make a good choice after seeing a lot of puppies. The only way to know for sure if the pup you choose is going to grow up to look the way you want is to see both its parents. Don't buy a dog from a breeder who won't let you do this. By the way, don't be put off if a breeder offers you a less expensive "pet-quality" puppy. This is not an inferior dog. It probably has a tiny imperfec-tion that disqualifies it as a show specimen but will not affect its suitability as a pet at all.

Breed clubs and associations often have list-ings of purebreds who have been given up by their owners. These dogs will often make ex-cellent pets and are, of course, a great deal less expensive than a new purebred puppy.

Caring for a Dog

Once you have chosen and brought home a dog, the information in this book will help you make decisions about everyday care—choos-ing a veterinarian, feeding and exercising a dog, and so forth.

New pet owners are very often confused about the specifics of health care. One of the most common health care issues is learning to recognize when a dog requires medical atten-tion. Many owners simply do not know and end up making errors that range from panic over a slight limp to waiting to "see what will happen" to a dog who's been struck by a car. There are several chapters in this book de-signed to help owners avoid these mistakes: Chapter 11 includes the symptoms most com-monly seen in dogs and their possible signifi-cance. The Encyclopedia of Diseases of Dogs has more detail about specific illnesses and diseases of dogs. There is also a complete Emergencies section.

Many owners are under the mistaken impression that they have to live with their dog's misbehavior. Not so. Chapter 8 discusses the most common canine behavior problems and helps owners to know how to deal with them.

All of this information will help a dog owner know what to do about what's going on with a pet. It will also help an owner to know when to seek help and to be able to judge the effec-tiveness of that help intelligently so that fur-ther steps can be taken if needed.

This book is unique in its scope, diversity, and expert sources of information. There is no other book like it. It is written to give dog own-ers all the help they need to have mutually satisfying experiences with their dogs.

William J. Kay, DVM, Chief of Staff
The Animal Medical Center

PART ONE

A

HEALTHY

DOG

1

Veterinary Care

WILLIAM J. KAY, DVM

The Rise of Companion-
Animal Veterinary Medicine

People have had dogs as pets and helpers for hundreds of years, but until the second or third decade of the twentieth century, the large-scale practice of companion-animal veterinary medicine did not exist. In the past, dogs and other pets did receive some sort of medical care when they were ill or injured, but this care was often performed either by physicians or laymen who had little if any scientific knowledge about small-animal medicine.

Early in this century, most veterinarians maintained large-animal practices, treating mainly food-producing animals and horses. At about the time of the Great Depression, several factors combined to cause more veterinarians to concentrate on "small companion animals," or pets. Many farmers were unable to spend a great deal of money on veterinary care for their livestock, and horses were nearly replaced by the automobile. At the same time, animal hospitals and veterinary practices devoted to small-animal care were rapidly multiplying, especially in urban areas.

At this point small-animal care was generally unsophisticated and often poor. There were few standards or guidelines covering the essentials of a good small-animal hospital or clinic, and the scientific information available on the care of pets was relatively meager. In 1933, the American Animal Hospital Association (AAHA) was founded by a small group of veterinarians to establish standards for facilities, equipment, and procedures and also to serve as a continuing-education and information-sharing organ for companion-animal veterinarians and the pet-owning public.

With the establishment of the AAHA, small-animal care became a well-defined area of veterinary medicine. However, modern pet practice really began to develop with the evolution of veterinary medical colleges. At the end of World War II, there were only ten accredited veterinary medical colleges in the United States. Now there are twenty-seven, with more in the process of development. As these colleges developed, they began to change their emphasis. Schools that once primarily produced veterinarians trained in the arts and skills of food-animal and equine practice, today train veterinarians skilled in all animal species, including pets. Now, more and more of the curriculum in veterinary schools is devoted to the study of the diseases of pets (including small birds, reptiles, etc.). And as the public's interest grows, state legislatures implement more curriculum changes, both for reasons of public health and from a growing awareness of the importance of pets to the well-being of people.

A second development that has helped to legitimize pet practice is the formation of specialties in small-animal medicine. Specialization in the study of small-animal veterinary medicine began in the late 1940s and has grown to the point where now about 6–7 percent of the veterinarians in this country have practical expertise in one of about a dozen areas. These areas of expertise include: cardi-ology, clinical pathology, dermatology, internal medicine (which includes gastroenterology, nephrology, oncology, etc.), neurology, ophthalmology, pathology, reproductive disorders, respiratory medicine, surgery, and zoological medicine. Veterinarians must take special training and pass rigorous examinations to become specialists, or Diplomates, in their areas of expertise. These specialists often practice in large veterinary institutions, including veterinary universities throughout the country. There are also many in private practice.

Veterinary Medicine Today

Today, we have a large number of professionals directing a significant amount of time, energy, and talent into training young people to be veterinarians. When they graduate, these young veterinarians may go to postgraduate studies and specialization, or they may go directly into pet practice.

We also have a higher and higher level of skill, and an emerging body of knowledge, either research-based or founded on scientific clinical experience. This growing data base gives veterinarians access to more and more information that they can use to ascertain what can be done to cure pets and improve their health. In this way, the development of veterinary medicine parallels the development of human medicine.

Veterinary medicine is a field in which new scientific developments and treatments arise continuously. There are new areas, new skills, new methods of treatment (acupuncture is now practiced at The AMC, for example), even newly recognized disciplines developing regularly. Within each general discipline there may be six or seven different subdisciplines. For example, as we mentioned, there are a number of subdisciplines in internal medicine. Generally, specialists in these very specific subdisciplines limit their practice to institutions, urban areas, and large groups of veterinarians who have gathered together to form a clinic, or group practice. There are now a number of veterinarians skilled and certified in general veterinary practice, which is comparable to the popular family general practice. Members of this group are called Diplomates, The American Board of Veterinary Practitioners.

Cost of Veterinary Care

This brings us to an emerging problem: The cost of this new technology and specialization will in many cases outstrip the public's ability to pay. Even now, pet owners who are aware of available services may have to make difficult choices about the level and amount of medical care they can and want to provide for their dogs. This distance between what is available and what the public can pay will widen as time goes on. And there will be an increasing differential in pet health care, based on an owner's personal economics, his or her understanding of the types of pet health care available, and his or her willingness to seek or choose a particular level of care. Some owners will choose to provide as much care as is available, but many others will not.

Although a relatively large medical bill for a dog only ranges between $500 and $3,000, as opposed to $20,000 to $30,000 or more for comparable human care, this places a financial burden on many people. Pet health insurance (PHI) may be the answer. In the past, many PHI plans failed, leading to skepticism and mistrust. However, now several companies have developed PHI plans that are viable and relatively inexpensive. These plans are available in several states, and it is reasonable to expect that as pet health care costs rise there will be more plans available within easy economic reach of the pet-owning public. Although health insurance for dogs is not necessarily a lifesaving issue, since a terminally ill pet may still be euthanized at its owner's discretion, PHI is a good idea for people who want to protect themselves against a large pet medical bill. Because PHI is not available in all areas and plans differ widely, and new plans are becoming available all the time, an owner interested in PHI should discuss it with her veterinarian.

Connections Between Human Medicine and Veterinary Medicine

Human beings and other animals share the same environment, and in the biological domain of dogs and humans there are diseases common to both species and diseases that are similar in both species. The more we know and understand about diseases and disease processes in dogs, the more we will know about these same diseases in people. The process of studying a specific disease in dogs and using what is learned to treat humans with the same disease is called comparative medicine. Veterinarians and physicians often work together and use data gathered from one species in treating another. Moreover, diseases need not be identical to be useful as study models. More and more articles are written, lectures given, and study groups held about this cross-referencing of knowledge in human and animal medicine.

There are many examples in which a disease or condition in dogs has had an impact on the further understanding or treatment of the same disease or condition in humans. The most useful thing for dog owners to know in this context is that dogs can, and do, suffer from many of the same diseases and disorders as humans.

Choosing a Veterinarian

With all of the knowledge and specialization in the field of small-animal and companion-animal medicine, how can dog owners know which veterinarian listed in the phone book will be a satisfactory doctor for them and their pets? Like dentists, lawyers, and physicians, veterinarians vary a great deal in qualifications and ability. A dog owner may be disappointed in the veterinarian he has chosen. Often the discovery that the choice of doctor has been unsatisfactory does not occur until an emergency, serious illness, or other health crisis arises.

Dog owners should have an idea of what services they expect from a veterinarian before they choose one. If what is wanted is solely routine care—yearly immunizations and possibly routine surgery, such as an ovariohysterectomy or a neutering operation—the choice may not be that crucial. Most veterinary services can be delivered by all veterinarians, and if an owner does not feel the need for a full-service doctor for a dog, he can shop around and find low-cost clinics that will perform most routine procedures. And for the ultimate in convenience, there are even mobile veterinarians who travel through communities in vans.

But the dog owner whose pet is an important part of the family will want more than this kind of piecemeal doctoring. Most dog owners want to establish a sound relationship with a veterinarian, just as they would with a pediatrician or dentist. The veterinarian, too, requires some time and experience with both the animal and owner in order to be truly effective.

A good first step in selecting a veterinarian is to ask someone who is knowledgeable about dogs and who has had extensive experience with dogs. A local breeder is often a good source of information. Other pet owners and neighbors are not necessarily the best people to ask for recommendations, as their standards may differ, and their assessment of a veterinarian may be based on subjective, rather than objective, measures.

A prospective client should make an objective evaluation of an animal hospital or clinic. The building need not be supermodern or fancy, but: Is the physical plant clean? Are the personnel dressed neatly and attractively? Does the business appear to be well-run, with good record-keeping and accounting procedures? Are the equipment and facilities up-to-date and adequate?

Since there is no way that an average owner can make an intelligent assessment of the equipment and facilities required for pet medical care, it is good to know that there are professional associations that set high standards as prerequisites for membership. The American Animal Hospital Association and the state veterinary medical associations have very exacting standards regarding the equipment, procedures, and physical facilities of animal hospitals. Animal hospitals that are members of one of these organizations must comply with strict standards and are subjected to periodic examinations. Membership in the AAHA, for example, indicates that a doctor follows a set of standards for pet medical care and hospital management. For a list of local AAHA-member hospitals, interested pet owners can write to AAHA headquarters.* AAHA can also be helpful to dog owners who are moving to another community or state by providing them with a list of local member hospitals.

There is a variety of different types of pet medical-care facilities to choose from. In large urban areas and in locations where there is a veterinary medical college, dog owners have access to large veterinary hospitals where there are specialists in nearly every facet of small-animal medicine and surgery. In many urban areas small groups of veterinarians with different specialties have joined together to form group practices. Many private practitioners have also formed group practices and have

*Send a self-addressed stamped envelope to: American Animal Hospital Association, P.O. Box 768, Mishawaka, IN 46544

arrangements with specialists to visit on a regular basis. In smaller communities and areas, three or more veterinarians may practice together, often pooling their resources to purchase sophisticated equipment and to subscribe to one or more of the many services now available, such as phone-accessed electrocardiograms, etc. About 75 percent of the veterinarians in the United States practice with one or two other veterinarians.

A dog owner should know what kind of veterinarian she wants before selecting a doctor for her pet. Is the veterinarian a generalist or a specialist? If he is a specialist, in what area? If he is not a specialist, can arrangements be made when one is needed? Does he have a working relationship or referral arrangement with a cardiologist, a surgeon, and an ophthalmologist, or with a larger hospital or institution

Photograph 2: Small dogs are usually placed on a table to be examined by a veterinarian. Here, Dr. William J. Kay looks over a dog, assisted by Dr. Karen A. Helton.

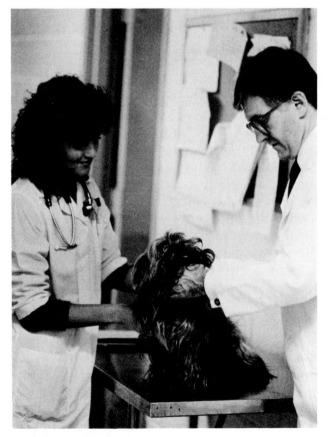

with specialists on staff? If a generalist claims not to need access to these kinds of specialties, the dog owner should probably go elsewhere. The owner should also find out if the doctor's practice is limited to small-animal medicine or is a mixed practice. Bear in mind that it is hard to be an expert in several different species today.

These are legitimate questions to ask in order to assess a veterinarian's suitability to be a particular pet's doctor. All practicing veterinarians have extensive university training and are licensed in the state in which they practice.

Although it is not necessary for a dog owner to like a veterinarian, the relationship will be more workable if the owner and veterinarian share a compatability of objectives. In a relationship that may last for years, it is important for an owner to feel comfortable and at ease

Photograph 3: It is usually easier for a veterinarian to examine a large dog while it sits or stands on the floor, as Dr. Kathleen E. Noone is doing.

with the doctor. In addition to objective assessments, there are several subjective questions that dog owners can ask themselves before deciding to choose a veterinarian.

• Is the veterinarian easy to talk to? Is she old/young enough to inspire confidence? Does she seem interested or impatient and offhand when answering questions? Does she talk more about herself than about the animal?

• Does the veterinarian seem to like the dog, and does the dog seem to be reasonably at ease with the veterinarian? Or is there some underlying sense of mistrust?

• Will the veterinarian's hours fit the owner's schedule?

• What arrangements does the veterinarian make for emergencies? Is someone from the staff on call twenty-four hours a day, seven days a week, or must a dog be taken somewhere else if it gets sick or is injured on a Sunday?

• Are there other services, such as grooming and boarding, available at the hospital, or must the dog be taken somewhere else?

• If a dog is ill or injured, are there hospital facilities? If so, is there around-the-clock supervision?

• Does the veterinarian keep accurate, up-to-date records of immunizations, etc., and send reminders when necessary? Or is it up to the owner to keep these records? (See Chapter 3 for sample health records for owners to keep.)

• Are there regular telephone hours when the veterinarian can be reached to discuss ongoing or possible problems?

Responsible dog ownership has many facets, one of which is the selection of the best available medical care. There is certainly no reason why a dog owner should be unhappy or uncomfortable with a veterinarian's manner or personality. While charm does not equal veterinary skill, a small-animal veterinarian should have a good relationship with the pet's owner as well as the animal patient to be truly effective. An intelligent dog owner should use common sense in selecting a veterinarian who meets his own and his dog's needs and expectations and should be aware that a pleasant manner is not always the measure of a good animal doctor.

First-time dog owners going to a new veterinarian may find it helpful to ascertain ahead of time exactly what the particular veterinary practice offers. Often a receptionist or secretary can answer questions over the telephone. Many veterinary establishments now have pamphlets that outline their services and owners' responsibilities.

In addition to finding out about office and telephone hours, fee schedules, emergency and boarding policies, and any other services, owners will need to ask what is expected of them.

• What, if anything, should the owner bring on the first visit? Will the doctor want a stool sample (almost always required in the case of a puppy), previous immunization records, and so forth?

• Must a dog be leashed or in a carrying case?

• Will the owner be expected to stay during the examination or medical procedure? Will she need to hold or restrain the dog, or will attendants do this?

• What are the hospital's policies about payment? Is the owner expected to pay before leaving, or will a bill be sent? Are credit cards or checks accepted?

An owner should ask these and any other necessary questions ahead of time so that there are no surprises.

What to Expect on the First Visit to the Veterinarian

On a first visit, the doctor will usually take an oral history of the dog from the owner, asking questions about where the dog was obtained, his parentage if known, and any observations the owner may have about the dog's appetite, digestion, sleep, and activity level. If the patient is an older dog that has been cared for by another doctor, a written health record is very helpful. (This is one reason why it's always a good idea for owners to maintain their own pet's health records. See Chapter 3.) This is the time for an owner to voice any concerns and ask any questions about the dog's well-being so that the doctor can bear them in mind as he examines the dog.

A thorough physical examination should include inspection of all parts of a dog's body, including the insides of the mouth and ears. The veterinarian will listen to the dog's heart with a stethoscope and palpate the animal's abdomen and a male dog's testicles. He will examine the skin and extremities carefully. If there is any evidence of a problem, the doctor may suggest further testing or evaluation. This may be done while the owner waits, or the dog may have to be left at the hospital for a few hours. Owners should never be afraid to ask questions in order to understand the purpose of a recommended procedure and what that procedure entails. The veterinarian should apprise owners of the cost of any test or procedure ahead of time. If he does not, the owner should ask.

Young pups visiting the veterinarian for the first time are usually examined for intestinal parasites. As we discuss in several of the following chapters, pups usually have roundworms at birth. Often it requires more than one deworming to rid them of these parasites. The veterinarian will also establish a schedule for immunizations (see Chapter 3).

At this time the veterinarian may schedule future visits. The owner should ask that reminders be sent if he wants them.

If medications are to be used at home, it is very important—especially for the inexperienced dog owner—to understand how a particular medication should be given. Ask for a demonstration, or try the procedure yourself in the doctor's office. In the end, it will save time and will assure that the dog is properly medicated. (See Chapter 12 for how to give various types of medication.)

Conclusion

Outstanding veterinary medical care covering a wide spectrum of expertise is readily available in the 1980s. An owner who wants and can afford the time and money can obtain highly sophisticated skills and the expertise of veterinary specialists for his pet. But, in order to obtain good medical care for a dog, an owner must be willing to take time, use common sense, and pay attention to objective and subjective criteria when choosing a veterinarian.

2

Your Dog's Body And How It Works

DENNIS A. ZAWIE, DVM

This chapter contains a brief rundown of the major systems in a dog's body and their functions, as well as some of the more common problems to which these systems are prone. All of these problems will be handled in greater detail in later chapters, especially in the Encyclopedia of Diseases of Dogs. In addition, we will include the few special senses, such as acute sense of smell and excellent hearing and vision, that are peculiar to dogs.

Before we begin, however, it is interesting to note that, in general, dogs' bodies are very much like those of all other animals, including humans. There are, of course, some minor differences that have evolved over the ages. But, contrary to what some veterinarians would like dog owners to believe, there is no great mystery about a dog's physique or physiology.

The Skeletal System

The average dog's skeleton contains 319 bones, including the skull, vertebrae, ribs, tail, etc. (see Illustration 19, page 209). A dog's bones perform several very important functions. In addition to supporting the dog's body and providing a system of levers that are necessary for muscles to work, they act as a protective mechanism for the internal organs. The skull protects the brain, the rib cage the lungs, the spinal vertebrae the spinal cord, and so

forth. The skeletal bones also act as storage areas, housing bone marrow and minerals (primarily calcium and phosphorous) until the body needs them.

The muscles and tendons of a dog are essentially the same as those in humans except that a dog's upper-body muscles bear half of its body weight and are therefore better developed than those of a human.

The Nervous System

Dogs' nervous systems can be broken down into two parts—the central nervous system and the peripheral nervous system. The central nervous system includes the brain and spinal

16

cord. Within the brain, there is the cerebral cortex, which houses the reasoning capacity of a dog—that which enables him to see, hear, and feel. This is also the center of a dog's behavioral or instinctual patterns (sexual behavior; maternal, defensive, and survival instincts; etc.). The brain also contains the cerebellum, which is responsible for coordinated movement and equilibrium. The spinal cord is necessary for a dog to interpret the input of sensations in his legs and feet. This interpretation of sensations is called proprioception. When there is damage to the spinal cord it can cause an interruption in the messages to and from the limbs, and varying degrees of leg weakness or paralysis may occur. (See "Neurologic Diseases and Disorders" in the Encyclopedia.)

The peripheral nerves include the twelve cranial nerves, which emanate from the brain and are responsible for all of the actions that occur from the neck up, and the spinal nerves, which innervate the rest of the body. After the peripheral nerves branch out of the brain or the spinal cord, they transmit messages to the muscles, telling them either to expand or contract.

Eyes

A dog's vision is directly controlled by the peripheral cranial nerves. Dogs' eyes have essentially the same parts as those of humans: the cornea (the clear part of the eye), the sclera (the white part), the pupil, the iris (the colored part), the lens, and the retina (see Illustrations 20 and 21, page 214). However, there are some notable differences between dogs' eyes and human eyes. Dogs' eyes have more rods than cones, while human eyes contain more cones than rods. Since rods are tiny cells that respond to very dim light, this means that dogs are better able to see at night than people. By the same token, their vision is not as good as ours is in bright light. Because of the lack of many cones, which are responsible for color perception, the dog's color vision is limited. Contrary to myth, dogs are not completely color blind, but we know that they have poor color perception.

Another way in which dogs' eyes differ from humans' is that they contain a membranous region around the retina called the tapetum, which reflects light back to the retina after it has passed through once, giving the dog two chances to capture an image and further enhancing the animal's night vision. Sometimes owners will notice a blue or yellow glare in a dog's eye when he's looking straight at the light. This is a reflection from the tapetum. This shouldn't be confused with another phenomenon common in dogs over eight years of age, which creates a bluish tinge in the lens. This is caused when the lens fibers become denser with age and refract light differently than they formerly did, imparting a different, bluish, color. This condition, called lenticular sclerosis, is often misdiagnosed as cataracts, but does not affect a dog's vision. (See also "Ophthalmic Diseases and Disorders" in the Encyclopedia.)

One other thing worth mentioning about a dog's eyes is the third eyelid. Along with all other animals except humans, the dog has a third eyelid, which is a membrane between the outer lid and the eye itself. This membrane serves to protect and clean the eyeball and sometimes appears in front of the eye. It is more prominent and noticeable in some breeds of dog than in others, and owners are often unnecessarily concerned by its appearance. There is a very common genetic eye disorder in some canines, called cherry eye, in which the lymph glands within the third eyelid become irritated and cause the lid to pop out. More about this in the Encyclopedia of Diseases of Dogs.

Ears

A dog's hearing is also controlled by the peripheral cranial nerves. The ear is divided into three parts: the external ear, the middle ear, and the inner ear (see Illustration 17, page

177). The outer part of a dog's ear, called the pinna, is made up of cartilage and serves to capture sound vibrations and direct them down into the ear canals so that they will reach the eardrum. That is why dogs are often observed pricking up their ears to catch sound waves. The middle ear contains the eardrum and three small bones that do nothing more than transmit sound vibrations from the eardrum down into the inner ear, where nerves register the sounds and transmit them to the brain. The inner ear is also responsible for balance. Dogs' good hearing is a product of the evolutionary process. Some say it developed to compensate for their relatively poor vision.

Digestive Tract

A dog's digestive tract is made up of a number of parts that transport food and water from the oral cavity where it is ingested; through the body where it is broken down, digested, and the nutrients absorbed; to the rectum, from which waste material is ejected.

Before discussing the digestive process itself, let's look at a dog's oral cavity, and in particular at the teeth. Teeth serve an adult dog in two ways: as weapons for both offense and defense and as tools used to procure and cut, or tear, food. Dogs' mouths and teeth are designed to meet their particular style of eating. As opposed to humans, who are omnivores and chew and taste their food, dogs are carnivores and rarely chew or taste food. Instead, they usually gulp it down, sometimes seeming to virtually inhale it.

Teeth provide an excellent way to tell the age of a puppy. By eight weeks, a puppy should have a full complement of twenty-eight baby teeth, consisting of six incisors (I), two canines (C), and six premolars (PM), equally divided between the upper and lower jaws on each side as follows:

$$I \frac{3}{3} C \frac{1}{1} PM \frac{3}{3} = 14 \times 2 = 28$$

By the time the puppy is six to seven months old its baby teeth should be replaced by a full complement of adult teeth (see Table 1, page 19). If this does not occur on time, the baby teeth may have to be extracted so that the adult teeth do not become deformed. (See Chapter 4, "Deciduous Tooth Extraction.") An adult dog should have forty-two teeth, including mo-

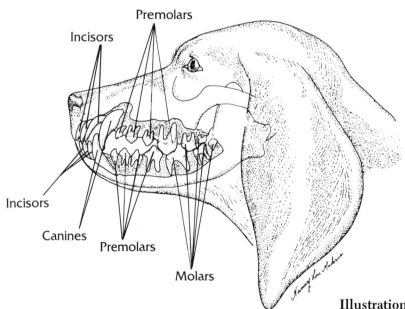

Illustration 1: A dog's permanent teeth

lars (M), as follows (see also Illustration 1, page 18):

$$I\frac{3}{3} \, C\frac{1}{1} \, PM\frac{4}{4} \, M\frac{2}{3} = 21 \times 2 = 42$$

Moving down into the dog's body from the oral cavity, we come to the esophagus, a long, tubular muscle, or organ, whose only function is to propel food from the oral cavity to the stomach by means of muscular contractions called peristaltic waves, which function throughout the digestive tract. When a dog swallows, a hinged cartilage called the glottis automatically covers up the trachea, or windpipe, to prevent food or water from entering it.

The food then enters the stomach, which acts primarily as a storage area, but also starts breaking the food down with digestive enzymes and hydrochloric acid. Very little digestion actually occurs in dogs' stomachs. The food then passes on to the small intestine, which is responsible for the digestion and absorption of water, electrolytes, and nutrients. Its spongelike surface is full of folds and turns to increase its absorptive area. The small intestine consists of three parts: the duodenum, the jejunum, and the ileum. In addition to its digestive and absorptive functions, the duodenum stimulates the secretion of enzymes from the pancreas. These help to digest the food as well as to stimulate contraction of the gallbladder to release bile into the small intestine. Bile serves to digest and emulsify fat.

At the junction of the small and large intestines, dogs have a small pocket, similar to a human's appendix, called the cecum, which can be the site of gastrointestinal difficulties. In particular, whipworms usually reside in the cecum.

The large intestine serves mainly as a storage area for waste material, but it also reabsorbs any remaining nutrients and water, which are extracted by the colon. Leftover material is fecal matter, which is then expelled through the rectum.

Other parts of the digestive tract are the pancreas and the liver. The pancreas has an endocrine function, secreting the hormones insulin and glucagon, which are necessary for the regulation of glucose. It also has an exocrine function, manufacturing and releasing digestive enzymes and bicarbonate into the small intestine. A dog's liver is the largest organ in its body. It has six lobes in contrast to the human liver, which has only one large lobe. The liver is responsible for a myriad of functions, all of which are very important. It aids digestion by producing bile, which aids in the absorption of fat; by metabolizing protein and carbohydrates; and by acting to detoxify the byproducts of digestion. In addition, the liver acts to metabolize and degrade any drugs, chemicals, or poisons that might get into a dog's body through environmental exposure. It also manufactures the major blood-clotting factors. (See also "Gastrointestinal Diseases and Disorders" in the Encyclopedia.)

TABLE 1

ERUPTION OF A DOG'S PERMANENT TEETH

Group	Tooth	Eruption Period
Incisors: (6 on each side, 3 uppers and 3 lowers)	Central Intermediate Corner	2 to 5 months 2 to 5 months Most breeds— 4 to 5 months
Canine: (2 on each side, 1 upper and 1 lower)		5 to 6 months
Premolars: (8 on each side, 4 upper and 4 lower)	First Second Third Fourth	4 to 5 months 6 months 6 months 4 to 5 months
Molars: (5 on each side, 2 upper and 3 lower)	First Second Third	5 to 6 months 6 to 7 months 6 to 7 months

Cardiovascular and Respiratory Systems

Next, let's travel to the dog's heart and lungs, which also are very similar to those of all other animals, including humans.

The cardiovascular system consists of the heart, which pumps blood, and the arteries and veins, which carry it. Blood from the circulatory system enters the right atrium of the heart, passes through the tricuspid valve into the right ventricle, which pumps it through the pulmonary valve into the pulmonary artery and on to the lungs for a fresh supply of oxygen. The oxygenated blood flows back into the heart (the left atrium), passing through the mitral valve into the left ventricle, the heart's main pumping chamber, which forces blood through the aortic valve into the aorta, the body's major artery. This artery branches into smaller arteries, arterioles, and finally capillaries, which carry oxygen and nutrients to every cell in the body.

The respiratory tract carries air into the lungs, where oxygen enters the bloodstream and carbon dioxide is removed from the blood. The respiratory tract begins with the nose. The primary function of the nose in respiration is to act as a filter, removing large particles the dog inhales. These particles are filtered out all along the respiratory tract, but the nose is the first, and most efficient, filter. The nose is also an olfactory organ, providing a sense of smell. In dogs, the olfactory nerves of the brain are highly developed. The dog has a much better sense of smell than we do.

When air leaves the nose, it travels down through an opening in the throat to the larynx; the larynx contains the vocal cords, which vibrate to produce sound when air is forced over them. Air then enters the trachea, or windpipe, a long tube that serves only to convey it to the bronchi and the lungs. As we mentioned before, the windpipe is protected by a hinged membrane called the glottis, which protects against accidental choking. From the windpipe, air travels through the various bronchial tubes and then into the lungs. It is in the lung tissue that the gaseous exchange of waste and oxygen occurs. (See also "Cardiac Diseases" and "Respiratory Diseases and Disorders" in the Encyclopedia.)

Genitourinary System

The reproductive tract of a male dog consists of testicles, which manufacture sperm and are housed within a membranous pouch called the scrotum; the epididymis, an area that stores sperm prior to ejaculation; the vas deferens, a duct that carries sperm into the ejaculatory duct; and the prostate gland, which secretes the alkaline prostatic fluid that transports the sperm and makes it viable in the female vaginal tract (see Illustration 2, page 21).

Undescended testicles are a very common problem seen in male pups. If the testicles have not appeared by the time a dog is at least four months old they probably will remain undescended. Dogs with this problem are called cryptorchid and are sterile. When only one testicle is retained it is usually the right, as the right kidney is higher than the left, leaving more space inside the right abdomen. Dogs with only one descended testicle are called monorchid and may be fertile. There is a high incidence of cancer in older males with undescended testicles (see "Testicular Cancer" in the Encyclopedia). Another common problem among older male dogs is an enlarged prostate. These diseases are often benign but infectious, and cancer may develop. Neutering a male dog will usually prevent these prostatic problems.

The female reproductive-urinary tract consists of the external genitalia, or vulva; the vagina, a passage leading from the vulva to the cervix, the narrow outer end of the uterus, or womb, which holds the fertilized ova, or eggs, during their development as fetuses; and the two uterine horns, which lead via the ovaducts to the ovaries, which produce the eggs (see Illustration 3, page 21). Most commonly, problems of the female genital tract occur in older,

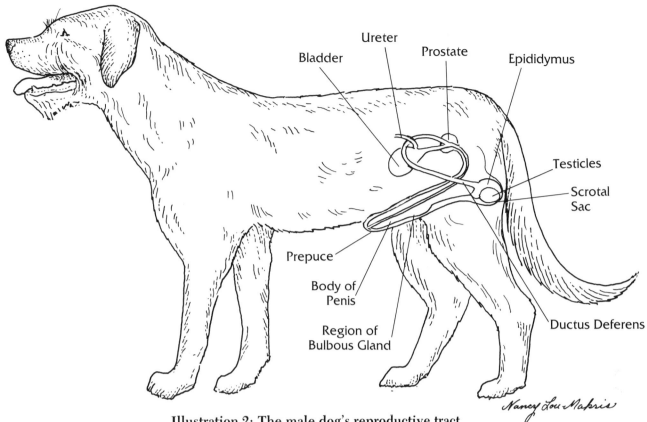

Illustration 2: The male dog's reproductive tract

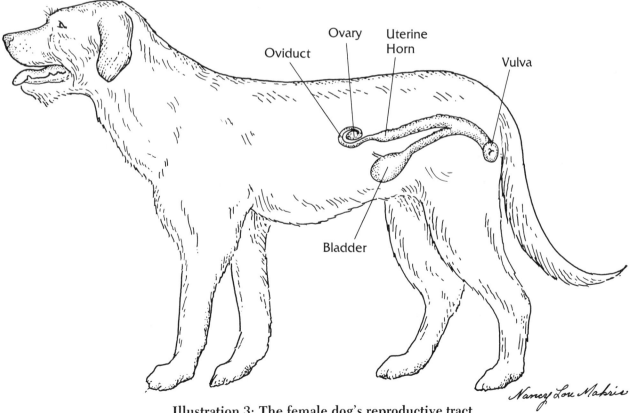

Illustration 3: The female dog's reproductive tract

unspayed bitches. (See also Chapter 5 and "Reproductive Disorders" in the Encyclopedia of Diseases of Dogs.)

The urinary tracts of both male and female dogs contain two kidneys, which serve as filters for waste materials in the bloodstream, ridding the body of the different byproducts, toxins, and poisons that can build up. The kidneys concentrate these wastes into urine by passing the blood through a system of filters. The urine is then conveyed through the ureter into the bladder, which serves as a reservoir until it is full and reaches a certain pressure point. At this point, the sphincter muscle relaxes and allows the stored urine to go out of the body through the urethra. Older dogs often suffer from various urinary tract disorders. Kidney disease is a common problem as are bladder diseases such as bladder stones and urinary incontinence. See Chapter 7 and "Renal Diseases and Disorders" in the Encyclopedia for symptoms and treatment of genitourinary diseases.

Endocrine System

The endocrine glands, located throughout a dog's body (see Illustration 18, page 191), manufacture and release hormones into the bloodstream. The pituitary gland controls and regulates many of the other endocrine glands by the hormones it produces (there are actually six hormones produced by the pituitary) and is a major control site for the entire body. Other endocrine glands are the thyroid, the parathyroid, the adrenal cortex, the adrenal medulla, the pancreas, and the gonads. For a detailed discussion of the endocrine system of dogs, see "Endocrine Diseases" in the Encyclopedia.

Hemic-Lymphatic System

The hemic-lymphatic system includes the spleen, the lymph nodes, and the bone marrow. Bone marrow is primarily responsible for the production of the different blood cells (red and white blood cells and platelets). Platelets help blood to coagulate; red blood cells carry oxygen to the tissues; and white blood cells perform various tasks. They ward off infection, clear debris from the body, and produce antibodies. White blood cells live about 7 days, while red blood cells have an average lifespan of 120 days. The clearinghouse for old red blood cells is the spleen, which also serves as an organ for the secondary production of red blood cells. Splenic tumors, or Hemangiosarcomas (see the Encyclopedia of Diseases of Dogs and the Emergencies section), rarely seen in humans, are very common in older dogs, especially German shepherds. Because the spleen is a nonvital organ, it is often surgically removed when diseased.

There are literally hundreds of lymph nodes located in various areas throughout a dog's body. They are responsible for the production of lymphocytes, which are special cells that control and regulate the body's immune system. Tonsils are specialized lymph nodes/glands, or lymph tissue in the throat, and are necessary to ward off infections. They rarely cause any problems, but many dogs are misdiagnosed as having tonsillitis and are given unnecessary tonsillectomies. Dogs are very prone to cancer of the lymph nodes (see "Lymphosarcoma" in the Encyclopedia), a disease that produces symptoms somewhat similar to those of Hodgkin's disease in people.

The Integumentary System

In this category we include the dog's hair, skin, anal glands (or sacs), claws, and feet.

A dog's hair, or coat, is an important system of his body. It forms a physical barrier between the environment and the skin and, with the skin, helps to create homeostasis (a balance between the external world and the internal dog). There are three basic types of canine haircoats.

The coat of the German shepherd is used as the standard for a normal coat because it is closest to that of a coyote or wolf. On this basis, coats are classified as short, normal, and long. Within these categories, there is a further division into coarse and fine. Thus, a wirehaired terrier has a short, coarse coat, while a short-haired dachshund's coat is classified as short and fine. Collies and spaniels have long, fine coats, and Bedlington terriers' and poodles' coats are labeled long and coarse, etc.

Amazingly, all dogs' coats are made up of only two basic colors: brown and yellow. Depending on the degree of melanin (dark pigmentation), the particular combination of yellow and brown, the reflection of light, and the way the color is deposited on the hair shaft, these two colors combine to form what we see as black, white, tan, and so forth. Sometimes there will be different colors combined on each hair shaft—this is called agouti, after a small, burrowing tropical rodent that has grizzled fur.

All dogs shed; this is a natural cycle of hair replacement that has more to do with the photoperiod than with temperature. For example, in the fall as the days grow shorter, a dog's coat will grow more slowly and shed less, resulting in a thicker coat. The reverse happens as days grow longer in the spring, stimulating the hair to grow faster and, therefore, to shed at a faster rate. Of course, there may be artificial stimulae to hair growth, and dogs under stress will always shed excessively, but all dogs, even the so-called "shedless" breeds, lose hair all year long. Variations of degrees of shedding noted in breeds are usually due to a difference in the length and thickness of the coat and the hair itself, and the location of hair on the body. When left ungroomed, the shed hairs of long-coated breeds will form mats and tangles instead of falling out.

Under the coat is the dog's skin, a very important organ that is often overlooked. Along with the coat, the skin protects the dog's internal organs and helps to provide a balance with the external world. Because dogs perspire only by panting and through their foot pads, their skin helps to dissipate heat. The blood vessels dilate, helping to cool the body off. When it is cold, the skin's vessels constrict to retain body heat. One of the most important functions of the skin is its action as a sensory perceptor, conveying sensations of touch, pain, and so forth to the brain. Another positive role that the skin plays is as a synthesizer of vitamin D. A dog's skin is also an important indicator of disease. Dogs with jaundice, for instance, will turn yellow all over, while the skin of a dog with congestive heart failure may have a blue tinge. In addition, if there's no dermatological problem, poor-looking, dry skin and coat often signal illness. Dogs' skin has antimicrobial and antibacterial capabilities as well; these help to protect the body from infection. See "Dermatologic Diseases and Disorders" in the Encyclopedia for canine skin problems.

The claws and feet are also part of a dog's integumentary system. Although a dog's foot pads are thick and calloused and are probably the strongest area of its body, they are nevertheless very susceptible to all kinds of problems and should be protected against extreme cold and any chemicals that are put in streets or gardens. As dogs age, their foot pads very often spread, or splay, and particular care must be taken to protect the spaces between them from irritation. Dogs' claws are not used as weapons, but are primarily for foot protection. They must be clipped if they don't wear down naturally. See "Grooming and Cleanliness," Chapter 3, for how to do this. See also "Dewclaw Removal" in Chapter 4.

The anal glands, or sacs, are small glands located roughly at the eight and four o'clock positions on either side of the rectum of both male and female dogs. At one point during the dog's evolution, the foul-smelling secretion from these glands was used as a territorial marker, but they now serve no useful purpose. Usually, the secreted matter in the anal glands is forced out by pressure from the feces when the dog has a bowel movement. Occasionally, however, the secretion itself will be very thick, will become impacted, and will not express. Owners will notice a dog scooting his rear end along the ground or licking excessively. If this happens, the dog should be seen immediately by a veterinarian or groomer who can express the secretion before the anal glands become infected. If the glands do become infected or abscessed there will be swelling, inflammation, draining, and a foul odor. Anal gland problems often become chronic. If they do, surgical removal of these glands is recommended. See "Anal Sac (Gland) Impaction" in the Encyclopedia.

Physiological Differences Among Breeds of Dogs

Despite differences in size, ear shape, tail length, or haircoat, and the possible specific problems these external dissimilarities may cause, all dogs are essentially the same physiologically. Great Danes and Chihuahuas have all the same parts, which work in the same way.

The only exception to this is the racing greyhound. Racing greyhounds have a red-blood-cell volume (hematocrit) of sixty, while every other dog's red-blood-cell volume averages about forty to forty-five. This phenomenon probably evolved over the years to compensate for the greyhound's greater oxygen requirements when racing.

3

Keeping Your Dog Healthy

Michael S. Garvey, DVM, with a note by

Peter L. Borchelt, Ph.D., on the Importance of Routine

The Importance of Routine

Dogs, like all animals, are creatures of habit. If a dog is to know how to behave and react, it will need some idea of what to expect. This does not mean that it is necessary to have a rigid routine but, in general, a dog should know when it is time to be taken out, fed, put to bed, and so forth.

A dog should never be left alone for long periods of time without some arrangements for its care being made. Dogs are completely dependent on owners for their most basic needs, and a pet who is ignored, or forgotten often, will suffer a great deal. An owner cannot tell a dog not to worry, that a walk and dinner will be a couple of hours late that evening. The unattended dog may feel forgotten and frustrated, to say nothing of hungry and uncomfortable. Dogs' and owners' schedules should be arranged so that this doesn't happen too often. If evening feedings become a problem, the main meal can be given in the morning. If unexpected delays or absences come up, owners should arrange for someone to take care of feeding and walking the dog at the usual time.

It is a good idea to hold a family meeting when a dog first comes into the household, or even beforehand, to decide who is going to be responsible for various aspects of the pet's care. Children can, and should, be assigned pet-care tasks. Gearing the difficulty of a job to the ability of a child is an excellent way to foster responsibility. Even the youngest family member can help to get dog food out and put it away, while older children can be given more difficult jobs, such as walking, grooming, feeding, and watering. Family circumstances and the age of the dog may make it practical to change the routine from time to time, but it is a good practice to discuss any changes, so that the dog does not become lost in the shuffle of family changes.

At the same time, the family should decide on other details of taking care of a new dog. Will it be allowed to sleep on beds and furniture or go into the dining room at mealtimes? Will one person be mainly in charge of training and housebreaking, or will everyone? What commands will be used? If all family members can agree on the basics and stick to them as much as possible, it will be much easier on both the dog and the family.

Dogs really want to please and to do what is wanted, as long as they know what to expect. For more about dog behavior and training, see Chapter 8.

Checkups

One of the most important routines a dog owner can establish is taking his pet to the veterinarian periodically. By seeing a dog on a regular basis, a doctor can spot any abnormalities or differences much more easily. An office visit is also an excellent time for an owner to discuss any concerns about a dog that may have developed, such as a change in habits, weight loss or gain, and so forth.

One of the easiest and best ways to be sure that a dog receives regular health examinations is to combine a checkup with necessary immunizations or booster shots. Since puppies require immunizations every few weeks until they are four months old, this presents an excellent opportunity for the doctor to assess a young dog's development. After that, yearly visits for booster shots allow an adult dog to be looked over. Of course, special circumstances may call for additional visits, and once a dog becomes a senior citizen it may need more frequent exams; but, in general, an annual visit combining boosters with a general checkup will provide good care for a healthy adult dog.

Vaccinations: What Do They Do?

One of the most important aspects of preventive medicine for dogs is periodic vaccination for serious infectious diseases. Infectious diseases are those that are caused by the invasion of the body by living organisms, usually bacteria or viruses. An infectious disease may or may not be contagious, depending on the organism involved and its tendency to pass from one animal to another. Most of the infectious diseases for which vaccinations are available are highly contagious, through either direct contact, airborne viruses, indirect contact, such as stools of infected animals, or through an intermediate host such as a mosquito or flea.

The infectious dog diseases for which vaccines have been developed are canine distemper, hepatitis, leptospirosis (all usually combined in one vaccine called DHL), para-influenza (CPI), canine parvovirus, and rabies. Dogs are protected from heartworm disease by preventive medication, given after a blood test to determine that there are no heartworms present in the animal's bloodstream. More about these diseases, their symptoms and treatment will be found in the Encyclopedia of Diseases of Dogs.

Vaccinations are given to "teach" a dog's immune system (defense system) about a particular disease organism. Once the body's defenses are primed or awakened to a particular bacterium or virus, the body is ready to do battle when the real disease organism is encountered because antibodies have been manufactured.

An antibody is a protein that body cells manufacture in response to exposure to a disease organism or to a vaccine. Thus, when an animal has been vaccinated against a particular disease, the antibody is in its body. This antibody helps to fight off the invading infection and obviously does a better job of it if it is already present and circulating in the dog's body when the disease enters. This, then, is the basic rationale for vaccination. It allows a dog to have antibody already present and ready to fight against a disease, instead of having to become sick and recover in order to have that antibody form naturally.

Vaccines are not effective once an animal becomes infected. They are used to prevent diseases, not to treat or cure them.

Incubation Periods of Diseases

One of the most confusing things about an infectious disease is its incubation period, or the time that lapses between exposure of an animal to an infectious disease and the first signs or symptoms of the disease. No disease organisms produce signs or symptoms immediately after they enter the body. The bacteria or viruses settle in the body and begin a process of multiplication. This period is known as the incubation period, and during it a dog will show no signs of illness. It is only after the disease organisms have reached a critical number, destroyed enough tissue, or spread to another area of the body or the bloodstream, that the animal will begin to appear ill.

It is especially crucial to be aware of the incubation period when getting a new puppy. The puppy may show no signs of illness, even to a veterinarian, but it can actually be incubating a disease that will surface some time later. That is why it is so important to get a puppy from a good source—a reliable breeder, a well-run shelter or adoption agency, or a caring family—to be sure that the pup has been protected against infectious diseases. Even the most careful breeders, agencies, or owners may not be able to prevent all contact with disease, however, so it is equally important to start a puppy's vaccinations right away. So-called "temporary" shots have very limited effect against disease, as we will discuss in the next section.

When a puppy or dog is vaccinated during the incubation period of an infectious disease (in other words, after the disease has already entered its body), a race is set up within the dog's body. Will the vaccine stimulate enough immunity quickly enough to protect the dog from the disease? Or has the disease gotten such a head start that the infection will still

FIGURE 1

IMMUNIZATION CHART FOR PUPPIES

(Note: This chart is a representative example of immunizations.
Many veterinarians recommend slightly different intervals.)

Disease	Age: 5–8 wks.	9–12 weeks.	13–15 wks.	16 –24 wks.	12 mos.
Parvovirus	x	x	x	x	x
Distemper (DHL)		x	x	x	x
Measles*	x				
Parainfluenza (CPI)		x	x	x	x
Hepatitis (DHL)		x	x	x	x
Leptospirosis (DHL)		x	x		
Rabies				x	x
Heartworm					
(test and preventive medication) Between 6 and 12 months, depending upon time of year					

*Sometimes given to young puppies as a substitute for distemper vaccine, as it is not inactivated by maternal immunity.

cause the animal to become ill despite the vaccination? Usually, the disease will win out and the animal will be come ill. This is often misinterpreted by owners, who attribute the dog's illness to the vaccination itself. It is extremely rare that a vaccination will cause an animal to become really ill.

Heartworm disease also goes through an incubation period, which is discussed in detail in the Encyclopedia of Diseases of Dogs.

Vaccinations for Puppies

Vaccinations are usually given to puppies under four months in a series every two to four weeks. This is necessary because although puppies receive antibodies against disease from their mother's milk, these antibodies are short-lived. While these maternal antibodies are alive, they will automatically inactivate a vaccination. But, since we do not know exactly how short-lived these maternal antibodies are, a series of vaccinations is given to be sure that at least one or two vaccinations are in effect after the pup's natural immunity is gone. Hence the limited effect of one "temporary" shot. (See also Chapter 6).

After a puppy has been successfully vaccinated by a series of injections (see Figure 1, page 27), it usually can be assumed that immunity has been achieved for a period of time. However, it is important to realize that *no vaccine* is 100 percent effective in all cases. Some dogs have more sluggish immune systems than others, and not all respond as well to vaccination as we would hope. It is always possible for an animal to contract a disease even when properly vaccinated.

FIGURE 2

IMMUNIZATION CHART FOR ADULT DOGS

Disease	Yearly	Every 1–3 Years	More Often When Indicated
Heartworm (test and preventive medication)	x		x
Rabies		x	
Distemper/ Hepatitis/ Leptospirosis (DPL)	x (Leptospirosis optional)		
Parainfluenza (CPI)	x (optional)		
Parvovirus	x		x

(All first vaccinations should be followed by a booster in 2–3 weeks; after that, a booster is given yearly.)

Booster Shots

Immunity to a disease from a vaccination, or even from the disease itself, is not a lifelong matter. Vaccinations must be given periodically to make sure that immunity continues. As a rule, these revaccinations, or booster shots, are given annually, but there are some exceptions. Figure 2, opposite, shows the normal frequency of boosters for most infectious diseases, but in some instances a doctor may recommend more frequent boosters. A booster, by the way, is the same kind and strength of vaccine as the original vaccination. The name developed because it is intended to further strengthen, or "boost," the original immunization.

Do All Dogs Need Vaccinations?

"My old dog never leaves the front yard. Why should I spend money on shots for it?" or "We live way out in the country, and there are no other dogs within miles. Do I really have to bother with vaccinations?" The answer to both questions is Yes.

Regardless of age or living situation, every dog should be protected. For one thing, dogs who are not regularly exposed to other dogs lose their immunity to infectious diseases quickly. Dogs who are exposed to others on a regular basis may encounter an infectious disease from time to time and be naturally boostered through the encounter. (This can, of course, be risky if the dog is not vaccinated.)

Even a dog who never leaves the yard or never sees another dog can be exposed to diseases through airborne viruses, from infectious feces brought into the house on peoples' shoes, bacteria carried on hands and clothing, and bites by host carriers such as mosquitoes and fleas. Encounters with other dogs or their droppings on walks and visits to the veterinarian or a boarding kennel can also expose a nonimmunized dog to the risk of serious illness. The possibilities of even the most well-protected house dog encountering disease are so numerous that regular vaccination is the only sensible course for dog owners to follow.

Keeping a Dog's Health Records

Many veterinarians keep health records for their patients and send cards or call to remind owners when it is time for a dog to have a vaccination or booster. However, cards do get lost in the mail and call messages can be forgotten, so the best and easiest thing for careful dog owners to do is to keep their own records. Up-to-date records will come in very handy, too, in case of a move or change of doctor.

We have included a sample health chart on this page (Figure 3). If there is more than one pet in the household, a ready reference of immunizations and boosters due is an invaluable aid in keeping records straight.

FIGURE 3

SAMPLE DOG'S HEALTH CHART

Dog's Name: Rover

Birth Date: Sept. 8, 1983

Age When Acquired: 8 weeks

PUPPY RECORD:

Age: 8 weeks   Date: November 9, 1983

Weight: 5 pounds

Length: 15 inches

Height: 10 inches

Remarks: Dr. Smith says Rover is sturdy and
    healthy.

Immunizations Given: Distemper, hepatitis,
    parvovirus, parainfluenza

Next Visit: November 30

Immunizations Due: Same as above.

Age: 11 weeks   Date: November 30

Weight: _____

Length: _____

Height: _____

Remarks: _____

Immunizations Given: _____

Next Visit: _____

Immunizations Due: _____

Etc., until adulthood.

Date When Spayed or Neutered: _____

ADULT RECORD:

Age: 1 year   Date:

Remarks: _____

Boosters Given: _____

Next Boosters Due: _____

Nutrition: Feeding a Dog Right

Note: Pages 30–49 are based, in part, on a monograph prepared for ALPO Products Company, Inc., by Michael S. Garvey, DVM, with their permission.

Mealtimes can be an important positive aspect of an owner-dog relationship, providing an opportunity for socialization and mutual satisfaction. But what to feed a dog may also cause an owner some concern. Just as everyone has become increasingly aware of the importance of good nutrition for the human members of the family, dog owners, too, are aware of the role proper nutrition plays for their pets. Questions about food additives, supplementary vitamins, and the pros and cons of "natural" foods for dogs may all have crossed a dog owner's mind. With all of the special-purpose dog foods on the market, there may also be confusion about the proper diet for puppies, older dogs, breeding bitches, overweight dogs, and dogs with specific medical problems.

Our knowledge of what constitutes good canine nutrition has grown by leaps and bounds over the past decade. For example, we know much more about the varying dietary needs of dogs at different stages of life; about dogs' food needs when they are suffering from disease; and about the relationship between diet and a dog's ability to deal with stress. What follows is a summary of that knowledge.

A Balanced Diet

The optimal amount of a given nutrient in a dog's diet is usually given as a range, rather than a single value. There are several reasons for this, primarily having to do with differences in individual animals and how each uses nutrients. As soon as a dog is living in a stress situation, such as growth, breeding, lactating, hard work, or emotional/psychological pressure, however, its nutritional needs become better defined and more rigid (see Figure 4, page 31). More about these specific needs later on.

The single most important requirement in nutrition is to provide the optimal intake of food energy for an individual dog. Individual needs are influenced by:

- Environment (shelter)
- The individual dog's own chemical or metabolic efficiency
- The physical or emotional demands an owner puts on a dog
- The age of the dog

Food energy is made available in the body's cells through the breakdown of carbohydrates, fats, and proteins, which oxidize to yield heat and to capture chemical energy, or ATP (adenosine triphosphate). ATP is the common currency of energy transactions, or metabolism, within living cells. The actual usable energy in food can be determined by subtracting the energy lost in waste from the gross energy contained in a given food. A gram of fat supplies nine calories of metabolizable energy, while proteins and carbohydrates each supply four calories per gram.

Here, briefly, are the dietary elements that are necessary to provide dogs with usable food energy:

Carbohydrates

Carbohydrates consist mainly of starch, sugars, and roughage, or fiber, and are introduced into the diet primarily through vegetable matter, including grains and cereals. There is no established dietary requirement of carbohydrate for dogs,[1] but carbohydrates form a valuable component of many commercial dog foods providing a ready source of energy. Dogs can use carbohydrates efficiently in fairly large amounts.

Too much fiber is not recommended for dogs, however. It is not a nutrient; it is largely indigestible; and it prevents the absorption of necessary nutrients in the digestive tract, leading to large, poorly formed stools. Giving adult dogs excessive amounts of dairy products should also be avoided; they are not well handled and often cause diarrhea.

FIGURE 4
OPTIMAL DAILY DIETARY INTAKE FOR DOGS
IN DIFFERENT SITUATIONS

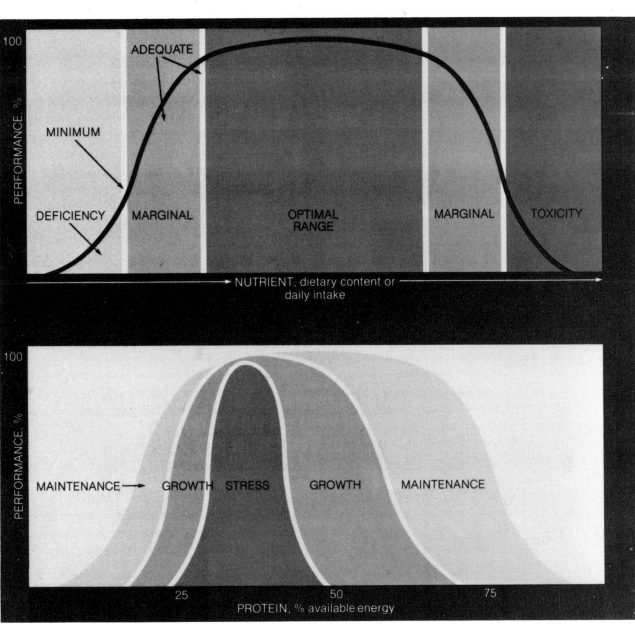

Figure 4. The optimal daily intake or dietary content of a nutrient is represented better by a plateau rather than a peak, because of imperfections in methods of determination, variation between animals, and homeostatic responses within animals.

The upper figure is redrawn from Mertz (2), with added indications of the minimum nutrient requirements and the indeterminate "adequate" (3,4).

The lower figure concerns the protein requirements of dogs, comparing optimal ranges for maintenance of adults, growth of pups, and stress.

The range is broad for the undemanding situation, but becomes more narrow as nutritional demands increase and constrain homeostasis. Ranges covering about 85 percent of maximal performance are 15 to 65 percent for maintenance, 25 to 50 percent for growth, and 30 to 40 percent for the stress of repeated exhaustive exercise.

Canine Nutrition and Feeding Management, ALPO Pet Center, Allentown, PA 18001, 1984.

Fats

Fats and oils are the most concentrated sources of food energy in a dog's diet. They also contribute to a healthy skin and coat and aid in the absorption of the fat-soluble vitamins (A, D, E, K). The minimum recommendation for fat in a dog's diet is 5 percent, but many breeders and owners of show or work dogs prefer a range of 15–35 percent.

Since fat contains more than twice the calories of either protein or carbohydrate, care must be taken to maintain a caloric balance of these and other nutrients if fat is added to a dog's diet. For the same reason, a dog's total daily food intake must be reduced when fat is added, or the dog will gain weight. Increasing the amount of fat in a dog's diet rapidly can also lead to digestive difficulties and diarrhea.

Proteins

Proteins supply a dog with amino acids, the body's building blocks. There are twenty-two amino acids, many of them called "essential" because they are not manufactured in a dog's body and must be supplied daily. Not all proteins supply all of these amino acids in the same proportion. Many vegetable proteins, for example, must be combined in the correct proportions in order to provide the same high-quality or complete protein as that found in meats, eggs, and dairy products. For this reason, it is very difficult to establish a minimum protein requirement for dogs, but reasonable estimates of mixed animal and plant protein sufficient to reach optimal ranges for a dog's daily requirement are 15 percent for maintenance, 25 percent for growth and breeding, and 30 percent for severe stress.

Vitamins

Although specific data on all of the vitamin requirements of dogs is limited, it is safe to assume that since most vitamins cannot be manufactured in a dog's body, they should be present in the diet. Exceptions are ascorbic acid (vitamin C), niacin, retinol, and choline, which are synthesized naturally by dogs.

Vitamins are usually divided into two groups:

The water-soluble vitamins, including vitamin C (not required by dogs) and all of the B-complex vitamins, which must be replaced daily.

The fat-soluble vitamins, including A, D, E, K, which are stored in the body. A continuous supply of these vitamins is not crucial, and owners should be aware that *oversupplementation of these vitamins can have toxic effects on a dog.*

Some vitamins may be destroyed in the cooking and processing of commercial dog foods. The major pet-food manufacturers take that into account and add sufficient vitamins to compensate for those lost in processing. They also carefully monitor batches of food for full vitamin content.

A dog's vitamin requirements may vary because of illness or other special conditions. The veterinarian will know if a pet needs any kind of vitamin supplementation. Otherwise, we do not recommend any kind of vitamin supplements without the specific recommendation of a doctor. Oversupplementation can be risky.

Minerals

Proper levels and combinations of minerals are known to be essential to maintaining a dog's health. There are basically two groups of minerals: the trace elements, such as iodine, iron, copper, cobalt, zinc, manganese, molybdenum, fluorine, and chromium, which dogs need only in extremely small amounts, and the macro-minerals, which are needed in large quantities. These include sodium, potassium, magnesium, calcium, and phosphorus.

Many factors, including vitamin intake, affect the proper absorption of minerals into a dog's body. In addition, if the proper ratio of certain minerals to others is not maintained, absorption is depressed. *Dog owners should never attempt to supplement a pet's diet with minerals without professional advice.* For example, the practice of adding large amounts of calcium and phosphorous to a large, growing pup's food by supplementing his diet with bone meal or other preparations can lead to serious skeletal problems.

Water

Dogs need sufficient water to maintain the proper level of body fluids, to carry nutrients throughout the body, and to flush waste from it. They lose a great deal of water daily through urination, respiration, and evaporation, so it is very important that an adequate water supply be available at all times. When water is accessible, a dog will normally drink enough to maintain the proper balance of body fluids. (See also "Polydipsia" in the Encyclopedia.)

Types of Commercial Dog Foods

There are four distinct types of commercial dog food on the market: dry, semi-moist, canned ration-type, and canned meat-type. Within each of these types of food, there are also special-purpose dog foods, which are described below. The four types of food differ in the way they are processed and preserved, in predominant ingredients, and in nutrient composition. They also differ greatly in moisture content. Since water has no nutritional value, foods should always be compared on a dry-weight basis. Tables 2, 3, and 4 compare these major types of commercial dog food.

Dry Dog Foods

The main source of food energy in dry dog foods is carbohydrate provided by starches from cereal grains and cereal grain by-products,[5] which must be cooked for optimum utilization. Table 2, below, shows the main ingredients; these are mixed with supplementary vitamins and minerals and run through large cooker-extruders, cooking the starches and giving the finished product a texture that dogs like. Fat is usually sprayed on the outside of the already cooked product to add to the fat content and to improve palatability.

Dry dog foods are easy to store, can be left out without spoiling, and are less expensive than canned foods. The addition of flavorings and aromas make them acceptable for most dogs, and they are generally well digested. The action of chewing dry dog food can also be beneficial to a dog's teeth and gums.

TABLE 2

PREDOMINANT INGREDIENTS
OF COMMERCIAL DOG FOODS

Dry	Semimoist	Canned Ration-Type	Canned Meat-Type
Corn	Corn	Barley	Meat by-products
Soybean meal	Meat by-products	Meat by-products	Meat
Wheat midds	Soybean meal	Wheat grain	Poultry by-products
Meat and bone meal	Corn syrup	Soy flour	Soy flour

Canine Nutrition and Feeding Management, ALPO Pet Center, Allentown, PA 18001, 1984.

TABLE 3
REPRESENTATIVE VALUES OF NUTRIENT COMPOSITION
OF COMMERCIAL DOG FOODS

		0	10	20	30	40	50	60	70	80	90	100
Dry	Moisture %	10.0										
	Protein %		21.0									
	Fat %	8.0										
	Fiber %	5.0										
	Ash %	9.0										
	Energy kcal/g	3.3										
Semi-Moist	Moisture %			30.0								
	Protein %		18.0									
	Fat %	6.0										
	Fiber %	3.0										
	Ash %	6.0										
	Energy kcal/g	2.6										
Canned Ration Type	Moisture %								75.0			
	Protein %	8.0										
	Fat %	4.0										
	Fiber %	2.0										
	Ash %	3.0										
	Energy kcal/g	1.0										
Canned Meat Type	Moisture %								75.0			
	Protein %	11.0										
	Fat %	8.0										
	Fiber %	1.0										
	Ash %	3.0										
	Energy kcal/g	1.2										

A major difference among dog foods is the content of moisture. Water has no caloric value. More meaningful comparisons can be made by determining the dry matter composition. This is determined by the following formula:

$$\text{Nutrient (\% of DM)} = \frac{\text{Nutrient (as is)}}{100 - \% \text{ Moisture}} \times 100$$

The dry matter protein content for the dry food listed in Table 3 would be:

$$\frac{21\%}{100 - 10} \times 100 = 23.3\%$$

The dry matter composition of the foods shown in Table 3 is shown in Table 4.

Canine Nutrition and Feeding Management, ALPO Pet Center, Allentown, PA 18001, 1984.

TABLE 4
DRY MATTER COMPOSITION OF
COMMERCIAL DOG FOODS

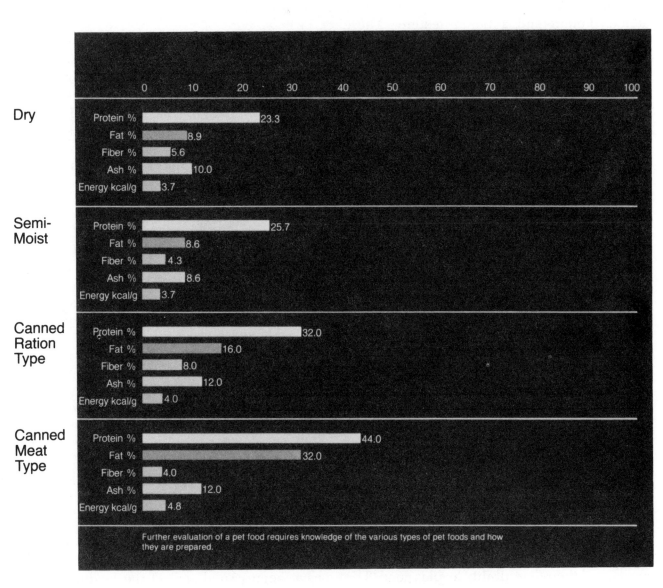

		0	10	20	30	40	50	60	70	80	90	100

Dry
- Protein % — 23.3
- Fat % — 8.9
- Fiber % — 5.6
- Ash % — 10.0
- Energy kcal/g — 3.7

Semi-Moist
- Protein % — 25.7
- Fat % — 8.6
- Fiber % — 4.3
- Ash % — 8.6
- Energy kcal/g — 3.7

Canned Ration Type
- Protein % — 32.0
- Fat % — 16.0
- Fiber % — 8.0
- Ash % — 12.0
- Energy kcal/g — 4.0

Canned Meat Type
- Protein % — 44.0
- Fat % — 32.0
- Fiber % — 4.0
- Ash % — 12.0
- Energy kcal/g — 4.8

Further evaluation of a pet food requires knowledge of the various types of pet foods and how they are prepared.

Canine Nutrition and Feeding Management, ALPO Pet Center, Allentown, PA 18001, 1984.

Canned Dog Foods

The main ingredients of both types of canned dog foods can also be found in Table 2.

The primary energy source of canned meat-type foods is fat, but up to 44 percent of the metabolizable calories is supplied by protein, as shown in Table 4, page 35. Soy flour gives added protein and a better texture. These foods are also supplemented with vitamins and minerals to provide complete nutrition.

The energy from canned rations is derived equally from carbohydrates, fats, and protein. Like meat-type foods, they are supplemented with vitamins and minerals to provide complete nutrition.

Both types of canned dog food are processed the same way; they are sterilized for preservation and to cook the grain ingredients, providing more usable carbohydrates.

Canned dog foods are well digested, especially the canned meat-type. The canned meat-type is also very palatable and serves as a good mixer to improve the flavor and nutrient density of dry foods. Canned rations are more palatable than dry foods, but not as tasty as the canned meat-types. The main advantage of canned rations over canned meats is lower cost.

Semimoist Dog Foods

Semimoist dog foods vary a great deal in formula and in moisture content. Modern semimoist dog food range in moisture from 15 to 50 percent, and in make-up from very near dry food to very near the canned meat-type. All are treated to retard spoilage.

The taste appeal of semimoist foods is somewhere between that of dry food and canned meats, and their digestibility level is good. The main appeal of semimoist foods is convenience. They have better flavor than dry foods and do not need to be refrigerated after opening.

Special-Purpose Dog Foods

The three main types of dog foods described above are most commonly fed to all healthy adult dogs. Special-purpose dog foods to meet the needs of definite classes of dogs have been developed in recent years. Because they are specifically formulated to meet particular needs, they are a great convenience for the dog owner who would otherwise have to learn what these particular needs are and feed a dog accordingly.

Puppy food: Puppy foods are found in all of the basic types. Designed to meet the greater energy and nutrient requirements of young, rapidly growing puppies, they have higher quality ingredients than general-purpose foods, improving digestibility. Owners should realize, however, that the same good puppy nutrition can be achieved by feeding larger quantities of general-purpose foods or by mixing a good general-purpose dry food with a canned meat food.

Stress diets: Dogs who are called upon to perform in shows, hunting, racing, or breeding are under stress, and their bodies need more protein and energy. Special stress diets are more nutrient dense and provide more metabolizable energy through protein and fat.

Geriatric diets: In general, older dogs are less active than younger ones and need fewer calories. At the same time, however, their bodies become less able to utilize the protein they eat. Therefore, although their daily calorie intake should decrease, older dogs still require the same amount of protein. Many commercial geriatric diets have greatly reduced protein contents. This lowered protein level is intended to reduce the workload of the kidneys, but it also has the negative effect of reducing many vital bodily functions. Cautions have been issued against the feeding of low-protein diets to older dogs when there is no evidence of severe kidney failure.[6]

Reducing diets: Reducing diets for dogs generally have reduced caloric densities achieved through the addition of nonnutritive bulk filler. These fillers also lower palatability and digestibility, which in turn serves to reduce total intake and utilization. Owners should re-

TABLE 5

PRESCRIPTION DIETS
AND THEIR USES

Following is a list of the most frequently used prescription diets for dogs, manufactured by two major producers, Hills Pet Products, Inc., and Cadillac.

	Hills	Cadillac
Low salt diet for heart patients	h/d	H diet
Low protein and mineral diet for impaired kidney and liver function	k/d	N diet
Lower protein and mineral diet for advanced kidney disease	u/d	—
Low protein, magnesium, calcium, phosphorus for bladder stones	s/d	—
Lamb-and-rice-based diet for food-induced allergies	d/d	—
Special diet tailored for older dogs	g/d	—
Highly digestible restricted-fat diet for intestinal upsets	i/d	E diet
Increased protein and fat for puppies, pregnant or nursing bitches, recuperating dogs, and dogs with infectious diseases	p/d	S diet
Low calorie, for obesity	r/d	O diet
General maintenance dog food	—	M diet

member that the only really effective way to help a dog reduce is to restrict the intake of calories and increase exercise. The advantage of these special reducing diets is that even though caloric density is decreased, bulk is provided. This fills a dog up and tends to prevent him from begging excessively, making it easier on the owner.

Prescription Diets: These special-formula diets, prepared by commercial manufacturers, are designed to meet the needs of dogs with severe medical conditions, such as food-related allergies, heart condition, kidney failure, and so forth. Their formulas are so precise (for example, the diet intended for kidney failure only contains 3.5 percent protein) that they can only be purchased by prescription from a veterinarian.

The two major producers of prescription diets for dogs are Hills Pet Products, Inc., and Cadillac. Table 5, opposite, lists their diets and the specific use of each.

Reading the Labels

The major pet-food manufacturers are very responsible when it comes to the products they sell for pets. Years of research and strict adherence to dogs' nutritional needs make it safe to say that feeding a dog one of the many types of food produced by any of the better-known companies will result in good nutrition.

One of the best ways to make an intelligent decision about dog food is to read the labels. Pet-food labels are made up of a number of different components, most of which are regulated under one or more state or federal laws. The Association of American Feed Control Officials (AAFCO) was formed to coordinate the various agencies involved and to bring some measure of uniformity to the laws governing pet foods. AAFCO has developed a uniform feed bill and regulations that govern pet-food labeling in most states.

There are two main parts of a pet-food label: The principal display panel and the information panel. The principal display panel must have an identity statement, including a brand

and product name, and a designator, such as "for dogs," or "for dogs and puppies," etc. This panel may also contain additional information or sales copy, as long as it doesn't hide the required information and isn't false or misleading. The information panel, which contains the ingredient listing, the list of guaranteed analyses, and the name and address of the manufacturer, packer, or distributor of the pet food. A typical pet-food label is shown in Illustration 4, below.

The Principal Display Panel

Much of the information on the principal display panel is regulated by law. The product name, which is often the same as the brand name, is covered by a variety of regulations:

The Flavored Food: A food need not contain any of the flavor ingredient itself, as long as the flavor source is clearly identified in the ingredient list and does, in fact, impart the named flavor.

The Percentage Rules: In order to be mentioned in the product name, an ingredient or combination of ingredients must make up at least 25 percent of the total diet and must be modified in some way to show that other ingredients are present. In other words, "Beef Dinner" identifies a product that contains at least 25 percent beef, as well as a number of other ingredients. Other descriptive terms, such as "chunks," etc., may also be used to indicate the form of the product.

If a product name is derived solely from a poultry, animal, or fish ingredient or combination of these, and no modifying term as "dinner" is used, the product must contain at least 95 percent of the named ingredient or ingredients.

Minor ingredients may form a part of the product name if they add a distinctive characteristic or have a significant effect on cost or the product's acceptance by the consumer. Thus, a name such as "Beef Dinner with Cheese" would indicate at least 25 percent beef and enough cheese to affect the price or

Illustration 4: A typical dog food label

the buyer's acceptance of the product. These rules hinge on whether a name would be deceptive or misleading, as determined by the AAFCO Pet Food Committee.

A final AAFCO rule regarding the naming of products requires that meats or meat by-products from animals other than cattle, pigs, sheep, or goats be identified. Horsemeat, for example, must be identified separately. If a meat is identified, it must correspond to the source (beef from cattle, etc.).

The Designator: This defines the purpose of the food, i.e., "dog food," "for dogs and puppies," etc. It is the only component of the identity statement specifically required by regulation, and in the case of some generic (white label) products, the designator is the only statement of identity.

The Declaration of Net Quantity of Contents: A statement of net weight is also required on the principal display panel. It must appear in the lower third of the display space and be printed or displayed in lines generally parallel to the base on which the package normally rests or is designed to be displayed.

The Product Vignette: If a picture of the product appears on the label, it must truly represent the product inside.

Nutrition Statements: These may be on either the principal display panel or the information panel, or both. They may be simple statements as to the adequacy of the diet ("Complete and Balanced," "Totally Nutritious," etc.), or they may be more explicit and show the basis of the claim ("Meets National Research Council Requirements," "Tested by Procedures Established by the Association of American Feed Control Officials," etc.).

Statements such as "Nutritious" and "Complete" mean that the diet contains all of the nutrients required by dogs in amounts needed for maintenance throughout life. They are suitable for feeding from puppyhood through old age, including special times like pregnancy and lactation. Such statements must be backed by facts that should be either chemical analy-

ses to show that the product meets the requirements established by a recognized authority such as the National Research Council or actual feeding tests on dogs as prescribed by AAFCO.

Nutrition statements may be more limited when the diet is formulated for a special or limited purpose. "Complete Diet for Puppies," "Reducing Diet," etc., are examples of limited-purpose statements. These products are formulated to meet only specific needs.

Pet foods labeled "snacks" or "treats," which carry no statements of adequacy, are generally not complete and should make up no more than 10–15 percent of a dog's total diet. A 1984 AAFCO regulation requires that pet foods that are not labeled as snacks or treats and have not been shown to be complete must carry a statement that the "product is intended for intermittent or supplemental feeding only."

The Information Panel

Laws governing the information panel include:

The Ingredient List: Each ingredient of a pet food must appear in decreasing order by weight or percentage. Most ingredients used in pet foods have been given official names and definitions by AAFCO, and this terminology must be used. More than six hundred ingredients are listed in the official publication of the association. It may be helpful for dog owners to understand a few of the more popular ingredients in order to evaluate a pet food on the basis of the ingredient list.

Meat is generally found only in canned and semimoist foods. It is limited to the "clean flesh derived from slaughtered mammals . . . [and] is limited to that part of the striate muscle which is skeletal, or that which is found in the tongue, in the diaphragm, in the heart, or in the esophagus."

Meat by-products are usually only found in canned and semimoist dog foods. The term refers to the "nonrendered, clean parts, other than meat, derived from slaughtered mammals." It includes but is not limited to lungs, spleen, kidneys, brain, livers, blood, bone, partially defatted low-temperature fatty tissue, and stomachs and intestines freed of their contents. It does *not* include hair, horns, teeth, and hooves.

Meat meal and meat and bone meal are distinct from meat and meat by-products and are usually found in dry pet foods, but may also be used in other types. They are defined as "the dry rendered product from mammal tissues, exclusive of hair, hoof, horn and hide trimmings, manure, and stomach contents, except in such amounts as may occur unavoidably in good factory practice." These two ingredients are distinguished from one another by their levels of phosphorus and pepsin-indigestible residue.

Cereal grains include corn, wheat, and oats, and a number of the by-products from cereal milling such as wheat middlings and corn gluten meal. These are found as major ingredients in dry pet foods. They serve primarily as sources of carbohydrate energy, although corn gluten meal and others can be sources of vegetable protein.

Soybean meal and soy flour are by-products of soybean-oil production and serve as a source of high-quality vegetable protein in all types of pet foods.

An ingredient in pet food that is not generally listed is "water sufficient for processing." This includes water used in the hydration of dry ingredients and water that enters the product as steam during the cooking process. The steam is required to ensure heat penetration for adequate sterilization of the finished food.

Many other ingredients are found on most pet-food labels. The long list of chemical names indicates the vitamin and mineral fortifiers added to achieve nutritional adequacy and balance.

The Guaranteed Analysis: The guarantees required on all pet foods include minimum crude protein and crude fat and maximum crude fiber and moisture. Other guarantees may be listed, but they are not required. Ash is often listed as a measure of the mineral content of the food.

Crude protein is based on nitrogen in the product. It is a fairly accurate index of protein quantity but gives no indication at all of the quality of the protein. Protein quality (e.g., vegetable vs. animal sources) can be judged on the basis of the listed ingredients.

Crude fat is a measure of the total content of substances soluble in ether. This ether extract includes neutral fats, fat-soluble vitamins, and phospholipids. Since neutral fats are by far the greatest portion of the ether extract, the crude-fat listing may be used as a true estimate of the energy density of the food.

Crude fiber is the indigestible part of the product. Crude fiber is not totally indigestible in a dog, but a high-fiber value indicates a large amount of lower-quality ingredients. As with crude protein, the ingredient list will give a better understanding of just what the crude fiber in a given product is made up of.

Moisture is a measure of the product's water content. It has little to do with the nutrient value of a given food.

What About Additives?

There has been some discussion in recent years about the dangers of additives in commercial dog foods. Many commercial dog foods do contain small amounts of various types of preservatives, which are a necessity to prevent the growth of bacteria. And most have food colorings, which are apparently a necessity to make the product appeal to human buyers. Semimoist dog foods often have corn syrup and/or other humectants in them to keep them moist. Some diets also contain artificial flavorings.

In our experience, these additives appear in such small amounts that there is no evidence that they are harmful or carcinogenic in any way. However, if their very presence is disturbing, see the section on noncommercial diets.

How Much of What to Feed

Theoretically, one properly balanced diet, high in nutrient density, would be suitable for all dogs at all stages of life if properly fed. The National Research Council has recommended one set of "Nutrient requirement values that provide for adequate nutrition of both growing puppies and adult dogs . . . the nutrients required for the entire life cycle of all breeds of dogs."[7] However, the committee recognized the limitations of applying this standard and amended their recommendations by stating that they were intended only as general guides and might require modification. A diet suitable for all dogs at all stages of life would have to be one of extremely high quality, well above the nutrient density of the "adequate" diet of the NRC,[8] and would be very expensive. That's why we recommend that owners choose dog foods based on the nutritional needs of a pet at each stage in life.

Optimal Ranges and Economic Considerations

An adult dog living in comfortable surroundings needs only a maintenance diet in order to prosper. However, when conditions are more nutritionally demanding, optimal ranges of nutrients tend to become narrower. Figure 4, page 31, demonstrates the narrower acceptable range of dietary protein for growth and the still narrower range during stress.

Carbohydrates found in cereal grains are the least expensive source of calories for dogs. Therefore, dry dog foods, which are composed mostly of grain, are the least expensive maintenance diet in terms of dietary energy and will usually provide adequate nutrition for a healthy adult dog who is relatively inactive and lives in comfortable conditions. But a least-cost maintenance diet composed entirely of dry foods will not contain an adequate percentage of high-quality protein for growth or stress conditions.

Semimoist foods cost two or three times more than dry, and canned foods that contain high-quality protein and fats are four or five times as expensive as dry foods on an energy (caloric) basis. One of these higher-cost diets is necessary when conditions demand a higher level of performance (puppy growth, show ring competition, etc.) or when dry foods alone fail to produce the expected result.

You may use a combination of foods and supplement dry foods to enhance their nutritive value (see "What Kind of Food?" page 43).

Avoiding Obesity: Recommended Daily Intake

There are two distinct ways to feed a dog: free-choice feeding when food is left available for the dog to eat at will; and feeding by eye or hand, when an owner feeds a dog a predetermined amount of food based on judgment and observation.

Most maintenance-only dry dog foods can be safely used for free-choice feeding, because their lack of enticing taste appeal will generally prevent a dog from overeating. This system of feeding is most often used in kennels, but it can have advantages at home, allowing an owner to leave dry food available for the dog all of the time. Take care, however, because while dry dog foods intended for maintenance-only use usually have a guaranteed analysis of 18 percent or less protein and 6 percent or less fat, general-use dry foods often have a much higher protein and fat content (up to 23 percent protein and 10 percent fat). Because of their greater appeal, free-choice feeding of these foods may encourage a dog to overeat. Nor should dry puppy foods or high-protein dry foods ever be fed free-choice to adult dogs on maintenance, as they are very likely to be too palatable and lead to overfeeding and overnutrition, resulting in obesity in adults and possible skeletal problems in young, growing dogs.

Individual dogs vary a great deal in the amount of food they need to maintain desired body weight, depending on how efficiently their bodies utilize food. Table 6, page 43, shows the average daily intake of food for dogs in a wide range of body weights. Owners may notice that the daily intakes of food recommended on commercial dog-food labels show that manufacturers generally call for a far greater quantity of food per day than the average amounts given in Table 6. This is usually done to ensure that the needs of all dogs are met, but it can lead to overfeeding and overnutrition for some dogs.

By far the most prevalent methods of feeding pet dogs are either by eye or by hand. When an owner feeds a pet by eye, he gives the dog amounts that result in a generally pleasing appearance. However, this method can be deceiving. Overweight people tend to prefer chubby dogs, for instance. Also, when indul-

gent owners offer unlimited amounts of good things to eat, most dogs invariably will consume much more food than necessary and will become obese.

A much more accurate method of determining how much to feed a dog to maintain ideal weight is by hand. Stand behind the dog, place both thumbs side-by-side on the midline, or spine, above the chest with fingers spread over the ribs (see Photograph 4, below). With thumbs pressing on vertebrae and fingers on ribs, slide the hands gently backward and forward. Ideally, you should feel a moderately thin layer of fat. Visibly protruding bones sug-

Photograph 4: Position of hands for judging a dog's weight

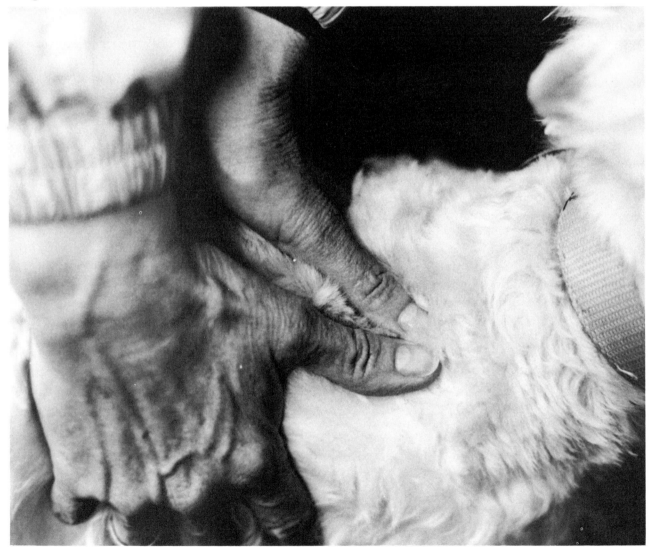

gest that the dog is too thin. A cushion of fat that hides the edges of the ribs, allowing only a smooth wavy feel to the chest, suggests that the dog is too fat and should be fed less.

To determine the correct amount to feed a dog, use the general guidelines provided in Table 6 (or the advice of your veterinarian), and assess the results at intervals by hand.

What Kind of Food?

Armed with knowledge about types of dog foods, nutritional requirements of dogs, and the proper amount of food to give on a daily basis, an owner still must decide exactly how to meet these needs. Owners usually choose the types of food they feed their pets based on their own preferences and those of their dogs. There are always several good choices of food, each of which will meet a dog's nutritional needs very well.

It is important to note that any change in a dog's diet must be gradual, or it will lead to upsets. Whether adding a new food, or changing rations altogether, continue feeding the old diet with a small bit of the new food mixed in for several days, and begin to observe the dog's stools and general appetite carefully. A good rule of thumb is to increase the amount of the new food by 10 percent each day until the old diet is completely replaced.

Dry vs. Moist Food: Dry dog food is usually used on a maintenance diet when costs must be kept low, but there are good reasons for feeding moist or canned products instead. Many dog owners are concerned about the appearance of a pet's coat, commonly known as bloom. Some dogs won't have this bloom when fed on dry food alone, and owners often supplement with liver, egg, or corn oil. The problem with this kind of supplementation is that it can be overdone and lead to an unbalanced diet. Using a complete, balanced canned meat diet is a safer way to increase protein and fat in a dog's diet.

Some dogs react badly to the large amounts of fiber and starch found in many dry dog foods and will develop flatulence, abundant sloppy stools, and occasionally chronic diarrhea.

These dogs probably will react better to the higher-quality meat-based canned products or high-quality dry dog food with less bulk and greater digestibility.

There are other reasons for feeding more expensive meat-based products. One of the most obvious is a dog's preference. Some dogs seem to be born finicky and greatly prefer the animal protein and fat found in canned foods. These dogs often fare poorly on dry food alone.

Foods of high nutrient density are particularly well suited for the toy or miniature breeds, which have a high requirement of food energy per unit of body weight.

TABLE 6

AVERAGE DAILY FOOD INTAKES FOR MAINTENANCE OF MATURE DOGS [1]

Weight Lbs.	Energy[2] kcal ME/day	Food			
		Dry[3] cup[4]	Semi-moist[3] oz.	Canned Ration[3] cans[4]	Canned Meat[3] cans[4]
5	245	¾	3¼	½	½
10	411	1½	5½	1	¾
15	557	2	7½	1½	1¼
20	691	2⅓	9½	1¾	1½
25	817	2¾	11	2	1¾
30	937	3¼	13	2¼	2
40	1162	4	16	3	2½
50	1374	4¾	19	3½	2¾
60	1575	5¼	22	4	3¼
80	1955	6½	27	5	4
100	2311	7¾	32	5¾	4¾
120	2650	9	36	6½	5½
150	3132	10½	43	7¾	6½
180	3591	12	49	9	7½

[1] Adapted from NRC(3)
[2] Energy in kilocalories of metabolizable energy per day
[3] See Table 4 for average analyses
[4] Household measure based on 8 oz. household measuring cup for dry and 14 oz. for canned products

Canine Nutrition and Feeding Management, the ALPO Pet Center, Allentown, PA, 1984.

Probably the most important reason why many people opt to feed their dogs more expensive rations than necessary is the satisfaction that they derive from seeing a dog obviously enjoying a meal.

Supplementing Dry Food: Another way to give a dog enjoyment is to supplement dry dog food in one of several ways. (Note: Don't leave moistened dry food out for more than an hour or two, or it will spoil.)

• Moisten dry food with about 1 part water to 4 parts food. Most dogs prefer moistened food to dry and, if allowed, consume 10–20 percent more.

• Whole milk in a ratio of 1 part to 4 parts dry food, or one-half part evaporated milk to 4 parts food, may also be mixed with dry rations, adding protein and fat as well as additional taste appeal. If milk has been part of a dog's diet since weaning or is reintroduced gradu-

ally over a period of 5–6 days, it will not cause diarrhea.

• A teaspoon of supplementary fat, such as meat drippings, chicken fat, or corn oil per half pound of dry food will raise the fat content.

• Small amounts of supplementary protein such as milk, meat, cottage cheese (1 tablespoon per half pound of food), or cheese (1–2 tablespoons per half pound) may be added. An excellent supplement is $1/16$ pound of liver per pound of dry food. An egg is best of all. One cooked egg per half pound of diet will supply excellent supplementary protein and fat.

• The simplest and safest way to improve the quality of dry dog food is to mix it with canned meat dinner, as long as both products are complete and balanced, so that nutritional deficiencies, imbalances, or harmful excesses will not occur. See Table 7, page 45, for how to vary the proportions of dry and canned foods in order to meet different levels of protein and fat.

Feeding to Meet Special Needs

Breeding

Gestation and lactation are the most nutritionally demanding stages in the normal adult life of the bitch, and the owner must pay careful attention to proper feeding and, in particular, provide adequate calcium for the dog.

Gestation: Two or three weeks before breeding, food intake should be increased slightly. Bitches maintained on cereal-based diets will benefit from increased protein. The best way to increase protein is to add moderate amounts of fortified meat-based canned dog foods.

Gestation lasts an average of sixty-three days, and the bitch needs little or no increase in nutrient level during the first five to six weeks. At four to five weeks, the dog should begin to receive more food (see Table 8, page 46) until the ratio of meat-based dog food reaches a proportion of 3 to 1, dry to canned, by volume, during the last ten days of gestation for medium or large dogs. Smaller dogs will benefit from a richer mixture of 1 to 1, by volume.

Monitor weight gain carefully. For a rough approximation of acceptable weight gain, multiply the expected birth weight of the puppies by the expected number of puppies in the litter and add 10 percent of the bitch's initial weight.

It's not uncommon for a bitch to experience two distinct periods of anorexia during pregnancy. The first may occur during the fourth and fifth weeks of pregnancy as a result of discomfort or hormonal changes. At about this time, her feedings should be divided in half, giving one portion in the morning and the other at night. Just before parturition the bitch may again lose her appetite. Do not force feed her, and take away any uneaten food. If she refuses to eat for longer than forty-eight hours, consult a veterinarian.

Lactation: The nutrition demands on the lactating bitch to produce milk and to cope with the stress of nursing will quickly deplete her nutrient reserves unless she is fed a high-quality diet.

TABLE 7
NUTRITION ACHIEVED BY
MIXING DRY AND CANNED DOG FOODS

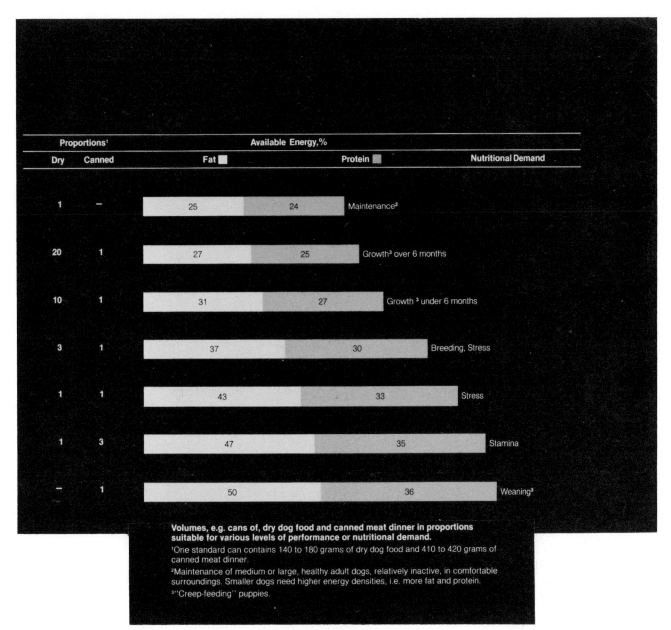

Proportions[1]		Available Energy,%		Nutritional Demand
Dry	Canned	Fat ■	Protein ■	
1	–	25	24	Maintenance[2]
20	1	27	25	Growth[3] over 6 months
10	1	31	27	Growth[3] under 6 months
3	1	37	30	Breeding, Stress
1	1	43	33	Stress
1	3	47	35	Stamina
–	1	50	36	Weaning[3]

Volumes, e.g. cans of, dry dog food and canned meat dinner in proportions suitable for various levels of performance or nutritional demand.

[1]One standard can contains 140 to 180 grams of dry dog food and 410 to 420 grams of canned meat dinner.

[2]Maintenance of medium or large, healthy adult dogs, relatively inactive, in comfortable surroundings. Smaller dogs need higher energy densities, i.e. more fat and protein.

[3]"Creep-feeding" puppies.

Canine Nutrition and Feeding Management, ALPO Pet Center, Allentown, PA 18001, 1984.

TABLE 8
SUGGESTED INCREASE/DECREASE IN DIET
FOR THE GESTATING/LACTATING BITCH

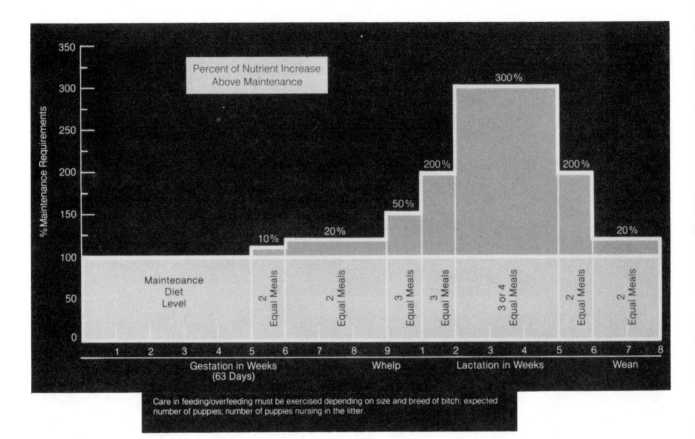

Canine Nutrition and Feeding Management, ALPO Pet Center, Allentown, PA 18001, 1984.

Studies show that dietary protein greatly influences milk production.[9] The bitch will develop a tremendous appetite while nursing, and will consume up to three or four times her maintenance intake. Her suggested diet intake is shown in Table 8. Adjust feeding levels according to her litter size.

Three or four meals a day will be easier on the bitch's digestive system than two large daily meals. If her stomach appears upset and she has sloppy stools or diarrhea, reduce the quantity, but not the quality, of the daily intake, keeping up the intake of fat and protein by using less carbohydrate food and the same amount, or more, of meat-based canned food.

Puppies During Growth

After the puppies are weaned (see Chapter 6), add moistened dry dog food gradually. Aim for a proportion of one part dry dog food to three parts canned by the time the pups are ten weeks old. You may change this ratio to reach a proportion of 1 to 1 by the time they reach approximately 20 percent of mature weight.

Puppies need twice an adult's maintenance requirements of energy and nutrients for proper growth from weaning until about half their expected mature weight. It is usually best to feed them three or four times a day.

It's impossible to prescribe exact amounts to feed pups. Any changes in, or additions to, a puppy's diet should be made very gradually. Abrupt changes will probably result in digestive upsets. It's particularly important not to overfeed growing puppies. Overfeeding may result in obesity or in overly rapid growth. Normal bones of young, fat puppies may not be adequately developed to carry their excess weight. Underfeeding, on the other hand, may result in poor growth and limited activity.

Proper feeding is best determined by using the eye and hand methods (see page 42). A puppy should look trim with only a slight layer of fat over the ribs. It is too fat if the ribs can't be felt with gentle pressure and too thin if the ribs can be easily seen when it moves. A puppy's diet should be adjusted every week to obtain the desired rate of growth, coat, body conformation, and spontaneous activity level, under the owner's careful observation.

Older Dogs

As dogs get older, their metabolisms slow down, and they burn fewer calories than when they were young and active. Care must be taken to feed an older dog adequate amounts of quality protein. At the same time, the older dog's fat intake may need to be lowered to reduce calories.

Unless an older dog requires a prescription diet, which can only be determined by a veterinarian, the best rule to follow is to continue feeding the dog the diet it has been used to all along if it is doing well.

If an older dog's daily intake of food has to be cut back, it will be much less noticeable to the dog if it is fed two or three small meals a day instead of one big one. It's a good idea to feed all older dogs several meals a day, in general. Smaller meals are easier to digest and more readily assimilated.

Hard Work, Stamina, and Stress

Hard work demands extra nutrients as fuel for muscles. Work also induces a variable degree of *stress*, which can be defined as the general response of the body to any extra demand, physical or emotional.

A stress reaction can be triggered in a dog by a change in environment, threat, or the need to react to an unusual demand from the environment. A situation need not be dire or life-threatening in order to produce a stress response in a dog. Events such as an infection, a bite from another animal, broken bones or other injuries, travel, breeding, showing, strenuous athletics, or deprivation of accustomed affection can all cause stress in a dog. The stress reaction signals a dog's internal system to go on alert, causing heartbeat and breathing rates to accelerate and muscles to tense. Extra food energy is needed to enable a dog's body to cope with any type of stress.

Studies of sled dogs in the field and of beagles on treadmills have shown that the optimal diet for hard work, stress, and stamina should be very digestible, low in bulk, and have the caloric proportions of 50–60 percent fat, 30–40 percent protein, and 10–20 percent carbohydrate.[10, 11]

In the past, the extra food energy for work was often provided for dogs by increasing the intake of carbohydrates, just as in the practice of carbohydrate-loading for human marathon runners that prevailed until recently. Recent studies show, however, that this may lead to blood in the urine of dogs because of a chemical change, and it is *not* recommended.

A better method of providing extra high energy for dogs is through a high-fat diet. High-fat diets are also highly digestible, and their lower bulk contributes further to stamina.[12] They are recommended with the following precautions:

• Introduce high-fat diets gradually to allow the digestive tract to adjust. Otherwise the fat may be digested poorly.

• Restrict the total amount of food fed daily in line with the increase in energy density caused by the higher fat level. At the same time increase the essential nutrient contents to maintain the necessary balance (see "Fats," page 32).

Two field studies of racing sled dogs indicate that even 23–28 percent protein is not enough to prevent mild "sports anemia," and that the optimal range of protein for these dogs is 32–39 percent. Since a low red-blood-cell count is characteristic of all overstressed individuals,[13] this finding can be applied to all dogs subjected to stress and hard work. High-quality protein, as found in eggs, dairy products, meat, and meat by-products, should constitute at least 30 percent of the metabolizable energy of a stress diet.

To reach the optimal ranges of these nutrients for a working dog, change the diet to include more fat and protein a week or so before training begins. For example, if a dog is maintained on dry food, replace part of that food gradually with canned meat dinner until the ratio of dry to canned is 1 to 3. The amount fed should be sufficient to keep the dog in the desired condition. Working dogs should be kept lean and trim. Evaluate the dog daily to make sure he is maintaining the correct weight.

Never feed dogs immediately before they are to indulge in strenuous exercise or heavy work. In general, it's always best to feed physically active dogs several small meals a day rather than one large one.

Nonphysical stressful situations, such as illness, travel, or separation from owners, also call for added food energy. This is usually supplied best by higher protein levels, but in some situations you may need to supplement. A veterinarian should assess the individual dog's needs.

Noncommercial Foods for Dogs

Commercial dog foods produced by the major manufacturers are designed to meet completely the nutritional needs of a dog at any stage of life or in any special situation when properly used. Some owners, however, prefer to feed home-prepared meals or meals composed of nothing but "natural" ingredients.

Home-Cooked Meals

Many adult dogs living in nonstressful situations seem to get along pretty well on nothing but table scraps. This kind of diet is not adequate for many other dogs, however.

Owners who have the time and are willing to learn about canine nutrition undoubtedly can create a home-prepared diet that will meet the needs of a dog at any stage of life. Advocates of home cooking for dogs maintain that the time spent is well worth the results of lowered feeding costs and healthy pets that are free from the possible ill effects of additives.

Aside from the tremendous amount of time spent shopping for ingredients and cooking meals for a dog, there are several problems with this theory. It's extremely difficult to purchase raw materials that don't contain some additives or preservatives. By substituting home-prepared foods for those processed under strict government regulations for composition, cleanliness, and sterilization, an owner may simply be exchanging one set of additives for another and introducing dietary imbalances at the same time. It is also difficult to maintain precise measurements and combinations of vitamins, minerals, and other nutritional elements at home. We advise owners to be extremely cautious about embarking on an entirely home-prepared regimen for a dog. If a dog is doing well on home-cooked meals, do not change; on the other hand, if an animal's faring well on a commercial diet, do not change either. There are several books in print that take the reader on a step-by-step routine for the choice and preparation of home-cooked pet foods. It's a good idea to read all of them before making a decision that will affect a dog's entire life, to say nothing of the owner's.

Of course, occasional treats of leftovers won't hurt most dogs at all, as long as they're not too frequent or excessive. Some dogs, however, cannot tolerate anything but their "regular" food. This will be quickly evident to an owner, as the dog will either vomit or develop diarrhea.

Vegetarian Diets

While on the topic of home-prepared diets for dogs, we should touch on the recently all-too-prevalent fad of feeding dogs all-vegetable diets. Dogs are carnivores, and their digestive organs have evolved over hundreds of years to derive proper nutrition mainly from meat, meat by-products, and other high-protein foods such as poultry, eggs, dairy products, and fish. These constitute the dog's "natural" diet. Feeding a dog nothing but vegetables and grains forces his body to work twice as hard in order to derive even minimal nutrition. In addition, as we mentioned before, too much cellulose, or fiber, found in vegetables and grains, prevents the absorption of necessary nutrients in the dog's small intestine and leads to large, poorly formed stools. In short, dogs' bodies are not equipped to handle a completely vegetarian diet, and they will not fare well on such a regimen in the long run.

Other Alternatives

There are several manufacturers of natural pet diets in various parts of the country, and many of them have national distribution. These companies produce pet food in various forms that contain no sugar, flavoring, coloring, preservatives, or other additives. Owners should check the ingredient lists and guaranteed analyses on the labels themselves. The only drawback to these foods is that they are usually very expensive. (See Bibliography for a few of these companies.)

Exercise

All dogs need some kind of regular daily exercise to keep in shape. The amount each dog needs will vary according to its size and genetics and will also depend, in part, on what physical demands the owner imposes. For example, if a dog is going to have to indulge in hard physical work, it will have to be conditioned for that work with vigorous exercise.

There are a few general guidelines pertaining to exercise for dogs that should be mentioned here:

• Don't exercise any dog strenuously immediately (less than two hours) after it eats a large meal.

• Before embarking on a vigorous exercise or training routine, a dog should have a physical exam to rule out cardiac or circulatory problems and skeletal or joint disorders.

• Just like human athletes, dogs need gradual conditioning in order to strengthen muscles, joints, and cardiac systems and to toughen foot pads.

• Owners should be alert to signs of fatigue and/or heat stress: excessive panting, loss of color in lips and face, a vacant stare. Dogs often won't give up or stop until they collapse.

How Much Is Enough?

Before discussing dogs' specific exercise needs, a differentiation must be made between "exercise" and "activity level." When we talk about exercise in this section, it refers generally to outdoor undertakings or indoor substitutes for outdoor work. Activity level, on the other hand, refers to the normal, everyday actions of a dog, usually in the home. Many dogs tend to run around indoors a lot, while others spend most of their indoor time sleeping or sitting quietly. Some small dogs have a very high activity level and scurry around almost continuously indoors, playing with toys or other pets, jumping up and down on furniture, going up and down stairs, and keeping an eye on the passing world outside. In many instances, this constant activity of small dogs adds up to almost enough daily exercise. Large dogs, however, may have very low indoor activity levels but require a great deal of outdoor exercise.

Probably the single most important factor to consider in determining just how much exercise is enough for a dog is genetics. What was this kind of dog bred to do? Over the years, dogs have been bred selectively to meet certain needs or serve particular purposes. Some breeds have been developed to be hunters or retrievers, some to work at tasks such as herding or pulling heavy loads, and others to serve only as companions for humans.

In general, dogs who were developed for hunting and retrieving, including hounds and terriers, have very high energy and require a lot of daily exercise to stay in shape and work off excess pep and ginger.

On the other hand, dogs developed primarily as companions (the nonsporting, nonworking breeds and the toys) are usually not as highly energetic and can get along quite well with moderate daily exercise.

Size and shape are also factors. Short-legged dogs such as dachshunds and tiny toy dogs will use up a lot of energy simply running around the house or on a short walk. Usually, males of all breeds are more energetic and need more exercise than females do. Most dogs are remarkably adaptable, however, and can adjust to less-than-ideal conditions.

In addition to appetite and general behavior, assessment of a dog's weight by hand, as discussed earlier in this chapter, is a good way to tell if it is in good condition and getting enough exercise.

Ways to Exercise a Dog

Location, climate, and the makeup of the family a dog lives with will certainly determine what kind of exercise predominates. A dog who lives in a household with several active youngsters probably doesn't need any extra exercise after romping in the yard with the children. On the other hand, a dog living alone with working adults in a city apartment will need a planned, appropriate exercise regimen.

Walking

Walking is the first thing that comes to mind when we talk about exercising a dog. In the city and the suburbs, where dogs are generally indoors most of the time, a walk on a leash several times a day is a necessity for sanitary reasons as well as for exercise. A short turn around the block morning and evening and a quick trip out to the nearest hydrant before bedtime are probably sufficient for most small housedogs. Larger and more energetic dogs will need additional, longer walks or a run in the park or the country.

Running Free

There are fewer and fewer communities in which dogs are allowed to run completely free. However, many owners of dogs in restricted areas still allow their dogs to run during off-hours, when dog-control personnel are not on duty.

Dogs who are kept in all day and allowed out to run only at specified times will usually be sufficiently elated at their freedom to take at least a short run and get some exercise. But dogs who are allowed to be loose all of the time or who are kept in large, enclosed yards often fail to exercise at all. If Rover chooses to sleep on the lawn all day instead of running around, owners should be sure to give him some supplementary exercise.

Most hunting dogs and retrievers, especially males, will take off for the next county if they're allowed complete freedom. Responsible dog ownership doesn't mean letting a dog do whatever comes naturally when it comes to running free. Take care to protect dogs who tend to roam from injury, loss, and even theft —a big price to pay for exercise that's effortless for the owner. These dogs would do better in an enclosed yard with daily vigorous play or controlled runs.

Running a Dog

There are two ways of running a dog: letting it run under controlled conditions and running with it.

If a dog is going to be run in a park or school-yard, in the country, or at the beach, it should be under some control. Even out in the country an owner has to be sure that the dog won't take off after a squirrel, skunk, or another dog, and disappear. Games such as fetch may seem to be a good idea, but there's no assurance that a dog won't be distracted and run off, especially if it is young and high-spirited.

The best form of control is a leash and a choke collar. Even the smallest dog is easier to handle with this type of collar. An owner can signal the dog to stop or come with a short, quick motion instead of having to haul and tug as he would on a regular collar, running the risk that the dog will pull his head through the collar and get loose. Choke collars are made in all sizes, weights, and materials and are in no way uncomfortable for the dog or "cruel" to use. A length of clothesline will do very well for a running leash, and there are long, spring-controlled retracting leads on the market that are excellent. A dog on a long lead should not be allowed to get out of sight in case the leash becomes tangled.

Some active owners take their dogs jogging with them. This is very good exercise, but it is important not to overdo. Just because a dog looks and seems healthy is no assurance that it doesn't have heart trouble or potential joint disorders. Before beginning to jog with a dog, have it examined by a veterinarian to be sure that its body can withstand the strain. Dogs generally will not complain, and in their eagerness to be with and please their owners, they may overdo to the point of exhaustion. Running on hard surfaces like concrete or asphalt for long periods can wear a dog's foot pads raw. A soft surface, like grass or dirt, is better.

It is not a good idea to exercise a dog by having it run behind a bicycle or car. Even if it can be managed without using a well-traveled road, there are great potential risks. If the animal is attached to a moving vehicle by a line or leash, there is a serious possibility that it might fall, or the line might become snagged and the dog dragged or choked. If the dog is not attached in some way, there is no assurance that it won't run off or get hit by a passing vehicle even if it stands still. Also even a slow-moving bicycle or car will maintain a speed level that even the best-conditioned dog cannot keep up with for more than a few minutes without badly straining its heart and skeletal system.

Games to Play—Toys

If it is not possible or practical to run a dog, there are a number of excellent ways of exercising a dog while playing with him.

One of the best and most enjoyable games to play with a dog is catch, or fetch. A dog need not be a retriever to enjoy chasing a ball or fetching a stick. A major pet-food manufacturer has even established a nationwide competition for Frisbee-catching dogs. The nicest thing about a game of catch or fetch is that the dog does all of the work and gets a great deal of good exercise, running out to retrieve an object and then returning it to the owner to throw again. Water-loving dogs who are good swimmers can get excellent exercise retrieving an object tossed in the water. Owners should be sure that there is a way for the dog to get out of the water. It is very hard (perhaps impossible) for most dogs to climb up on a dock or boat unaided. Owners must think for their pets when playing catch or fetch in or out of the water: watch for cars or other hazards and keep an eye out to see that the dog doesn't become exhausted.

Tug-of-war is another good game to play with a dog. Large dogs and breeds with under-shot jaws and good grips, such as bulldogs and boxers, particularly love this game, and it is excellent exercise for a dog's legs and shoulder muscles. There are rubber toys and leather straps on the market specifically designed for tugging. Or a tugging toy can easily be made by knotting a sturdy sock. Care should be taken not to pull too hard with a teething pup or with an older animal that has any loose teeth. (See also Chapter 8.)

Indoor Exercise

Small and medium-sized dogs can get a lot of exercise indoors playing fetch or tug-of-war, and even big dogs can play modified games of tug-of-war inside.

It is hard for large or giant dogs to get sufficient exercise indoors, however, unless an owner is able and willing to invest in special equipment. For example, there are treadmills intended for indoor home use on the market; they are usually available through mail-order houses that serve kennels or breeders. These may serve a useful purpose, but only on a temporary or part-time basis.

Exercising a Fat Dog

Dogs who need to lose weight can be helped to burn up calories and develop muscle tone by increasing the time spent walking, running, or playing games, indoors or out. Every time an overweight dog moves, it is putting a great deal of strain on its heart, circulatory system, and joints, so owners should be particularly careful to increase exercise gradually, never exceeding the point when a dog becomes obviously tired. Eventually, an added half-hour a day of some kind of fairly vigorous exercise may help Fido shed those extra pounds and stay slim and trim.

Training for Vigorous Exercise or Hard Work

If a dog is going to take part in vigorous exercise, such as racing or hunting, or indulge in hard work pulling a sled or herding cattle, it must, of course, be conditioned well ahead of time. As we mentioned above, the increased dietary requirements needed for these special conditions must be added gradually, in advance. The same rule applies to conditioning a dog's body to withstand heavy strain. Just because a dog is in the prime of life, looks strong and vigorous, and has a high energy level doesn't mean that it can suddenly be asked to do hard physical work without building up to it.

We will not discuss specific training programs here. There are a number of good ways to condition a dog to be able to perform various physical tasks; there are also a great many incorrect ways to train a dog, and a number of pitfalls that should be avoided. Owners who are not trainers should not attempt to train a dog for a special task without professional advice and help. Breed associations and interest clubs and groups will recommend a good professional trainer for almost any type of special task an owner wants a dog to learn.

Special Exercise Considerations

There are some times in a dog's life when it is best to go very easy on the exercise or even to restrain a very active dog from exercising too much.

Young, growing puppies, for instance, need no exercise beyond what they get naturally playing with their littermates. Once a pup is taken away from its brothers and sisters, it will still get a lot of exercise running around the house. Puppy bones are very soft and their joints are tender; and owners have to be careful not to let them run wildly on slippery surfaces or they may break a bone. Overweight puppies and pups of very large breeds with heavy bones and bodies are particularly susceptible to joint disorders and can develop skeletal deformities if they are allowed to jump or run excessively. Puppies usually sleep immediately after eating. If they are forced to exercise, they will probably throw up. Puppies under six months of age tire very quickly and should be allowed to exercise at their own pace and stop whenever they want. After a pup is half-grown, a normal but moderate exercise regimen can be started.

Although it's very important that a pregnant bitch be in good physical condition, it's also important that as the pregnancy progresses some care is taken. Jumping and exercise that involves any kind of twisting motion should be avoided as the bitch becomes big. Vigorous exercise should always be avoided right after meals, but it is particularly important that pregnant bitches avoid after-eating exercise, which might lead to extreme discomfort. As the time for delivery approaches, it is best to let a bitch determine for herself how much exercise she wants to do.

Old dogs must continue to move every day, but they should not be required to indulge in overstrenuous exercise. A walk is more suitable for a senior citizen than a brisk run, and shorter play periods several times a day are a good replacement for an extended playtime. Controlled, frequent movement rather than vigorous physical exercise is the key for all older dogs. Thoughtful owners will never let an older dog be pushed into doing too much, nor will they let it get into the habit of being completely sedentary. More about this in Chapter 7.

There's no point in trying to interest a sick dog in a game of catch or a run. Owners should take the signal from a dog who is not well and allow it to set its own pace when it comes to exercise. As soon as it feels better and is ready to run around again, it will let its owners know.

Grooming and Cleanliness

Grooming a dog is the process of keeping its coat, skin, eyes, ears, and extremities clean and neat. It may include clipping and/or plucking the coat, but it is not confined to these procedures.

Regular grooming is a good routine to establish with a dog. Not only will frequent brushing and combing keep the dog clean and free from snarls and mats. it will also do a great deal to keep a dog's skin and coat healthy and free from problems. A grooming session also provides an excellent opportunity for the owner to look the animal over for changes and abnormalities (parasites, lumps, rashes, wounds, or sores). The process itself is usually mutually enjoyable for both dog and owner, providing a quiet time for togetherness.

Many owners who take care of their pets' everyday grooming still opt to take their dogs to a professional groomer on a regular basis for bathing, clipping, nail trimming, and other routines.

Young puppies should be accustomed to handling as soon as possible (see Chapter 6). If this has been done and grooming is introduced gradually in short sessions, there should be no problem. If, however, a dog is skittish and frightened, even of brushing, it has probably had a bad experience and will have to be shown gradually and calmly that there is nothing to fear. Owners sometimes become irritated and upset when a dog shies from them or runs away when it is grooming time. What they need to realize is that it is not them but the routine or the tools that the dog is afraid of and that their annoyance will only frighten and confuse the animal even more. It may take some patient observation to determine the problem. With a little time and a lot of patience, almost all dogs will learn to like being handled and brushed and will soon stay still for a complete grooming.

It is a good idea to assemble the tools that will be used for grooming and put them somewhere handy in a box, bag, or drawer. A brush and comb and a pair of blunt-nosed scissors for long-haired dogs are all that most owners will require. Other tools such as nail clippers can be included.

A Grooming Routine

Even if a dog does not absolutely need it, a quick brushing and combing every few days will help to keep its coat shiny and will remove loose hairs that would otherwise end up on the carpet.

All dogs need some regular grooming, even short-haired breeds. The frequency and extent of brushing and combing depends on the kind of coat a dog has and on what he might get into. A long-haired dog who romps in a yard full of bushes and burrs will need to be brushed and combed thoroughly more often than a short-haired animal who spends its time in an apartment.

There is no hard and fast rule as to the best time to have a grooming session, but it is not a good idea to handle any dog, especially a young pup, immediately after it has eaten. Nor is it practical to expect a dog to stay quiet for brushing and combing when it needs to go out.

The quickest way to turn a grooming session into a circus is by chasing a dog around the house with a brush. It really does not matter where a dog is groomed. Professional dog groomers always put the animals up on a table to work on them. The dog tends to stay quiet, and it saves the groomer's back. Laps work well for grooming small dogs, and it is easiest to brush a big dog while he is standing and you're sitting on the floor. Some dogs prefer to lie down while being groomed and will often be so relaxed that they fall asleep.

Both dog and owner should be able to look on grooming as a pleasant experience, rather than a scary and hurtful one, and the onus is on the owner to provide a calm, relaxed atmosphere for grooming.

Brushing and Combing

It is easy to brush a dog's back and throat, but many animals balk at having their legs and feet handled. Owners of dogs with touchy legs and feet will have to experiment with the most satisfactory way to work on them. If a dog pulls away when its leg or foot is held to be brushed, let go. Usually it is not the actual brushing or combing that the dog objects to, but the fact of having its leg restrained. Try resting the foot in your palm, as if the dog is shaking hands, and use gentle brush strokes. When the dog realizes that it will not be held tightly by the foot, it will probably permit its legs and feet to be groomed. Other dogs like to have their feet and legs worked on when they are lying on their backs or sides, legs extended. Some never do learn to like having their feet and legs touched, and owners will just have to be as gentle and quick as they can about the whole thing.

Dogs often also object to having their faces, tail areas, and tummies touched. Gentle hand stroking and patience will usually bring a dog around. These are all delicate areas, so care must be taken not to pinch, pull, or hurt a dog or its trust will be shaken.

Ears, especially long ones, are often tender and need a very gentle touch. If a dog steadfastly refuses to let its ears be brushed or cries when its ears are touched, suspect an ear infection (see "Aural Diseases and Disorders" in the Encyclopedia).

In very dry weather, a slightly damp terry washcloth rubbed over a short-haired coat may help to settle it down and remove remaining loose hairs.

Double-coated dogs (collies, German shepherds, etc.) require special attention to remove loose hairs and should be brushed from the skin outward.

If there are mats or tangles in a long-coated dog, they should never be yanked out, but should either be "worked out" gently with fingers and a wide-toothed comb or snipped out with scissors. Sometimes a drop or two of mineral oil will help loosen mats.

Some breeds have special coat-care needs, which are best learned from a breeder or veterinarian. For more about dogs' haircoats in general, see Chapter 2.

For details about skin problems, see "Dermatologic Diseases and Disorders" in the Encyclopedia.

Fleas and Ticks

When grooming a dog, an owner may come across either of these parasites. Fleas usually appear in the thick fur at the base of dog's tail, or around the neck; often, the small black exudate is all that is visible. Ticks are likely to adhere to a dog around the head, in the ears, and between foot pads. They can appear as small, flat, dark brown beetlelike bugs, or have a large tan beanlike appearance when they are engorged with blood. They adhere firmly and must be pulled off with a tweezers. If the engorged females are allowed to drop off a dog, they will eventually lay many thousands of eggs.

The most important thing for dog owners to know about controlling these two parasites is that they do not *live* on the dog but *feed* on the dog. Therefore it is not enough to rid an animal of ticks or fleas; the environment must be rid of them also. In cases of severe infestations it is often necessary to use strong "bombs" or foggers in a home, and a professional exterminator may be required. Eggs, larvae, and parasites can also live in an outdoor location such

as a doghouse or run, and it may be necessary to exterminate them too. In warm climates this can be a year-long problem. A local veterinarian will be able to advise a dog owner about the best control methods for each geographical location.

Flea and tick collars, tags, and medallions are usually effective in preventing a dog from picking up these parasites, but they will not kill fleas or ticks that are already on the dog, and they have limited preventive powers when an infestation is severe. Some owners claim success with "natural" control methods such as giving brewer's yeast to a dog. In our experience, these methods work only if an infestation is very mild.

The first step in control is to rid the animal of parasites with a flea and tick bath, or "dip." As mentioned above, firmly attached ticks must be removed by hand, but an insecticide dip will help to loosen them. Powders and sprays are useful for some dogs, but a bath is more apt to reach all areas, especially in a long- or thick-coated animal. At the same time, the indoor environment must be exterminated: wash bedding and fog or spray the entire house.

Preventing reinfestation is essential also. This can be accomplished by the use of flea collars or sprays on the animal, regular washing and spraying of the indoor environment, and regular professional extermination of the indoor and outdoor environment in areas where flea and tick infestation is a serious year-round problem. (See also in the Encyclopedia, "Allergic Skin Diseases," "Intestinal Parasites —Tapeworms," and "Parasitic Diseases of the Skin.")

Looking a Dog Over

Once in a while, it is a good idea to make a thorough head-to-toe examination of a dog. Check eyes, nose, ears, and mouth, and lift the dog's tail and look at the anal area for soreness or redness or any dried fecal matter. Long-haired dogs in particular often have problems with pieces of stool that get caught in their fur. If this should happen, wash with warm water, or cut any dried matter out with a blunt scissor. Trim the fur in this area. Swelling or redness may be a sign of anal sac (gland) impaction (see the Encyclopedia of Diseases of Dogs).

Foot Pads

Hold the dog's foot gently upside-down and run a fingertip between each pad to check for stuck material or sore spots. Foot pads should be hard and leathery, and the spaces between them should not be wide or spread. Old dogs' foot pads sometimes splay, or spread, due to arthritis or other conditions. If this should happen, take care that the feet do not become irritated by too much abrasion on hard surfaces or by chemicals used to remove ice or snow in the winter and in gardens in the spring and summer. Gently rinse the feet with warm water and baking soda if the spaces between the pads look sore, and then make it a practice to rinse the dog's feet each time it comes in. If a dog exercises vigorously on a hard surface, check to be sure that the pads have not become tender or overcalloused. Any severe or persistent foot problems should be seen by a veterinarian.

Eyes

While brushing a dog's face, gently clean away any dried matter in the corners of the eyes with a washcloth or cotton swab moistened with warm water, a mixture of warm water and baking soda, or a mild saline solution. A healthy dog's eyes should be clear, not red, and have no discharge except for a few tears. Some dogs do have a normal watery eye syndrome that causes brown stains on either side of the nose. This can be taken care of cosmetically, but the dog should be seen by a doctor first to rule out disease or other physical cause. (See the Encyclopedia, "Overflow of Tears.")

Long-haired dogs may need to have the hair around their eyes trimmed to avoid irritation; use a curved blunt-nosed scissor.

Ears

A dog's ears should be looked over once in a while in the course of grooming. If the inside of the ear flap, or pinna, looks dirty, it can be cleaned gently with a small piece of cloth or cotton wrapped around a fingertip and moistened with mineral oil. Nothing should ever be poked into a dog's ear canal. The folds of skin around the ear should also be cleaned. A cotton swab will reach into small crevices. Long-haired and long-eared dogs sometimes get a heavy growth of hair on the undersides of their ears, or at the opening of the inner ear, which can collect dirt and eventually interfere with hearing. This excess hair should be removed. This is best done by a professional. (See the Encyclopedia, "Aural Diseases and Disorders.") Ear mites are also covered in detail in this section.

Mouth and Teeth

With the dog's mouth closed, pull back on his lips to expose gums and teeth. Healthy gums are pink and firm, and the teeth should be firm and free from any bad stains. Pushing gently on the corners of the jaw, open the dog's mouth and examine the tongue and the insides of the teeth.

If the gums are pale or bleed when touched, or if there are any swellings or red marks inside a dog's mouth, they should be seen by a veterinarian.

We recommend that owners brush, or clean, their dogs' teeth regularly to remove tartar and invisible plaque, which can cause tooth loss. An adult dog who has never had proper tooth care should have an initial scaling performed by a veterinarian to remove hard tartar that will have built up over the years. As with all routines, the younger the dog, the easier it is to get it used to having its teeth cleaned. Begin by using a rough cloth, such as a washcloth or gauze square wrapped around a finger, and rub the teeth from gum to tip (see Illustration 5, below). Work up to a rougher cloth and then to a toothbrush. Using a child-sized toothbrush with medium bristles, brush each tooth from the gumline to the tip with a mixture of one-half salt and one-half baking soda, slightly moistened. Do not use toothpaste designed for humans, as it can cause stomach irritation, and dogs don't like the foaming. Sensitive, loose, or broken teeth should be seen to immediately by a veterinarian. (See Chapter 2 for the normal eruption of a dog's teeth, Chapter 4 for deciduous tooth extraction, and Chapter 7 for problems relating to older dogs' teeth.)

Illustration 5: "Brushing" a dog's teeth with a cloth

Nancy Lou Makris

Less Frequent Routines

Some kinds of dog care are only done on an "as needed" basis.

Nail Clipping

Unless a dog is walked daily on pavement, its nails will need regular clipping. Dogs are born with a dewclaw, an extra claw that grows just above the foot on the inside of the dog's leg. In some breeds, this claw is removed when a dog is young (see Chapter 4). If not, it must also be trimmed. If a dog's nails are allowed to grow too long, they can cause the toes to spread, or splay, making it difficult for the dog to walk; they can catch on things, and tear; or they may become ingrown, curling back painfully into the foot pads. Too-long nails can also snag furniture and carpets and scratch floors and people.

If a dog is groomed commercially, nail clipping will usually be done when needed. Some veterinarians will also clip dogs' nails as part of their regular service. Many owners prefer to do this job themselves, however.

Although nail clipping is not painful, most dogs do not like it very much, and owners need a firm, sure hand to accomplish it successfully. An owner who is at all nervous or apprehensive about nail clipping probably should not attempt it. Before clipping a dog's nails at home, it is important to have a grooming professional or veterinarian demonstrate the proper procedure.

A good-quality clipper designed specifically for dogs' nails should be used. Human nail clippers are not strong or sharp enough. Hold the dog's paw gently so that it does not try to pull away. Having someone to calm and soothe the dog will be very helpful the first few times. The nail should be clipped halfway between where the vein, or "quick," ends and the tip of the nail. If a dog has clear nails, it is not hard to see where the vein, or "quick," ends. If the nails are dark, it is a good deal more difficult, and it is best to take off just a little at a time. It is far better to clip too little than to take a chance of cutting into the vein. If you do, it

will hurt and bleed a lot. A cotton ball or gauze pad held tightly over the end of the nail will usually stop the bleeding, but a styptic pencil, special powder, or a silver nitrate stick may sometimes be needed. The problem is rarely serious, but it will be very hard to convince the dog that it will not happen again.

After clipping all of the nails, smooth the ends with an emery board or nail file to remove sharp or rough edges.

Bathing

How often a dog is bathed depends a great deal on coat type and the wishes of the owners. A dog who is going to spend a lot of time in very close quarters with people, sleeping on laps and sharing beds with children, will probably be required to have a bath more frequently than one who spends most of its time outdoors.

Many dogs never have or need a bath for their entire lives. Others are bathed weekly. A good average for a normal housedog is about every four to six weeks. Bathing too often will remove natural oils and may lead to dry skin and excessive shedding.

In general, dogs with smooth, oily coats such as beagles and Labrador retrievers should only be bathed when absolutely necessary. Their coats can usually be kept clean with regular brushing. Dogs with undercoats are very difficult to bathe and dry and should be bathed every six months at the most. On the other hand, long-haired or curly-haired dogs will probably need a bath every month to six weeks to keep clean. Breeders and veterinarians are good resources for owners who need to know more about their dogs' specific bathing needs.

Before bathing a dog, brush out its coat to remove any tangles or mats, which will be much harder to get out when the fur is wet.

If a dog's skin is especially sensitive, human baby shampoo or a special medicated preparation can be used. Flea and tick shampoos may be prescribed by a veterinarian. See Chapter 12 for the use of medicated shampoos.

Always bathe a dog in a warm, draft-free spot. A large dog can be washed outdoors on a summer day, but most dogs will fare better in small, indoor areas. Many owners bathe their large dogs by getting into the shower with them. Little dogs do well in the kitchen sink. If the tub or sink is slippery, line it with an old towel. Fill partly with warm water, lift the dog into the water, and gently wet its head and neck with a washcloth. Soap, lather, and rinse very thoroughly in several changes of water. Next, wet the body and legs with a hose or spray, soap and rub, and rinse again and again. Especially dirty spots, such as legs and feet and tail areas can be rewashed, using a cloth or sponge. Be sure to rinse all of the soap out of the dog's coat, as soap residue can cause itching and irritation.

A cream rinse can make it easier to comb out a long-haired dog.

Dry the dog immediately, rubbing gently with towels. If a dog has been accustomed to it, a hair dryer does a wonderful job of drying, but many dogs are frightened of the noise. Particular attention should be paid to the insides of the ears and other cracks and crevices such as armpits. A dog should not be let outdoors until completely dry. It can take several hours for a dog's coat to dry thoroughly. If in doubt, feel the skin under the thickest part of the coat. Brushing long, damp hair tends to tear the coat. A wide-toothed comb can be used to straighten out a long coat while it is drying. After the coat is completely dry, a gentle brushing will restore sheen.

If a dog has gotten involved with a skunk, soak the dog completely in tomato juice and then bathe.

Dry Baths

Sometimes a dog may get dirty when bathing is not convenient, or it may get dirty too frequently for bathing. There are a number of dry dog shampoos on the market designed to remove excess oil and other dirt between shampoos. Cornstarch, talcum powder, and fuller's earth can also be used as dry cleansers. These products are simply rubbed in all over the dog and then completely brushed out; take care to remove all traces of powder next to the skin by brushing the coat backward, against the growth of the hair. In our experience, dry shampoos are very difficult to get out of a dog's coat and do not work very well, but many owners like them.

Clipping, Plucking, Trimming, Professional Grooming

Some breeds of dogs require regular additional coat care. Curly-haired dogs must be clipped and trimmed, and some wirehaireds need plucking. Other dogs may look better and stay cleaner and neater with regular coat cutting.

There are books on the market that show owners how to perform various clipping and trimming jobs at home. These are helpful. However it is almost impossible to learn how to clip a dog through pictures alone. If an owner wants to take care of a dog's coat at home, the best thing to do is to take a class or ask a local groomer or veterinarian if it is possible to watch while the dog is worked on.

Owners who do not have the time, patience, skill, or interest to clip or pluck their own dogs should find a professional groomer. Most communities have more than one. In some areas, there are even traveling dog groomers who will bathe and trim a dog at home. The best way to locate a good dog groomer is to ask other owners or a veterinarian for recommendations.

A well-run grooming establishment should be clean and neat, and the dogs should be calm. A dog who is being worked on will usually be standing quietly on a table with a minimum of restraint. However, the dogs should not be overcalm or lethargic and dopey. This might indicate that the establishment routinely uses tranquilizers, a practice that is not only unnecessary in most cases but that might be harmful. A good professional groomer should only resort to drugs in exceptional cases.

A dog who has become used to being groomed professionally early in life will have no problems with the procedure. A first-time adult dog may be understandably nervous and apprehensive. Once an owner has made a thoughtful choice of groomer, the best thing to do is to leave the dog quickly, with a minimum of fuss. The groomer has had to deal with new customers before. Very often the continued presence of the dog owner makes the situation more difficult.

References: Chapter 3

1. Exceptions are pregnant bitches, who need small amounts of dietary carbohydrate, and formulas for hand-fed pups, which should contain 10–15% carbohydrate.

2. Mertz, W.: The essential trace elements. *Science* 213, 1332–1338, 1981.

3. Anon.: *Nutrient Requirements of Dogs.* National Research Council, National Academy of Sciences, Washington, D.C., 1974.

4. Anon.: *Official Publication.* Association of American Feed Control Officials Inc., Baton Rouge, Louisiana, 1974.

5. Kronfeld, D. S.: Nature and uses of commercial dog foods. *JAVMA* 166, 487–493, 1975.

6. Kronfeld, D. S.: Geriatric Diets for Dogs. *The Compendium for Continuing Education of the Practicing Veterinarian,* Vol. 5, No. 2, February 1983.

7. Anon.: *Nutrient Requirements of Dogs.*

8. Ibid.

9. Downey, R. L., Kronfeld, D. S., and Banta, C. A.: Diet of beagles affects stamina. *JAAHA* 16, 273–277, 1980.

10. Kronfeld, D. S., and Downey, R. L.: Nutritional strategies for stamina in dogs and horses. *Proc. Nutr. Soc. Aust.* 6, 21–29, 1981.

11. Karlsson, J., and Saltin, B.: Diet, muscle glycogen, and endurance performance. *J. Appl. Physiol.* 31, 203–206, 1971.

12. Kronfeld and Downey, Nutritional strategies for stamina in dogs and horses.

13. Hammel, E. P., Kronfeld, D. S., Ganjam, V. K., and Dunlap, H. L.: Metabolic responses to exhaustive exercise in racing sled dogs fed diets containing medium, low and zero carbohydrate. *Am. J. Clin. Nutr.* 30, 409–418, 1977.

(Pages 30–49 are based, in part, on a monograph prepared for ALPO Products Company Inc., by Michael S. Garvey, DVM, with their permission.)

4

Common Surgical Procedures

CHERYL J. MEHLHAFF, DVM

Surgery for dogs falls into several classifications. There are purely elective procedures, performed on healthy animals; and there are operations that are necessary, dictated by an existing disease condition. There are two kinds of necessary operations. Surgery may be semielective, with ample time available for preoperative planning and assessment; or it may have to be performed in an emergency as a lifesaving act. In this chapter, we will focus on elective and semielective surgery and describe some operations that are commonly performed on dogs.

Stages of Surgery

Any operation has four distinct phases: the preoperative, or evaluation and planning stage; the induction stage, when the anesthetic is given; the intraoperative stage, when the surgery is actually performed; and the postoperative, or recovery, stage. Let's look at each of these stages.

Preoperative Period

The preoperative period begins when the veterinarian decides to perform surgery. It is a planning and information-gathering period, during which the veterinarian must consider a number of factors. These include the indications for the operation, possible alternatives to surgery, and the risks involved for the dog.

When elective surgery will be performed on a young, healthy animal, only a minimum of preparation may be needed. The veterinarian will want to perform a general physical examination of the dog in order to rule out any hidden problems, to determine the animal's age and weight, and to be sure that all immunizations are up-to-date. The veterinarian may order a more elaborate preoperative screening for older dogs or for more complicated cases. When surgery is going to be performed on an older dog that may have more than one problem, preoperative testing might include X

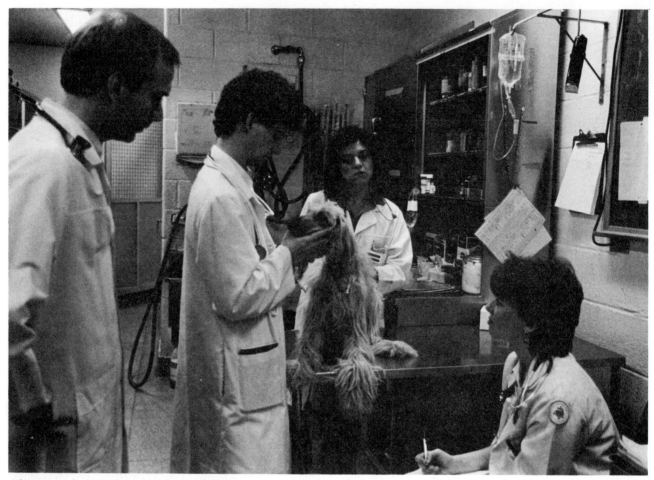

Photograph 5: A thorough preoperative examination is given a patient by a team of veterinarians at The AMC.

rays, various blood and urine tests, and certain specialized tests to evaluate specific organs (e.g., an electrocardiogram).

Whatever the age of the dog, the aim of preoperative planning is to gather information. With this information, the veterinarian will be able to predict the animal's risk from anesthesia and can then carefully select the appropriate anesthetic for the dog.

Because a dog who is going to have elective surgery is usually allowed to remain at home up until the morning of surgery, it is important for owners to remember that the animal's stomach must be empty. This is to prevent vomiting during recovery from the anesthesia, when the dog may inhale the vomitus into its lungs. Generally, the dog should not be fed for eight to ten hours preceding surgery and should not be allowed water for the last two to three hours before the operation.

Induction Period—General Anesthesia

The purpose of anesthesia is to block the dog's perception of pain and to keep the patient still while an operation is in progress. General anesthesia, rather than local anesthesia, is usually necessary for dogs. A dog cannot understand the need to stay still; so many procedures, such as dentistry, that might be performed on people with a local anesthetic require a general anesthetic when performed on dogs. Under general anesthesia, the patient is completely unconscious, with muscles relaxed. The dog feels no pain and has no recall of the procedures once it is waked. If the dog has been carefully evaluated before the operation, general anesthesia carries a minimum risk for most animals, even those who are seriously ill.

A dog usually receives a tranquilizer or sedative a few minutes before it is brought into the prep room to be anesthetized and prepared for the operating room. It may also receive other preanesthetic drugs at this time to help maintain heart rate, control salivation, and so forth.

In the prep room, the now calm dog is placed on a table, and a catheter is put into a leg vein. Hair is often clipped from the area where the catheter will be placed. A general anesthetic is then carefully injected through the catheter, and in seconds the dog is relaxed and unconscious.

Once the dog is under anesthesia, it receives a maintenance anesthetic for the duration of the operation. For short procedures, it may simply be small additional doses of the injectable drug. For longer surgeries, a gas or inhalant anesthetic is used. The gas is a mixture of oxygen and one or more modern drugs—not ether—and is administered via a rubber or plastic endotracheal tube, which is gently passed down the dog's trachea toward his lungs and fastened in place. Occasionally a dog may have a temporary sore throat and a cough

Photograph 6: A little dog awaiting surgery. Notice the sign on the left side of the picture.

Photograph 7: The animal is carefully monitored during surgery. Notice the cardiac oscilloscope in the background.

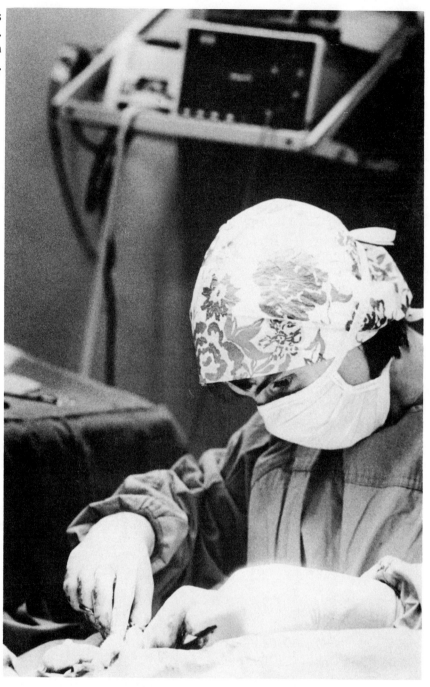

following surgery when an endotracheal tube has been used. This will usually clear up without treatment, and should not concern an owner unduly. But if it is severe or lasts for more than twenty-four hours, consult the veterinarian.

A dog under anesthesia may breathe on its own, spontaneously, or in certain cases breathing may be assisted or controlled by the anesthetist. This can be done manually, by squeezing a bag containing the anesthetic gas, or by using a mechanical ventilator or respirator. Once the dog is under anesthesia, an intravenous drip of fluids is attached to the catheter. Blood transfusions are rarely necessary and are almost never used in routine operations.

Before the dog is moved to the operating room, where the actual surgery will take place, the hair around the area intended for surgery must be shaved. When the shaved hair is vacuumed away, the dog is moved to the operating table.

Intraoperative Period—Surgery

We at The AMC have a standard surgical procedure, which is followed by each doctor with every surgical patient. This procedure may vary in individual practices, but in general, veterinarians follow certain working procedures. The dog is carefully monitored during surgery. This includes monitoring heart function on a cardiac oscilloscope and continuous regulation of the intravenous fluids and anesthetic gas. The dog's breathing, pulse, and color are checked frequently, and it is kept warm with a special circulating-water heating pad.

Before the operation actually begins, the shaved area is repeatedly scrubbed with a soap solution and then alcohol to sterilize the skin. Special sterile towels and drapes are used to cover all of the table, instrument stands, and all of the animal except for the surgical field itself. The staff takes care throughout the operation to prevent contamination or contact with anything that is not sterile.

Photograph 8: Special sterile towels and drapes are used to cover a dog during surgery. Dr. Cheryl J. Mehlhaff is the surgeon.

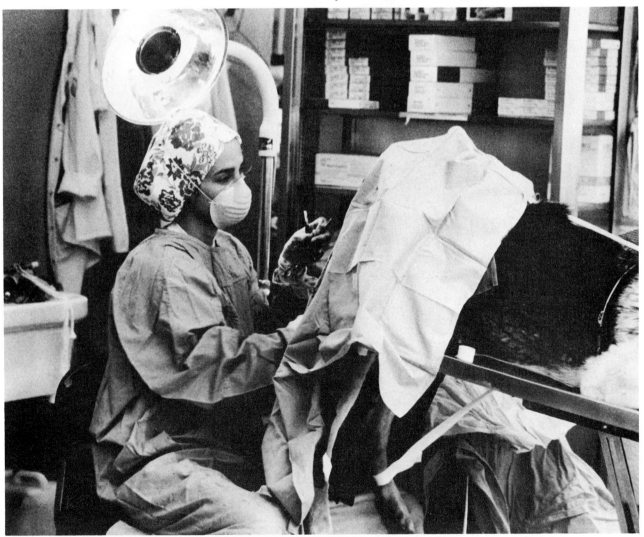

Postoperative Period—Recovery

When the operation is completed, the anesthetic is turned off and the dog is allowed to wake up. Depending on the type of anesthetic used, the length of the operation, and the age of the dog, the return to consciousness can take anywhere from minutes to several hours. This is why a postoperative hospital stay of anywhere from several hours to several days is necessary to ensure an uncomplicated recovery.

Bandages are usually unnecessary, and most dogs do not tolerate them well. They are rarely used, except for support in certain orthopedic cases. See Chapter 12 for bandage care.

After a dog is released from the hospital, the owner continues the postoperative care. Even routine surgery such as an ovariohysterectomy, or "spay," is a major operation and requires a certain convalescent period. Animals should be allowed to rest and not be asked to play, jump, or run when they first return home.

The experience of having surgery may upset a dog's stomach. This is perfectly normal, and owners should not expect a pet to be hungry when it first comes home. Rewarding a brave postoperative dog with extra treats is only inviting trouble. The best thing to do is feed the dog small amounts of its regular diet at frequent intervals, returning it gradually to a normal feeding schedule over the course of a few days.

Check incisions once or twice a day. Pay attention to the sutures, if present; look for evidence that the dog is licking or chewing them.

Photograph 9: A postoperative dog wearing an Elizabethan collar to prevent it from chewing the incision

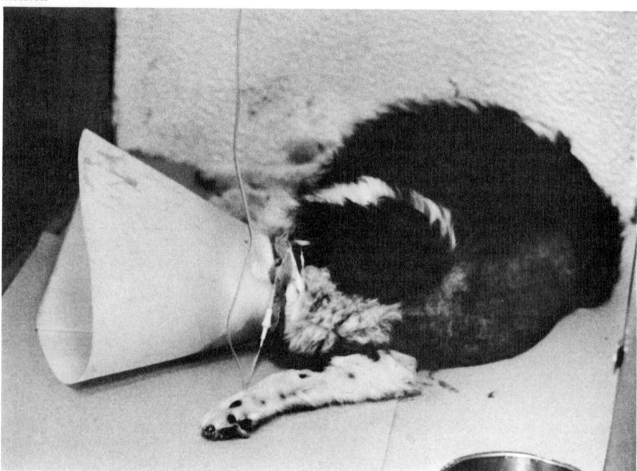

(See "Ovariohysterectomy" below for a discussion of kinds of sutures.) Excessive swelling, redness, or any discharge are all warning signs and should be called to the veterinarian's attention as soon as possible. The doctor may put an Elizabethan collar on the dog. This is a plastic cone that fits around the pet's neck and prevents it from reaching around and chewing the incision. (See Photograph 9, page 66.) Some veterinarians use an alternative device called a "side brace." It also mechanically prevents a pet from reaching an incision. See Chapter 12 for how to make a temporary Elizabethan collar.

Most dogs do not suffer great pain or discomfort during their recovery period. If they do feel discomfort, most dogs tolerate it very well. Only rarely do veterinarians prescribe analgesics for postoperative dogs. Analgesics will cause grogginess and may mask signs of complications. Owners should always consult with the veterinarian before giving any medication to a postoperative dog.

Ovariohysterectomy (OHE, "Spay")

The main reason this operation is performed is that it provides permanent sterilization of female dogs. Although there are other, medical means of contraception, they are not recommended for a number of reasons, discussed in Chapter 5. Besides the very important benefit of preventing unwanted heat periods and pregnancies, there are several extremely important medical benefits to be gained by an OHE. These include the reduction or virtual elimination of the chances of a dog developing breast cancer, uterine infections, tumors of the reproductive tract, "false pregnancy," and certain dermatological conditions. See Chapter 5 and the Encyclopedia of Diseases of Dogs for more about these problems.

If an owner decides to have an OHE performed, the optimal age for the dog is about six to eight months. If the dog is spayed at this time, the procedure will precede the first heat. The only requirement is that the dog be relatively mature in growth. Depending on the breed of dog, this usually occurs at around six to seven months of age. There is no reason to wait until the first heat or until after the bitch has had one litter. In fact, an OHE greatly reduces her risk of developing mammary gland cancer when she has it before her second heat. After that, the benefits decline rapidly, and if the animal is two-and-a-half years old or older when spayed, the expected mammary gland cancer rate is the same as for unspayed females.

Older unspayed ("intact") dogs are prone to developing uterine infections, or pyometras (see the Encyclopedia of Diseases of Dogs). These infections can be life-threatening and often require a semielective or emergency OHE, which can present a potential risk to the patient.

The Operation

The bitch is prepared for the operation as described in the previous section. Even though the actual incision is usually only one or two inches long, her hair is clipped in a wide area to prevent contamination and to allow for a longer incision if necessary.

The doctor uses a sterile scalpel to incise the skin just below the belly button and divides several layers of fat and muscle until the abdominal cavity is reached. The doctor then locates the uterus and removes it and the attached ovaries. The surgeon makes sure to remove all of the ovarian tissue, because the ovaries are the source of the female hormones that cause heatlike behavior. Only a stump of the uterus is left behind. All the layers previously opened are sutured closed with materials that do not have to be removed later.

The skin is closed in one of two ways. The usual method is to use nonabsorbable stitches, which are removed approximately ten to fourteen days later (see Figure 5, page 68). An alternative is to use subcuticular stitches. These

FIGURE 5
GRAPH OF THE HEALING PROCESS,
DEMONSTRATING WHY SUTURES ARE REMOVED
10 TO 14 DAYS FOLLOWING SURGERY

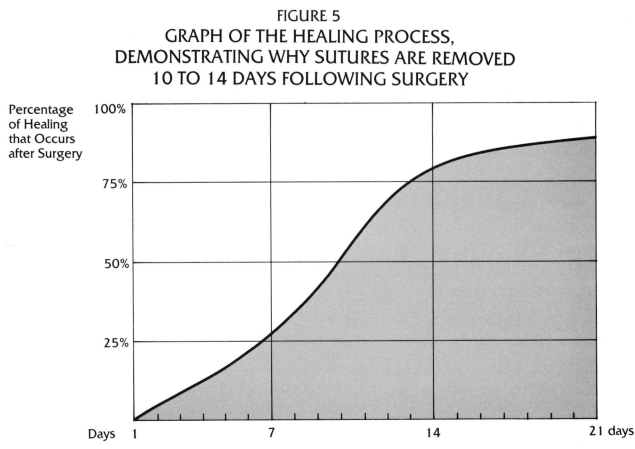

sutures are below the skin and are dissolved by the body over time. The choice is based on the surgeon's preference and the personalities of the dog and owner.

Remember that there are multiple layers of stitches. If the skin stitches come out or the edges gap, there is no need to panic. Just make sure that the abdominal contents are not visible. Cover the wound with a clean dressing, or leave it alone. Do not allow the dog to chew, lick, or scratch the incision until you see the veterinarian.

Despite the "routine" nature of an OHE, it is a major abdominal surgical procedure and requires ample postoperative rest and care.

With proper care at all stages of surgery, complications following a canine OHE are rare. Once in a while, a dog will appear to come into heat after being spayed. This may indicate the presence of ovarian tissue somewhere in the abdomen and may require a second, exploratory operation. Even more rare is an infection of the tiny stump of the uterus sometimes left behind during the operation.

Should this occur, the dog may need a second operation to remove the stump.

Personality Changes and Weight Gain Following an OHE

Since an OHE is usually performed just as the dog is going through puberty, the normal changes in temperament, playfulness, and sleeping patterns that occur at this age are sometimes attributed to the operation. A pet may seem calmer, less anxious, and more responsive after an OHE, but there is no real evidence to link those changes to the OHE procedure.

Similarly, many people believe that dogs routinely gain weight after an OHE. As with personality "changes," it is the age at which most dogs are spayed that brings about most of these changes, though the OHE is often blamed. All dogs approaching maturity undergo normal changes in metabolic rate, activity level, and food utilization. A one-year-old dog requires less food per pound than a puppy does. To avoid the problem of weight gain, be sure to adjust the amount and frequency of feedings and to exercise a dog regularly. See the "Nutrition" and "Exercise" sections in Chapter 3 for more details.

Castration (Neutering, Altering)

Castration involves the removal of a male dog's testicles, which, like the female's ovaries, are the main source of sex hormones. Removal of the testicles also eliminates the source of sperm cells, and so is the most effective permanent means of birth control for the male. The operation can be performed as early as six to seven months of age.

Just as female hormones (estrogens and progesterones) influence certain diseases, testosterone, the male testicular hormone, has been implicated in a number of medical problems. Prostatitis, perianal hernias, perianal tumors, and hair loss are just a few of the testosterone-related problems (see the Encyclopedia of Diseases of Dogs for details). The testicles themselves are also vulnerable to tumors (cancer) and infection. Thus, castration may be recommended as an elective procedure to reduce the risk of medical problems or as part of the medical or surgical treatment of any of them.

Castration also reduces the dog's aggressive behavior as well as his roaming behavior. Early castration is often recommended to eliminate these behavior problems before they become habits.

Many owners object to the castration of a male dog believing that the operation will make the dog less brave and "macho." It is important to remember that a dog's personality is only minimally determined by sex hormones, but rather is a product of his breeding and environment. Sex hormones may enhance aggressiveness, and castration may temper it, but the basic tendency of a dog to be docile or aggressive depends on a brain-level phenomenon.

The Operation

Once anesthetized, the dog is placed on his back, and the area around the scrotum, groin, and base of the penis are shaved and sterilized. A small, one- to two-inch incision is made just in front of the scrotum, through which the testicles are removed. The vessels and vas deferens (a duct that carries sperm into the urethra) are clamped and tied off, and the testicles are removed. Closure of the incision is performed the same way as it is after an OHE. Subcuticular stitches are often used to reduce the dog's urge to lick the incision. The dog may be discharged the same day as the operation, but usually he is kept overnight.

Because the scrotum is left intact and may swell, it may appear to the owner that the dog was never castrated. Over time, the scrotum usually shrinks, and hair will eventually grow over it.

In some instances, the scrotum is removed along with the testicles. This is usually only done in cases when the scrotum itself is diseased or when infection of the testicles is suspected.

Complications are rare following routine castration. In a few cases a dog's scrotum may be irritated by the clipper blades or develop a rash in reaction to the surgical iodine solution. More often, persistent licking can lead to swelling of the scrotum and inflammation. This problem can be controlled with an Elizabethan collar (see pages 66 and 67) and the use of warm compresses for several days. If swelling of the scrotum is severe, bring the dog to a veterinarian.

Personality Changes and Weight Gain After Castration

As with OHEs for female dogs, castrations are often performed while the male dog is maturing. So, some owners falsely attribute normal changes in activity level, food utilization, and so forth to the surgery. We have noticed that some dogs increase their appetite after castration. To avoid weight gain be careful not to indulge a pet's increased desire for food. Giving a dog low-calorie snacks such as celery and carrots may satisfy his hunger. Decreased roaming behavior may also result in weight gain. Make sure that the dog has a regular exercise schedule (see Chapter 3).

A last point on the subject of personality change is to remind owners that dogs are far less "hung up" about the presence or absence of testicles than many people are. Dogs do not have a sexual ego that needs protection.

Alternatives to Castration

Long-term alternatives to castration are not routinely available for the male dog. Vasec-

tomy, which entails surgically cutting and tying off the tubes that transmit sperm from the testicles to the urethra, is effective for contraception. Vasectomy, however, does nothing to eliminate the sex-hormone production, and so a vasectomized dog will still face all of the behavioral and potential medical risks of the non-vasectomized dog.

Newer methods are being investigated, including oral contraceptives, injections into the testicles, and others, but as yet none has found wide acceptance. Interested owners should check with their veterinarians.

Caesarean Section (C-Section)

Certain breeds of dogs, either because of their particular body conformation or other problems, will predictably need to have their puppies born via C-section. Still other bitches develop complications during pregnancy or labor, and a C-section may become necessary. See Chapter 5.

Medications can be given to a bitch who is having difficulty delivering, which may make it possible for her to deliver without a C-section. But, if the operation does become necessary, it will be the veterinarian's decision as to when it should be done, so that the bitch doesn't become too exhausted from unfruitful labor.

The Operation

Preparation for a Caesarean section follows the same steps as for other surgery. An incision

is made into the abdomen. The uterus is then incised, or opened up, in order to remove the puppies. The puppies are each taken out, cleaned, and their umbilical cords cut, as described in Chapter 5. The uterus is then closed. This procedure must be done very carefully, especially in a breeding bitch, to prevent scarring of the uterus, which might prevent her from successfully whelping in the future.

Closure of the incision and postoperative care follow the same pattern as described above. Usually, because the puppies will be nursing, we use subcuticular sutures after a C-section.

Other Surgical Procedures

Deciduous Tooth Extraction

A dog's deciduous, or "baby," teeth should all be gone by the time the pup is six or seven months old. (See Table 1, p. 19). Occasionally, one or more of these teeth will be retained and can cause an orthodontic problem by displacing the permanent teeth. The "canine" teeth are most commonly affected.

Removal is usually quite simple and requires only sedation or minimal anesthetic. Since many dogs are brought in for an OHE or

castration around this time, the extraction of the deciduous teeth is often performed concurrently with these other procedures, under general anesthesia.

Dewclaw Removal

The dewclaws are the vestigial, unneeded thumbs and big toes of dogs. Many dogs are born without them. Many dogs born with dewclaws have them removed by a veterinarian shortly after birth. Some breeds, however, require rear dewclaws if they are going to be shown. These "extra" toes with their long, unworn nails tend to catch easily on objects as the dog walks by, causing them to tear and bleed.

Removal is simple, since the dewclaws are often attached to the dog's leg by no more than some loose skin. The operation requires general anesthesia, and it is best to coordinate it with other procedures, such as an OHE, castration, or dentistry.

Tail Docking and Ear Cropping

Tail docking and ear cropping fall into a category known as "cosmetic surgery." These surgeries are performed to change the appearance of the animal, not for any potential health benefits. *The Animal Medical Center does not routinely perform these procedures.* An increasing number of veterinarians across the country object to this practice, as well.

Historically, tail docking was performed to protect working dogs' tails from injury. Many

TABLE 9

GUIDELINES FOR TAIL DOCKING WHEN PERFORMED

Breed	Amount of Tail to Leave on Dog	Breed	Amount of Tail to Leave on Dog
Affenpinscher	One-third		
Airedale terrier	Three-quarters	Rottweiler (usually born tailless)	One vertebra
Australian terrier	Two-fifths		
Bouvier des Flandres	About one-half inch †	Schipperke	One vertebra
		Schnauzer, giant	Three vertebrae (approx.)
Boxer	One-half to three-quarters inch †	Schnauzer, miniature	One-fourth
Brussels griffon	One-fourth	Schnauzer, standard	Two vertebrae (approx.)
Doberman pinscher	Two vertebrae (approx.)	Sealyham terrier	One-half
English toy spaniel	One-third	Silky terrier	One-third
Fox terrier	Two-thirds	Soft-coated Wheaten terrier	One-fourth
Irish terrier	Three-quarters		
Kerry blue terrier	One-half	Spaniel, Brittany	Three vertebrae
Lakeland terrier	Two-thirds	Spaniel, Clumber	One-third
Norfolk and Norwich terriers	One-fourth	Cocker	One-third
		English cocker	One-third
Old English sheepdog (usually born tailless)	One vertebra	English springer	One-third
		Field	One-third
Pinscher, miniature	One-fourth	Sussex	One-third
Pointer, German shorthaired	Two-fifths	Spaniel, Welsh springer	One-half
		Viszla	Two-thirds
Pointer, German wirehaired	Two-fifths	Weimaraner	Three-fifths
		Welsh corgi (Pembroke)	One vertebra
Poodle—all sizes	One-third to one-half	Welsh terrier	Two-thirds
		Yorkshire terrier	One-third

† When docked at one week of age.
Note: Approximate guides only. Consult breeders, judges, etc., for further information.
Adapted from *JAVMA*, January 1, 1968.

breeds now require tail docking because of tradition. Inexperienced owners may not be aware that a puppy's tail has been docked because the operation is usually done simultaneously with dewclaw removal, when the puppy is only two to three days old. Anesthesia is not required, but an experienced veterinarian should perform the procedure to ensure the proper length as set out in the various breed specifications. An improperly performed tail dock may disqualify a dog for showing. Table 9 on page 71 lists the breeds that traditionally have their tails docked.

Ear cropping has no practical or medical justification, but is a purely cosmetic surgery designed to give a dog a more "alert" appearance. The surgery is done on older puppies, at three to four months of age, and requires general anesthesia. Part of each ear is cut off to an appropriate size and shape, and the free edges are sutured. After initial healing, the ears are taped, braced, or otherwise forced into an erect position to encourage the growing cartilage to assume the "correct" upright stance. This can take anywhere from one to four weeks or longer.

Major complications, such as infection, gangrene, improper size and shape, etc., can ensue from a poorly performed ear crop. It is imperative for an owner who wants the operation for her dog to select a qualified veterinarian who has experience with the procedure in general and particular knowledge of the breed's specifications as to length and shape. Breeders and others unfamiliar with sterile surgical techniques should not do ear crops. It can be difficult to find an experienced veterinarian for ear cropping, since many doctors now prefer not to perform the operation. The best sources of information are local veterinarians, breeders, and owners of the same breed who have had successful ear crops performed on their dogs.

5

Breeding and Reproduction

KATHLEEN E. NOONE, VMD

There are three kinds of dog owners whose pets have puppies: experienced, professional breeders of purebred animals who breed selectively in order to produce particular physical or personality traits and to make money selling the puppies; individuals who breed a pet bitch because they want her to experience maternity, think that she would be a good mother, and usually intend to keep one of her pups; and individuals whose pet becomes pregnant accidentally. This chapter is intended for the inexperienced, nonprofessional breeder.

The first thing for a nonprofessional breeder to bear in mind is, What will happen to the puppies? It does not take more than one visit to any pound or shelter to realize that, despite a great deal of publicity on the subject, dog overpopulation continues to be a major problem. Owners of pet bitches who are thinking of breeding them, or of unspayed bitches who stand a chance of becoming accidentally pregnant, should think long and hard about the necessity of providing good homes for all the offspring of their pets.

Another important consideration is an owner's willingness and ability to spend the time, money, and energy required to breed a dog successfully and raise a litter of puppies. There are a great many time-consuming and expensive steps to take in order to ensure a good outcome. We will cover many of them in this chapter.

Birth Control

Owners of dogs or bitches that they do not want to breed may want to have their pets surgically neutered for several reasons:

In the case of the bitch, an ovariohysterectomy, or spaying operation, described in Chapter 4, will, of course, prevent accidental pregnancy. It will also prevent having to deal with a biyearly heat (or estrous) cycle, the attraction of male dogs, and possible mating. Even more important, if spaying is done early, the bitch's health will benefit.

There are hormonal birth control pills and liquids (Ovaban and Cheque). Owners who wish to use these forms of birth control should check with their veterinarians, as there are possible side effects associated with the use of either of these drugs.

In addition to keeping a male dog from fathering pups, castration may prevent him from roaming and reduce aggressive behavior. The operation, described in Chapter 4, can also have health benefits.

Accidental Breeding

Owners of unspayed or unprotected female dogs in heat may have an extremely hard time keeping males away; they may come from afar and often stay around day and night for the duration of the heat period. If an accidental breeding does take place, there are several things that can be done:

• When owners do not intend to breed a female later, she should be confined and then spayed two or three weeks after her heat period has ended.
• The bitch can be allowed to have the litter if the owner is ready and able to care for the pups and find homes for them.
• Hormonal mismating shots will alter the transit of the egg through the reproductive tract and change the receptivity of the uterus, causing it to become an unsuitable environment for the eggs so that they do not become fertilized. Although there are supposedly safe dosages for this drug, we consider it risky and do not recommend it for several reasons: Hormone shots have a high potential for upsetting the body's estrogen levels and can cause a serious uterine inflammation called pyometra (see the Encyclopedia of Diseases of Dogs); they can also predispose a dog to future mammary gland problems; in addition, if hormones are used at too high a dosage they can cause bone marrow destruction, or aplastic anemia, which can be irreversible and cause death due to lack of blood components (see the Encyclopedia).

Breeding

There are a number of points to consider before attempting to breed a dog. Not all veterinary practices are equally well-equipped to perform all of the complex tests and procedures described below (e.g., a sperm count or vaginal cytology). If problems arise and an owner wishes these or other sophisticated procedures to be performed, he should discuss this with his regular veterinarian, who will be able to direct him to a specialist if necessary.

Choosing a Suitable Mate

Because of the selective process that goes into developing a purebred animal and the inbreeding and line breeding necessary to this process, some breeds have developed specific predispositions toward genetic defects. Some large breeds, for instance, are predisposed toward hip dysplasia; prominent-eyed breeds can develop eye problems; and some breeds are prone to congenital heart defects. There are literally hundreds of congenital canine defects and medical disorders that we know are inherited.

Some professional breeders line breed intentionally in order to achieve specific physical characteristics—a particular haircoat color or body size, for example. A problem may arise if an undesirable gene is also passed along in this line. Fortunately, the majority of professionals are responsible people who care about continuing a line of dogs that are sound in body and mind. Home breeders, however, often accidentally contribute to overbreeding through ignorance. For example, by mating their cute little Boston terrier to the cute little Boston terrier across the street without checking on the ancestry of each, they may end up with pups who have severe congenital disorders.

Sometimes veterinarians can suggest a suitable mate or stud service. Dog fancier magazines and journals often have advertisements from owners looking for mates for their bitches or studs. It is the owner's responsibility to check into the line of each dog very carefully, whether the dog belongs to a friend or is a professional stud, bearing in mind the particular breed's predisposition toward various diseases and disorders. The line check should go back as far as possible, because although recessive genes may not show up in each generation, one parent can be a carrier who will transmit the problem to pups. Owners of large dogs should be sure to have both partners X-rayed for hip dysplasia, which may not show up until an animal is two years of age or older (see the Encyclopedia of Diseases of Dogs). Prospective mates should also be given complete physical examinations by a veterinarian, including testing for venereal diseases.

If all of this sounds very difficult, it is. Responsible dog owners should not indulge in casual breeding just because they think that "Fluffy would make a good mother," or they may end up with pups with severe birth defects.

Owners of mixed-breed dogs have a much less difficult job if they want to mate their pets, as long as they are not particular about size, color, and conformation of the pups. Health measures must, of course, be taken, but the problems attendant on overbreeding do not apply to them. If the parents are healthy, the resulting puppies should be, too.

Age to Breed

Puberty in a dog occurs anywhere between six and eighteen months of age, and sexual maturity is reached about two to three months after an animal attains adult body weight. Females usually become sexually mature a few weeks prior to males of the same breed and because small dogs reach adult weight sooner than larger breeds, they are sexually mature at an earlier age. Giant breeds, such as the Irish wolfhound, often do not have their first heat until they are a year-and-a-half old and may not be sexually mature until two or two-and-a-half years of age. However, in general a bitch who has not begun to cycle when she is over one year of age and yet has reached her full adult body weight several months earlier should be evaluated for infertility. More about this later on. Interestingly, environmental as well as physiological factors play a part in maturation age. Free-roaming dogs, like street children, grow up and mature sexually earlier than their home- or kennel-bound cousins.

Owners usually judge the proper age for breeding a bitch. It is best not to breed a dog until her second or third heat, as very young bitches tend to have small litters, which can lead to difficult births, or dystocias. Also, first heats may often be very mild and barely noticeable. These early mild cycles are often referred to as "silent heats."

The Heat Cycle: When to Breed

The canine heat cycle classically occurs twice a year, but it is often variable. Larger dogs may cycle only once every nine months, and some breeds, such as the Basenji, only once a year.

The heat cycle has several stages. The first stage is called proestrus; during this stage there is a vaginal discharge of blood, the vulva becomes firm, swollen, and red, and the female secretes pheromones, which are sex attractants for male dogs. She, however, is not yet receptive to males and will not permit mounting, avoiding advances and sometimes snapping. This stage usually lasts an average of nine days, although there is a great individual variation, and it may last much longer.

Following proestrus is the estrus stage, which also lasts around nine days, with individual variations. During this period, the female is receptive to the stud and will stand and permit him to mount her.

It is recommended that most bitches be bred nine, eleven, and thirteen days after the start of vaginal bleeding, but, because proestrus can last for up to twenty-two days, the time to breed the bitch can be highly variable. Lay owners can have a hard time judging the proper time because some dogs bleed very little, and others are very fastidious and lick their hindquarters so that no discharge is evident. Sometimes the bitch's behavior toward the male is the best indication of when she is receptive. A veterinarian who specializes in canine breeding and reproductive medicine can determine just what stage the heat cycle is in by examining vaginal cells (a procedure known as vaginal cytology).

In order to ensure success, breeders usually allow a bitch to mate once every forty-eight hours, or at least two or three times between the ninth and fourteenth days after the onset of bleeding.

When the estrus stage is over, the bitch enters the luteal phase, during which she either becomes pregnant or does not. This stage lasts for two or three months, and it is during this period that some bitches experience an odd syndrome, false pregnancy, which actually mimics real pregnancy, including some hormonal changes. Even though there are no fertilized eggs and often no mating has occurred, the bitch may show abdominal enlargement, swelling of the breasts, and perhaps have milk in her mammary glands. Toward the end of the "pregnancy" period the bitch will often indulge in nesting behavior. With the lack of a birth, the behavior will stop when the next stage of the heat cycle begins. If a bitch goes through a false pregnancy with each heat—which often happens—the kindest thing that owners can do is to have her spayed.

Between the luteal phase and the beginning of a new cycle with the proestrus stage, the dog is in the anestrus period, a time of lessened ovarian activity. This stage will last an average of three months but can continue for anywhere from two to eight months, depending on the dog's normal cycle.

Breeding Soundness

The soundness of both the bitch and dog is as important to success as the proper age and time for breeding, and it is best to plan ahead so that all will go well when the bitch is ready.

At least one month ahead of mating, both the bitch and dog should have a complete physical examination, at which time the veterinarian needs a detailed health history. For both, this will include a fertility record—past litters mothered or sired and/or unsuccessful attempts—and an evaluation of pedigree, paying particular attention to past genetic defects that may have cropped up, in either a dog's ancestry or offspring.

Systemic or infectious diseases must also be ruled out, and all immunizations brought up to date. Each dog should also be given a blood test for brucellosis, a disease that is transmitted primarily through sexual contact and that has major reproductive repercussions. In addition to taking these physical measures, the doctor should also observe the personalities of both dogs. If either is excessively shy or overly aggressive, breeding may be very difficult.

The bitch's history in relation to her estrous cycles, pregnancies, births, condition of puppies, and any previous urogenital problems should also be explored. Any previous use of sex hormones or prophylactic medications should be noted. A complete urogenital examination is necessary to assure that there are no infections or structural deformities that might interfere with conception or birth. The doctor will perform this examination by manual palpation of the urethra, bladder, and vagina, by direct visual observation and with the use of a speculum. This is especially important for a first-time breeder, to be certain that the bitch does not have any vaginal masses, tumors, growths, or muscular or vascular rings that would impede mating and/or delivery or make them painful. A bitch who has ever had a traumatic injury, such as being hit by a car, should be carefully assessed for pelvic damage, a badly healed fracture, for instance. If there are any signs of inflammation or infection, or if there is a tumor, a vaginal swab culture and or biopsy (in the case of a tumor) may be necessary for diagnosis.

It is also essential for the bitch to be dewormed thoroughly at least a month prior to conception. Worms are often present in the female's musculature and will travel across the placenta into the puppies and into the bitch's mammary glands when she becomes pregnant. Although deworming the bitch may not rid her entirely of these parasites, at least it will cut back on the number of them that can be passed along to the fetuses and newborns.

Probably the single most important health

measure that can be taken for a bitch who is to be bred is to be sure that she is not overweight. An obese dog has neither the stamina nor energy needed for birth and nursing. The bitch's body weight should be stable. She should be trim and not in the process of either losing or gaining weight at the time of conception.

In addition to the complete general physical examination and health checkup described above, first-time stud dogs should have a urogenital examination. The testicles will be palpated to be sure that they feel normal, and the epididymus, the area located between the testicles and the urethra in which semen is transported during ejaculation will be felt to be sure that it is not warm or swollen. The doctor should also check to be sure that the dog's penis and prostate are normal.

The Mating Act

Once it has been ascertained that the bitch is ready for mating, the partners should be introduced gradually, preferably while on leads if they do not already know each other. Some breeders suggest that virgin bitches be muzzled so that they do not bite the male in fear and confusion.

The dogs should be confined in an enclosed room or outdoor pen that allows them space to move around but from which they cannot escape.

The male will usually sniff and lick at the bitch's external genitals. Depending on her age and experience, the bitch will either want to play and romp for a while or will immediately be ready to mate. When she is ready, she will stand still, tail to one side. The male will then stand behind her on his hind legs and hold her by the hips with his front legs, thrusting his penis violently into her vulva, ejaculating semen (see Illustration 6, below). After ejaculation of semen, the dog will dismount and rotate so that the two animals are standing back to back, his penis still inside her vagina, while continuing to ejaculate a fluid originat-

Illustration 6: A male dog mounting a female

Nancy Lou Mahrie

ing from the prostate that does not contain sperm in high numbers. This is called the coital lock, or "tie." It can last anywhere from five minutes to forty-five minutes, and no attempt should be made to separate the dogs during this period, as injury to the dog or bitch could result (see Illustration 7, below).

Mating Problems

The description above is of a normal mating between dogs. Problems can often occur, however, especially when neither animals nor owners are experienced.

As we mentioned before, nervousness or shyness can create a problem. An animal who is a household pet, not used to meeting strange dogs or being in unfamiliar places, often will be much too upset by the whole procedure to pay any serious attention to mating. Recognizing this, owners should try to arrange to have a shy dog mated at home or introduce her or him to the mating location well ahead of time.

Male dogs who are primarily pets may simply be lacking in sufficient aggressiveness or libido to be interested in mating. If a male fails to perform at all after several attempts to mate him, owners may have to conclude that he simply is not cut out to be a father. If, however, a male dog is interested in the female, but stops abruptly after attempting to mount her, the problem could be physical. If he has not been thoroughly examined beforehand, it may be found that an abnormality of the penis is preventing normal breeding.

A bitch who refuses to allow a stud to mount her at all is probably simply not ready to mate. Owners have misjudged the time. If she seems interested, but forces the male to dismount, she may have a physical condition that is causing her severe pain. Most often the cause is some kind of stricture, or abnormal narrowing, of the vaginal area. This can be caused by a badly healed pelvic fracture or tight bands in the posterior vagina. Sometimes, a condition called persistent hymen, when the membrane does not break, may be the problem. In all of these cases, the bitch will allow herself to be mounted but will be in obvious pain upon intromission of the stud's penis. These condi-

Illustration 7: The coital lock, or "tie," can last anywhere from five to forty-five minutes.

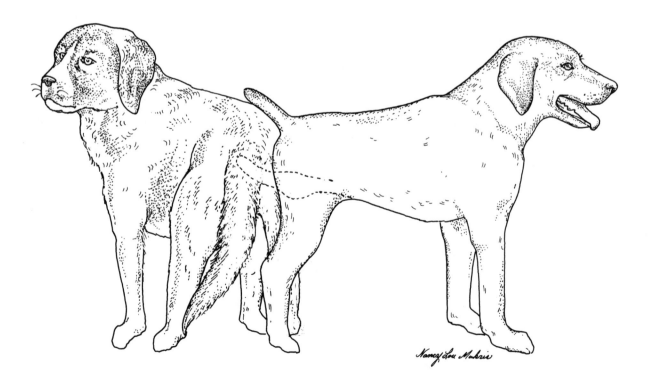

tions can usually be diagnosed by means of digital palpation by a veterinarian experienced in breeding problems, and they can occasionally be corrected either manually or surgically.

Infertility

When the mating goes smoothly but no pregnancy follows, it is possible that one of the partners is infertile. Consult a veterinarian who specializes in canine breeding and reproduction problems.

It may be easier to determine whether or not a stud is infertile, so breeders usually focus on the male first before submitting a bitch to elaborate tests and examinations. The first step is to find out whether or not he has successfully impregnated a female during the same time period. If so, this, of course, is proof of his past fertility. If not, the stud should have a semen collection and evaluation to assess the sperm count, its forward motility, and its morphology. If it has not been done already, a complete physical should be given to the stud to rule out urogenital problems.

If the stud is fertile, the bitch must then be evaluated. There can be a number of reasons why a bitch fails to conceive. Sometimes apparent infertility is simply a matter of timing. Mating a bitch at the wrong time is probably the most common cause of so-called infertility. This is particularly true if a bitch has irregular or abnormal heat cycles. Owners should also remember that large breed bitches begin to have their heat cycles late and that older dogs tend to cycle fewer times per year.

There can be several reasons why a bitch fails to cycle at all, or appears to. Sometimes a bitch continues to have silent heats. That is, her heats are very mild, and she keeps herself clean so that owners are unaware of them. Not infrequently, people don't know that a bitch has been previously spayed by another owner. There are also rare cases of dogs who, although they appear to be females, have two sets of sex organs and are actually hermaphrodites. Most commonly, bitches who fail to have heat cycles or have overlong intervals between cycles are suffering from hormonal problems—disorders of the thyroid, adrenal, ovarian, or pituitary glands.

A bitch's physical abnormalities can prevent the semen from traveling to the ovaries to be fertilized, even though a successful breeding has apparently taken place. Physical causes of infertility in a bitch who has normal heat cycles are incomplete development of the uterine horns and an occlusion of both oviducts. Both of these conditions will prevent the fertilization of eggs and can be diagnosed by the use of dye studies or exploratory abdominal surgery.

An infectious disease can also make a bitch infertile. The most common illnesses that can prevent a bitch from conceiving are brucellosis, which we mentioned earlier; a herpes virus; and chronic endometritis, or uterine and vaginal infections. A veterinarian can advise owners how to deal with these diseases. Careful isolation of the causative organisms via culture tests and appropriate therapy can often result in a return of fertility if no permanent damage has occurred.

Barring one of these disorders or diseases, a bitch who still fails to conceive should have her heat cycle carefully studied. Daily evaluations of her vaginal cells by the use of a vaginal cytology can often help to determine optimal breeding time so that a successful breeding can take place.

Pregnancy

Because heat periods are so widely spaced, a bitch's pregnancy cannot be determined simply because her next heat cycle does not begin.

Twenty-one days after breeding is the earliest possible time that a veterinarian can feel the slightest enlargements in the uterus by palpation, and this is only possible in a very thin, trim bitch. At about twenty-eight to thirty days, the fetuses can be felt better. It will take much longer before anything can be felt in large breeds, and if a bitch is obese the puppies often cannot be detected at all. Bitches carrying several pups will often have increased abdominal size at around five weeks of gestation. Radiology may be used to determine pregnancy, but only during the last three weeks of gestation.

After about thirty-five days, the bitch's teats will become enlarged and turgid, and ten days later they will be larger but softer. At around fifty days, the breast tissue itself will enlarge.

A couple of days before whelping, there will be a little bit of watery secretion from the teats in a first-time mother. Actual milk secretion will commence immediately after birth. Bitches who have been pregnant many times will not have any teat development until fifty days, and their milk secretion may start a couple of days before whelping.

Whelping usually occurs around sixty-three days after breeding, but the range can be anywhere from fifty-nine to sixty-six days. This variation is due to a possible time lapse between the time the sperm enters the female and the time of actual fertilization. Small breeds tend to whelp earlier than large dogs.

General Care During Pregnancy

If a bitch is in good health and at a desirable weight at conception, the pregnancy should go without a hitch and no special care is necessary. Unless there is a problem, there is no need for veterinary checkups during pregnancy.

A pregnant bitch should be allowed to exercise as usual up until the last week or two before delivery, when heavy exercise should be restricted. If there is a great deal of abdominal swelling because the litter is large, the bitch herself will probably slow down; she should never be pushed or urged to exercise more than she wants to.

Small dogs who usually jump up and down onto furniture a lot are usually self-restricting as they get larger, but owner awareness and restraint may sometimes be necessary.

Nutrition for the pregnant bitch is discussed in detail in Chapter 3, but it bears repeating that sometimes bitches become anorexic shortly before delivery (and often immediately after). Highly nutritious, low-bulk meals should be offered several times a day in small portions, but the bitch should never be forced to eat.

Pregnancy Disorders

Pregnant bitches may sometimes have a slight clear or milky discharge from the vagina, which is nothing to worry about. A bloody or pus-filled discharge, however, is abnormal and indicates infection. It requires immediate veterinary attention.

Hemorrhaging may be a sign of impending abortion. Spontaneous abortions early in pregnancy can occur for many reasons: because of fetal defects; a traumatic injury to the mother; an abnormal maternal environment—the bitch is suffering from a thyroid disorder, for instance; or because the mother is suffering from one of a number of viral, bacterial, or protozoan diseases. Pups born before eight weeks of pregnancy seldom survive.

Ectopic pregnancies and uterine torsion are problems that can occur in the dog but are very rare.

Hypocalcemia, or eclampsia, can occur either toward the end of pregnancy or postpartum. It is usually seen in small-breed dogs and is caused by a lack of sufficient calcium in the diet during late pregnancy and nursing. During late pregnancy and lactation, a bitch's system is drained of calcium first to form skeletons and later to produce milk. If this calcium is not replaced by a high-calcium commercial diet during the time of need, the bitch will become very ill. Symptoms include restlessness, trembling, high fever, muscle spasms, and eventually convulsions. This is an emergency situation, requiring immediate professional care (see also the Emergencies section).

Owners should remember that birth, or parturition, will occur approximately sixty-three days after fertilization of the egg, which is *not* necessarily sixty-three days after mating. Therefore, there is no need to panic and assume that something is wrong if the pups are not born on exactly the day they are expected.

Whelping

About two weeks prior to the expected birth, the mother should be introduced to the whelping box, which will be used for the delivery of the pups and in which they will live with their mother afterward. Ideally the box should be made of wood so that it is sturdy, draft-free, and easy to keep clean. The dimensions of the box will depend on the dog's size, but it should be large enough for her to move around in comfortably. Height of the sides will also depend, in part, on the dog's size and the expected dimensions of the pups. The sides should be high enough to prevent the pups from crawling and, later, walking out and also to prevent drafts; six to eight inches is probably sufficient for average-sized dogs. An opening should be cut in one side to provide easy access for the bitch. This opening can be closed when needed with a loose board. The entire bottom of the box should be lined with many layers of newspaper. After birth, old towels or blankets can be substituted, but papers that can be removed and disposed of are necessary during birth.

For large dogs, a wooden pole or board should be mounted across the center of the box about four or five inches from the bottom so that the puppies can get through but the mother cannot. Alternately, a shelf can be built all round the inside walls of the box, about four to six inches from the bottom. These devices will protect the puppies from accidentally being rolled or stepped on by their mother.

It is very important that the temperature in the box remain even and warm. If necessary, a heat light or lamp should be rigged up well above the box so that the temperature never falls below seventy degrees Fahrenheit.

The bitch's temperature is going to drop immediately before birth begins, so a week before expected delivery, owners should start taking the bitch's temperature twice a day in order to know what her normal temperature is and to determine its usual daily fluctuations. See Chapter 12, under "General Care," for how to do this.

In very long-haired bitches, the hair around the mammary glands and vulva may need to be clipped.

This is also the time to assemble any equipment that may be needed to assist in whelping. In addition to a rectal thermometer, cotton thread to tie off the umbilical cord, clean scissors to sever the cord, and towels to rub the puppies down may all be needed.

Signs That Delivery Is Imminent

Two to three days before the delivery of the puppies, the dam may lose her appetite. Her vulva may appear somewhat swollen, and there may be a slight discharge. Nesting behavior will become evident, with the bitch carrying favorite objects into the whelping box and tearing up the newspaper in it.

Anywhere from twenty-four to forty-eight hours preceding birth, there will be a sudden drop in body temperature to below normal; this may last only a very short time and is easily missed unless a regular temperature-taking routine has been established.

Being nervous and upset because she is in a strange place can delay labor and delivery. All bitches are better off delivering their pups in familiar surroundings with people they know, but if a physical condition demands that the bitch be moved to the doctor's office, or if the whelping box must be placed in a strange place, she should be familiarized with the location at least a week ahead of delivery time.

Labor and Delivery

There are three distinct stages of labor and delivery. During the first stage the cervix relaxes and dilates, and mild contractions, which are not usually noticeable to owners, occur. The bitch will be restless, visiting the whelping box frequently, panting, and shivering. If she has eaten recently, she may vomit. Some bitches want company and companionship at this time, while others prefer solitude. Individual preferences should be honored. This stage usually lasts anywhere from six to twelve hours, but can be longer, especially with first-time mothers.

Labor, during which contractions of the uterus propel the fetus through the cervix into the vagina, then begins. Owners should be aware that first-time mothers often interpret the onset of labor as the need to urinate and will attempt to run outside. When strong contractions begin, most bitches lie on one side, straining and often licking the vulva. Some groan, and very nervous bitches may scream. Between contractions, the bitch will pant rapidly.

First, the water bag, or chorioalantois, will appear between the lips of the vulva. It will either break by itself or be ruptured by the mother, releasing some fluid. Next, the head of the pup, surrounded by the amniotic sac, will appear. Once the puppy's head passes through the lips of the vulva, the rest of its body will slide out easily, lubricated by the amniotic fluid. The mother will then break the sac, lick the pup vigorously, and bite off the umbilical cord. This entire process usually lasts anywhere from fifteen minutes to an hour.

The third stage of delivery is the expulsion of the placenta, or "afterbirth," which the bitch will probably eat. Sometimes the placenta will not be expelled until after the birth of another pup. This is perfectly natural, but care must be taken that a placenta is not retained after all of the pups are born.

In between births the bitch will often relax, seeming to think that the job is over. Pups should be allowed to nurse. Intervals between puppies will vary considerably, but are usually shorter if there is a large litter. The range can be anywhere from fifteen minutes to an hour. Sometimes the time between the first and second pups is a great deal longer than that between subsequent births—up to two or three hours. Delivery time of an entire litter can take from four to twenty-four hours, and there is no need for concern as long as the bitch is not constantly straining or in obvious pain.

Delivery Problems

Problems should be anticipated if a bitch has had trouble in previous deliveries, or if a first-time mother is known to have had a pelvic injury. Older or obese bitches are definitely in the risk category and should be monitored by a veterinarian. Certain breeds are known to have difficulty delivering either because of the puppies' large heads or for other anatomical reasons. Owners of these breeds should always discuss the possibility of a Caesarean section with their veterinarians. The operation itself is described in Chapter 4.

Trouble should be suspected if a bitch strains hard for more than four to five hours with the first pup or strains for three hours between pups without successful delivery; if labor does not begin when it seems imminent, but there is a dark green discharge from the vagina; or if labor suddenly stops and the bitch seems restless and weak. A Caesarean section may be necessary in all of these instances.

Dystocia, or difficult birth, can occur either because there is something wrong with the mother or because there is something wrong with one or more of the fetuses. The cause can be an inadequate maternal birth canal caused by impediments from old pelvic fractures or a vaginal mass. Uterine inertia (or atony), or weak expulsive efforts on the part of the mother, can also cause dystocia. This is commonly seen in fat old dogs, very small dogs, dogs who have very large litters, or in dogs who are suffering from low blood calcium or low blood glucose. An exceptionally large fetus or one with a very big head can cause a difficult birth, as can a fetus that is in an abnormal position in the birth canal. Sometimes a dead fetus can become lodged in the birth canal, blocking delivery of other pups (see also the Emergencies section).

If you suspect trouble, it is better to be over-cautious about calling the veterinarian than to wait too long, possibly risking the lives of both mother and puppies.

Helping in a Normal Delivery

It is best not to interfere in a delivery when all is going well, but sometimes a bitch may need some assistance from owners even when there is no problem, especially if she is a first-time mother.

If a pup seems to become stuck, it is important to complete the birth as quickly as possible or the puppy will die from lack of oxygen. Grasp the puppy firmly but gently by the body with clean hands and turn and pull in a downward direction until it can be slid out. Don't pull a puppy by the head or a limb, or it may be injured.

Sometimes the mother fails to break the amniotic sac and lick a pup. If this should happen, an owner should immediately break the sac and rub the puppy briskly with a cloth towel until it begins to breathe and return it to the mother to lick right away. It may also be necessary to tie off the umbilical cord if the dam does not bite it off properly. Allow the pup to remain attached to the placenta for about five or ten minutes, and then tie the cord with cotton thread approximately one inch from the puppy, being careful not to apply traction to the puppy's abdomen. Sever the cord on the placenta side of the tie with scissors.

Puppies should always be returned to the mother immediately to be nursed. If a bitch completely ignores the pups, they may have to be removed and cared for by hand (see Chapter 6).

Postpartum Care

When the birth appears to have been completed, the bitch's abdomen should be checked for any undelivered puppies or remaining placentas. Owners of small dogs can usually do this themselves, but large or obese dogs need to be checked by a veterinarian.

The bitch's vulva should be bathed with warm water and dried thoroughly, and the whelping box should be cleaned up, any uneaten placentas removed, and the newspapers changed. For several hours, keep a close watch to be sure that none of the pups is rejected. Rejection usually occurs because of some defect, and a puppy who is not accepted by its mother should be examined by a veterinarian right away. If there is no defect, the pup may have to be raised by hand (see Chapter 6).

The dam will probably be reluctant to leave her puppies for a few hours, and owners may have to carry or coax her outside to relieve herself. She should be offered water and small amounts of food but should not be forced to eat until she is ready, which may be several days after delivery. She may vomit some of the placentas she has eaten. This is nothing to worry about, but they should be removed before she can eat them again. Her stools may be loose and darker than usual for up to a week after delivery. During lactation, the bitch's food intake must be increased considerably. See Chapter 3, "Feeding to Meet Special Needs," for exact amounts and kinds of food to give. As mentioned, small, frequent meals will be easier to digest than larger ones.

For about three weeks after delivery, the dam may have a vaginal discharge, which can be brownish or reddish. If the discharge persists, is a dark color, contains blood, clots, or pus, or has a foul odor, consult a veterinarian.

The dam's temperature should be taken two times a day for about a week after delivery (see Chapter 12). If her temperature rises above 103 degrees, she may have an infection and need veterinary attention.

Her mammary glands should be checked daily for any signs of heat, redness, pain, or swelling. The milk should also be observed for abnormal discharges. Any blood or clots in it is a sign of a problem.

Some new mothers want to be left entirely alone with their puppies, while others crave company. Bitches who have very close relationships with their owners and some very high-strung animals may tire of the puppies and want to be out with their human families more and more. Owners of these dogs will need to recognize this and coax or urge the mother back to her pups. Sometimes it may be necessary for someone to sit with her and the puppies to ensure that she spends enough time with them.

Postpartum Diseases of the Mother

Sudden neglect of the litter is a sure sign that all is not well with the bitch. As we mentioned before, an elevated temperature, vaginal bleeding, or a foul-smelling vaginal discharge are all signs of disease and require immediate attention. When the mother is ill the pups should be weaned immediately if they are old enough (three weeks). Otherwise they will probably have to be raised by hand, at least until the dam recovers.

If the dam is restless and seems to have abdominal discomfort, a retained placenta or uterine infection can be the cause, and the owner should seek veterinary help immediately.

An infected uterus, or metritis, is a condition that usually occurs within three days after delivery. This is a disease that is preventable by strict attention to cleanliness, since it is usually caused by a bacterial infection that spreads from the vagina to the uterus when the cervix is dilated during delivery. The dam will have a high fever, lose her appetite, be very thirsty, and have a foul-smelling vaginal discharge. This is an emergency, requiring immediate professional attention.

Rejection of the puppies can be caused by an infection of one or more of the mammary glands a condition called mastitis. The glands become hard and swollen and very red. A brownish or bloody watery fluid is seen. Sometimes, an abscess can form and rupture, discharging foul-smelling pus. Treatment is with antibiotics, hot compresses, and expression of the infected fluid. If the mammary glands are not abscessed and the milk is not affected, the pups can usually continue to nurse after the bitch is made more comfortable.

Agalactia is the absence of lactation in a bitch. Treatment is directed at stimulating milk production with the use of drugs. If this technique fails, the pups will then have to be hand raised.

We spoke of hypocalcemia, or eclampsia, under "Pregnancy Disorders." This condition can occur within three weeks after delivery, as well as in the latter stages of pregnancy. If the litter is old enough, it should be weaned immediately; otherwise, alternate hand feeding and nursing can carry the pups over until they can be returned full time to the dam. At the same time, the bitch should receive calcium supplements.

Care of newborns, or neonatals, including the care and feeding of orphaned pups, is covered in detail in the next chapter.

6

Care of Newborns

PHILIP R. FOX, DVM

It bears repeating that in order to have healthy newborn puppies, or neonatals, both the sire and dam must be in good physical condition. This will prevent the passing along of any diseases or parasites to the pups. In addition, a bitch who is sick, over-weight, infected with worms, poorly vaccinated, or fed a nonnutritious diet will not have the strength and stamina necessary to support puppies during pregnancy, whelping, and nursing.

General Care of Newborns

Owners must be sure that the dam has adequate food and water available at all times during lactation. Actual amounts of food for nursing dams will vary according to the size of the dam and the litter, but most bitches' appetites increase tremendously during this period. In the nutrition section of Chapter 3, we discuss amounts and types of food for lactating bitches in detail.

When there is a very large litter, even a healthy bitch may not be able to nurse all of the pups at the same time, and supplementary feedings of the puppies may be necessary. This can be accomplished by allowing half of the litter to nurse, while feeding formula to the other half (see below for types of formula and ways of feeding), then reversing the process at the next feeding. Some breeders advocate allowing the smallest puppies to remain with the mother all of the time, while supplementing only the larger pups. Whichever method is used, take care not to let any newborn pup remain away from the mother for very long.

Cleanliness and warmth are extremely important for newborns. Puppies must be kept at an even, warm temperature for at least the first four to six weeks of life. A high-sided whelping box, as described in the previous chapter, will help keep the newborns free from drafts. Body heat from the mother and littermates also will provide warmth, but take special care to avoid sharp temperature changes. Even though the dam will lick her puppies clean when they urinate or defecate, the papers or rags covering the bottom of the whelping box should be changed regularly to guard against dampness and bacterial growth.

Weight gain is the single most important criterion of how a puppy is doing. A healthy pup should just about double its birth weight by the time it is ten days old.

When puppies nurse, they receive colostrum from their mother. This contains antibodies that protect the pups against disease. While these maternal antibodies can protect a puppy, they can also interfere with the effectiveness of vaccines (see "Vaccinations for Puppies," Chapter 3). That is why we give puppies a se-ries of three to four vaccinations spaced over a period of time until the age of eighteen weeks. Problems occur when a pup isn't immunized at all or gets only part of the series. *Until a puppy is eighteen weeks old and has had all of the required series of vaccinations, it may not be immune to infectious disease.* Keep it away from environments, such as kennels or grooming establishments, where there are other dogs.

Raising an Orphaned Pup

An orphaned puppy, deprived of the care of its mother and the warmth and companionship of littermates, needs special supportive care and attention.

General Care

The first two weeks of life are most critical for an orphan. A warm environment is especially important for a pup who is alone. If a pup is separated from its mother and littermates, an outside source of heat is necessary. A puppy that becomes chilled may sicken and die. (See also "Hypothermia," page 90.) For the first seven days of life, the puppy should be maintained at an even temperature of ninety degrees Fahrenheit. This can gradually be reduced to eighty-five degrees when the pup is seven to twenty-one days old, then to seventy-five degrees until the puppy is thirty days of age, and eventually to about seventy degrees from thirty to sixty days. The best way to accomplish this is by using a high-sided whelping box, or incubator, placed near a heating vent. If this does not provide sufficient warmth, a heating light or lamp should be assembled above the box, and left on all of the time. Half of the incubator should be covered in some way to provide escape from the constant light. A shoe box placed upside-down can be used for this. *Electric heating pads or hot water bottles are not recommended.* They can easily burn a tiny puppy, and the heat they give out is not sufficiently diffused.

A clean environment is also extremely important for an orphaned puppy who is without a mother to lick it clean. Wipe the baby gently, and change bedding regularly to be sure that it is kept dry.

Puppies less than one week old need assistance in defecating and urinating. They do not have the ability to move their bowels or empty their bladders consciously and must be stimulated to do so. This is usually taken care of by the dam, but owners of orphans will have to perform this function. Six or eight times a day, or after each feeding, hold the puppy gently in the palm of one hand and gently rub the anus or genital area with a Q-tip, cotton ball, or cloth moistened with water or baby oil. Wipe the pup's eyes several times daily with a Q-tip moistened with mineral oil, until they open.

Since they lack the exercise and stimulation a mother's licking and nudging gives them and the competition to nurse that their litter-mates provide, orphan puppies need to be handled gently at least six or eight times daily. They should be allowed to walk and move around rather than be left to lie quietly all the time.

It is especially important to keep track of an orphan puppy's weight gain. A pup who is being raised by hand should be weighed at birth on a small gram scale (available at a pharmacy) and again every eight to ten hours for the first four or five days. A puppy should gain one to one-and-one-half grams per pound of anticipated adult weight per day. The pup should double its birth weight at around ten days of age. Daily weighings should continue until an orphaned neonatal is about two-and-a-half to three weeks old.

What to Feed Orphan Pups

By far the best substitute for a puppy's own mother's milk is that of another nursing bitch. Take care to be sure that the foster mother is in good health, and watch carefully to see that the mother does not reject the pup.

If a foster mother is not available, an orphan pup must be given a substitute formula. Pure cow's milk is a very poor choice, because it does not provide nearly enough calories and nutrients to support a puppy, is poorly digested, and often leads to diarrhea. There are good commercial simulated bitch's milk products on the market. They are generally available at drugstores or from the veterinarian.

Home formulas can be used in a pinch, although they are not nearly as well-balanced or nutritious as the commercial products. A good home formula is:

8 ounces of cow's milk (3.5 percent fat content)
1 egg yolk
2–4 drops of human infants' liquid multiple vitamins

All formulas should be prepared fresh daily and served at room temperature, using one of the methods described below.

As to frequency of feeding, it is a good general rule that pups be fed six to eight times a day up to three weeks and four times a day from three to six weeks of age. Solid food should begin to be introduced at about three weeks of age. More about weaning later on.

The following table indicates the recommended caloric intake for neonatals.

Owners should bear in mind that these recommendations for frequency of feeding and amounts to feed are only general guidelines, which ideally will result in a plump, contented pup who sleeps most of the time. Thin, restless, crying pups are either not receiving the correct nutrition or are ill.

TABLE 10

CALORIC INTAKE FOR NEONATALS

Age in days	Kilocalories per pound per day
Up to 7	60
7–14	70
14–21	80–90
Over 21	Over 90

How to Feed Orphan Pups

There are several ways to feed orphan puppies.

The least desirable but most common and frequently used method is with an eyedropper. The drawbacks to this way of feeding are:

• A lack of accuracy in administering the correct amount of food.

• A tendency to give food too rapidly when the bulb of the eyedropper is squeezed, causing food to be taken into the lungs, which can result in pneumonia.

• The inflexibility and rigidity of the dropper, which can injure the puppy's mouth and throat.

Far better than eyedroppers are nursing bottles (either those designed specifically for dogs, those used for human babies, or small doll bottles). It is very important to fit the size of the bottle and nipple to that of the puppy so that neither the bottle itself nor the nipple can possibly be swallowed. The owner should adjust the hole in the nipple to ensure the proper flow of formula. If the hole is too large, the pup may gag and drool formula from the corners of his mouth. If it is too small, it will take too long for the pup to take in the meal, and it will become fatigued. After a pup has been fed from a bottle, it must be burped to avoid indigestion from swallowed air. Holding the animal in the palm of the hand, gently rock it and/or massage its abdomen with two fingers until an air bubble comes up.

The third way of feeding neonatals under ten days of age is with a gastric or stomach tube, a procedure called gavage. This is an especially good method for very young orphans who are ill and/or unable or unwilling to suckle. It will only work, however, for very young puppies who don't have a well-developed gag reflex. A soft, flexible feeding tube, or human male urethral catheter, should be premeasured. Place it along the outside of the pup's body from the tip of the mouth to just in front of the last rib; mark this length. Insert the tube into the pup's mouth (it may need to be lightly lubricated with mineral oil) and gently push down into the stomach, up to the marked spot (see Illustration 8, page 89). If the tube hangs up anywhere, withdraw it and gently restart it. Attach a syringe containing a premeasured amount of formula to the free end of the tube, and administer it very gently and slowly. One further word, using a stomach tube may prevent a pup from developing a strong sucking instinct. So, if a pup is going to be returned to the dam later on, it is best not to use this method of feeding.

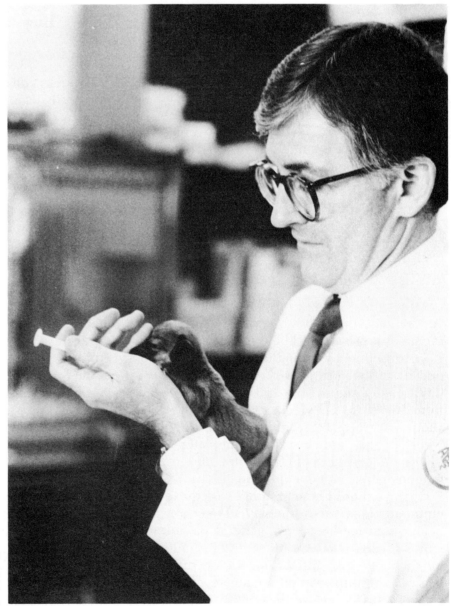

**Photograph 10:
Dr. William J. Kay giving
medication to an orphaned
newborn pup with a syringe**

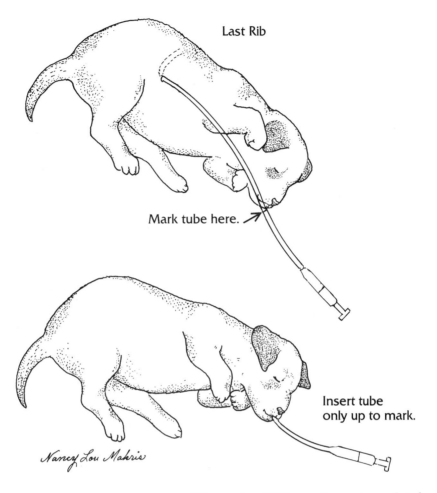

Last Rib

Mark tube here.

Insert tube
only up to mark.

Nancy Lou Mahris

Illustration 8: Measuring a stomach tube for feeding a neonatal

Weaning

Weaning is a very gradual process that has several steps. It should begin when the puppies are about three weeks old.

The first step in weaning is to remove the dam from the puppies for at least an hour prior to feeding time so that they will be hungry. The dam should also be kept away from the pups while they are eating.

Then, place a small, shallow dish of gruel in the puppies' environment. The gruel should consist of a little bit of commercial dog food mixed with water or whatever formula the puppies have been taking, or with some diluted strained baby food. Some of the pups will be aggressive enough to eat immediately. Others will need to be coaxed by placing a little bit of the food on the tips of their noses or tongues.

When the pups start to take this gruel, begin to decrease the bitch's food intake so that she produces less milk. At the same time, gradually give the puppies more and more food, making it less and less "gruelly" and more solid, by degrees.

Toward the end of the weaning process, allow the pups to eat as much food as they want, unless they look bloated. Ideally, puppies should appear rotund. If they seem bloated, cut back on their rations. See "Nutrition," Chapter 3, for more details on amounts and proportions of food for puppies.

Puppies should be completely weaned at about six to eight weeks of age.

A Healthy Puppy

A healthy puppy is round and firm with good body and muscle tone. It will spend 90 percent of the time or more sleeping, either on its stomach with head extended or on its side. When awakened, a healthy pup will yawn and will not be especially vocal. A pup who cries or vocalizes for more than ten or fifteen minutes is expressing pain, discomfort, chilling, or stress. If so, it has some kind of health problem.

The veterinarian sees the dog more frequently during the period between six weeks and six months of age than at any other time during its life. It is very important during this developmental period to consult with the vet on proper nutrition, vaccinations, deworming, and evaluations of possible congenital or hereditary disorders.

Regular stool-sample evaluations and treatment for parasites are next in importance to proper immunizations for keeping a puppy healthy. Virtually all dogs are born with the potential for having roundworms. Some say that all puppies are born with roundworms. Owners should not think that just because they see no worms there are none. Worms are not always visible to the naked eye. Have the veterinarian check stool samples frequently and have the pup dewormed at least once, whether or not the sample was positive; no stool-sample evaluation is 100 percent accurate. (See also "Intestinal Parasites" in the Encyclopedia.)

A Sick Puppy

A neonatal puppy who is not well has three things to contend with:

Dehydration: A puppy who does not take in food or water in adequate amounts or is exposed to chills, excess moisture, or low humidity may become dehydrated very quickly. Since the majority of its body is water, this can be devastating.

Hypothermia, or Low Body Temperature: Neonatal dogs are dependent to a large extent on the radiant heat they receive from their dam. If they are separated from their mothers, they require an increased outside source of heat. Chilling increases the pup's respiratory rate and causes it to feel cool to the touch. If this situation is allowed to continue, a puppy may go into a coma and die.

Diarrhea: While it is perfectly natural for neonatal dogs younger than three weeks to have soft stools, changes in the diet of the bitch or the pup can produce excessive diarrhea in puppies. If allowed to persist, diarrhea can be very debilitating. It causes severe dehydration, which can be fatal to a young pup. (See "Gastrointestinal Diseases and Disorders" in the Encyclopedia.)

Infectious Diseases and Illnesses of Neonatals

If a puppy seems sick, several diseases should immediately be suspected.

The most common infectious canine diseases, which we will discuss in detail under infectious and contagious diseases in the Encyclopedia, are canine distemper, a highly contagious virus, transmitted from dog to dog via the aerosol route, frequently through sneezing; and canine parvovirus, spread by infected feces. It is also highly contagious. Both of these diseases are very serious and often fatal and can leave recovered dogs with lasting aftereffects. Prevention by proper vaccination is by far the best course to take.

Other diseases that affect both adult dogs and puppies are infectious canine hepatitis (canine adenovirus type), which now is seen rarely because of the protective effects of vaccination; and infectious tracheobronchitis ("kennel cough"), which is also introduced via the aerosol route. In addition, there are a number of viral gastrointestinal diseases, many of which do not even have names, that can cause symptoms similar to canine parvovirus.

Diseases Peculiar to Puppies

There are some diseases and disorders that are normally seen only in young puppies.

Oral Papillomatosis: This an uncommon canine infectious viral disease of young dogs, causing benign but terrible-looking wartlike growths on the tongue and mouth. It is transmitted from dog to dog by direct contact and licking and through commonly used dishes and toys. It is usually self-limiting, going away by itself as the dog gets older and gains immunity. Occasionally surgery is used to remove these growths.

Canine Herpes: Often referred to as the "fading puppy syndrome," canine herpes affects one- to three-week-old puppies, who can die it within hours. A formerly healthy, vigorous pup will suddenly become acutely ill, crying and not nursing. Often there is no fever. Affected bitches may have nodules on the vagina, accompanied by inflammation. The puppies who do recover will remain carriers for months. Treatment simply involves supportive care.

Umbilical Cord Infection: Puppies can also contract an umbilical cord infection, from which they can become very sick and die if not treated by a veterinarian.

Ophthalmis Neonatorum: This acute, pussy bacterial eyelid infection is fairly common in newborns. Both eyelids become swollen, and the eyes must be bathed regularly and treated with antibiotic ointment prescribed by a veterinarian.

Toxic Milk Syndrome: Puppies suffering from toxic milk syndrome become bloated, cry, have greenish diarrhea and swollen, distended, red anuses. This indicates incompatability with the bitch's milk. Take the bitch to the doctor and have her treated with hormones and antibiotics, while the pups remain at home and are given supportive care.

Hypoglycemia, or Low Blood Sugar: This is very common in small-breed neonatals. Acute stress and/or enzyme and hormonal systems that are inadequately developed at birth can be the causes. Symptoms are muscle weakness, twitching, depression, and eventual collapse. Immediate veterinary attention is necessary. The doctor will give an intraveneous injection of 50 percent dextrose to bring the pup's blood-sugar level up rapidly. An emergency home remedy, until a doctor see the pup, is to give the pup honey or corn syrup by mouth. It will be absorbed through the oral membranes very quickly. See also the Emergencies section.

Mange: Young puppies are also quite susceptible to mites. These can cause scarcoptic or demodectic mange. Both types will show up as little bald spots in the haircoat around a pup's muzzle, ears, legs, and extremities. Although puppies can sometimes outgrow the demodectic form of mange, the scarcoptic form is usually more severe, causing intense scratching and chewing. If you suspect mange, see the veterinarian immediately. (See "Dermatologic Diseases and Disorders" in the Encyclopedia).

Physical Abnormalities and Deformities of Newborn Pups

If there are no signs or symptoms of illness or disease, but a pup still is not doing well, it may be a congenital physical abnormality.

Puppies can be born with several different types of congenital heart disease. A neonatal who is not thriving and/or appears to have breathing difficulty should be examined to es-

tablish a diagnosis. The prognosis for recovery varies, depending on the severity of the problem. For more details see the Encyclopedia of Diseases of Dogs.

Sometimes puppies around two weeks old develop a hernia, a protrusion of an organ, or a a part of one, through an opening in the abdominal wall, either around the groin or navel. To the naked eye it will appear as a small, round bulge in the skin. If a hernia shows, have the puppy seen by a veterinarian, who will either suggest waiting to see if the hernia will close by itself or will advise that it be surgically repaired.

In toy breeds, an unusually large head dome may indicate hydrocephalus, or an accumulation of fluid in the brain. This may or may not cause problems.

A puppy who is noticeably smaller than its littermates is usually referred to as the runt of the litter. These litttle pups may have some sort of birth defect or illness and should be examined immediately by a veterinarian.

Socialization

In addition to having their physical needs taken care of, it is important that young puppies begin to learn about the world around them at an early age.

The critical period for socialization of a puppy is between six and sixteen weeks of age. During this time, it is important for a puppy to have interaction with household members, including supervised introductions to other pets. Owners should remember, however, that a dog this age is still a baby. Make sure that young children or other animals do not handle it too roughly or wear it out.

Although owners may begin some sort of housebreaking when a puppy is very young, it is important to realize that little puppies lack control of their bowels and bladders and have very low storage capacities. They usually urinate every two to three hours and urinate and defecate immediately after exercise, eating, and drinking. Therefore, they have to be taken to the paper very frequently when they are young if owners want to have any measure of "success" in the housebreaking process. Pups begin to have some control over elimination somewhere around three months of age.

A puppy is never too young to begin to learn when its owner is pleased or unhappy with its behavior. Reinforcing good behavior with an approving tone of voice, a pat, or a treat, and showing disapproval for unacceptable actions will usually give a pup the idea very quickly. (See also Chapter 8.)

Sensitivity training should also start when a pup is young. If, for example, a dog will need grooming regularly, it should be gradually introduced to the sound of a hair dryer or electric clipper at an early age. It is also a good idea to get a puppy used to being handled and examined, especially in sensitive spots such as feet, tail, mouth, and ears. By accustoming a young puppy to the sights, sounds, and sensations of the world it will be exposed to as an adult, reassuring it if it is nervous or frightened, and enabling it to feel secure, an owner can prevent many problems from arising in the future.

7

Care of Older Dogs

Connie E. Leifer, DVM, and

Robert E. Matus, DVM

The age at which a dog becomes a senior citizen depends in part on its anticipated life span. Giant breeds, with a life expectancy of about ten years, begin to seem old at six or seven, while small dogs, who can live to be twenty, aren't considered old until they are fifteen or so. Within these averages, a dog's aging will vary just as a person's will, depending on its general health and condition. Thus, an obese dog or a very sedentary animal will show signs of age sooner than one who is trim and active. Finally, illness or disease will, of course, take a toll.

Signs of Aging

An owner should be able to notice when a dog begins to slow down, but sometimes changes are so gradual that a more objective observer such as the veterinarian or a family member who has been away for a while will be the first to notice.

Probably the first and most obvious sign is amount and kind of sleep. Older dogs sleep a great deal and seem to sleep very soundly. While young dogs usually wake up easily, apparently sleeping "with one ear open," ready to jump up and follow their owners to another room, for instance, old dogs often have to be waked.

When they do get up after sleeping, old dogs may be stiff and slow to start, just like older people. This can be due to normal aging and stiffening up of joints, but it may have more serious causes.

Personality changes can also occur. An old dog may become cranky and unwilling to be handled or bothered, especially by children. Owners should realize that some reluctance to being mauled or tugged around is natural for older dogs, but if personality changes become extreme they may be caused by pain, severe discomfort, or illness.

General Care of Older Dogs

An important thing that owners can do to keep older dogs healthy is to prevent them from becoming obese. As a dog's body ages, metabolism slows down, causing a different use of nutrients to occur. Lean body mass decreases while fatty deposits increase. Therefore, daily food intake must be tailored to meet an older dog's particular needs and at the same time prevent excessive weight gain. In the "Nutrition" section of Chapter 3, there is a detailed discussion of how to meet the dietary needs of older dogs. It bears repeating, however, that older dogs continue to require high-quality protein, and that frequent, small meals are easier for them to digest than single, large ones. Sometimes an older dog requires a prescription diet because of a specific medical problem. Many of these diets are also described in Chapter 3.

How much exercise an older dog should have depends, in part, on what it's accustomed to. Allowing a dog to become completely sedentary will adversely affect cardiac function and hasten bone wasting (osteoporosis) and muscle atrophy. Bones build up and continue to be strong in direct relation to the stress that is put on them. Muscles also retain their strength and resiliency in direct proportion to their use.

Older dogs may develop arthritis, a "cold" lameness, which causes joints to stiffen with prolonged rest. As the joints "warm up" with movement, much of the pain of arthritis diminishes. Therefore, moderate exercise may be helpful. Take care not to overdo it, however, or an arthritic dog will have pain the next day.

The general loss of moisture throughout a dog's body as a result of aging may make its skin excessively dry and itchy. Owners should brush and comb older dogs regularly to stimulate oil production, cleanse the skin, and remove loose hair and dandruff.

Recent studies show that the T-lymphocyte-suppressor cells that govern the body's immune system diminish and possibly are less active with advancing age. This means that as a dog becomes older its immune system becomes less effective, and it becomes more susceptible to infectious diseases as well as to cancer and degenerative diseases than it was when it was younger. What this means to owners of older dogs is that whenever possible their animals should be protected against exposure to disease, chilling, excessive dampness, and extreme environmental changes.

In general, the important thing is to keep the older dog on an even keel as much as possible as far as nutrition, exercise, and environment are concerned.

Avoiding Stress: Boarding an Older Dog

All dogs need to know what to expect and will thrive in a well-established routine. As dogs age, they become even less able to tolerate the stress of sudden change. Not only does an older dog become more "set in its ways," but it can often have an undetected disease or disorder that its system is compensating for and is keeping in delicate balance. A sudden change in routine or environment may cause stress that can disrupt this fine homeostatic balance and cause the animal to sicken suddenly.

Owners of old dogs should recognize this and handle potentially stressful situations with common sense. If they are going to be moving or taking a dog away on vacation, for example, they should be especially careful that the older dog's routine is not upset. Meals and exercise should be on time. A senior citizen will also appreciate a little security from home. A familiar blanket or bed will help to reassure the dog that all is well and it has not been forgotten.

If owners are going to be away, it may be best to arrange for an old dog to stay at home with an experienced "sitter" who knows its routine, rather than taking it along or boarding it in a kennel.

When an older dog does have to be kenneled, it is important to choose the facility carefully. Recommendations from other dog owners may be helpful, but what is acceptable care for a young, healthy animal may not be adequate for a senior citizen. Veterinarians also generally have a list of kennels they trust. It is the dog owner's responsibility, however, to visit the facility, talk to the owners or managers, and check on details of care, such as:

• Are up-to-date immunizations and medical histories required for potential boarders?

• Is there a veterinarian on call for emergencies?

• Will the kennel give medications?

• What about climate control (e.g., air conditioning in summer; heat in winter)?

• What are the dogs fed? Will the kennel give special diets and are they willing and able to feed a dog more than once a day?

• What kind of supervision and companionship is available? How often are the animals visited each day? Is anyone there at night?

• Are the dogs taken out or expected to relieve themselves in their cages? How often are they exercised?

• What are the cages like? How large? How clean?

• Are owners permitted to bring blankets or beds, and if so, is the bedding actually put in the cages?

Although kennels have a responsibility to the animals they are boarding not to allow people to troop through the cage area continuously, an owner who explains the reason for his concern should at least be allowed to take a quick look around. The American Boarding Kennels Association (ABKA) is an association of boarding kennel operators devoted to providing good care for their charges. They will provide a list of member kennels to dog owners.*

What About Getting a New Pet?

For some old dogs, a new puppy or kitten in the household provides a new lease on life, giving them a release from boredom, renewed interest in playing and being active, and even an increased appetite. Others resent the newcomer, feel pushed out of their owners' lives, become depressed and fretful. In extreme cases, an older dog's health can suffer.

A dog who has spent at least part of its life in a household with other pets will probably accept a youngster better than one who has always been an "only child"; and an animal who feels well will react better to the upset of a newcomer than one who does not. Owners are generally the best judges of how a pet will accept the situation.

No matter how good-natured or accepting an older dog is of a new animal in the household,

this is bound to be a stressful situation, and the owner must protect the older dog as much as possible. Again, common sense is necessary. A young animal may be more aggressive and energetic than an old-timer, and care must be taken not to engender a competitive situation. The older dog's food bowls, bed, favorite toys, etc., must be off-limits to the newcomer, and if one of the animals has to be restrained or confined to prevent a confrontation, it should generally be the new pet. In addition, the older dog's accustomed routines should be followed religiously, and its own private time with its people protected.

An older dog who feels secure and unthreatened by a new, younger animal will usually accept the situation with grace, as long as it is allowed to remain boss.

Health Care

An older dog may require more frequent veterinary visits than the regular annual trip for boosters. Some veterinarians prefer to see their elderly patients on at least a biyearly basis in order to head off potential problems, and, of course, a dog with an ongoing medical problem may require more regular visits.

Owners should make it a point to observe

their old pets, paying particular attention to any change. Changes in habits can be very gradual and barely noticed on a daily basis. That is why the veterinarian probably will ask a number of questions: Is the dog getting

---

* Write to: American Boarding Kennels Association, 311 N. Union Blvd., Colorado Springs, CO 80909

around pretty well, or is it slowing down? Is there any weight loss or gain? Is its appetite good? How about its digestive system? Is it vomiting? Does it have diarrhea? Is it constipated, or straining to defecate? How much water does it drink? Does it have to urinate more frequently or have accidents in the house? Is it coughing? Sneezing? Is there any discharge from its nose or eyes? How about personality changes?

These questions are easy to answer if a dog is a house pet. Owners of dogs who live outdoors all the time should make it a point to observe their older pets' habits on a regular basis to know if any changes have occurred.

Health Problems

There are a number of canine health problems that are not confined to old dogs but are much more apt to occur after middle age.

Among the more common systemic diseases and disorders, which are discussed in detail in the Encyclopedia of Diseases of Dogs, are general heart and circulatory changes, which can lead to heart failure, and endocrine disorders, such as Cushing's syndrome and diabetes mellitus. Kidney (renal) failure is also an important disease that more often occurs in the older dog.

Owners are sometimes concerned that their dogs are going blind when they see the lenses of the eyes take on a hazy appearance. This condition, known as lenticular sclerosis, is a normal aging change and does not ordinarily affect vision. Older dogs also often develop iris atrophy, which causes them to squint in bright light, but this condition does not affect vision either. Cataracts, often the result of diabetes mellitus, may eventually cause blindness. If blindness is gradual, most dogs adjust very well after a short time as long as their environment remains the same. More about this under "Ophthalmic Diseases and Disorders" in the Encyclopedia.

Many older dogs become partially deaf, although they rarely suffer a complete hearing loss. There is usually no medical treatment for this, and most dogs seem to get along well with impaired hearing, although some may bark continuously. When an old dog suddenly does not obey or seems not to pay attention, its owner should realize that it may be due to deafness rather than sudden disobedience. Take care to protect a deaf dog from dangers, such as cars.

Dental disease is very common as dogs age, and an oral examination should be part of an older dog's regular veterinary examination. If a dog's teeth have not been cleaned regularly, plaque and tarter build up, and cavities, or caries, can form. Owners should suspect problems if an older dog has bad breath, bleeding gums, eats less, or refuses to chew hard biscuits or toys. A dog with a painful mouth will approach food, want to eat, and then back away or stand looking sadly at its plate. Sometimes food will fall out of its mouth. The dog's teeth will have to be professionally scaled and deep cleaned. After that, regular tooth cleaning at home will help to keep a dog's mouth free from problems. See Chapter 3 for instructions. Older dogs can develop oral tumors, which will also show up in an oral examination. See the Encyclopedia of Diseases of Dogs.

Many older dogs suffer from painful joints and stiff backs, which usually manifest themselves in a generalized arthritic stiffness. It can be very difficult to pin down the exact cause of this lameness and pain. It can result from degenerative joint disease, a congenital malformation that has worsened over the years due to constant wear and tear, or from an old injury or trauma. If an animal seems to be in constant pain, consult the veterinarian. There are medications that can be prescribed to alleviate the pain of stiff joints when no other more serious disease is present.

Older dogs are also prone to various types of urinary disorders. A distinction should be made between excessive urination (polyuria), frequent urination (pollakiuria), and urinary incontinence, each of which can have a number of different causes.

The instigating causes of excessive urination fall into two categories: failure of the body to conserve water adequately and excessive thirst. Failure to conserve water may result from kidney failure, certain endocrine diseases such as diabetes mellitus, or a uterine infection of older, unspayed female dogs known as pyometra, which may affect the kidneys and lead to excessive loss of body water. An increase in thirst may also be due to certain endocrine disorders, such as Cushing's syndrome, liver disease, or a disease of the central nervous system.

Frequent urination may result from such things as irritation of the bladder walls (cystitis), which manifests itself in frequent urination of small, often bloody, amounts. It may also be due to other types of bladder infection, urinary tract stones, or a urogenital tumor.

Another urinary disorder occurs when the bladder fails to retain normal amounts of urine. Urine then actually "leaks" out. The condition is called urinary incontinence. When an older spayed female only leaks urine while asleep, it may be due to a hormone imbalance, a condition that usually can be medically treated by a veterinarian. Other causes of urinary incontinence in an older animal may be related to the nervous system and in such cases the incontinence is often accompanied by a weakening of the hind limbs.

Finally, whatever the underlying cause of a urinary disorder in an older dog, water should always be available. *Never withhold water*; it may create dehydration, which will exacerbate existing diseases or disorders. (See "Renal Diseases and Disorders" in the Encyclopedia.)

Anesthesia and the Older Dog

Owners are often very concerned about surgery for an older dog, no matter how minor, and are especially fearful about the use of an anesthetic.

Although anesthesia used to be risky for older animals, today's testing procedures and methods of giving anesthetics minimize the risk to the extent that we can safely perform anesthesia on most older patients. (See Chapter 4.)

Here at The AMC, to recognize a risk patient who may require special care before, during, and after an operation, we routinely do a complete medical workup, as described in Chapter 12, on any dog over six years of age before performing even minor surgery. With the information from these tests, we can often safely operate on even very old, diseased dogs by using the proper support systems. Most veterinarians perform these tests as a matter of course, but owners should always ask to be sure that they are carried out. Testing does involve additional cost, however.

Of course, no matter how carefully preparations are made and anesthetic given, there can be unexplained deaths of animals in the operating room, just as there are of humans. But by using testing procedures and controlled anesthetic, the risks have been greatly minimized, and no owners need deprive pets of needed surgery because they fear the use of anesthetics.

Euthanasia

The reasons for euthanizing a pet, how euthanasia is performed, an owner's presence during the procedure, memorials to pets, and ways in which a pet's death can affect an owner are discussed in detail in Chapter 10. In this chapter, however, we will touch briefly on making that decision for an old dog.

As we emphasize in Chapter 10, the decision to euthanatize must be an individual one, and there is no right or wrong involved in whatever decision an owner makes. Some pet owners are unable to cope with disease and/or illness of any kind. For them, the daily care of a sick old dog would be extremely difficult and would only serve to rob them of any happy memories they might have of their pet.

Other owners want to keep an old dog alive as long as possible, provided that it is not suffering, and they are willing and able to do all of the things necessary to keep the dog as comfortable as they can. Then the difficulty may lie in judging whether or not the animal is in pain, and if so, how much. A sick dog is not necessarily in a lot of pain, and sometimes owners can judge from the way the animal acts just how much it is hurting. It is pretty safe to assume that a dog who eats reasonably well, is attentive and happy to see its family, and is fairly active in relation to its age is not in severe pain.

Because a veterinarian will probably know when a dog will be likely to experience pain or cease to have a meaningful life, owners should always consult a veterinarian when considering euthanasia for an older dog. Doctors can help with this difficult decision based on their knowledge of the normal course of most diseases.

Emergencies

Michael S. Garvey, DVM

The word *emergency* can be very frightening in its implications of a sudden, life-threatening occurrence. For the dog owner, the sense of panic and helplessness can often be heightened by the fact that animal accidents and sudden illnesses usually seem to happen "off-hours," when the regular veterinarian's office is closed. One thing that dog owners can do to alleviate part of the problem is to prepare ahead of time for this situation. What does the veterinarian recommend doing? Where is the nearest emergency veterinary clinic or hospital? What is their telephone number? This information can be placed in a convenient spot along with other emergency information, so that time isn't wasted wondering what to do when the need arises. Dog owners who travel with their pets or take them to vacation homes should take a few moments to obtain the same information wherever they are.

The fact remains that the best thing to do for any dog in any kind of emergency is to get him to a veterinarian right away. Owners have neither the knowledge nor equipment to accomplish much in the way of real help when a dog is seriously ill or injured. In our estimation, many so-called emergency techniques and measures, which have been touted in the past and are still put forth in many pet-care books and articles, at best serve no constructive purpose and at worst only tend to complicate problems by wasting precious time.

There are, however, some steps that can sometimes be taken by owners in certain situations to make a dog comfortable and possibly prevent further damage until a doctor can be reached. We will outline these steps in this section. We will also discuss the signs of a real emergency so that dog owners can make intelligent judgments regarding their pets' well-being.

Canine emergency situations are usually due to either accidental injury or illness. An illness can be an emergency because it is acute or of sudden onset; an ongoing illness can develop into an emergency for a variety of reasons. Accidental injuries that are emergencies can include trauma, such as a bad fall, hard blow, or being hit by a moving vehicle, which may involve fractures and other internal injuries; lacerations or wounds; the ingestion of poisons or other harmful substances; burns; electrocution; smoke inhalation; etc. In a category of its own, heat prostration is a frequent, serious emergency for dogs.

Avoiding Accidents

WHEN IS IT AN EMERGENCY?

It is an emergency requiring immediate veterinary attention when:

- A dog has received any kind of traumatic injury—a fall, being hit by a car or bicycle

- A fracture is suspected

- There is *significant bleeding* from any part of the body, including in the stool and urine

- Any kind of eye injury has occurred, no matter how seemingly slight

- A dog's gums or mouth are pale and/or purplish blue

- A dog is having difficulty breathing

- A dog is severely trembling, shaking, or in obvious discomfort

- A dog collapses, seems suddenly weak, loses consciousness, and/or has more than one seizure

- A dog suddenly becomes depressed or feverish

- Vomiting and/or diarrhea lasts for more than twenty-four hours

- A dog is unable to urinate

- A dog is choking or is known to have swallowed a foreign object

- A dog is known to have ingested drugs, medications, or poison

- A whelping bitch is unable to pass a puppy after five to six hours of labor

Any of these signs or occurrences or any combination of these signs constitutes an emergency.

Dog owners can often avert an emergency situation if they are aware of the kinds of accidents that frequently occur to puppies and dogs and use common sense to try to prevent them. First-time dog owners especially should realize that puppies and dogs have no way of knowing about the possibilities of injury. They should remember to anticipate danger for a pet, just as they would for a small child. Some accidental causes of injury to dogs and ways to avoid them include:

- Trauma from being hit by a car, motorcycle, or bicycle: Careful control of a dog, wherever it is, can usually avoid this kind of accident. Keeping a dog leashed or in a carrying case when traveling in a car and making sure car windows are only opened halfway can protect a dog from accidental injury. If a dog is on a leash at all times, scratch and bite wounds from other animals can usually also be prevented.

- Trauma from falls from windows: The "high-rise syndrome" isn't limited to cats, nor to animals who live in large cities. Owners should realize that puppies are just as curious and incautious as kittens, and a fall from a second-story window to a concrete walk in the suburbs can be almost as damaging as one from a fifth-floor city apartment. Pups should never be left unattended in a room with fully opened windows. Even when people are present, screens, bars, or windows opened from the top are good safety measures until a puppy grows up a bit and develops some judgment.

- Young puppies will chew almost anything, especially when they are left alone for long periods of time and become bored. Plugged-in electrical wires, if chewed, can cause electrocution. Again, pups should never be left alone for even short periods in rooms where lamps, radios, etc., are plugged in, until owners are sure that they aren't going to chew the wires.

- Swallowed objects, such as bones, toys, and other small things, can become lodged in a dog's esophagus and have to be removed by a veterinarian. They can also damage a dog's pharynx, or throat. Usually, young dogs or puppies are more prone to swallowing these types of objects than older animals are. Again, the owner's caution and common sense can be helpful in averting these kinds of occurrences.

• The ingestion of substances such as human medications can cause drug intoxication, and dogs are often poisoned when they eat or drink various other substances. No medications should be given to a dog except on the advice of a veterinarian (see also Appendix). It is particularly important for dog owners to know that antifreeze (ethylene glycol) is extremely attractive to dogs and potentially fatal. Antifreeze should be kept in tightly sealed containers or disposed of immediately and not left lying around the garage or property.

• Despite a great deal of publicity about this problem, owners still take their dogs with them in the car on hot days. Leaving a dog closed in a car in the sun for even brief periods of time can quickly result in heat prostration. In warm weather, dogs are best left at home.

SHOCK

This is the number-one condition that dogs sustain from trauma, including fractures, and severe bleeding or hemorrhaging. It is a collapse of the cardiovascular system and is characterized by rapid heartbeat; confusion; collapse; shivering; weak pulse; and pallor, which can be detected by lifting up a corner of the dog's lip and examining the gums and mucous membranes in the mouth. Normally, the insides of a dog's mouth are bright pink. If they are pale pink, there is a problem. If they are white, the problem is serious. Shock brought about by severe blood loss is called hemorrhagic shock. Dogs who are suspected of being in shock should be kept quiet and warm and be given prompt veterinary attention. Treatment for shock includes rapid intravenous fluid therapy. *Unless shock is treated promptly, the damage to the cardiovascular system will be irreversible.*

Emergency Conditions and Situations

The signs and symptoms listed above can often be caused by one or more conditions. As we said earlier, there is usually nothing helpful that an owner can do while waiting for veterinary care, but we have included any first-aid measures that are applicable. (See also Figures 6 and 7, pages 113–115.)

Bleeding or Hemorrhaging

Bleeding or hemorrhaging from any part of a dog's body can be an emergency if the bleeding is profuse or if it is at a slow pace and lasts for a long period of time. Owners can assess the seriousness of bleeding by checking for pallor and other signs of shock.

Nasal or oral bleeding: If profuse, this can be life-threatening. Ice packs or cold com-

presses over the nose or mouth area may help to slow bleeding, but it is usually impossible to get a compress to the problem area. Therefore, there is very little that an owner can do to stop this kind of bleeding except to get a dog emergency veterinary attention as quickly as possible.

Skin or surface bleeding: Lacerations, wounds, or puncture wounds in any part of the body can cause bleeding. Usually wounds in the skin surface cause minimal bleeding. The exception is a deep wound that involves a vein or blood vessel underneath the surface. This is most likely to occur in the neck area, where the jugular vein is or with cuts of the leg or foot. If there is significant bleeding from the skin, manual pressure should be applied in places that are not easily bandaged. Use a clean cloth or bandage and apply pressure next to the wound until the bleeding stops. Use a compression bandage in areas that can be readily bandaged (see Illustration 9, below). *We do not advocate the use of tourniquets.* They are very dangerous, may cause the loss of a limb due to prolonged interruption of the blood supply, and are not as effective as properly applied pressure.

Bleeding on feet and legs: Probably most problem surface bleeding in dogs involves either the feet or limbs. Lacerations of the foot pads tend to bleed a lot. This is very spongy tissue, and while the bleeding will often stop, it will begin again as soon as the dog steps on the foot and spreads the foot pad. If this process continues for too long, a dog can lose a significant amount of blood. Treat foot pad lacerations with a compression or pressure bandage if possible; it can be held in place temporarily with an old sock.

There is a small but significant artery behind the foot pads, at the back of the foot. This is a prime spot for dogs to cut when they step in broken glass or something sharp, causing arterial bleeding, with the blood spurting or pumping out. This is more serious than venous bleeding, in which the blood oozes out. Apply a compression bandage, not only over the wound itself, but around the whole foot. Again, a sock is useful to hold the bandage in place temporarily. *It is important not to tie a constrictive band over the cut*; this will cut off circulation to the rest of the foot. When an owner is going to bandage the lower part of a dog's limb, the entire lower part of the limb should always be bandaged to avoid swelling.

Bleeding that occurs higher on the legs can be significant when superficial veins and arteries are punctured or lacerated. As a general rule, a soft-padded compression bandage should be used in these areas.

Vomiting blood: This can be a cause of great concern for dog owners. However, if fluid is being vomited, vomiting is frequent, and the extent of the bleeding is flecks or streaks of

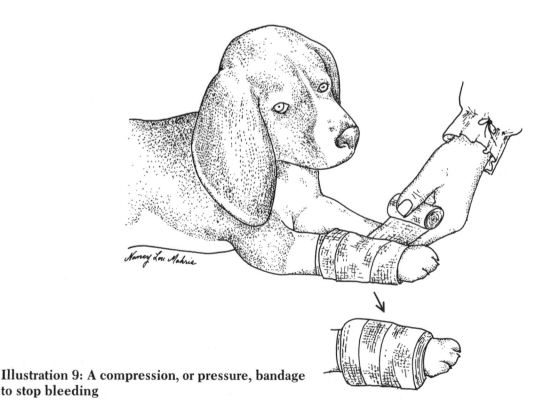

Illustration 9: A compression, or pressure, bandage to stop bleeding

blood in the vomitus, this is not a life-threatening emergency. If there is a profuse amount of blood thrown up, or if there are blood clots present, it can indicate significant bleeding in the stomach. In that case, veterinary attention should be sought quickly. There is no emergency treatment for this condition, and oral medication is not advised.

Bloody diarrhea or stool: If the blood is confined to streaks or flecks, with normal stool or diarrhea, it is not a severe emergency. If, however, the stool becomes pools of dark, foul-smelling blood and that is all that is passed from the rectum, it may be hemorrhagic gastroenteritis (HGE), which is a severe and life-threatening emergency. Small dogs may go into shock within hours with HGE; it will take a longer time for larger dogs to reach this condition. A great deal of water will be mixed with the blood, and this can lead to a specific type of shock, called hypovolemic shock, caused by too much fluid being lost from the bloodstream. There is no home emergency treatment for profuse blood in the stool. Immediate emergency veterinary care must be sought.

Blood in the urine: This is usually a sign of a urinary-tract infection such as cystitis (see the Encyclopedia of Diseases of Dogs) or a bladder infection, and it is usually not a significant emergency. Often, a dog has symptoms of straining to urinate (see "Stranguria" in the Encyclopedia), passing urine but in small amounts. But if there is significant bleeding in the urinary tract, the urine becomes very dark red, and/or there are blood clots passed, it is the sign of significant bleeding from the urinary tract and requires prompt veterinary attention. Again, there is no first aid or medication that can be given at home.

Spontaneous bruising: This type of bleeding can be the most difficult for an owner to recognize, but it can be significant. Large purple splotches on the skin, particularly on dependent areas such as the abdomen, can indicate a bleeding disorder. Little purple or red spots on the insides of the dog's ears or the gums may indicate a low platelet count, rat poison (see

"Warfarin Poisoning," in the Encyclopedia), or some other type of bleeding disorder. The animal can bleed into areas such as the brain, which can cause acute problems, and so all of those types of bleeding disorders should be taken very seriously and considered medical emergencies.

Burns

Dogs are usually not burned with fire, but a dog sometimes falls into a tub of scalding water, or boiling water or grease may fall onto a dog, scalding the animal all over his body, causing diffuse burns that can be extremely serious. No first aid is advised, but prompt medical attention is crucial. Dogs can also suffer from thermal burns of the esophagus if they swallow very hot food. Veterinary treatment is advised, but a mild coating-type antacid medication, such as Maalox, can provide immediate relief.

Cardiovascular Emergencies

Cardiac arrhythmia: An irregular heartbeat, either an extreme increase of the heart rate above normal (tachycardia) or an abnormally slow heart rhythm (bradycardia), will look very much like shock. The animal will become confused and weak and may collapse, and the heart rate will be abnormal. Examination of the dog's mouth will show extreme pallor, with white mucous membranes—in this case because the heart is not pumping blood properly. These are severe emergencies. The animal should be kept free of stress and brought to a veterinarian as quickly as possible.

Congestive heart failure: This is a significant problem in old dogs, particularly the small, toy breeds. Usually there are some symptoms preceding an emergency heart failure. For instance a dog may have an ongoing cough that usually occurs in the middle of the night. This can sometimes be difficult to differentiate from a collapsed trachea with an accompanying cough, which small dogs often develop. However, dogs with a collapsed trachea usually breath normally without coughing when they are quiet. Once congestive heart failure is in the coughing-and-wandering-at-night stage, the animals will also have difficulty breathing. This will appear as rapid, or deep, breathing movements in the chest as if the dog is not able to get enough oxygen, or as abdominal breathing in which the abdomen sucks in or extends every time a breath is taken. This is because the dog's lungs are full of water, and oxygen is not really being absorbed into the bloodstream. It is very important once an animal gets to this stage to keep it absolutely quiet and stress-free and to get it to a veterinarian quickly. Any undue excitement, stress, or hassles can cause the animal to collapse or have a cardiac arrest. Again, the owner should examine the dog's mucous membranes. Just as they are white during shock or hemorrhage, they can be various shades of purple or blue when a dog is having respiratory difficulties. This is called cyanosis, is indicative of a lack of oxygen in the bloodstream, and is always a very serious problem.

Collapse

It can be very difficult to know what causes a dog to collapse suddenly and not be able to get up. A dog will often collapse as a result of shock following a traumatic injury or severe blood loss. Collapse can also be caused by congestive heart failure, hypoglycemia, and heat prostration. True collapse is usually the result of some metabolic or systemic disease, such as an hemangiosarcoma that has gone too far, causing the animal to become too weak to rise; or it can be because of a ruptured spinal disc (intervertebral disc disease). Entries describing these diseases and conditions will be found in this section and in the Encyclopedia.

Diarrhea

Dogs get diarrhea from time to time for a variety of reasons (see Chapter 11). Usually, it should be of no serious concern. For treatment of common diarrhea, see "Gastrointestinal Diseases and Disorders" in the Encyclopedia. Diarrhea becomes an emergency when it is bloody or contains blood clots (see Bleeding Disorders), or when it lasts for more than twenty-four hours or is accompanied by any one or a combination of vomiting, listlessness, depression, loss of appetite, or fever, or the dog seeming or acting ill. In any of these cases, immediate veterinary help is necessary. It can be an indication of a serious infectious illness, such as canine distemper or canine parvovirus (see the section on infectious diseases in the Encyclopedia), of poisoning, or a number of other systemic illnesses.

Drug Intoxication

If a dog ingests a lot of just about any normal human medicines including heart medications, blood pressure pills, antidepressants, tranquilizers, etc., it is an emergency. In addition, "recreational drugs," such as marijuana, hashish, hallucinogenics, etc., can cause severe problems for a dog. Reactions of dogs are unpredictable. An animal can overdose on Valium and either become extremely excited or get an upper and become depressed. The ingestion of any of these things requires a rapid trip to the veterinarian. When an owner is sure that a dog has eaten medicine or other drugs, an appropriate first-aid measure is to get them out of the dog before significant absorption takes place. If an owner *is sure that the material is not caustic* (see Poisoning), he can induce vomiting by giving hydrogen peroxide orally, by tablespoonfuls, until vomiting occurs. Hydrogen peroxide will not harm a dog and is usually effective (see also Appendix).

Dystocia

This is a whelping problem that occurs when a bitch is unable to pass a puppy. It can often be difficult, even for a veterinarian, to tell whether an animal is in normal labor or dystocia. The general rule of thumb is that if more than five or six hours elapse between pups and the mother is still in labor, there is a problem. If dystocia is not taken care of, the puppy most certainly will die, and the mother will certainly develop problems as well. Another form of dystocia is uterine atony, or uterine inertia, in which the animal will be in labor for an extended period of time and all of a sudden start to become weak and stop pushing. Any dog who suddenly becomes weak during labor needs prompt veterinary attention (see also Chapter 5).

Eclampsia or Hypocalcemia

This is another problem associated with whelping. It usually occurs after normal delivery, when the mother has been nursing the pups for a while. It is a condition in which the blood calcium drops rapidly because of excessive calcium demand both prior to birth and for milk for the puppies after birth. It most often occurs in toy breeds (Chihuahuas, toy poodles, and Yorkshire terriers), particularly those who have big litters, although it can occur with only one puppy. Signs include high fever, excessive panting, trembling, shaking, all the way to collapse. This requires immediate veterinary treatment with intravenous calcium. It can be a fatal condition or can cause coma or irreversible central-nervous-system damage. Any dog—particularly a toy breed— who develops severe panting and trembling within a week or so before whelping, right after whelping, or during the period when she is nursing puppies should be suspected of having eclampsia (see also Chapter 5).

Electrocution

This is a problem that is usually confined to puppies, who will chew on anything they can find, including a plugged-in electric cord. They will sustain a nasty shock to the mouth area and electrocution. Electrocution can be mild and present very few signs, but as a rule it will cause significant pulmonary edema (fluid in the lungs), resulting in extreme breathing difficulty. If severe cyanosis (blue mucous membranes) is noted, or white mucous membranes, indicating shock, immediate veterinary treatment is necessary. If treatment with diuretics and oxygen is fast enough, the puppy can usually be saved. If an owner comes home and finds a puppy lying prostrate somewhere unable to move and having difficulty breathing, he should suspect that the pup has bitten an electric cord and get immediate help.

Eye Trauma

Because eyes are very intolerant of trauma, any eye injury must be handled quickly and appropriately or the eye may not be salvagable. A severe emergency that commonly occurs in the brachycephalic breeds of dogs (Boston terriers, boxers, English bulldogs, Lhasa apsos, Pekingese, pugs), but can happen to any breed, is a proctosed globe, or eye out of the socket, where the eyeball bulges out of its socket (see the Encyclopedia). This requires immediate veterinary treatment to replace the eyeball in the socket quickly. If the eyeball remains exposed for too long, the cornea will dry out and it may not be possible to save the eye. Emergency first aid can consist of applying ophthalmic eye wash or ointment to keep the cornea moist. *CAUTION: Tap water or anything that is not the right osmotic concentration may cause more damage than leaving the eye dry.*

Fractures

Virtually every bone in a dog's body can be affected by fractures. Fractures of the limbs are very common. Usually, dogs with fractured limbs are not in a great deal of pain provided that they are not walking around and the fracture is not being moved around. *Attempts to immobilize a fracture with splints or any other kind of hard apparatus usually causes more discomfort and pain to the animal than leaving it alone.* What's more, many of the fractures that are high on the leg cannot be splinted appropriately. The splint is usually placed where it's convenient for the owner, and the end of the splint comes right at the fracture, which then causes the fracture to separate more than it would have normally. The best thing to do for small dogs with limb fractures is to pick them up by the chest and/or abdomen, and carry them with their limbs hanging free (see Photograph 11, page 106). If the bouncing movement of walking causes the limb to move too much, or if the animal is too large for this, the dog can be placed on a stretcher or some other hard object such as a dog bed, basket, bassinette, dishpan, carton, tightly stretched blanket—anything that will support the animal so it can be transported without a great deal of pain (see Photograph 12, page 107). If other types of fracture are suspected, a stretcher or hard object should also be used. There is almost always shock when there is a fracture, so the dog should be kept as quiet as possible, wrapped in a blanket for warmth, and brought to the veterinarian with a minimum of jostling and movement.

Gastric Dilatation/Torsion Complex— "Bloat"

This usually affects large-breed dogs, weighing fifty to sixty pounds or more. Signs include nausea and frequent attempts to throw up, usually followed by dilatation of the abdomen, as the stomach becomes very large and fills up with gas. This is a severe emergency. As the

stomach gets very large in the abdomen, it puts pressure on all of the abdominal organs, including the diaphragm, which can make it difficult for the animal to breathe. Pressure on the veins returning blood to the heart traps blood in the dog's back end and keeps blood from returning to the heart to be repumped. Eventually the animal will go into shock from lack of blood, in this case not from hemorrhage but from blood trapped in its posterior. The dog will become confused and weak and will collapse and have a rapid heart rate and pale mucous membranes. Immediate veterinary help is necessary.

Gastrointestinal Upsets

Gastrointestinal upsets can be caused by a variety of problems, many of which are not

Photograph 11: The best thing for small dogs with limb fractures is to pick them up by the chest or abdomen and carry them with their limbs hanging free.

Photograph 12: A small dog who is hurt can also be transported in a carton.

emergencies (see "Gastrointestinal Diseases and Disorders" in the Encyclopedia). Most serious emergency situations, however, will cause a dog to suffer from some form of gastrointestinal upset, and sudden loss of appetite is almost always a sign of illness or pain. Owners must use their judgment as to cause and severity of these kinds of upsets. See Diarrhea, Gastric Dilatation/Torsion Complex, Poisoning, Pyometra, Vomiting.

Heat Prostration

This is an emergency that naturally occurs in warm weather. Heat prostration develops in dogs because they do not sweat, and the only way they have to remove excess heat from their bodies is by panting, which allows moisture to evaporate from the tongue, mouth, and mucous membranes, providing some cooling. This is obviously a very inefficient system to try to get rid of heat from a dog's entire body, and there is a limit to how fast an animal can breathe and

pant and continue to oxygenate itself. That is why dogs are particularly susceptible to heat prostration. The three most common causes of heat prostration are: (1) An owner closes a dog in a car in the sun while running an errand. Result—hot car, poor ventilation, poor air circulation, and the dog develops heat prostration. (2) A dog is kept in a hot room or apartment without much ventilation and develops heat prostration. (3) Dogs who have difficulty breathing in the first place—the brachycephalic breeds with pushed-in faces, overweight dogs, dogs with cardiac problems, etc.—will start to breathe more rapidly than normal when it becomes very hot and/or very humid, especially if they overexert; this can develop into heat prostration.

Dogs with heat prostration will often develop thick saliva and foam in their mouths from blowing bubbles through it. They will start to make noisy respirations, and their tongues will hang out. In severe cases, the dog's mouth will become cyanotic and the animal's body temperature will be very high. It is best to rush the dog to the veterinarian as quickly as possible so that the animal can be cooled, receive medication to protect the brain from the heat and the hypoxia (deficiency of oxygen), be given fluids if in shock, and be given oxygen if necessary. It is all right to try to cool the animal with cool water, sprayed all over the dog's body, but if this is not done well, it may take up valuable time. The leading cause of death from heat prostration is cardiovascular collapse, shock, and DIC, a bleeding disorder brought on by long-term excess body heat. The condition usually starts with trickles of blood from the nostrils and progresses to profuse hemorrhaging. Once DIC starts, there is usually nothing that can be done to save the animal.

Hemangiosarcoma, Ruptured

A hemangiosarcoma, or tumor in the spleen or liver, can rupture. These tumors are seen most frequently in large-breed dogs, particularly German shepherds. If the tumor ruptures, the dog will become weak and collapse, and the dog's mucous membranes will be pallid, in this case because of a combination of shock and internal hemorrhaging, or bleeding into the body cavity. If the condition continues for a period of time, there will be abdominal distention, although it may not be visible at first. This is an emergency because of the shock and hemorrhaging, and the dog must be seen by a veterinarian quickly.

Hypoglycemia

Hypoglycemia, or low blood sugar, is most likely to occur when puppies don't eat properly for even very short periods of time. Yorkshire terrier puppies, in particular, are susceptible to hypoglycemia (see Chapter 6, "General Care of Newborns"). Older dogs of any size can develop an insulin-producing abdominal tumor that will secrete large amounts of insulin periodically and cause hypoglycemia. And a dog with diabetes mellitus on insulin treatment who either receives too much insulin or receives a normal amount of

insulin and doesn't consume a normal amount of food will also develop hypoglycemia. Signs of hypoglycemia vary. The affected dog will usually begin to show weakness and mental confusion. The animal may pace, wander aimlessly for a period of time, and be unresponsive to its name. Weakness usually starts in the dog's rear limbs and then progresses to the front legs, and the animal may eventually collapse and be unable to stand. But often the neck and the head seem to move normally and the dog seems to be aware of its surroundings; it is just too weak to get up.

There is a variant form characterized by an acute onset of seizures or convulsions. The dog will roll over on its side, make rapid jaw movements, salivate profusely, let go of bowel and bladder, and shake violently with its limbs. If hypoglycemia is too severe and goes on for too long, seizures and eventual coma are inevitable. There may be brain damage, even after proper treatment. This is a condition in which first-aid treatment may help. If a puppy who has not been eating properly starts to get weak or confused, some honey, Karo syrup, sugar water, or anything containing sugar given orally may reverse the problem quickly. If the situation has been going on for a long time, however, attempts at home treatment may not be productive. Giving an older animal with an insulin-producing tumor, or insulinoma, sugar while it is still awake may help to reverse the problem (see in the Encyclopedia, "Digestive System Tumors"). Certainly, oral sugar given before seizures or collapse occur can be very helpful for a diabetic dog who has overdosed on insulin. There is no specific dosage. However, it would be good to get at least a tablespoonful of honey or syrup into a small animal, a little bit at a time, and multiple tablespoons into larger animals.

Inability to Urinate

It can be very difficult for an owner to know whether a seeming inability to urinate constitutes an emergency for a dog. Owners should pay particular attention to the attitude of a dog with urinary difficulty. For example, a dog with cystitis will assume a normal urinating posture and push and push and get out only drops or tiny puddles of urine; it will attempt to go very frequently (pollakiuria), because the infection makes it feel as if the bladder is full even though it is not. In contrast, if there is an obstruction in the urinary tract, such as a urinary tract stone, some other obstruction, or an injury as a result of a urinary tract trauma, a dog will attempt to go frequently because its bladder is indeed full. The dog with a urinary tract infection, such as cystitis, does not have an emergency condition; it will be able to pass urine in small amounts. The dog will usually continue to eat and feel well. The obstructed animal will not be able to pass urine at all and will eventually become sick, very uncomfortable and quiet, lose its appetite, and vomit. This is an emergency, requiring immediate veterinary care.

Poisoning

Unfortunately, poison is usually ingested by a dog outside or in dark corners, and an owner very rarely knows what the animal has eaten or how long ago. Often, owners first become aware that something is wrong when the dog starts to show symptoms. *If an owner knows that a dog has ingested something caustic, such as Drāno, or other acids, no attempt should be made to make the animal throw up.* Milk can be given to provide protein for the acid or caustic alkali to work on so that it will leave the stomach and esophageal lining alone. When in doubt, and if a veterinarian cannot be reached immediately, owners can call the nearest poison-control center to find out what to do for known ingestants. See Appendix for how to induce vomiting *if known* that the dog has ingested a noncaustic substance.

As mentioned before, ethylene glycol, the active ingredient in antifreeze, is one of the most toxic substances for dogs. Any animal that gets anywhere near antifreeze should be brought to the veterinarian immediately. Symptoms are usually mental confusion, vomiting, and eventual collapse. If symptoms begin before treatment is started, the animal will usually go into kidney failure and die. Dog owners should be warned that antifreeze should be disposed of or locked up in tight drums or closed-cap containers. Once a dog tastes antifreeze, it starts to crave it and may drink an entire bucket. This is a seasonal problem, occurring in both the fall and the spring, when people normally add antifreeze to car radiators or flush it out of them.

Toxic plants are not usually a problem with dogs, because most dogs are not big plant eaters, and most plants, even the poisonous ones, only have irritating saps that cause dogs to vomit or perhaps get diarrhea. The only exception is dumbcane (*Dieffenbachia*), which contains an ingredient that can cause profuse swelling of the tissues in the mouth and throat, which could cause a dog to suffocate if it gets enough. This is a rare problem. With all poisonings, particularly in the case of caustic substances, rapid treatment by a veterinarian is helpful. The doctor can give cathartics, flushes, or whatever is needed to neutralize or remove the poison before it is absorbed.

Pyometra

This is a surgical emergency that occurs in older, unspayed female dogs, usually two to three weeks after a heat cycle. It is an infection of the uterus and is characterized by appetite loss, vomiting, diarrhea, depression, possible fever, and increased thirst and urination (see Chapter 5 and the Encyclopedia). It must be treated immediately by surgical removal of the uterus.

Respiratory Difficulty

Whenever a dog is having difficulty breathing, it should be considered a very severe emergency. Breathing difficulty can be caused by congestive heart failure, severe pneumonia, or a traumatic chest injury, any of which can result in fluid in the lungs, fluid in the chest cavity around the lungs, or air in the chest cavity around the lungs (pneumothorax). The dog will make deep excursions of the chest to try to get oxygen and will often be cyanotic as well. Immediate veterinary help is essential to draw the air and/or excess fluid out of the dog's chest cavity.

Smoke Inhalation: Dogs who have been in burning buildings can develop serious respiratory problems from smoke inhalation, even though they have not actually been burned. Sometimes the problem is not obvious right away, but within a few days the dog may have severe difficulty breathing quickly (e.g., after exertion). Again, veterinary help is advised.

Ruptured (Slipped) Spinal Discs (Intervertebral Disc Disease)

When a dog suddenly or gradually becomes unable to get up, it is an emergency, and the dog should be seen by a veterinarian as quickly as possible. Because the cause is rarely known, there is very little for the owner to do. The cause could be ruptured discs in the back, which usually occur in small, toy-breed dogs and long dogs, such as beagles, basset hounds, dachshunds, etc., who carry too much weight on their backs. There are two kinds of rupture: In one, an animal has pain in the back, shakes, trembles, hides, and acts as if it is in discomfort, but continues to walk, even though the rear legs function poorly. In the other, a dog lets out a scream or groan and its back legs collapse. The dog often still has control of its front legs and may drag its back end around, using its front legs. Some disc ruptures damage the spinal cord badly, and within minutes after the rupture the spinal cord is already damaged beyond repair, and the dog is permanently paralyzed. The faster a veterinarian sees a dog with a slipped disc, the better the dog can be evaluated and the more likely rear limb function can be restored.

Seizure Disorders/Convulsions

Seizures or convulsions can range from momentary loss of consciousness to severe, violent seizures, in which a dog will roll over on its side, paddle ferociously with its legs, and let go of its bowel and bladder. These seizures can last anywhere from fifteen seconds to several minutes and are usually followed by a postictal period during which the animal is very quiet, stays in position, breathes rapidly or pants, and gradually returns to normal. One short seizure followed by a brief postictal period after which the dog returns to normal is not a severe emergency. A seizure becomes a severe emergency if a dog has cluster seizures, or one seizure after another, for prolonged periods of time (status epilecticus). A dog can die during these seizures, become hypoxic (a condition brought about by loss of oxygen in the tissues), and suffer from permanent brain damage. There is little an owner can do when an animal is suffering from a seizure except to prevent the dog from hurting itself by removing heavy objects from the vicinity. *Never poke fingers in or around the mouth of a dog having a seizure;* dogs do not swallow their tongues, and you can get badly bitten. Seizures are most commonly caused by hypoglycemia, canine distemper in puppies, and idiopathic epilepsy, which usually starts to show up when a dog is somewhere between one and three years of age, particularly in toy breeds. Any seizure should be treated promptly by a veterinarian.

Unconsciousness

See Collapse.

Whelping Emergencies

See Dystocia and Eclampsia.

Vomiting

Dogs vomit a great deal more than humans do, for a variety of reasons, most of which are not emergencies. For treatment of common vomiting, see in the Encyclopedia, "Gastrointestinal Diseases and Disorders." However, vomiting becomes an emergency when there is a profuse amount of blood or blood clots in the vomitus (see Bleeding or Hemorrhaging) or if it persists for more than twenty-four hours and is accompanied by one or more of the following other symptoms: diarrhea, fever, abdominal distention, listlessness or weakness, loss of appetite, obvious discomfort, or illness. In these cases, vomiting can be a symptom of many conditions and/or illnesses, including shock, gastric dilatation/torsion complex (bloat), kidney (renal) disease, liver disease, pancreatitis, poisoning, drug intoxication, pyometra, canine distemper, canine parvovirus, etc. (see entries in this section and in the Encyclopedia.)

Handling an Injured or Very Ill Dog

Common sense is again the best guide for handling an injured or very ill dog. An owner must realize that a dog in shock and severe pain is also probably very frightened. Even the best-tempered pet may strike out in this kind of situation. Before approaching a dog who has been injured, an owner should protect her hands and arms if possible and should avoid putting her face close to the dog's. If a dog tries to bite, a temporary muzzle can be fashioned out of a belt, handkerchief, or necktie (see Chapter 12).

Needless to say, if an animal is lying on a busy roadway, it will be necessary to move it as quickly as possible, taking care not to cause further injury. An owner who is alone should not hesitate to ask for help in stopping traffic. If the dog is large, the owner may need help to move it, as any attempt to lift the dog alone or drag it can be painful to the dog and may do it harm. An old board can serve as a good stretcher, or lacking that, a blanket or coat can be held tautly enough by two people to carry a large dog a short distance (see Photograph 13,

Photograph 13: An injured large dog can be moved on a "stretcher" made of a blanket.

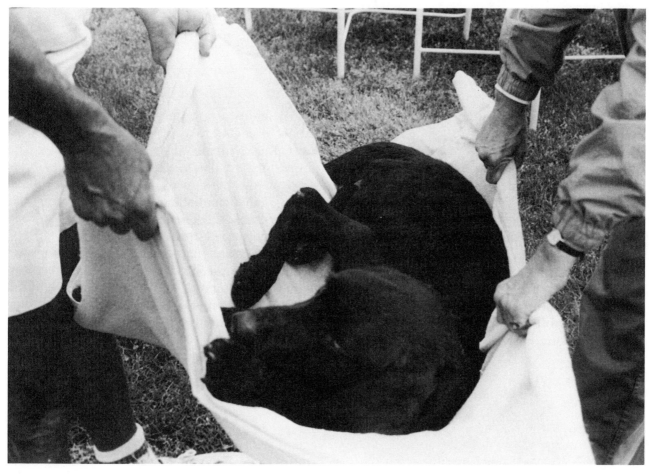

A FIRST-AID KIT FOR DOGS

The following items should be kept handy in
a box or bag at home or in the car. Take them
with you when traveling with a dog:

Gauze pads, size depending on size of dog

Gauze rolls

Old sock or two to protect foot bandaging and
hold it in place

Adhesive tape—athletic tape is very good

Sterile cotton or cotton swabs

Tweezer

Blunt-tipped scissor to cut away hair, especially for long-haired dogs

Hydrogen peroxide—to induce vomiting and
to use as a wound-cleaner

Veterinary ointment for superficial wounds or
burns

Ophthalmic drops or ointment

Tablespoon or syringe for administering liquids

Old towel, blanket, or carton to transport a
hurt dog and/or to serve as a wrap while
medicating

Rectal thermometer

Any medications the dog usually/sometimes
takes

Also useful (check with veterinarian for dosage and use first):

Maalox or other coating-type antacid

Kaopectate or other antidiarrheal medication

Buffered aspirin

---

page 111). Again, muzzling the dog is a good
precaution.

A dog who is very frightened may try to run
off, despite its injuries. If possible, the owner
should stay with the animal while someone
else goes for help. Talking to the animal in a
soothing manner may help to calm it, but if it
is really frightened and hurt it may not even
hear.

It is safe to assume that any dog who is injured or seriously ill will be suffering from
shock and should be kept warm, dry, and as
quiet as possible.

Under no circumstances should an injured or

unconscious dog be given anything by mouth
or be forced to take liquids or medication. At
best, they will do no good, and at worst, the
animal may choke to death. (Exceptions to this
arise in the case of hypoglycemia; the ingestion of caustic substances; and when a dog has
suffered thermal burns in its mouth or throat.
See previous section.)

If an owner is in a strange place and does not
know where the nearest veterinarian or emergency veterinary clinic is, a local branch of the
ASPCA or Humane Society or the local police
or fire department may be able to help.

FIGURE 6

CHART OF ACCIDENTAL EMERGENCIES

Injury	What to Look for	First-Aid Measures	Degree of Emergency*

Animal bites:
   Known animal
   Unknown/wild animal
	Excessive Bleeding
	 Locate biter/check for rabies
		Clean with antiseptic
		 Pressure bandage
			e to E
			 E

Arterial bleeding	Spurting blood	Manual pressure Compression bandage	LTE

Burns:
   Extensive external
   Mouth/throat
	Shock	Keep warm, quiet
		 Coating-type antacid
			LTE
			 E to SE

Drug/medication ingestion	Reaction	Induce vomiting	SE
Electrocution	Unconsciousness, shock, cyanosis, breathing difficulty	Keep quiet, warm	LTE

Eye Injury:
   Scratch-cut
   Eyeball out of socket
	—
	 —
		Keep eyeball moist with ophthalmic drops or ointment. Wet compress.	E
			 SE

Foot/leg bleeding	Arterial bleeding	Manual pressure Compression bandage	E to LTE
Fractures	Shock	Keep quiet, warm	E to SE
Heat Prostration	Respiratory difficulty, excessive panting, cyanosis, high body temperature, collapse, bleeding from nose	Spray with cool water	LTE
Mouth, nasal bleeding	Shock	Ice packs/cool compresses	SE to LTE
Poisoning/caustic sub's.	Vomiting, collapse	Milk	LTE
Skin-surface bleeding Neck area	Significant bleeding	Manual pressure/ compression bandage	E to SE
Swallowed objects	Choking/difficulty breathing	—	E to SE

Trauma:
   Fall from height
   Hit by vehicle
	Shock, fractures, difficulty breathing, inability to urinate, weakness, collapse	Keep quiet, warm	E to LTE

* e = *emergency*—requires *prompt* veterinary attention (within 24 hours)
  E = *Emergency*—requires veterinary attention *as soon as possible*
  SE = *Serious Emergency*—requires quick veterinary attention
  LTE = *Life-Threatening Emergency*—requires immediate veterinary attention

FIGURE 7

CHART OF MEDICAL EMERGENCIES

Illness/ Condition	Symptoms	First-Aid Measures	Degree of Emergency*
Bleeding disorder	Easy bruising, bloody stools/urine, anemia, pale mucous membranes, nosebleeds, difficulty breathing	Protect from trauma and jostling	SE to LTE
Bloody diarrhea/stool	Foul-smelling, dark	—	LTE
Blood in urine	Clots, dark-colored	—	SE
Bruising	Purple splotches on skin/abdomen. Purple/red spots on insides of ears or gums	Protect from trauma and jostling	SE
Cardiovascular emergencies	Confusion, weakness, white mucous membranes, irregular heartbeat, collapse	Keep stress-free	LTE
Congestive heart failure	Night coughing, difficulty breathing, cyanosis, collapse	Absolute quiet, stress-free	LTE
Convulsions/seizures	Shaking, rolling over on side, paddling with limbs, loss of bladder/bowel control	Protect from harm	E to SE
Repeated seizures			LTE
Gastric dilatation/torsion complex—"bloat"	Frequent ineffective attempts to vomit, abdominal distention, confusion, weakness, shock, pale mucous membranes, rapid heart rate (large-breed dogs)	—	LTE
Hemangiosarcoma, ruptured	Collapse, pale mucous membranes, shock, abdominal distention (large-breed dogs, German shepherds)	—	SE to LTE
Hemorrhagic gastroenteritis (HGE)	Profuse, foul-smelling rectal bleeding	—	LTE (small dogs) SE (large dogs)

Illness/ Condition	Symptoms	First-Aid Measures	Degree of Emergency*
Hypoglycemia	Weakness, mental confusion, aimless wandering, collapse, possible seizures (small-breed puppies, dogs with diabetes mellitus)	Oral sugar	SE to LTE
Pneumonia, severe	Difficulty breathing, cyanosis, collapse	—	LTE
Pyometra	Loss of appetite, vomiting, diarrhea, depression, fever, increased thirst and urination (unspayed females)	—	SE
Slipped disc Severe	Pain, trembling, hiding, collapse, rear-end paralysis, severe pain	—	E SE
Urinary stoppage	Inability to urinate, vomiting, very quiet, sick	—	SE to LTE
Warfarin poisoning	Anemia, nosebleeds, pale mucous membranes, difficulty breathing, blood in stools or urine, bruising	—	E to LTE
Whelping problems: Dystocia	Inability to pass a puppy for 5–6 hours while still in labor	—	SE
Eclampsia	High fever, excessive panting, trembling, shaking, collapse (small-breed dogs)	—	LTE
Uterine inertia	Sudden weakness during labor	—	SE

* e = *emergency*—requires veterinary attention within 24 hours
E = *Emergency*—requires veterinary attention *as soon as possible*
SE = *Serious Emergency*—requires quick veterinary attention
LTE = *Life-Threatening Emergency*—requires immediate veterinary attention

PART TWO

PEOPLE-PET RELATIONSHIPS

8

Canine Behavior

PETER L. BORCHELT, PH.D.

Most dog owners are interested in and curious about their pet's behavior. Of the many questions dog owners ask, four general concerns stand out. One question is about the dog's concept of time: can a dog tell time, and what is its "attention span?" Another has to do with personality: does a dog have a "personality," do dogs differ in "personality," and what do these differences mean? The third question concerns the dog's ability to show "guilt" and to know when it has done something wrong. This question also involves the uses and misuses of punishment. The last question concerns obedience and obedience training. Is it helpful or necessary, and will it help with behavior problems?

These four questions will form the basis for this chapter. They will allow us to discuss some of the basics of behavior, to point out information in the scientific field of animal behavior that is relevant to pet dogs, and to highlight some recent findings regarding the prevention and treatment of canine behavior problems. Using this scientific data about canine behavior as a springboard, we will also show dog owners how to deal with some everyday behavior problems in a practical way.

Dogs and Time

Do dogs have a sense of time? In order to discuss this question we first need to define how we experience time. The passage of time can be judged by external stimuli and measured in objective units, such as hours and seconds. It can also be judged by internal evidence, such as hunger or boredom, and measured subjectively.

Unlike humans, dogs cannot tell time from a clock or watch; nor do they have a concept of numbers or of hours, minutes, and seconds as we measure them. The "counting" trick sometimes demonstrated by some animal species in circuses or sideshow acts indicates at best an ability to tell one from a few and from many. It does not indicate an understanding of numerical concepts. But there is abundant evidence that animals can and do use their own internal "clocks" to measure seasons, months, days, and even hours.

119

A seasonal clock is probably based on simple external stimuli, such as the number of hours of daylight per day or the change in temperature. As the days get warmer and longer in spring, for example, an animal's physiology changes. One such change is in the level of hormones, which influence seasonal breeding and the raising of the young.

Monthly clocks may be phased by the tide or amount of moonlight and daily clocks by light-dark and temperature cycles. Animals can learn to "set their clocks" by any number of environmental events that occur at consistent times. For instance, dogs readily learn to antic-ipate mealtimes, play periods, and other activ-ities that are motivating and occur at regular times. A typical positive signal is the sound of a can opener or a cupboard door, to which a dog responds by running to be fed. A noon whistle or siren that frightens a dog might be a regularly occurring negative event that the an-imal might learn to anticipate, hiding regularly before it goes off.

In addition to being measured into objective units such as days or seconds, time can also have a psychological, subjective aspect. The old saying "times flies when you are having fun" is only half of the truth and implies a less cheerful counterpart, that time drags when you are not having fun. In other words, good things go by fast, and bad things drag on and on and on, or at least it seems that way to dogs as well as people. This psychological component is useful in addressing the two questions that dog owners ask most often about dogs and time. They want to know about their dog's attention span and its perception of time when it is left alone.

Some dog books state that the dog's attention span is very short and that therefore obedi-ence-training sessions, for instance, should be limited to ten or fifteen minutes. In fact, a dog will pay attention to something for as long as it finds it interesting. Many people play with their dogs for hours at a time. A playful dog can keep its attention on an interesting game for a long, long time. On the other hand, when an owner wants to indulge in some other activity, such as obedience training or a boring game, the dog may lose interest very quickly.

So if the question of attention span arises in the context of obedience or any other type of training, the way to keep the dog paying atten-tion is to motivate it properly. Almost any dog has its "price." Some dogs can be had for food, some for play, some for praise, and some for any of the above. An owner who knows his dog well will usually be the best judge of how to keep that dog motivated.

On a subjective level there is the question of a dog's ability to tell how long it has been left alone. To answer this question, we first have to discuss a very important behavior called attachment and its sometime partner called separation anxiety. Attachment, or social at-tachment, is necessary for any social species. The young must become socially attached to their parents; they do this by seeking contact through following and staying close and by maintaining contact through vocalizing (crying, whining, howling) and increased activity (searching) when they are separated from the parents. Separation-related behavior in puppies usually consists of vocalizing. A puppy whines, cries, and howls when it is taken from its mother and littermates and when it is left alone in the kitchen or bathroom the first night it is brought home. There are numerous reasons why even an adult dog might continue to show separation-related be-havior; we will discuss these later in this chap-ter. If an owner's absence provokes anxiety in a dog, that dog will become acutely aware of the time the owner leaves and of how long the owner is gone. The dog's increasing level of anxiety after the owner leaves serves as a good internal clock. Thus, there is usually a consis-tent behavior pattern for each dog with this problem. Some dogs learn to anticipate accu-rately the time at which the owner will return and even to recognize the sounds of their own-er's car or footsteps from a distance. The stim-uli a dog might use to judge the passing of time could be the amount of daylight outside, traffic patterns, or the activity of neighbors.

So, can dogs tell time? Yes, they are aware of time. Not as we are, with our calendars and clocks, but as the passage of events that are particularly important to them. When it is im-portant for a dog to be aware of time, it will be aware of it. On the other hand, as with people, if a dog is having fun, it does not follow a time clock, and it has no necessary limit to span of attention.

Dog "Personality"

The word *personality* has several meanings. If we say of a human that "she has a wonderful personality," we probably are using the word to connote social skill(s), adroitness, or the capability to elicit positive reactions from a variety of other people under different circumstances. Another aspect of the common definition of personality focuses on the most obvious or salient impression that the person gives to others. For example, a person may be described as "aggressive," "boring," "fearful," or "shy." There is often an element of evaluation involved in these assessments, and a given personality may be deemed good or bad. These definitions of personality aim at what the nature or essence of a person is. That question has intrigued and puzzled philosophers and other people since before the time of the ancient Greeks.

What does this have to do with dogs? We will show how a short review of the scientific study of human personality is relevant to a pet dog. From the beginning of the science of psychology over one hundred years ago, a major area of interest has been the description and measurement of human personality. Originally, this study was closely related to the science of human medicine. Clinicians such as Freud were concerned with individuals who had obvious "personality problems"; there was a concern for how the person was, or was not, functioning in, or adjusting to, the environment. The focus was on what motivates a person to act the way he does and to observe the whole person in his natural habitat. Later on, as psychology became more experimental, data from laboratory studies of humans and other animals, such as rats, pigeons, and monkeys, would be used to try to help answer these theoretical and practical questions. At the present time, the question of what personality actually is involves everything we know about psychology: behavioral genetics, biochemistry of the nervous system, early experience, learn-ing and conditioning, and social and environmental influences.

The science of animal behavior has also been around for over one hundred years, and thousands of animal behaviorists have labored to describe the behavior of many hundreds of species of animals in their natural habitats. People who are concerned with what animals do in "real world" situations are called comparative psychologists, animal behaviorists, or ethologists.

The question of a dog's "personality" (what makes up an individual animal's nature and behavior) is really very complicated, and cannot yet be fully answered. But one thing that makes it somewhat easier is the realization that dogs are less complex than humans. With dogs we can safely ignore the complicated human issues of language and symbolic thinking and can concentrate on behavior and emotions.

An important beginning concept in animal behavior is the ethogram, a descriptive list of all the various behaviors of a particular species. An ethogram can be general, very specific, or a combination of both. For instance, an important behavior of animals is the ability to eat. This can be classified generally as feeding, or we could list all of the various behavior patterns involved in feeding such as biting, chewing, or swallowing. Such preparatory feeding behaviors as searching for, stalking, and chasing prey could also be included. Even more specifically, particular muscle movements entailed in feeding could be described. Most ethograms comprise several different levels of description simultaneously, arranged into behavior systems and subsystems. A behavior system is a functional class of behavior; that is, it includes important behaviors that the animal is motivated to do; they have an evolutionary base and occur in most or all members of the species.

Table 11, page 123, is a general ethogram of the major classes of behavior or behavior systems of the dog. When we speak of a dog's personality, we will be considering (at least potentially) all of these behavior systems. At a general level, we list seven major classes of behavior that apply to most animals to some degree. These systems are then subdivided into additional behavior subsystems and then further subdivided into specific behaviors that apply only to dogs or closely related species, such as wolves and foxes. This list of behaviors and behavior systems can be very useful because it allows us to define and agree upon what we are talking about. It forces us to give specific descriptions of what an animal is doing, and it often leads to discovering either general principles of behavior or relationships between and among behaviors. More on all this later on.

Two classes of behavior, locomotion and social behavior, are not included in Table 11. This is because neither of these types of action are functional systems of behavior. Locomotion can occur at some point in just about any behavioral system. For instance, a dog may walk or run to food, water, novel areas, after toys, to or from other dogs, and so forth. By the same token, several major behavior systems are always social (e.g., reproduction), and some, like grooming, are sometimes social activities and sometimes not.

This table of behavioral systems serves as the start of a list of what dogs can do. What they actually do at any given time is more complicated and harder to understand. We know that dogs do not engage in these various behavior systems in a random manner and that observable environmental stimuli are important predictors of what an animal will do. For instance, dogs do not eat just anything at just any time. Rather, they eat when food is available and they are hungry. Two general sets of stimuli interact here: an external stimulus perceived in the environment—food—and an internal stimulus, which we label as hunger. High hunger will lead to a less restrictive definition of food, and a starving animal will eat just about anything it can. However, when a dog is full, it may not even eat a tasty morsel that is right in front of it.

An important part of the job of an animal be-

haviorist is to understand what internal and external stimuli are involved with each behavior system. Some behavior systems such as feeding, drinking, and mating have been extensively researched, whereas other systems, such as grooming and play, have not. In spite of the fact that the science of animal behavior has learned a lot, much remains a mystery. However, we can state some general principles. One is that each behavior system is influenced by many factors. There is evidence that each behavior system is influenced by genes, by learning, by early experience, by social variables (such as the presence or behavior of other animals), as well as by complicated internal physiological and biochemical factors. Behavior is very complicated because it involves the functioning of a living organism in a complex and intricate world.

This means that every dog will be unique. Each animal starts off different because of its genes (identical twins, however, start out with the same genes). Further variation is introduced cumulatively because each animal's prenatal and postnatal environment is different and itself changes constantly. Dog owners should expect different dogs to be similar in some respects (after all, a dog is a dog—they all have four legs, hair, and a full list of normal behavior systems). But each individual dog is different from every other, physically and behaviorally, in many respects.

The second principle makes it a bit easier to understand each dog's unique personality. That is, animals usually only do one thing at a time. So even though a dog may shift from one behavior system to another rather quickly, the stimuli to which it is responding at any given time are somewhat restricted. If we understand what stimuli a dog is paying attention to, we can more accurately predict its behavior. The third principle is that an animal's behavior is generally stimulus-specific and that the stimuli can often be observed by us. But in observing those stimuli we must not forget that despite many sensory and perceptual similarities between dogs and humans, there are profound differences. For instance, dogs' ears and noses are much more sensitive than ours.

How do these principles relate to personal-

TABLE 11

ETHOGRAM OF MAJOR CANINE BEHAVIOR SYSTEMS

Behavior System	Subsystem	Behavior	Problems
INGESTION	*Feeding*	Hunting, chasing, chewing, swallowing	Predation, possessive aggression, begging
	Drinking	Lapping, licking	
ELIMINATION	*Defecation*	Circling, scratching ground with back legs	Housebreaking, submissive or excitement urination, marking
	Urination	Leg lifting, squatting	
RESTING/ SLEEPING		Circling, going under furniture, lying down	Sleeping on furniture
CARE OF BODY SURFACE		Grooming (washing, scratching)	
CONTACTING	*Investigating*	Sniffing, pawing, searching	Pulling on leash
	Play	Playing "boo," chase, fetch, tug-of-war	Play nip, mouthing
	Social Attachment	Maintaining contact— following, staying close Seeking contact— vocalizing, searching, escaping	Separation anxiety
REPRODUCTION	*Nesting*	Digging, circling	
	Mating	Courtship, copulation	Mounting people
	Care of young	Nursing, retrieving	
AGONISTIC	*Fighting* ("aggression")	Barking, biting, growling	
	Dominance/ subordinance	Staring, ears/tail up, "standing over"	Dominance, aggression
	Defense/escape ("fear")	Ears back, tail tucked, shaking, shivering, running away	Fears, phobias

ity in the pet dog? We now know that there are many dimensions, or behavioral systems, that we can use to measure personality. We know that behavior is influenced by a multitude of internal and external factors, and we also know that an animal is perceiving and responding to a rather limited set of stimuli at any given time. So, a dog's personality is a complex interaction of its genes, early and later experiences, and environment. And all of these factors may lead to a different personality, depending on which behavior system is considered. A nice way to tie this information together is to look at how behavior develops in dogs.

Development of Personality in the Dog

The process of a dog's development from puppyhood to maturity is central to the issue of personality because so many factors throughout a dog's life can operate to influence its behavior. We will begin with an overview of the development of the dog and compare it to the development of the human child. Figure

FIGURE 8
A SCHEMATIC CHART
COMPARING DOG AND HUMAN DEVELOPMENT

DOG Age: Birth	Weeks			Months			Years	
	2–3	3	4	1–2	4	6–12	1–3	10–15
Sensory blind	eyes open							
anosmic		startle to sound		weaning				
deaf								
Motor suck, lick, crawl			baby teeth		permanent teeth		behavioral maturity	
				fear of strangers				
		social play		and environment				old age, death
					exploration of			
				begins to eat	environment			
cries, root to nipple			walk	solid food	dominates/subordinates (other dogs)			
withdraws from pain				attachment to other pups and people			sexual maturity	
no elimination reflexes		elimination reflexes						
				begins to eliminate out of nest			leg lifting in males	

HUMAN

Age:	Birth	\<— Months —\> 1	2	3	4	5	6	8–12	\<— Years —\> 1–3	10–15	20–30	60–80
Sensory												
	Can see shapes and patterns, hear, smell, taste											
		eye contact, focus, smile										
			visual following									
				discriminates between people								
						eats solid food						
							begins self-feeding					
								baby teeth				
								fear of strangers				
										sexual maturity		
Motor												
	suck											
	turn head											
	root to nipple											
	withdraws from pain											
	cries											
	smiles											
	elimination reflexes											
				vocalizes, babbles								
						imitates sounds, movement						
							sits					
							reaches, grabs					
							investigates with hands					
							interested in social play					
								crawls, stands				
								begins to use words				
								separation anxiety				
									walks			
									uses language			
									bladder and bowel control			
											behavioral maturity	
												old age, death

8, pages 124 and 125, is a general schematic chart comparing dog and child development (remember that there are large individual differences).

When a puppy first comes into the home, owners are immediately faced with a lot of decisions: where to keep it, how to housebreak it, what to feed it, how to protect belongings from being chewed, and so forth. Of course the pup will have been checked by a veterinarian, who will give advice about diet, immunizations, etc.

Most puppies are adopted at about two months of age. From birth to two months, the puppy will have developed considerably. It entered the world as a helpless, relatively immobile, blind and deaf creature that could suck and show rudimentary reflexes but was not able to eliminate by itself. The mother had to stimulate elimination reflexes by licking the pup. A human baby, in contrast, is in many respects more developed at birth. Humans can suck, hear, see, and eliminate by themselves.

However, a puppy develops much more rapidly than a human infant does. By two months, a pup has its baby teeth, can walk and run, eat solid food, and is weaned from its mother. It is already tending to eliminate out of the nest and even to show preferences for eliminating in certain locations; it may show fear of strange animals, people, and environments; it has an attachment to littermates; and it rapidly attaches to people. The human infant does not reach this level until a year of age or more and cannot fully control elimination behavior until about two years or so.

Space Management

When a new puppy comes into the home, it does not yet know about when and where to eliminate or that investigating and exploring things by chewing them is not desirable. Most owners try to manage these behaviors and prevent problems by restricting the space available to the puppy. We do the same for human infants, keeping them protected in cribs and playpens until they are old enough to have the "run of the house."

In properly managing a puppy's space in the home, we have to keep in mind three functions that should be provided for by the puppy's space. First, the puppy area must meet the pup's behavioral needs as well as protect it from household dangers; second, the space must meet the owner's needs to protect furniture, carpets, and household objects; third, and equally important, the pup's space must allow it to adjust easily to the human environment as it grows up and its behavior systems mature. As we talk about the development of a pup's behavior systems, we will see that its space requirements change. This means that an owner may have to change the way of managing the puppy's space and consider several different behavioral requirements as the puppy matures.

The "Crate" as a Space-Management Technique

Some people highly recommend a small crate or cage in which to keep a puppy, on the assumption that it aids in housebreaking and helps prevent destructive behavior. A few words about crates are necessary here. First, most pet owners don't like the idea of crates—there is something psychologically negative about keeping a puppy in a small crate. The image tends to conflict with the natural desire to have a cute, cuddly puppy with us to hold and play with.

Second, most breeders and trainers who recommend crates discuss their use in ways that are incorrect or counterproductive. For instance, one of the justifications for using a crate is that the dog, like its presumed ancestor the wolf, is a "den-dwelling" animal. Well, it is not! Wolves and other canids, such as coyotes and foxes, do dig dens for whelping and as places to keep the young pups as protection against inclement weather and predators. But wolves' dens do not have doors, and the pups are free to explore their immediate surroundings. Furthermore, there are usually several pups to keep each other company. Canids may also dig under snow and other materials to keep warm when sleeping and resting, but they keep in contact—at least in sight or hearing range if not in body contact—with fellow members of their social group. Thus, in the natural world, the den is used for shelter and protection and does not interfere with the normal development of social play, exploration, and attachment behavior.

However, it is also true that some degree of confinement of a new puppy is important at first. A pup can be confined in the kitchen or a small room such as a bathroom. A baby's play-pen also makes an excellent home for a small puppy. It is equally important, though, to arrange things so that confinement does not interfere with the other behaviors and development. To help this discussion, look at Table 12, below. It shows the behavior systems that are most important for the owner of a new puppy to manage properly. The most important thing to note from this table is that a particular problem may occur for more than one reason. For instance, urinating in the home could be a housebreaking problem, that is, the dog has not yet learned "where the bathroom is," or it could be because of submissive be-

TABLE 12

CANINE BEHAVIOR SYSTEMS
THAT ARE IMPORTANT FOR DOG OWNERS TO MANAGE

Behavior System	Behavior	Problems
Elimination	*Urinating* *Defecating*	*Housetraining*—location, surface preference *Submissive urination*—to owner, stranger. Fear, submission *Excitement urination*—to owner, stranger. Play, greeting *Marking*—usually urinating, hormone influenced
Attachment	*Vocalization* bark, whine, howl *Elimination* urinate, defecate *Destructive behavior* chew, dig *Psychosomatic response* *Behavioral depression* *"Hyperactivity"* play, attention-seeking	*Separation anxiety*
Investigation/ Exploration	*Chew, mouth, bite*	*Destructive behavior*

havior, overexcitement, or even marking, which develops after sexual maturity in males. Chewing of furniture could be misdirected play behavior or a sign of separation anxiety, or caused by "teething." Let's go through the list of problems in Table 12 and explore how an owner might manage them properly.

Paper Training and Housebreaking

We know that by two months of age pups are beginning to show a tendency to eliminate away from the nest area and even show preferences for eliminating in specific locations, regularly going back to the same spot. A pup may like the spot itself (location preference) or the texture of the surface (paper, grass, rug, etc.). These preferences are generally learned, which means that pups can usually also learn to use new locations or surfaces. Owners need not be too concerned about shifting a puppy from paper to outside, for instance. Most of the time there is no problem. Remembering that each animal is a bit different from any other, we can use these preferences to ease the task of housetraining a puppy.

If a pup is housed in a large crate, equivalent to the size of a baby's playpen, that is big enough for it to move around in, or perhaps confined in the kitchen or bathroom, and if that pup tends to eliminate in one area, an owner may want to put paper on that spot. As the pup continues to eliminate on that spot (location preference), it would learn to associate paper with eliminating (surface preference). Later when it is time to teach the puppy to eliminate outside, owners should look for any sign of location preferences outdoors. If the puppy develops a location preference that is inappropriate (the hallway or the sidewalk, for instance), the location can be shifted gradually over several weeks until the puppy learns a new spot. Or the pup could be taught to learn a new location or surface quickly by being taken to the new spot and made to stay there until it eliminates. Proper scheduling of walks with feeding and drinking schedules will facilitate this process.

A surface preference often shows up in the house when a young puppy prefers to elimi-
nate on rugs or carpets. Sometimes a pup that prefers a rug may readily shift to grass outside. Other times an owner may have to be creative and find a surface other than newspaper that attracts the puppy better than the living room carpet. Soft paper towels, for instance, may do the trick, or a rug remnant may even be used temporarily as a last resort.

As the puppy develops, its preferences usually become obvious, and the owner can use them to manipulate where the puppy eliminates. Again, judicious scheduling of feeding can also be used to manipulate when a puppy eliminates.

Submissive Urination and Excitement Urination

Notice from Table 12 that a puppy may urinate as a submissive response, at the same time rolling over on its side or back or squatting when a person approaches or bends over it. Excitement urination may occur during play or vigorous greeting behavior. These problems have nothing to do with housetraining and are treated differently. It probably does more harm than good to punish these behaviors by yelling or scolding. Notice that we did not mention punishment, even for housetraining. We will discuss uses and misuses of punishment later in this chapter. An overly submissive puppy will grow out of this behavior eventually, and the owner can help things along by being very careful not to elicit the behavior, although this can be difficult. It may require approaching the puppy from a kneeling or squatting posture rather than standing over it. Excitement urination also may be outgrown and is best treated by scheduling play in short bouts interspersed with going outside or to the papers. If the dog urinates from excitement when it greets its owner, it may also be showing signs of a separation problem (see following section).

Urine Marking

Urine marking is one of many territorial, competitive behaviors characteristic of social animals. It is displayed much more frequently by males than females. In dogs, urine marking involves leg lifting and the deposit of small amounts of urine throughout the home. It is usually not surface specific and may occur in one, a few, or—most usually—many locations. Often the dog will mark new objects that come into the home, such as shopping bags. Urine marking develops at or after sexual maturity and the first step for treatment is to remove the influence of male hormones by neutering, or castrating, the dog (see Chapter 4).

Attachment and Separation

The dog is a highly social animal that has evolved to show intense and continuous social attachment. This attachment can be directed to other dogs or to humans. Generally, when a puppy is brought into the home at about two months of age, it has just been weaned from its mother. It is beginning to learn independence and to accept absences from its mother, and it starts to attach strongly to humans. When first brought home, a pup usually cries when left alone—often for long periods of time. This may decrease within a few days as the puppy adjusts to being in the home environment.

A common recommendation to help a puppy bridge the first few days away from its mother and littermates is to provide it with a ticking clock and hot-water bottle at night. Providing this warmth and a steady repetitive noise may work in some cases. There is evidence that the young of some species of animals are calmed by repetitive sounds at frequencies near the maternal heart rate.

It is fairly common, however, for the owner to tolerate no more than one or two nights of whining and crying before bringing the puppy into the bedroom, whereupon it sleeps quietly. This is not necessarily a bad thing to do, assuming that the puppy is provided with paper or some other suitable surface on which to eliminate. Data from over seven hundred pet owners who filled out a questionnaire at the University of Pennsylvania indicates that over one-half of them allow their dog to sleep on the bed with them at least some of the time.

Table 12 shows that whining and crying are only some of the behaviors puppies and dogs exhibit when they are anxious about being left alone. Sometimes dogs will urinate and defecate because of anxiety; this is often misinterpreted as a housebreaking problem. Other times dogs chew and dig, either as a way of escaping (e.g., at the door) or redirecting their anxious feeling (e.g., at the couch). This is often misinterpreted as puppy "teething" or as "spite." Anxious dogs can also show psychosomatic symptoms such as vomiting or diarrhea. Behavioral depression is displayed by a lack of eating, drinking, or playing, during the owner's absence; often, on the owner's return, the dog displays an exuberant greeting, which in some rare cases can extend for hours and is described by owners as "hyperactivity." Behaviors that occur because of separation anxiety have been noted in many other species, including birds, monkeys, and people. These behaviors, caused by the owner's absence, may even occur when there are other dogs in the home.

Separation behaviors usually occur shortly after the dog is left alone, often within five to ten minutes after the owner leaves. In many cases, particularly when the problem has been going on for some time, the dog will become anxious even before the owner actually leaves. For instance, a dog can readily learn that particular owner behaviors, such as putting on work clothes, taking a purse or briefcase, and locking the door always occur before a long, anxiety-provoking absence. These actions will then come to elicit anxiety as well.

Separation-related behaviors in puppies are best avoided the same way that they are with human children—that is, by gradually exposing the puppy to longer and longer periods of separation until it gets used to reasonable absences of a few hours or more. In some cases, this involves simply leaving the puppy alone for a few minutes at a time ten to twenty times per day (say, during TV commercials) and then gradually building up the length of absences. Sometimes, the owner will have to start with absences of a few seconds only! By the way, it may not be necessary for the owner to leave the home. She could simply walk out of the room for a short while. As shown in Figure 8, pages 124–125, children begin to show separation anxiety at about one year of age, but no one would even think of leaving a one-year-old child alone, in or out of a playpen, for very long. Usually, a caretaker is with the child until he is old enough to go off to school, where he is then in a supervised social environment. In contrast, many puppies are left alone for the entire day while the owners are at work. It is not surprising, then, that so many problems arise.

Fortunately, preventing or treating separation-anxiety problems is simpler with puppies than with children. But the owner must be aware of reasonable limits as to what a dog can tolerate. A person who gets a two-month-old puppy and who is regularly out of the house ten hours a day probably has made a big mistake. This person should have gotten an older dog, or a cat, or a turtle! A puppy cannot easily tolerate such long absences of its social companions, and the owner will be faced with big problems. Confining the puppy during work hours might work as long as the puppy has acceptable levels of social contact for the rest of the day, but clearly this is not an ideal situation. Trying to prevent problem behaviors during day-long absences by confining a puppy or dog in a crate is likely to lead to problems. The crate does not, by itself, impart any "magical" feeling of comfort or relaxation—the puppy must be conditioned to relaxing or sleeping in an area or enclosure before it becomes a learned "safety" or relaxation area. Of course, the time spent conditioning the puppy to be nonanxious in an enclosure could be just as easily spent conditioning it to be nonanxious in larger areas of the home.

As a puppy starts to develop adult teeth, it will go through a chewing stage. If an owner is lucky, chewing will be restricted to chew toys only. Often, however, the puppy looks for novel and more interesting things to chew, such as furniture. It has been our experience, however, that the really bad cases of puppy chewing are not due to normal teething but instead arise out of separation problems. In these cases owners will have to take the time to get the dog gradually used to being alone.

For chewing caused by teething, owners usually provide an abundance of chew toys, which the dog relishes in play when the owners are around. But often, when the puppy is alone, it does not touch these toys and chews other objects instead. Sometimes, applying bitter-tasting substances to the chewed objects will help. Many times it does not, or the puppy will simply chew something else. Inappropriate chewing caused by teething can sometimes be alleviated, paradoxically, by providing fewer types of chew toys at one time and presenting them alternately so that each day the dog has something a bit different to chew. Or owners can try a variety of different materials to see if the dog prefers a certain type of chew toy.

Some Factors Influencing Separation Anxiety

Just as with any other behavior system, attachment and separation behaviors may differ greatly from one dog to the next. Some of these individual differences are due, of course, to experience and learning. But there probably are biological differences in dogs as well that are not fully understood. One of the obvious experiential factors is the amount and quality of time an owner spends with his dog. As discussed above, too little social contact will inevitably result in a problem. On the other hand, too much contact without any separation is not good either. An owner who is home all day every day and never leaves a puppy alone is preventing the pup from ever adjusting to even a very short separation. In these cases a problem will occur during an emergency separation or perhaps if the pup has to spend time at the veterinarian's.

A dog who experiences permanent separation from one owner and reattachment to a new owner has had a profound learning experience that will affect its attachment and separation behavior. Dogs from dog pounds and animal shelters often attach very strongly to the new owner and exhibit separation problems when the new owner leaves even for a short time. In these cases, confinement or crating is highly likely to make things worse. Owners frequently get frustrated and angry in these cases and resort to punishment, which usually only serves to raise the dog's anxiety level or may lead to the dog's shifting from one type of separation behavior to another. The only real solution to this is for the owner to be aware that the problem is likely and to spend a lot of time gradually accustoming the dog to being left alone.

Contacting: Play and Investigation

Puppies often mouth and bite during play. These behaviors are particularly likely to occur when play follows separation or if the puppy is deprived of play. Then the pup may react with "hyperactive" behavior. Escalated play is usually directed at parts of the human body that move, such as hands and feet. Attempts by the owner to shoo the puppy away or to hit it may escalate the mouthing and biting even further. Simply providing lots of chew toys may not help, because the toys do not allow for the key elements of movement and interaction with the owner.

In most cases, teaching the puppy to play tug-of-war games with specific toys will help solve this problem. Many dog books and trainers say that tug-of-war is bad for dogs, since it leads to aggression. It is true that puppies usually growl during tug-of-war, but it is a play growl of quite a different tone and intensity from aggressive growls. The pup is growling in play and nothing more. Done properly, tug-of-war games will exhaust play behavior and teach the puppy that mouthing and biting occur only when it has a toy in its mouth. The owner can play with the pup for progressively shorter periods of time so that brief play episodes can be used to reward quiet, nonplay behavior.

It is important to point out that most dogs can learn to distinguish a toy from a nontoy, even if they look similar. Many owners report that their dogs play only with their special shoes, socks, or towels, leaving all other shoes, socks, and towels alone. All that is necessary is for the owner to play consistently with the dog in amounts that satisfy the dog, using one or a few toys, and the dog will not be interested in playing with anything else.

Another technique for reducing mouthing and biting of hands and feet is to signal the dog the same way another puppy would if bitten too hard. Puppies cry when bitten too hard by littermates, letting out a high-pitched yip, which usually results in the biting puppy letting go. An owner can learn to make such a yip or yelp to help teach the pup about appropriate types of play.

Another common problem is the dog pulling on the leash. This usually occurs because the dog is simply intent on getting to an interesting stimulus in the environment, usually to smell it. Dogs investigate the world with their noses, and a walk is an introduction to a large array of fascinating new smells. Forcing a dog into a heel position all of the time deprives it of necessary levels of investigation and may lead to constant pulling on the leash. It is better to allow a dog to sniff and explore as much as possible when it is safe, and only demand a heel when necessary.

Guilt and Punishment

Guilt

A very common scenario is that of a dog owner coming home to find that the pet has done something bad and remarking that the dog looked "guilty" and slunk away. The guilty look may include not looking at the owner at all or looking with a "grin," ears flattened down a bit, or tail down or tucked between the legs.

This guilty look is actually submissive behavior, the purpose of which is to signal to another animal that "I give up," or "Please don't threaten me." Dogs readily show this behavior when they are threatened by a more dominant animal or when they anticipate such a threat. When owners tell me that they know their dog knows that it has done wrong, it merely means that the dog is showing submissive behavior to the owner's threat or anticipated threat. Dogs who show this so-called guilty behavior have been punished consistently when the owner arrives home. Usually, the misbehavior has been some form of separation behavior and has occurred long before the owner comes home. Typically, the first time the owner discovers the misbehavior (e.g., feces on floor, furniture chewed), the dog shows no guilt. If it then gets inappropriately punished, the dog quickly learns to expect punishment when the owner comes home and the evidence of misbehavior is present. Thus, the typical instance of guilty behavior is simply a learned association between consistent stimuli (owner's arrival, evidence of misbehavior usually done hours ago) and the dog's submissive behavior.

In this situation it is much more objective and simpler to interpret the dog's behavior as a simple conditioned submissive response rather than a complex behavior such as guilt. It is important to note that this interpretation allows us to solve the separation problem, whereas the concept of guilt leads an owner down a long, very winding and unproductive road of trying to explain to the dog what to do. That doesn't work.

But . . . what about the case of a dog who shows a guilty or submissive response the first time it misbehaves? Doesn't that show that the dog has a conscience and knows it has done wrong? After all, in this case, there has been no opportunity to associate the owner's threat or punishment with misbehavior. No, most of the instances we are aware of involve the dog misbehaving as either a separation problem or because of illness. In these cases, it is difficult to say whether guilt is a good term to use or not. Certainly a simpler explanation is that when a previously well-trained dog who has learned to eliminate outside the home, eliminates inside the home because of anxiety or illness, it senses that a social rule has been

violated. This can lead to anticipatory submission as if the dog had done something wrong.

Because we cannot ever know exactly what is going on in a dog's head, we must assume that this is what is happening. The important thing to remember here is that most, if not all, instances of what looks like the dog knowing it has done something wrong are not. When owners judge their dogs to be capable of guilt, they often erroneously judge them to be capable of understanding not to do it again when told not to! The only effective way to correct misbehavior is to understand behavior thoroughly. This is strong enough evidence for me that cognitive explanations are not very fruitful in dealing with dogs.

Punishment

There probably has been more confusion and misinformation concerning punishment than about any other concept or term in psychology. Punishment is technically defined as the application of an aversive stimulus to an animal contingent upon a response, which then lowers the future probability of the response. Let's dissect this definition and uncover the basic rules for the use of punishment. Doing so will also clarify the misuse of punishment and allow dog owners to avoid it.

The first rule of punishment is to punish the behavior, not the animal. Thus, the aversive stimulus must be contingent upon a response, which means it must occur while the dog is in the act of doing the behavior or misbehavior. For example, if an owner says "no," or claps her hands, the dog should cease the act. If an owner waits more than a second or so to punish, the animal will be doing something else, and the wrong behavior will end up being punished. For instance, if an owner wants to punish a dog for jumping up on the table, then the behavior to look for is jumping up. Applying an aversive stimulus (for example, a loud "no") just as the animal jumps up might work. But seeing a dog with its paws on the table and then running up to it and yelling as it runs away will be less likely to decrease the future likelihood of the animal's jumping up because the punishment (yell) occurred at least a few seconds or more after the jumping up. Even worse, if an owner comes home and yells at or hits a dog for some misbehavior that occurred long before, the dog will simply be taught to run away from its owner when the owner comes home. Obviously, if an owner cannot catch the dog in the act, punishment can't be used as a behavior-modification technique.

The second rule is to use a high level of punishment. The punishment level should be high enough to work but not so high as to elicit prolonged fear or an aggressive response. A good level is one that startles the dog and makes it back away a bit. If the dog runs, hides, and will not come when called, the level was too high. If the dog growls or snaps, an owner should switch to a different technique. A common mistake is to use "no" in a conversational tone, as if the dog understood English. This is not likely to be effective and the owner often then says "no" louder and then louder until he is screaming. Much experimental research has shown that gradually increasing the level of punishment serves to immunize a dog against the punishment. Thus, starting low and gradually increasing means that very high levels must eventually be used to be effective. On the other hand starting with a high level is more likely to be immediately effective. We recommend that if owners want to get verbal (actually vocal) control over a dog they should use a vocal signal that the dog will immediately understand as a reprimand or correction. A word such as "no" or, even worse, a long, drawn out signal like "nooooo, nooooo" may not be effective. More effective is a word such as "Hey!" or a grunt. Such a vocal signal is deeper in tone, more growl-like, and usually is a more effective punishment than the more verbal signal. It is important to realize that the dog perceives vocal signals differently from humans. Dogs really do not understand human language as we do.

A third rule is that for punishment to be effective it must be used frequently and consistently. This means that an owner needs to catch a dog in the act of misbehaving a high percentage of the time. Using an effective level of punishment at the right time but only 20 percent of the time that the animal misbehaves means that 80 percent of the time no punishment is delivered. To be effective, punishment must be highly probable when the misbehavior occurs. Of course, if an owner cannot catch the dog in the act a high percentage of the time, then punishment cannot be used as a behavior-modification technique.

A fourth rule is to make sure that the dog cannot escape the punishment. If an owner tries to use physical punishment such as a swat with his hand or newspaper, and the dog sees it coming and runs away, then it will learn to get better at running away, since that serves to avoid getting hit. Even worse, if the dog becomes aggressive (growls, bites) as a means of escaping and avoiding punishment, then punishment will succeed only in making the dog more aggressive.

The fifth rule of punishment is that if the other rules can be satisfied, but there is no decrease in problem behavior within a few punishments (say five to ten), then an owner should stop using punishment. It is unlikely to work if it doesn't work in a hurry.

The last, and probably most important, rule for the use of punishment is to lower the motivation for the misbehavior. It is certain that punishment is a relatively ineffective technique if the animal is highly motivated to misbehave. Of course, this rule requires an understanding of what does motivate the problem. Knowing the factors that influence or motivate a behavior problem opens up a variety of behavior techniques other than punishment that can be used to solve the problem. For instance, it does not make sense to try to punish an intact male dog for urine marking when castration is known to be likely to reduce the motivation for this behavior.

Most owners seem to try instinctively to use a punishment technique (correctly or incorrectly) for just about any misbehavior that angers them. The above rules make it clear how difficult it is to use punishment in the correct manner. Most pet behavior problems cannot be punished effectively because the owner cannot meet one or more of the rules. The owner will then have to seek another technique or the help of a professional animal behaviorist to help devise the appropriate technique. A list of doctoral-level animal behaviorists and veterinarians with animal-behavior training who specialize in pet behavior problems is included in the Bibliography.

Obedience Training

Notice that nothing has been said so far about obedience and obedience training. That was on purpose. Obedience training is irrelevant to most of the major issues and problems related to dog behavior. This is a strong and controversial statement and requires some explanation.

Let's begin with a discussion of the rationale most often given for why obedience training is important—namely, dominance and the dog's role in a social group. As discussed previously, the dog is a highly social animal. For most animals who live in groups, social behavior and relationships are regulated to a great extent by dominance and subordination. The terms *dominance hierarchy* and *pecking order* are used commonly. The term *dominance/subordinance hierarchy* is more accurate. The popular image of wolves or dogs in a pack is that all the animals aspire to dominance, only one can make it to the top, and the others try to get there at the first opportunity. Some people think that obedience training for the dog in the human family is the best and only way for the owner to ensure that the dog does not become dominant and thus cause behavior problems.

However, in the real world of animal behavior, dominance/subordination relationships are more complicated than the popular image described above. In complicated social animals, such as dogs and wolves, dominance is a relative not an absolute concept. A dog may be dominant in one situation and less dominant or even possibly submissive in another situation. Furthermore, there are large individual differences in dominance/subordination. At one end of the continuum are dogs who are highly likely to be dominant in many situations and at the other end are dogs highly likely to be submissive in many situations. Most dogs are somewhere between these extremes. Some other factors influencing dominance are sex, hormones, size, and age. In general, males are more dominant than females. Although young puppies will start showing dominance/subordination relationships within the litter by the age of two months, dominance in social groups is reserved for adult, behaviorally mature animals. Dogs do not usually display dominance-related aggression to human family members until they are about one or two years of age (if it is displayed at all). It is important to note that only about 10 percent or so of the cases of dog behavior problems presented to animal behaviorists involve dominance aggression.

Dominance is indicated by specific postures. These include standing over (head or front legs over the back of the subordinant), direct stare, "butting" with the shoulder or flank, and/or a stiff, tense straight-legged posture. A dog indicates submission by averting its gaze or rolling over on the side or back and sometimes urinating. Dominant dogs often obtain and maintain possession of food, bones, etc., although a subordinant (defined by posture) may not let a dominant take food or bones away. Dominant dogs are likely to growl, bare their teeth, and bite as a means of achieving and maintaining dominance.

A dog may exhibit dominance to humans in its family in a variety of ways: it may show dominant postures; it is likely to be possessive of food, treats, and toys, and may steal things such as clothing; and it is very likely to resist being placed into submissive postures. This last feature of dominant dogs is often subtle and causes great confusion among owners of such dogs. For instance, many dominant dogs will roll over readily in the context of play with their owners but will growl or bite if forced to roll over when they do not want (when groomed, for example). Some dominant dogs will tolerate a certain amount of petting, patting, or rubbing, but they perceive too much of it as the owner trying to dominate them so they may react aggressively. Almost all owners of dominant or aggressive dogs report that the dogs are unpredictably aggressive. But, in fact, a close behavioral analysis will usually reveal the stimulus situation that causes the problem.

Many, if not most, of the dogs presented to animal behaviorists for dominance-related aggression have been obedience trained and have done well. Why? Because dominance is generally situation-specific. If the dominant dog interprets obedience training (in a group class, with a private trainer, or with the owner) as play and fun, then obedience training is occurring out of the context of dominance and will have no effect on the dominance problem. If the dominant dog interprets obedience training as someone trying to dominate it, trying to force obedience with leash corrections *may* decrease the dog's dominance or *may* simply escalate the dog's aggression. We usually counsel owners not to get into a dog fight with the dog. Sometimes trainers or other strangers to the dog can get away with punishment and correction techniques but that is not fair to the owner, because strangers are not in the dog's social unit. The dog may be intimidated or afraid of an unfamiliar person.

Rather than fighting with the dog, let's see if scientific information can help us reduce the dog's dominance. Since about 90 percent or so of the cases of dominance/aggression occur in intact males, a relatively simple first step is to castrate the dog (see Chapter 4). We know that male hormones tend to increase dominant behavior in many species. However, the effects of hormones interact with other variables such as genes and experience. So if castration does not help, an owner might consult an animal behaviorist who can suggest a variety of techniques to help (see list in Bibliography).

It should go without saying, but will be said anyway, that all the other behavior problems in dogs such as housebreaking, separation problems, phobias, and other forms of aggression are even less likely to be related to the dog's obedience training or lack thereof. Of course, sometimes animal behaviorists can use some simple behaviors such as "sit" or "stay" to facilitate the treatment of some problems. Animal behaviorists usually teach owners how to teach the dog these and other behaviors without going to great lengths to teach behaviors that are irrelevant to the specific problem.

None of the above means that there is anything wrong with obedience training a dog. On the contrary, obedience training is a nice sport, and an owner and dog can have a lot of fun and meet many interesting people and animals along the way, if that interests them. There are also many dogs and dog owners who can benefit from group obedience classes. A group class is a readily available and generally safe way to expose a dog to other dogs and is a good way to pick up some basic skills about observing and controlling a dog. However, some people are not interested in obedience training their dog and that is all right, too.

All an owner really needs in order to enjoy his dog is to understand some of the principles of animal behavior and learning and to know when to seek help from an animal behaviorist if difficult problems arise. It is important to know that behavior problems with dogs are very common and that a problem dog does not mean that an owner is responsible or even irresponsible.

The general rule is to work with the dog's natural behavior systems rather than fight them. The game should involve two winners, not one winner and one loser—or two losers!

9

Dogs as Companions

WILLIAM J. KAY, DVM

Pet Ownership Throughout the World

Not all societies recognize or accept the naturalness of loving a pet. The reasons for this are generally either socio-psychic or economic.

In the Eastern countries, for example, pets do not have a role similar to their role in Western nations. But a fascinating thing has occurred in Japan. As Japan has become increasingly westernized, a tremendous change has occurred in the acceptance of pets and in the development of veterinary medicine to care for their needs. Pets have become extremely popular in Japan. The Japanese Veterinary Society is among the fastest-growing veterinary societies in the world, with many veterinarians turning from a research orientation to increasing their skills and commitments as pet doctors.

Economic considerations are among the big-gest reasons why pet ownership is neither condoned nor fostered in many countries. When human living conditions are at a subsistence level, there is neither enough space nor food to share with a dog.

Pet ownership and all of its attendant services, from veterinary care to pet food and pet-accessory manufacture, has flourished primarily in countries where society in general is rich enough to have the means to provide for pets. In affluent societies in Western Europe and the United States, dog ownership often takes on very elaborate forms, culminating in shows, clubs, and competitions, etc.

Dogs have special roles in peoples' lives, then, when society encourages and condones pet ownership and when people have sufficient leisure time, money, and interest to provide proper care for a pet.

Why People Own Dogs

People own dogs for a variety of reasons, including ego satisfaction, security for their possessions and themselves, friendship, and exercise. But the single most fundamental reason for dog ownership is love. Because dogs have characteristics possessed by few of us, they can often meet needs that society does not.

Dogs are true, loyal friends who give their owners and others nonjudgmental persistent affection and love throughout their entire lives. They are very easy to be with. They never grow up and never grow out of their complete affection, loyalty, and love. Not only are they companionable with their owners, but they also provide a focus of activity for them and can be a catalyst for developing relationships with other dog owners. Most dog owners are gratified and enriched by their relationships with their dogs. In short, dogs add to the human dynamic and are good for people. It is not hard to understand why people own dogs.

This is not to say that there are not some potentially negative aspects associated with dog ownership. Some owners substitute a relationship with a dog for meaningful human relationships because the dog relationship is so much easier and less demanding. Others become so involved with their pets that they suffer a great deal of pain and grief when the animal dies or becomes ill. In our opinion, the relatively few cases of negative dependence are far outweighed by the majority of cases in which dogs play a positive role in their owners' lives.

Photograph 14: Dogs give nonjudgmental, persistent affection and love throughout their entire lives. *(Photograph by Joan E. Billadello)*

Acknowledging the Role Dogs Play in Peoples' Lives

The Human/Companion Animal Bond (HCAB) is a term that has emerged in recent years as the result of society's new awareness of the important and positive role pets play in peoples' lives. The investigation of this role in all of its aspects has become a new social science. It is being studied by people in a variety of professional disciplines, many of whom have a special interest in it for reasons that range from the economic to the sociomedical. Among these professionals are animal behaviorists, dog trainers, health-care specialists, psychologists, social workers, and veterinarians.

Although the importance of pets to people is not new, the tremendous publicity received by The Bond in the past few years has had many positive results. Recognition that a person's relationship with a pet is significant has allowed grief over a pet's death to "come out of the closet." Not only are bereaved pet owners permitted to display their grief, but they may also bury a dog in a pet cemetery, or memorialize it in some other way, without society's rejection (see Chapter 10).

This new awareness of dogs' value to people has helped dogs to receive better understanding. Dogs are *not* unimportant objects, although we still have a long way to go before people completely accept this.

Another important aspect of this new concept is a growing movement to allow people to have pets in public housing. Last November, the President signed a bill prohibiting owners or managers of federally funded housing from denying occupancy solely on the basis of pet ownership. The bill has a year before being implemented and, of course, guidelines must be set. It is a step in the right direction. When people recognize the value of pets to people, dogs will no longer automatically be considered a "nuisance," forbidden completely as they once were. There are, of course, several problems associated with allowing pets, especially dogs, to live with people in close proximity. Now at least, however, some thought is being given to working out solutions to these problems. The day will soon come when an eighty-year-old will no longer have to give up her only friend, a twelve-year-old poodle, in order to move into a decent apartment.

Solutions must be worked out for older pet owners who may face hospitalization, a move to a nursing home, or death. Often, concern about what will happen to a beloved pet overrides these peoples' concerns about what will happen to themselves. At The AMC, a program called The Surviving Pet Maintenance and Placement Program was initiated in 1983. This guarantees a pet owner facing one of these situations that her pet will be well cared for the rest of its life. We should all be aware that a pet owner facing a personal situation of great significance and stress often becomes additionally upset if his pet's well-being has not been attended to.

"Helping" Dogs

Most people are aware that there are Seeing Eye Dogs (Guide Dogs for the Blind) who work with visually impaired people allowing them to lead independent lives.

There are now several Hearing Dog programs that operate in much the same way for the hearing impaired. Dogs act as their owners' "ears" to alert them of crying babies, ringing doorbells and telephones, and honking cars. Dogs are also taught to help wheelchair-bound or bedridden people by carrying and fetching things.

Guide dogs for the visually impaired have had special national legal status for many years. Restrictions concerning entry into public buildings and public transportation have been lifted for these guardians and friends. Many of the newer classifications of "helping dogs" are gaining special status in most states. Usually, they wear a distinctive collar for ready identification. Their owners often have to present identification cards in order to gain entry to many places, since public awareness is slow in developing.

Many different "pet therapy" programs with various names exist and/or are developing across this country. In these programs dogs are used as therapeutic tools in hospitals, nursing homes, homes for the elderly, hospices, and other health-care and caretaker institutions, where they are either visitors or live-in "mascots." Programs under the aegis of SPCAs, Humane Societies, veterinary medical schools, Junior Leagues, schools, and colleges abound. They are far too numerous to list here. Interested people can find out about these programs through one of the organizations listed above or in their local telephone directory. The Latham Foundation, which is concerned with humane education of all kinds, most particularly in the field of the HCAB, has information relating to every aspect of The Bond.*

More and more, doctors, social workers, and other health professionals recognize the positive role dogs play in the physical, emotional, and psychological well-being of lonely or isolated individuals. It is not only the elderly, ill, or physically handicapped who can benefit from a dog's companionship and devotion. Healthy adults can find themselves in situations in which they are alone and cut off from contact with familiar people and surroundings. Divorce, job loss, transfer to a strange city, and death or illness of a mate or relative are only a few of the circumstances that can lead to a sense of isolation and loneliness. Children, too, can feel bereft when mother suddenly goes back to work, leaving them to come home to an empty house after school, when a brother or sister goes away, when they move to a new town, or when they face divorce or separation. In all of these situations, the companionship of a dog can help. A pet can become a confidant, protector, ally, and simply a warm presence. A dog can also be a catalyst to get people up and out and often acts as a "third party" for conversation and contact with other people. It is a well-documented fact that people with pets weather storms and unrest in their lives better than those who are completely alone.

If mental and physical health is more than the absence of illness but includes, by definition, a feeling of well-being and comfort, then many people of all ages are healthier because of the companionship of a pet dog.

Traveling with a Dog

In this jet-age society, more and more pet owners are traveling and taking their companion dogs with them. Unfortunately, it is not as easy to take a dog as it is a favorite suitcase, and many owners are bitterly disappointed upon arriving at a motel or airport to find that Fido is not welcome or does not have the proper traveling papers. Owners who plan to take their dogs on even a short trip need to plan ahead for their pets' safety and acceptability.

Dogs tend to vomit much more readily than humans, and the combination of motion sickness and nervousness are often enough to set off all but the most seasoned canine travelers. On any but the shortest car trips (to the corner), dogs should not be fed for at least four hours before leaving. Owners should also ask their veterinarians about antinausea medication or tranquilizers, especially for long trips.

Dogs often become overexcited in strange places, especially if their owners seem nervous or preoccupied. They may panic and become single-minded in an effort to get away, seeming sometimes to have turned deaf and blind in their headlong rush to be anywhere but where they are. It is very important to protect a dog from escaping. For small dogs, a crate or carrying case works well. The case should be large enough for the animal to lie down and stand up in but not so big that the dog rattles around in it. Large dogs do not do as well in a crate (except on an airplane). They do better on a strong, short lead with a choke collar.

Dogs can get lost or stolen when they travel. There are pet-finding services throughout the country, but they generally rely on a dog's wearing a collar with an identifying tag. Unfor-

---

*Write to: The Latham Foundation, Clement and Schiller, Alameda, CA 94501.

tunately, dogs often pull out of their collars. Although at this time there is no good central registry for tattoo identification of dogs, tattooing does serve a purpose in that dognappers are often wary of stealing a pet with a tattoo because they are not certain whether or not the dog is registered. And a dog with a tattoo is hard to pass off on an unsuspecting buyer. Recently a system has been developed that uses a tiny microchip with an identifying code that can be injected under the skin of a dog and read by a special electronic device. This practice has been introduced by a private company and endorsed by some Humane Societies. The system is already being used for livestock and may become available to the pet-owning public in the future. In the meantime, the best insurance against a lost or stolen dog is awareness and care.

Except for older animals and those with ongoing medical problems, dogs who are only going to be traveling a short distance probably do not need to have a medical checkup before a trip. But any animal who will be traveling long distances or who will be going overseas certainly must have a complete medical examination and up-to-date immunizations. For entry into many countries, a current immunization record, signed by a veterinarian, is a must. Some states have immunization regulations for any dog entering via public transportation. In addition, a first-aid kit containing needed medications, including antidiarrhea medicine, for instance, is a good idea (see page 112). Changes in water and diet can have the same affect on dogs as they do on human travelers. It is a good idea to consult with the doctor about drinking water and to take along a full-trip supply of whatever food Rover is used to eating.

Pet-entry (and departure) regulations vary widely from country to country, and dog owners who plan to take their pets abroad should plan well ahead of time and know exactly what to bring with them. Some countries require lengthy (up to six months) quarantine periods for any entering animal. The ASPCA has prepared a booklet outlining regulations for 177 nations and dependencies and all fifty states. See the Bibliography for how to obtain a copy.

Going by Car

In addition to the above general rules for traveling with a dog, there are a few additional particulars about car travel.

• Dogs often get car sick, even when they take medication, so it is a good idea to take along a couple of old towels in the car.
• Be sure to bring an ample supply of drinking water.
• Dogs should never be allowed to hang their heads out of a moving car's window—something they love to do. In addition to the danger of falling or jumping, a dog's eyes can be badly damaged by the whipping wind and foreign matter.
• The first thing most dogs want to do when a car stops is get out. Owners must remember to leash a loose dog securely before opening a car door or before stopping if the car windows are open.
• Many motels and hotels do not welcome pets. Smart dog owners should make reservations ahead of time at a place where they know the dog can stay in the room with them (see Bibliography for a guide).
• Be very careful about leaving a dog in a parked car. Theft, which we discussed above, is a danger. A worse danger comes from heat prostration (see the Emergencies section), which can occur in a very short time and can cause serious illness or death.

Going by Train

Every railroad line has different rules and policies about allowing dogs to travel. Many allow no pets at all, while others permit an animal to travel in first class. Some will only allow dogs in carriers or crates in the baggage car. Check ahead of time. If travel will be in very hot or very cold weather and a dog is required to ride in the baggage car, determine if the car is heated or cooled.

Going by Bus

Again, bus lines differ on pet travel rules, but most do not allow pets except for "helping dogs." Those that allow dogs often require them to be confined in carrying cases or crates.

Going by Plane

Airlines also differ a great deal on their pet policies. On short domestic flights, some carriers permit a small dog to accompany an owner in the passenger compartment as long as it is in a carrying case and has a reservation. Other airlines put all animals in the baggage compartment. Many have very rigid regulations as to dimensions and material of shipping cases, and almost none will allow an owner's own case to be used. Most will sell a shipping case to an owner by prearrangement, but owners who arrive at an airport without having made arrangements ahead of time may find that there are no crates available and may not be able to ship a dog. Some airlines (TWA for example) have pamphlets that outline carrying-case requirements and availability and the costs of traveling with or shipping a dog. They are usually available free from travel agents or airline representatives. Make dog travel arrangements well ahead of time so that the dog can travel in off-peak hours if possible; that way it will receive more attention from airline personnel.

Some agencies specialize in animal travel and can help an owner ship a pet by air to almost anywhere in the world. Some will take care of pickup and delivery to and from the airport and will make arrangements for in-transit and stopover care of a dog. The ASPCA has a very well-regarded Animalport at JFK International Airport (see Bibliography for more information).

A final word: If a dog is traveling in a crate or case, place identification tags on the dog, on the outside of the crate, and inside the crate. If owners will also be in transit in different carriers or on a different schedule, include a third-party telephone number as well as the owner's final destination. Any special feeding, watering, or medicating instructions should be attached firmly to the outside of the crate or case in at least two clearly visible places and on a tag affixed to the dog's collar.

10

When a Dog Dies

SUSAN PHILLIPS COHEN, CSW, ACSW

Dog owners who turn to this chapter may be hurting and in distress. That is why we have chosen to write the following pages in a slightly more informal and personal style than the rest of this book.

When a dog dies, some people are able to accept it calmly, realizing that this, too, is part of the natural life cycle. Others, however, may be very surprised to find themselves gripped by powerful emotions. They may be stunned at how swiftly time has passed. When did that roly-poly pup, who could exhaust its human friends with endless games of catch, begin to have difficulty going up the stairs?

Dog owners whose pets live a normal life span and die in old age can take comfort and pride in the fact that their devotion and good care combined with luck and their pets' good genes helped their dogs have long, happy lives.

An owner who endures the premature death of a dog because of accident or illness often feels cheated or even punished by his pet's early death. Others have difficulty even considering a pet's mortality. Instead of being realistic about a dog's life span, these people almost seem to believe that if they give their pet perfect love and care, he will live as long as they do, or at least set a record for life expectancy! These people in particular often blame themselves for a pet's death. It is important for them to remind themselves that, even with the best of care, no one can live forever, not even a beloved pet.

After a well-loved dog has died, an owner can be bewildered at the intensity of her grief. She should realize that it is not surprising that she is so upset, considering what most dogs contribute to their owners' lives. Who is always glad to see us? Who makes sure we get enough exercise with daily walks or play periods? Who helps us to meet people in a new neighborhood or town? Who listens to our everyday joys and sorrows and never interrupts? Who cuddles up to keep us warm and cozy and keeps us company when we are alone? Who never complains about the money we have lost or the wrinkles we have gained? Who does not care how stylish our clothes are or how well-decorated our house is? Who likes us even when we do not even like ourselves and does not take offense when we are crabby or rude? Our dog. Of course it hurts to lose a friend like that.

Feelings at the death of a dog can be confusing and painful to many people. Sometimes these people consider themselves "odd" or "different" because of these strong emotions. In the following pages, we will tell grieving owners what to expect of themselves during this sad time and try to help them to help themselves, and others, through the period of bereavement.

Stages of Bereavement

Even though each individual's situation is unique, bereavement almost always follows a fairly regular pattern. For most, the stages of bereavement differ only in intensity and length.

Many people experience anticipatory grief from time to time—"What will I do when Daisy dies?" Unfortunately, this does not save anyone from experiencing real grief when it arises.

Once it becomes clear that a dog is too sick or hurt to live much longer, the owner often goes through a bargaining period, similar to a child's "I'll be good if. . . ." The bargain can be unspoken, like a prayer, or it can take the form of a plea to the doctor—"I'll give your hospital a big donation if you can keep Sunshine alive until my child comes home from school," or "until after Christmas," or whatever.

The first stage of grief is numbness, shock, and denial. How long this stage lasts depends, in part, on the nature of the death. If, for example, an old dog has gradually gone downhill, there will still be surprise and shock at its death, but these feelings may not be as intense or last as long as the complete disbelief felt when a healthy young animal is suddenly killed by a car or felled by an illness.

The middle period of grief is generally a mixed-up, upset feeling, characterized by depression and anger. Depression often hits people when they first get up in the morning momentarily forgetting their loss, which then comes rushing back full force in a few seconds. Dog owners often find returning home to an empty house without their pet's joyful welcome the worst part of the day. People are often angry with themselves, the driver of the car that killed their pet, or the veterinarian who could not save the dog. Guilt or anger at themselves can be an insidious emotion, causing people to feel terrible for a long time. Those who are inclined to take responsibility seriously often feel guilt intensely, blaming their own shortcomings for their pet's death.

The third and last stage of bereavement is acceptance. Acceptance does not imply being happy that the death occurred or feeling that everything is back to where it was before. What it does mean is believing and understanding that the death actually did happen and dealing with it in a realistic way.

Even some otherwise perfectly sane people end up doing and experiencing seemingly "crazy" or unusual things during the normal bereavement process. They may hear, see, and feel the presence of a dog who has recently died. Very commonly, completely rational people talk to their dead pets. These are all part of the bereavement process for many individuals.

It is possible that someone may get stuck in any of these stages of bereavement for a long time—constantly bursting into tears, unable to shake the feeling that the dog is still alive somewhere, or having problems getting up in the morning. This does not signify weakness or a complete emotional breakdown, but if it is troubling and persistent, it may be a good idea to seek counseling or other outside help.

Getting Help

The services of counselors who specialize in helping bereaved pet owners are available in only a few locations in the country at present. Here at The AMC we have a full-time social worker on staff; there is a social worker connected with the University of Pennsylvania

School of Veterinary Medicine; the Massachusetts SPCA has just hired a part-time social worker; and the San Francisco SPCA has held free monthly seminars given by a health professional for grieving pet owners. We hope that there will be more programs of this sort in other parts of the country soon. A few therapists with a special interest in the subject will treat bereaved pet owners in their private practices. More and more veterinarians are becoming aware of the importance of taking owners' grief seriously and are learning how to help.

Barring access to this kind of special care, the best solution for a grieving pet owner is self-help. Unfortunately, people often have to deal with a society that does not understand the depth of their pain. "If you miss Banjo so much, why don't you get another dog?" is an all-too-common piece of advice given to people who are hurting over the death of a pet. Even sympathetic friends may have difficulty knowing what to say and resort to the too-cheerful cliché often applied to human death —that it is "for the best."

If families, friends, and business associates offer little real solace, many people find that talking to someone else who has been through the same experience is comforting. This may seem impossible, especially in a big city, but it is often surprisingly easy. A woman who lives in New York was surprised when a complete stranger came up to her on the street and said,

Photograph 15: Susan Phillips Cohen, director of counseling at The AMC, talks to the grieving owners of an old dog facing euthanasia.

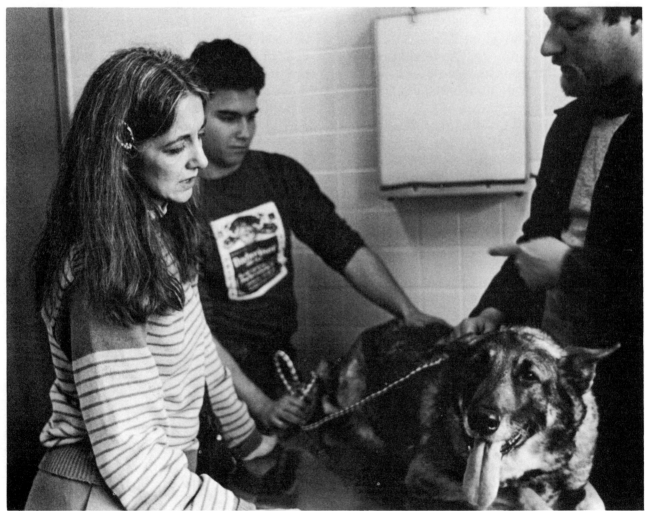

"I used to see you walking your dog, and I can't help but notice that you don't have him any more. My dog recently died. What happened to yours?" If asked, veterinarians can sometimes put grieving pet owners in touch with each other. Although it can be very hard to do, letting other people know about the hurt and its cause can be a step in the right direc- tion. What is most important is to do whatever is necessary to feel better.

One thing that everyone can do to help is to try to educate society in general to take this kind of grief seriously and not to dismiss people's pain when a pet dies by saying "It was only a dog."

Helping a Child Deal with a Dog's Death

Parents can anticipate problems and help their youngsters better when a pet dies or must be euthanized if they recognize the various stages of childrens' development as it affects their ability to understand death. In general, the older the child, the more she should be made aware of details and the more she should be allowed to participate in and control ultimate plans concerning a dog.

Children under five usually don't have a very clear idea of what death is, nor do they recognize cause and effect. Often, they cannot tell the difference between what has really happened and their dreams, fantasies, wishes, or something that they saw on television. Phrases like "put to sleep" are more than confusing; they can be terrifying to a child this age who may then think that every bedtime may be his last. Children this age have a hard time understanding that death is final and that their pets are never coming back. Because of their tenuous grasp of cause and effect, they can often suffer guilty pangs and believe that something they did, such as dressing the dog up in doll clothes, or some angry thought they had killed the animal.

Children between five and ten or twelve usually understand a bit of what death is all about but can have trouble really comprehending it. They often shock adults by wanting a lot of gory details about a pet's death. Parents should realize that this is not heartless curiosity, but that these children really want and need to know the details in order to grasp what happened. Straightforward, honest answers will usually help a child this age come to terms with the reality of a dog's death.

Young teenagers may be the most difficult to help when a pet dies. For years they have been told that the dog is "their" pet to care for and love; however, they are usually still not considered old enough to help make serious life and death decisions about that pet, especially if these decisions involve financial considerations. Parents should be completely honest with youngsters this age and try to give them as much control over the situation as possible. It can help a lot to take the child along to the veterinarian to hear firsthand, from an objective source, just what the situation with the pet is. Allowing a child to participate in decisions about a pet and to plan some sort of memorial service, for example, can help a great deal in his acceptance of the inevitable. A child who is not consulted in making decisions about what will happen to "his" dog may never forgive his parents.

A friend recently told about an incident that happened when he was ten. He came home from school one day to find that his dog was missing. When he ran into the house calling to his mother to get the car so that they could look for Okie, she calmly informed him that she had given his friend away "to a little crippled child who needs him more than you do." Thirty years later, that man is still bitter and has never forgiven his mother for giving away his dog.

Children should never be kept in the dark about final arrangements for a pet. It is often helpful to allow a child to see the dog's body after euthanasia or an accidental death. In our experience, children are more upset by their fantasies about what happened to a pet than they are by reality. If Tara is buried in a nearby field, tell the youngster where—do not let him wander around looking for the grave. If the dog was cremated, be honest about it; let a child have a memorial service. Or sit down as a family and talk about Otis, just as a recently departed cat is memorialized in *The Tenth Good Thing About Barney* (see Bibliography).

In other words, let children do as much or as little as they wish about the death of a dog—but give them the option to plan, and choose, what they really want to do.

Euthanasia

Dogs are euthanized for several reasons: because of failed or failing health; because owners can no longer keep them; and because of behavior problems.

Many healthy, young dogs are euthanized yearly because of behavior problems. Faced with a costly lawsuit, possible eviction, or a dog who barks continuously, an owner may feel that the only answer is to have the dog "put to sleep." There are solutions other than euthanasia to almost all dog behavior problems. If an owner really cares about a dog who is misbehaving and would like to keep it, Chapter 8 will help.

Another reason owners euthanize healthy dogs is because they are unable to keep their pets because of some outside circumstance, a move to an apartment with a no-pet rule, for example. People who are concerned about this kind of housing discrimination may want to help toward passing legislation against it. If possible, owners and their families should try to face facts and anticipate this kind of situation ahead of time, not waiting until the last minute to come to terms with it. It may be hard to admit that Prince could be happy with someone else, but it is really unfair to the dog not to try at least to find it a new home, especially if it is young. Perhaps a relative or friend would take Prince if his food and medical bills were subsidized by his former owner. Maybe the veterinarian knows someone who would like to have an adult dog as a pet. In some communities pet-placement services will match older animals with new owners for a fee. Even if none of these solutions turns out to be viable, at least an owner will be able to feel that he tried everything possible.

Caring owners should also plan ahead for the care of their dogs in case serious unanticipated illness or injury might force them to give up their pets. Barring the happy solution of adoption by family or friends, some people in this situation would not give a beloved dog to a shelter or pound, because they would have no control over who might adopt him. Nor would such owners ever consider turning a pet loose to fend for itself. When an owner has exhausted all other alternatives in these instances, euthanasia may well be the kindest solution, especially for an older dog.

When a well-loved older dog reaches the stage of not enjoying life anymore, becomes ill, or is in constant pain, its owner must face the fact that the best thing may be to let it go. The dog's regular veterinarian should always be consulted about this decision and, often, if an animal is not suffering, or if its pain can be alleviated by medication, a doctor will suggest waiting a while to take this step. It can help to take time to get used to the idea, to allow all family members to say good-bye and to finish the relationship, especially if a dog has been a family pet for a number of years.

Even so, it is never easy. A well-known veterinarian, who had for years been counseling his clients to face reality and make the decision to euthanize calmly, tells this story about himself: His thirteen-year-old retriever was blind, partially deaf, and her legs were starting to go. "As soon as she can no longer get up the stairs, I will put her to sleep," he told himself. Three months later, as he was carrying her up the stairs, he vowed, "If she becomes incontinent, then I'll do it." Three months later, as he mopped the floor for the second time that day, he thought, "As soon as she no longer enjoys her meals—that will be the deciding factor." And, when that did happen some time later, he finally euthanized his pet. But, as he says, he learned a great deal about the difficulty of making that particular decision and no longer becomes impatient with his clients who can't bring themselves to make up their minds.

Many families ask whether or not it is a good idea for an owner to be present when a pet is euthanized. Veterinarians have different feelings about this. For some, it would be personally disturbing to have owners present. They feel that most owners would be upset by the experience and that it is neither necessary nor desirable to allow anyone to witness a pet's death. An owner who feels strongly about wanting or needing to be there can certainly find a veterinarian who will allow it. But before rushing off to a new doctor, owners should discuss their feelings honestly with their regular veterinarians. By letting the doctor know how strongly they feel, and why, they may be able to help her change her position. Owners should realize that the doctor may want to say good-bye to a dog that she has taken care of for years, too.

Individuals should follow their own feelings and instincts about this. For some it would be awful to watch a pet leave, and these people should never feel guilty or ashamed if they do not want to be present. They will do better remembering their dogs as they were. Very responsible owners can feel strongly that they owe it to their dog to be there; and others may suffer if they're not present, imagining terrible scenes of what happened to a pet. The important thing to know is that there are options.

If an owner does opt to be with a pet in his final moments, the doctor should be asked to explain ahead of time what may happen. Even though the shot is painless, a dog may yelp or urinate, and sometimes the medication doesn't act right away. Some veterinarians have a policy of requesting an owner to sit in a chair during the process—it helps to relieve the doctor's anxieties about the possibility of having a fainting human on her hands.

While any family member who wishes to be there should be allowed, many families select one family member to act as a representative during the actual euthanasia. As we mentioned before, it often helps people a great deal to see the dog's body afterward—the reality is never as bad as their fantasies might be.

Memorializing a Dog

There are many options concerning what to do with a dog's body. When a dog dies at the doctor's office, the veterinarian will have some sort of cold storage in which an animal can be kept at least overnight, and owners should never allow themselves to be rushed into making a decision. If a dog dies at home, the veterinarian may be willing to hold the body briefly if the owner is able to transport it to the premises. In large cities, private organizations such as pet cemeteries or pet ambulance services and undertakers will pick up a dog's body for a fee. This can be a big help for an owner with no car or a very large dog.

People tend to feel the same way about burial for a pet as they would for any human family member. For some, once a pet is dead, the body is just an empty hull that no longer represents their friend, and what happens to it is not terribly important. For others what happens to a dog's body is very important. There are no right or wrong answers about what is best to do with a dog's body. Again, individuals and families should do whatever seems right to them.

The simplest thing to do when a dog has died is to leave the disposition of the body to the veterinarian who will take care of it in whatever way is usual.

If an owner lives where it is legal to do so, it may be possible to bury a dog in its favorite spot in the yard. A casket can usually be purchased from a pet cemetery, or the dog can be wrapped in its favorite blanket or sweater. Many families like to place a homemade marker fashioned from natural stone or perhaps will plant a flowering shrub over the grave.

If home burial is not possible, arrangements can be made with an outside agency for cremation or burial. Cremations can be handled in two ways: there are group or individual cremations. In the latter case, the ashes are returned to the owner. In many places, owners

Photograph 16: One way to memorialize a beloved dog who has died (Abbey Glen Pet Memorial Park in Lafayette, New Jersey). Insets: Two different types of memorial markers *(Photograph by Eric E. Laabs)*

can choose a memorial park, country, or farm burial, in which either a dog's ashes or its body is buried. Usually there are no markers allowed with this type of arrangement, but people can go to the cemetery where a pet is buried. Some owners prefer a formal burial for a pet. Once more, there are choices as to how this is done: a dog can be buried with or without a casket and/or a marker in a pet cemetery. Pet cemeteries also offer a wide variety of op-

tions to suit different tastes. In some, owners can erect any type or size of memorial marker they wish, while other cemeteries limit markers to one or two models.* (See Photograph 16, above.)

There are many other ways of memorializing a well-loved pet; they range from donations to animal hospitals or to organizations that help needy pet owners to simple family memorial services.

Other Pets

At times, having another household pet can help to alleviate the loss felt when a dog dies, but for some people the remaining pet only serves as a constant reminder of the one who is gone. There is no question that pets do grieve for each other. There are too many stories about animals refusing to eat, losing weight, and looking depressed to deny it. Remaining

animals will often look all over for a departed dog for a while, checking places it used to frequent.

---

* For information about reputable pet cemeteries, contact: International Association of Pet Cemeteries, P.O. Box 606, Elkhart, IN 46514.

After a while the remaining pet may start to take over the role of the dog who is gone, becoming more protective and affectionate or starting to sleep where the other pet did.

Some people get a new dog very shortly after a pet has died because they are used to the companionship of a dog and to the sounds it makes around the house. Their life-style is organized, in part, around dog ownership—walking, feeding, and caring for a dog. For others, changes in family makeup and life-style mean that dog ownership is no longer practical. These people may opt for a different kind of pet or no pet at all. Many people need time after the death of a dog before getting a new pet. They may feel disloyal to their old pet by getting a new one, or they may simply need a while to adjust before making a decision.

The worst mistake that grieving dog owners can make is to try actually to replace a departed dog by getting another animal of the same breed, sex, and color, naming it the same, and pretending that it is a clone of the first pet. This will lead to nothing but heartache for the owner and unhappiness for the new dog who, after all, has a right to live its own life in its own way and not as a carbon copy of another animal.

Family and friends can also make a bad mistake by presenting a grieving owner with a new dog. People should really choose their own pets, and the recipient may not be ready, or able, to care for a new dog right away. What starts out as a kind, loving gesture will probably only lead to unhappiness all around. A far better solution is to give a gift certificate for a dog that the former owner can cash in whenever he is ready to choose a new pet.

Conclusion

Most people will outlive their pets, and if a dog is well loved, losing it will hurt. A period of bereavement over the death of a dog is normal, but although the grief can be severe, it can be survived. People can help themselves and seek assistance from friends and family, the veterinary profession, organizations devoted to helping pets, professional counselors, and especially from other pet owners.

Certainly parents and other adults need to be sympathetic and helpful to children who are feeling pain, and possibly guilt, in this situation. People also need to know that it is all right to do whatever is necessary in order to handle their grief and should not allow themselves to be put off or made to feel foolish by others.

There are several books listed in the Bibliography that may help both adults and children deal better with the pain resulting from the death of a pet dog.

PART THREE

DISEASE AND ILLNESS

11

Symptoms of Illness

MICHAEL S. GARVEY, DVM

It is often very difficult for a dog owner to judge whether or not a pet requires veterinary care. In the Emergencies section we have included canine disorders and illnesses that a doctor must treat right away. In other chapters we also mention many diseases, disorders, and illnesses that can affect a dog. The Encyclopedia of Diseases of Dogs contains a complete alphabetical listing of most of the major canine diseases and the disorders that can occur in every part of a dog's body. In each instance symptoms or clinical signs of the specific illness or disorder are described. This chapter will serve as a cross-reference for owners whose dogs are showing certain symptoms or signs so that they can have an idea of what the trouble might be and look it up in the appropriate section. We must hasten to add, however, that dog owners should not attempt to diagnose their pets themselves. There are far too many variables for anyone but a trained professional to judge, and observable outward clinical signs are often only the tip of the iceberg. In order to make a firm diagnosis, it is usually necessary to perform one or more of the diagnostic tests described throughout this book. What follows is aimed only at helping dog owners make an intelligent decision about when to seek veterinary help.

Signs of Pain

Dog owners are often uncertain about how to know if their pets are in pain.

A dog who experiences mild discomfort after minor surgery or as a result of a passing stomach upset, for instance, may simply not want to be touched or handled. It probably will not be very hungry and may prefer to sleep undisturbed until it feels better. Owners need not be upset as long as this "leave me alone" attitude lasts no longer than twenty-four hours.

A dog who hurts because of an arthritic-joint condition or immediately following surgery or fracture repair, for example, will exhibit all of the above signs more strongly. The dog may limp, have difficulty getting up, or refuse to take stairs. An owner of a dog who is hurting

153

should allow the pet to set its own pace and should never force or urge a dog in this condition to do anything it does not want to do. If a dog continues to hurt for more than a day, a veterinarian should be consulted.

If a dog is experiencing severe pain, the signs will be more dramatic and obvious. A dog with a suddenly ruptured spinal disc, for instance, may cry out and collapse. Dogs in severe pain will often hide underneath things or in a corner or closet. Others may growl or even snap when approached. Many dogs pant when they are in discomfort. A dog who is displaying severe pain symptoms should have immediate medical attention (see also the Emergencies section).

Dogs do vary, however, in their acceptance of and reaction to pain. Some animals cry and limp when they twist an ankle a little bit or scream when they are given a routine immunization, while others may show no sign of pain even when they have a serious injury. Only an owner who knows her pet well can assess for sure just how much a dog is hurting.

Signs of Illness

Except for obvious, overt symptoms, the single most common sign that all is not well with a dog is a *change* in habits, personality, or activity level. A sudden change is usually easy to spot, but changes occurring over a period of time can be much more subtle.

Symptoms of illness, like signs of pain, can occur in varying degrees, and dogs can have widely different ways of handling them. A dog may have an ongoing, chronic condition that is barely noticeable to an owner. Signs or symptoms of illness frequently occur in combination with each other, and it is often not until a second symptom manifests itself that an owner is aware of a problem. For instance, a gradual increase in appetite by itself might not seem significant, but coupled with weight loss it could indicate pancreatic insufficiency.

A list of the major signs and symptoms of illness in dogs follows. The illnesses are cross-referenced to the Encyclopedia of Diseases of Dogs and/or the Emergencies section. We emphasize that this is intended only to be a general guide. The illnesses mentioned may not manifest themselves in the expected ways, and the fact that a dog is showing the symptoms listed does not necessarily mean that it is suffering from a given illness.

Symptoms of Illness

NOTE: DISEASES OR DISORDERS IN CAPITAL LETTERS WILL BE FOUND IN THE ENCYCLOPEDIA.
THOSE WITH AN * ARE INCLUDED IN THE EMERGENCIES SECTION.

Abdominal Distention: Enlargement, swelling, or puffing up of the abdomen usually indicates enlargement of an abdominal organ, an abdominal mass, or a buildup of fluid in the abdominal cavity. It can be due to: Gastric Dilatation/Torsion Complex ("Bloat"),* CONGESTIVE HEART FAILURE,* CUSHING'S SYNDROME, DIGESTIVE SYSTEM TUMOR, HEMANGIOSARCOMA (RUPTURED*), LIVER DISEASE, RENAL (KIDNEY) DISEASE, or Toxic Milk Syndrome in neonatals (see Chapter 6).

Absence of Blink: If one eye is involved, it could be an ophthalmic problem, such as EYE OUT OF SOCKET,* OCULAR TUMOR, or ULCERATED CORNEA or a neurologic problem, such as FACIAL PARALYSIS. If both eyes are involved, it is usually a neurologic problem, such as FACIAL PARALYSIS on both sides, or MYASTHENIA GRAVIS.

Anorexia (loss of appetite): Loss of appetite may occur in dogs for a variety of reasons. Owners should be concerned only if it lasts for more than twenty-four hours or is accompanied by other signs of illness. The exception is young puppies, who cannot go without food for more than a few hours (see Chapter 6). It can occur during pregnancy (see Chapter 5 and "Feeding to Meet Special Needs" in Chapter 3) or on hot, humid days. It can be a sign of many illnesses, from a mild intestinal upset (see GASTROINTESTINAL DISEASES AND DISORDERS) to a DIGESTIVE SYSTEM TUMOR or it can be caused by a number of diseases occurring in all parts of a dog's body.

Appetite, Increased: CUSHING'S SYNDROME, DIABETES MELLITUS, HYPOGLYCEMIA,* PANCREATIC INSUFFICIENCY.

Balance or Coordination Problems: These are usually of neurologic origin. See ATAXIA, BALANCE DISORDERS, DEGENERATIVE MYELOPATHY, DYSMETRIA, middle-ear infection, MYASTHENIA GRAVIS, NEUROLOGIC DISEASES AND DISORDERS.

Blindness: Signs of acute BLINDNESS include walking into walls or other objects or a reluctance to move from one spot. Acute BLINDNESS can be caused by CATARACTS, DETACHED RETINAS, NEUROLOGIC DISEASES AND DISORDERS, OPTIC NERVE COLOBOMAS, OPTIC NEURITIS, PANNUS. Chronic BLINDNESS usually has less dramatic signs as dogs can adjust to it gradually. See also OPHTHALMIC DISEASES AND DISORDERS.

Bleeding: Abnormal bleeding occurs with cuts and wounds (see Emergencies), bleeding tumors and cancers, and infections. It can also occur with WARFARIN POISONING* and with blood disorders, such as APLASTIC ANEMIA, HEMOPHILIA, IMMUNE-MEDIATED THROMBOCYTOPENIA, and LEUKEMIA.

Blood in Stool: This indicates a problem in the upper or lower gastrointestinal tract. If there are streaks or flecks, it is far less serious than if there are pools of blood. See Emergencies and also DIGESTIVE SYSTEM TUMORS, GASTROINTESTINAL DISEASES AND DISORDERS. Upper gastrointestinal bleeding may appear as melena (black, tarry stools), indicating digested blood. See also Hemorrhagic Gastroenteritis,* HEMOPHILIA, IMMUNE-MEDIATED THROMBOCYTOPENIA, PANCREATITIS.

Blood in Urine: This indicates a problem in the kidney, ureter, prostate, bladder, or urethra (see RENAL DISEASES AND DISORDERS). It can be a sign of a bladder infection (CYSTITIS) or HY-

DRONEPHROSIS, IMMUNE-MEDIATED THROMBOCYTOPENIA, PROSTATITIS (males), TRANSMISSIBLE VENEREAL TUMOR (females), RENAL CYSTS, URINARY TRACT STONES, URINARY TRACT TRAUMA,* UROGENITAL TUMOR.

Bowel Movement, Increased/Frequent: COLITIS, INTESTINAL PARASITES, rectal disorders.

Bowel Movement, Strained: COLITIS, INTESTINAL PARASITES, PERIANAL ADENOMAS, perianal hernias, PROSTATITIS.

Breathing Difficulty: Difficulty in breathing should always be taken seriously. It can be a sign of CARDIAC DISEASE, Electrocution,* ESOPHAGITIS, Heat Prostration,* LARYNGEAL DISEASE, MYASTHENIA GRAVIS, NASAL CANCER, NASAL DISEASE, RESPIRATORY DISEASES AND DISORDERS, Shock,* SOFT PALATE DISORDERS, Swallowed Objects,* TRACHEAL DISEASE, Traumatic Chest Injury,* VALVULAR HEART DISEASE, WARFARIN POISONING.*

Bruising: Abnormal bruising may indicate a bleeding disorder. See Emergencies, "Bleeding or Hemorrhaging," for a description. See also HEMOPHILIA, IMMUNE-MEDIATED THROMBOCYTOPENIA, WARFARIN POISONING.*

Changes in Gait: A change in a dog's gait can have neurologic origins such as a BALANCE DISORDER, or DYSMETRIA. It can also be a result of a MUSCULOSKELETAL DISEASE OR DISORDER such as HIP DYSPLASIA, MYOSITIS, or RADIAL NERVE PARALYSIS.

Choking/Gagging: This can, of course, be caused by a swallowed object,* but it can also be a sign of ESOPHAGITIS or PHARYNGEAL DISEASE.

Clouding of Lens: This can be caused by CATARACTS, LENTICULAR SCLEROSIS, OCULAR TUMORS.

Collapse: This may be caused by shock,* also ANEMIA, Cardiovascular Emergencies,* Electrocution,* HYPOGLYCEMIA,* INTERVERTEBRAL DISC DISEASE,* severe infections in any part of the body, TOXICITY, Trauma.*

Coughing: Can be the sign of a number of different illnesses or diseases: BRONCHIAL DISEASE, CARDIAC DISEASE, CONGESTIVE HEART FAILURE* (night cough), ESOPHAGITIS, HEARTWORM DISEASE, LUNG CANCER, PNEUMONIA,* RESPIRATORY DISEASES AND DISORDERS, TRACHEAL DISEASE, TRACHEOBRONCHITIS, VALVULAR HEART DISEASE.

Diarrhea: Dogs often get diarrhea, and it should not cause concern unless it persists for more than twenty-four hours or is accompanied by other signs or symptoms of illness. See GASTROINTESTINAL DISEASES AND DISORDERS for how to treat common diarrhea. If it persists, it can be a sign of DIGESTIVE SYSTEM TUMOR, CANINE DISTEMPER, COLITIS, ENTERITIS, GASTROENTERITIS, INTESTINAL PARASITES, PARVOVIRUS, or other systemic illness.

Drooling: This can be a sign of nausea, car sickness, or a foreign body in the mouth. May also indicate CRANIOMANDIBULAR OSTEOPATHY, DENTAL DISEASE, ESOPHAGITIS, FACIAL PARALYSIS, ORAL TUMORS.

Ear Flap Tenderness/Soreness: When accompanied by swelling, it can be a sign of an AURAL HEMATOMA, or it may be caused by an ear inflammation or infection (OTITIS EXTERNA), EAR FISSURES, or EAR MARGIN DERMATOSIS.

Ear Discharge/Odor: Sign of EAR MITES or of an ear inflammation/infection (OTITIS EXTERNA).

Eating Problems: See Mouth Discomfort.

Eye Redness: When accompanied by swelling, it may be a symptom of CHERRY EYE. It may also be due to CONJUNCTIVITIS, CORNEAL TRAUMA, DEFICIENCY OF TEAR PRODUCTION, DERMOID, GLAUCOMA (this requires immediate attention and can be painful), OCULAR TUMORS, PANNUS. See also RED EYES.

Eye Discharge: This may be due to CANINE DISTEMPER, CONJUNCTIVITIS, CORNEAL TRAUMA, DEFICIENCY OF TEAR PRODUCTION, or Ophthalmis Neonatorum in newborns (see Chapter 6).

Facial Distortion: Various types of facial distortion can be caused by FACIAL PARALYSIS, HORNER'S SYNDROME, MYASTHENIA GRAVIS, MYOSITIS, NASAL CANCER.

Facial Swelling: An acute allergic reaction called angioedema may cause facial swelling, as may ALLERGIC SKIN DISEASE, BACTERIAL DISEASE/INFECTION OF THE SKIN, CRANIOMANDIBULAR OSTEOPATHY.

Fever: (See Chapter 12, "General Care," for how to take a dog's temperature.) Fever can be caused by any kind of viral or bacterial infection, including CANINE DISTEMPER, CANINE PARVOVIRUS, or INFECTIOUS BACTERIAL ARTHRITIS. It is often accompanied by Anorexia and/or VOMITING and DIARRHEA. It should always be medically evaluated. It can also be a sign of AUTOIMMUNE DISEASE, cancer (see ONCOLOGY), Heat Prostration,* SYSTEMIC LUPUS ERYTHEMATOSUS. Other causes of fever that are not serious include agitation, environmental temperature, and exercise. If the temperature returns to normal after a rest, dog owners need not be concerned.

Hair Loss: Ears—PINNA ALOPECIA; Body—COLOR MUTANT ALOPECIA, CONTACT DERMATITIS, CUSHING'S SYNDROME, and other ENDOCRINE-RELATED SKIN DISORDERS, FUNGAL DISEASES OF THE SKIN, demodectic or SCARCOPTIC MANGE, TAIL GLAND HYPERPLASIA.

Head Shaking/Rubbing: This is usually an ear problem. See AURAL DISEASES AND DISORDERS, EAR MITES, OTITIS EXTERNA.

Head Tilt: May be a sign of a NEUROLOGIC DISEASE OR DISORDER (vestibular disorder), especially a BALANCE DISORDER or a middle-ear infection.

Jaundice: Yellow color to eyes, inside of ears, mucous membranes, skin, etc. Also urine may be dark yellow in color. Indicates AUTOIMMUNE HEMOLYTIC ANEMIA, DIGESTIVE SYSTEM TUMOR, LEPTOSPIROSIS, LIVER DISEASE, PANCREATITIS.

Joint/Limb Swelling: DEGENERATIVE ARTHRITIS, HYPERTROPHIC OSTEOARTHROPATHY, IDIOPATHIC IMMUNE-MEDIATED ARTHRITIS,

INFECTIOUS BACTERIAL ARTHRITIS, limb FRACTURE,* RHEUMATOID ARTHRITIS, SYSTEMIC LUPUS ERYTHEMATOSUS ARTHRITIS.

Lameness or Limping: The most obvious cause of lameness or limping is a minor foot injury such as a splinter or cut. A muscle pull or sprained ankle or knee joint can also cause temporary lameness. If it persists, it may be due to any of the many types of ARTHRITIS, BONE TUMORS, COXOFEMORAL LUXATION, FRAGMENTED MEDIAL CORONOID PROCESS, GROWTH PLATE DISORDERS, HIP DYSPLASIA, HYPERTROPHIC OSTEOARTHROPATHY, HYPERTROPHIC OSTEODYSTROPHY, INTERVERTEBRAL DISC DISEASE,* LEGG-CALVÉ PERTHES DISEASE, limb FRACTURES,* MUSCULOSKELETAL DISEASES AND DISORDERS, OSTEOCHONDRITIS DISSICANS, OSTEOMYELITIS, PANOSTEITIS, PATELLAR LUXATIONS, RADIAL NERVE PARALYSIS, UNUNITED ANCONEAL PROCESS.

Lethargy or Listlessness: This is a nonspecific sign that can be associated with any illness.

Licking: See Scratching.

Lumps/Bumps/Masses: These may be signs of tumors, cysts, cancers in any area. Often the only way to differentiate between them is by surgical biopsy (see Glossary 2). See also DERMATOLOGIC DISEASES AND DISORDERS, ONCOLOGY, and SKIN TUMORS.

Mouth Discomfort: If a dog exhibits pain when touched on the face or when eating, this can be a sign of foreign body in the mouth, or DENTAL DISEASE, ORAL TUMORS.

Mouth Odor: Can be a sign of DENTAL DISEASE, KIDNEY DISEASE, ORAL TUMORS.

Nasal Discharge: A nasal discharge can be caused by foreign body in the nose, an Infectious Disease such as CANINE DISTEMPER, or can be a sign of NASAL CANCER OR NASAL DISEASE.

Night Blindness: PROGRESSIVE RETINAL ATROPHY.

Nosebleeds: Heat Prostration,* IMMUNE-MEDIATED THROMBOCYTOPENIA, NASAL CANCER, NASAL DISEASE, VON WILLEBRAND'S DISEASE, WARFARIN POISONING.*

Panting: Discomfort, excitement, exercise, fear, Heat Prostration.*

Paralysis: This is of neurologic origin. See FACIAL PARALYSIS, INTERVERTEBRAL DISC DISEASE,* PARESIS, PLEGIA.

Seizures:* ECLAMPSIA (see also Chapter 5) EPILEPSY,* HYPOGLYCEMIA,* Hypoparathyroidism (see ENDOCRINE DISEASES), LIVER DISEASE, NEUROLOGIC DISEASES AND DISORDERS, RENAL (KIDNEY) FAILURE, TOXICITY.

Scooting on Rear End: ANAL SAC (GLAND) IMPACTION, tapeworms (see INTESTINAL PARASITES), Perianal Pyoderma (see BACTERIAL DISEASES/INFECTIONS OF THE SKIN).

Scratching/Pawing/Rubbing/Biting/Licking: When the dog scratches its body in any of these ways, it is evidence of skin disease (see DERMATOLOGIC DISEASES AND DISORDERS, ALLERGIC SKIN DISEASES, PARASITIC DISEASES OF THE SKIN). When a dog worries other areas, it indicates a problem in that area.

Shortness of Breath: Severe ANEMIA, CARDIAC DISEASE, LUNG CANCER.

Skin Eruptions: See DERMATOLOGIC DISEASES AND DISORDERS (especially demodectic MANGE), AUTOIMMUNE SKIN DISEASE, EAR MARGIN DERMATOSIS, PEMPHIGUS GROUP, SCARCOPTIC MANGE. MANGE.

Sneezing: This is not a problem unless continuous or very frequent. It often accompanies an ALLERGIC SKIN DISEASE. Also may be a sign of NASAL CANCER, NASAL DISEASE, RESPIRATORY DISEASES AND DISORDERS.

Snoring/snorting: This may be due to nasal obstructions or SOFT PALATE DISORDERS. Normal in brachycephalic breeds (see Glossary 1), unless excessive.

Spinal Pain: INTERVERTEBRAL DISC DISORDERS,* various forms of ARTHRITIS.

Swallowing Difficulty: ESOPHAGITIS, MYASTHENIA GRAVIS, PERSISTENT RIGHT AORTIC ARCH, PHARYNGEAL DISEASE, Poisoning,* TONSILLITIS.

Tail Biting: Skin problem (see DERMATOLOGIC DISEASES AND DISORDERS), ANAL SAC (GLAND) IMPACTION, tapeworms (see INTESTINAL PARASITES).

Tail Paralysis: Tail hanging limp. Can be due to a fractured tail or a fractured sacrum.

Thirst, Increased (POLYDIPSIA): See Urination, Increased/Frequent.

Urinary Incontinence: See URINARY INCONTINENCE, ECTOPIC URETER.

Urination, Increased/Frequent: This is usually accompanied by increased water drinking: CYSTITIS, CUSHING'S SYNDROME, DIABETES MELLITUS, ECLAMPSIA (see also Chapter 5), HYPERTHYROIDISM, PROSTATITIS, PYURIA, PYOMETRA, UREMIA, Urinary Tract Infections (see RENAL DISEASES AND DISORDERS), UROGENITAL TUMORS.

Urination Difficulty: URINARY TRACT STONES, URINARY TRACT TRAUMA.*

Urination, Strained (STRANGURIA): CYSTITIS, HEMATURIA, PROSTATITIS, PYURIA, URINARY TRACT STONES, URINARY TRACT TRAUMA, UROGENITAL TUMORS. (See also RENAL DISEASES AND DISORDERS.)

Vaginal Discharge: ENDOMETRITIS, normal estrus (heat) cycle (see Chapter 5), postpartum infection/problem (see Chapter 5), PYOMETRA,* TRANSMISSIBLE VENEREAL TUMORS.

Voice Change: LARYNGEAL DISEASE, MYASTHENIA GRAVIS, RESPIRATORY DISEASES AND DISORDERS.

Vomiting: Dogs vomit occasionally without being ill. It should be of no concern unless it persists or is accompanied by other symptoms of illness. See GASTROINTESTINAL DISEASES AND DISORDERS for treatment of ordinary vomiting. Vomiting, however, can be a sign of systemic or other disease, such as ADDISON'S DISEASE, BALANCE DISORDERS, CANINE DISTEMPER, CANINE PARVOVIRUS, DIABETES MELLITUS, DIGESTIVE SYSTEM TUMORS, GASTRITIS, INTESTINAL PARASITES, KIDNEY (RENAL) DISEASE, LIVER DISEASE, MYASTHENIA GRAVIS, PYOMETRA, etc.

Weakness: ADDISON'S DISEASE, APLASTIC ANEMIA, blood loss,* Cardiovascular Emergency,* CUSHING'S SYNDROME, DEGENERATIVE MYELOPATHY, DIABETES MELLITUS, HEMANGIOSARCOMAS,* HYPOGLYCEMIA,* MYASTHENIA GRAVIS, PERIPHERAL NEUROPATHY, Shock,* Traumatic Injury.*

Weight Gain: CUSHING'S SYNDROME, HYPOTHYROIDISM, obesity.

Weight Loss: CONGESTIVE HEART FAILURE,* DIABETES MELLITUS, GASTROINTESTINAL DISEASE, KIDNEY (RENAL) DISEASE, PANCREATIC INSUFFICIENCY.

12

Care of a Sick Dog

RICHARD C. SCOTT, DVM

In the previous chapter, we discussed symptoms of illness or disease that a dog may display. When a dog is brought to a veterinarian because an owner has noticed some symptoms, or signs, that the animal is not well, the first thing that the veterinarian must determine is exactly what the problem is. After that, he must prescribe appropriate treatment and/or medication. In the following pages, we will talk about the steps a veterinarian will usually take in order to make a diagnosis, and then we will describe some of the more common methods of treatment used in canine medicine.

To Hospitalize or Not?

Several factors will determine whether an animal requires hospitalization or can be treated entirely as an outpatient. This determination must be made by the veterinarian.

What considerations lead to a decision to hospitalize a dog? First, and most important, is the ability to make a diagnosis of the trouble. If, for example, an otherwise healthy dog is brought to a doctor with a set of symptoms, it is possible that that animal can be diagnosed on the basis of its medical history and a physical examination and that any further diagnostic tests can be performed on an outpatient basis. Unfortunately, however, things are often not that simple, and a dog may require a complete battery of tests, including a Complete Blood Count (CBC), X rays (radiographs), a Biochemical Profile (SMA-20), and possibly other more specialized tests, before the doctor can make a diagnosis. What it boils down to is this: If a diagnosis cannot be established right away, a dog will usually need to be hospitalized for testing and evaluation.

Owners are often concerned that a dog may be temperamentally unable to deal with hospitalization. In our experience, it is usually the owners who have problems with this because they are dependent on their pets and the separation of hospitalization is stressful for them. In general, dogs tend to adjust well and usually do not pine when hospitalized, and owners are able to get over their frustrations and fears in a short time. When a dog is released from the hospital, the joy expressed by both pet and owner reflects the degree to which they missed each other. But no permanent harm was done to either!

On the other side of the coin, owners' needs or desires can sometimes lead to the hospitalization of an animal who could do well with home care. There are situations in which owners are going to be away from home for an extended period of time. There are cases of extremely fractious dogs whom owners find impossible to medicate. And there are some owners who are deeply concerned about their ability to apply proper health care at home. In all of these circumstances, hospital care may be requested by an owner, even though a dog's condition does not necessarily warrant it.

There will always be a number of questions when a dog has to be hospitalized.

The first question usually has to do with length of stay. Here at The AMC, the average length of stay for a diagnostic workup is two days. After information about a dog's condition has been gathered from preliminary tests and X rays, a diagnosis may be made or further tests can be called for; and the length of any further hospitalization is based on whatever procedures or treatments are necessary. At this point, even in the case of a seriously ill animal with multiple-organ-system involvement, a five-day hospital visit is average, and any stay over ten days is rare.

An owner should never hesitate to ask what a dog's hospitalization will cost. But she should bear in mind that a final accounting will depend on the diagnosis of a dog's illness and the treatments needed. A veterinarian should be able to give a good estimate of the cost of a dog's initial two-day workup based on a standard battery of tests and X rays. After this, further tests may be needed in order to make a diagnosis, or a diagnosis may be made and a course of treatment indicated. In either case an owner is consulted, either by telephone or in person, and an estimate of further costs can usually be given. In some states, pet health insurance may help to offset the cost of treatment for certain illnesses. There is more about this in Chapter 1. Unfortunately, in general there is very little financial assistance available for veterinary costs, but elderly clients on fixed incomes may sometimes be able to get some help through special foundations or funds. Barring this kind of help, most veterinarians are willing to set up installment payments for their clients who are unable to pay an entire bill at once. An owner who feels unable to take on the financial burden of a dog's hospitalization and treatment has two choices: He may take the animal home to live out its life without further medical treatment, or he may have the animal euthanized right away. This kind of difficult decision should only be made after careful thought and discussion with the veterinarian as to the various options.

Consultation with specialists is not usual in the average private veterinary practice during the first few days of diagnosis. But often when a doctor in private practice faces a serious matter that may be beyond her hospital's facilities or that requires the expertise of a specialist, she will refer the dog to a veterinary hospital connected with a university or to a large institution such as The AMC. There are also a number of specialized services to which many private veterinarians subscribe, such as Cardiopet and Cardiotrace, both of which provide cardiac monitoring of a patient via the telephone for doctors who do not have electrocardiogram machines of their own.

Hospital Care of a Dog

Owners are often very concerned about just what will be happening to a dog when it is in the hospital. Although details may vary in individual hospitals, the following descriptions of routines and procedures will hold true in most veterinary practices.

At The AMC, owners are asked to sign an admission form when a dog enters the hospital; this gives permission for emergency procedures if the owner cannot be reached. Heroic attempts to reach an owner always take place, however, before a doctor will proceed on the basis of this document. Most private practices do not require admission forms, but doctors are usually in close touch with owners in these cases.

As far as actual physical care, here at The AMC, dogs are taken out to individual sanitized runs three times a day to relieve themselves. Every animal is visited by a number of people many times a day. At this hospital, animals are checked late in the evening as well.

We find it best to give an entire workup, or panel of tests, to a dog right away in order to get a complete picture of what is going on. Not only does it save money for the client in the long run, but it is far better for the animal to be subjected to only one set of tests rather than to have one or two tests one day, only to have it found that other tests are needed later on. The standard diagnostic procedures we perform are a Complete Blood Count (CBC) and SMA-20 Biochemical Profile (SMA-20). Beginning by patting and talking to the dog to get its confidence and calm it if necessary, a nurse and doctor hold off a vein by either wrapping the dog's leg tightly with a piece of rubber tubing or by holding off the vein manually. A needle is then inserted into the vein and blood is drawn. Because most blood tests can be performed on one sample, only one venipuncture is usually needed for these tests. This is almost always a painless procedure for a dog. Most dogs resist the restraint needed more than they mind the actual bloodtaking. The CBC determines the white- and red-blood-cell numbers and their status. The SMA-20 examines the functions of the liver, kidneys, and indirectly examines the functions of the heart, lungs, and intestines. Important body-fluid electrolytes are also examined.

A urinalysis is also part of the standard diagnostic procedures; it examines the urine for glucose, protein, bile, and any abnormal constituents, including red and white blood cells. The sample is collected by catching urine when it is voided or by fine-needle aspiration (cystocentesis). (See Glossary 2.) More rarely, a sample of urine is collected by inserting a sterile catheter through the external genitalia into the bladder.

Frequently, X rays of the chest cavity and abdomen are taken. The way this is done varies from one hospital to another. The animal must be held still, and in most practices this is accomplished by first using a mild tranquilizer and then gently strapping the dog in position while the X ray is taken.

Dogs who enter the hospital are also often given parenteral fluids to support them and fight disease. Fluids are given through a jugularvenous catheter. Usually no sedation is required to insert this. With the dog lying on its side, two animal-health technicians (AHT), or a technician and doctor, clip the fur and scrub an area over the jugular vein as if for surgery. They then insert a metal needle, or stylus, into the vein. A soft, polyurethane catheter which the animal cannot feel at all then replaces the metal stylus, allowing parenteral fluids to flow through a plastic tube and into the dog. On occasion, this jugularvenous catheter can also be used to remove blood samples painlessly from an animal. Parenteral fluids may also be given subcutaneously (SQ) in less critically ill animals. These parenteral fluids are balanced electrolyte solutions (sterile), which approximate the normal constituents of the body fluids. When given in appropriate volumes they assist in reestablishing the normal body-fluid status that was deranged by disease.

Antibiotics are frequently given to dogs who enter the hospital to treat or prevent infection. Many antibiotics are given through the jugularvenous catheter, but other are given by injection beneath the skin (SQ) or into the muscle (IM). Still others are administered orally (PO).

Most veterinary practices have regular daily call-in hours for clients, and doctors will, of course, call owners whenever necessary.

Should Owners Visit Dogs In the Hospital?

Often, when a hospitalized animal is critically ill or undergoing a lot of difficult diagnostic tests, a visit will help to set an owner's mind at ease and alleviate some worries about what is happening to his pet. A visit can also be beneficial for a dog. If an animal is not eating, for instance, a treat from home may do the trick. Common sense must prevail, of course. A lot of people should not troop in at once, nor should they visit more than once a day.

If a dog is simply undergoing routine tests or will only be hospitalized for a short time, it is probably best not to visit. Visiting can upset the normal routine of the hospital day (e.g., scheduled tests, X rays, etc.), and a dog who is feeling fine may very well think that it is going home when owners come and be upset when they leave without it.

Home Care of a Sick Dog

Owners may often be called upon to take care of a sick dog at home—to give medications, treatments, and so forth. In the case of a chronic illness, such as diabetes mellitus, these treatments may continue for the rest of the animal's life. In other cases, medication may only be required for a limited amount of time, until the disease or disorder has been brought under control.

Especially in the case of a serious or ongoing disease, an owner's life-style and ability to continue medication on a regular basis must be given careful consideration, and a decision about how to proceed has to be made by both the veterinarian and the owner.

Owners are often very concerned about the time required to medicate a dog. We find that most people can find the time if they really want to. For instance, when pills and liquids are called for three times a day, they are usually given morning, evening, and night, posing no problem for working owners.

Veterinarians are always willing to give careful instructions about medicating or treating a dog, and owners who are at all unsure or unclear about what is required should ask questions or request a demonstration. When a medication does not seem to be working, the failure frequently lies not in the medication itself but in an owner's inability to give it correctly. Owners should never be ashamed or embarrassed to ask for help, because there is often an easy solution to the problem. The form of medication can be changed, a different method of dosage used, etc., and veterinarians are always glad to help.

Sometimes even the most willing and able owners are faced with an unwilling patient. Even good-natured dogs may resist medication or treatment, especially if it has to be repeated frequently. Naturally stubborn or bad-tempered animals may prove impossible to treat without some help or restraint.

Help and Restraint

Before getting into the specifics of medicating and treating a dog, here are some ways to deal with a recalcitrant patient.

Sometimes all that is needed in order to get a dog to cooperate is to disarm it slightly. Small dogs are easier to treat or medicate if they are simply put up on a table or counter. The slippery surface surprises them so that they do not move around. Grasping a dog by the ear flap will usually have a restraining effect when applying ear medicine.

Often, however, these steps are not enough, and it will be necessary to enlist the aid of another person. A family member or a friend can often restrain a dog simply by holding its head or body and petting and soothing it while it is treated or medicated.

In the case of a dog who is biting, or attempting to bite, stronger steps must be taken. If it is not prohibited by the disease that is being treated, chemical restraint, or a mild tranquilizer, can be given, but even this may be difficult to administer.

The most effective way to restrain a biting dog is to use a muzzle. Two people are needed, one to hold the animal firmly from behind, while the other puts the muzzle on. Wrap a nylon stocking, a strip of gauze, or a soft piece

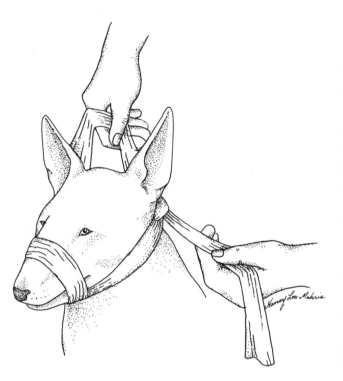

Illustration 10: A muzzle may be used to restrain a biting dog in order to medicate it.

To keep a dog from chewing off a bandage or licking a wound excessively, a homemade version of an Elizabethan collar is very effective until the animal can be seen by the doctor. For a large dog, cut out the bottom of a plastic bucket and tape the rough edge to protect the dog. Punch holes at regular intervals around the bottom edge, and thread a length of soft twine or gauze through the holes, forming loops. Put the dog's head through the bottom of the bucket, ears inside, and tie the bucket on by passing another length of twine or gauze through the already formed loops and then tying it snugly around the animal's neck (see Illustration 12, page 164). For a small dog, a plastic freezer or ice-cream container can be rigged up the same way (see Photograph 17, page 164). This device will prevent a dog from being able to lick or bite any part of its body and will also prevent it from scratching its head. Veterinarians have more professional devices that they can dispense when needed (see Photograph 9, page 66).

Illustration 11: Manual restraint is another way to restrain a dog who must be treated or medicated. An assistant will have to give the medication to the dog.

of rope such as clothesline tightly around the dog's muzzle, crossing the ends under the chin and bringing them around the neck and up to tie tightly behind the ears (see Illustration 10, above). The muzzle really needs to be snug, because if a dog can open its mouth even a tiny bit, it can bite. This, of course, precludes giving pills, and liquid medicine must be used (how to administer this later on).

Another way to restrain a biting dog or to keep an already muzzled dog from running off is by using manual restraint. To do this, put the dog's nose or bottom of its neck in the crook of one arm and pull its head in tightly against your body, folding the forearm up by flexing the elbow. Hold the back of the dog's head with the opposite hand. The same opposite arm can also be used to restrain the dog's body by pulling the elbow inward to trap the animal's body against yours. An assistant can then give medication to the dog (see Illustration 11, opposite).

Photograph 17: Two views of an ice cream container rigged up as a temporary Elizabethan collar on a small dog

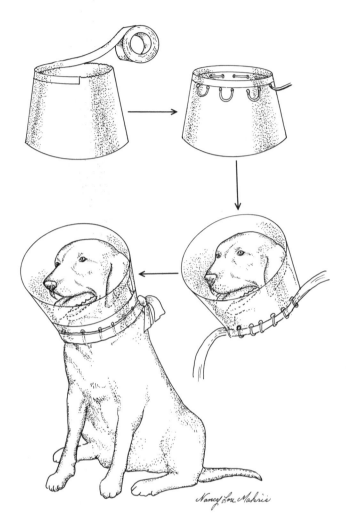

Illustration 12: How to fashion a homemade Elizabethan collar to prevent a dog from licking or chewing any part of its body.

General Care

Use common sense in caring for an ill or convalescent dog. The animal should be kept warm and isolated from a lot of noise and confusion if it is feeling poorly. The dog's own temperament and feelings should be considered when it comes to company. Some sick dogs want to be left alone, while others crave attention. Most owners give their recuperating dogs the run of the house if the animal is used to it, but if the dog is quite sick it is sometimes a good idea to set up one room or area of the house as a sickroom. This need not be any par-

ticular place; the place where the dog's bed is normally located is usually a good choice. Water and food can be placed nearby and the animal can be kept quiet and warm. It is especially helpful to isolate a dog if it is too sick to go out or has diarrhea or accidents indoors as a result of its illness. Sometimes a rubberized mattress or sheet may be necessary if an animal is incontinent of urine or feces. In this case, bedding must be cleaned/changed at least twice a day—more often if necessary.

Forcing Food and Fluid

If an animal has difficulty getting up to eat and drink, food and water must be brought to it. Occasionally, it is necessary to force-feed an animal. The easiest way to force fluid is with a large plastic medicine dropper, or a syringe with the needle removed, available from the veterinarian. Tilt the dog's head up toward the ceiling, and pull its cheek out by grasping it gently with thumb and forefinger. Baste the liquid slowly into its mouth through the funnel made by the cheek pouch (see Illustration 13, opposite). The liquid will flow into the mouth between the teeth. To force food, place some strained baby food on a standard wooden tongue depresser, grasp the animal's muzzle from the top with one hand, force its mouth open with the depresser, and wipe the food on the roof of the mouth. Alternatively, a syringe can be filled with strained baby food and then basted directly into the dog's mouth rather than into the cheek pouch.

Taking a Dog's Temperature

To take a dog's temperature, use a standard rectal thermometer. Shake down the thermometer and lubricate it with vaseline. With the dog standing, lift its tail, and insert the thermometer gently and very straight into the rectum, until only about one-half to one inch remains out. Leaving it in for one minute is

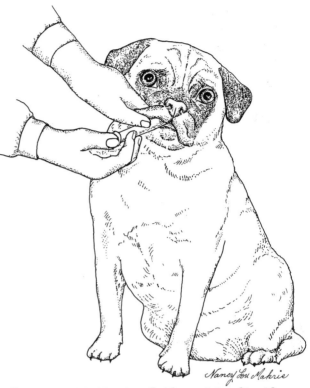

Illustration 13: Forcing fluid, or giving liquid medication, with a syringe

usually sufficient. A dog's normal body temperature is between 100 and 102.5 degrees. Anything above indicates an illness that is producing fever. Anything below indicates more critical illness or the impending delivery of pups in full-term pregnant bitches. (See Chapter 5.)

Medicating a Dog

The majority of home medications for dogs come either in the form of pills, capsules, or in liquid form. To give liquid medicine to a dog, follow the instructions given above for forcing fluids. Fortunately, most antibiotics and other medicines come in both pill and liquid form, so that if a dog has to be muzzled, for instance, a liquid medicine can be substituted for a pill or capsule.

Pills and Capsules

There are two ways to give a pill or capsule to a dog. If the animal is eating well, the easiest method is to hide the pill or capsule in a meat, cheese, or bread ball and toss it to the dog. Sometimes dogs get wary after a while and dissect the food ball before eating it. A trick we use here to fool even the most suspicious dog is to give a couple of "phantom" (nonmedicated) food balls first, and when the animal's guard is down, toss in the medicated treat. Don't, however, try to hide a pill or capsule in a big plate of food. The dog may not eat all the food or will find and avoid the medicine (and the food as well). If a dog is not eating well and will not accept food, the medicine will have to be given directly. Grease the pill or capsule

Illustration 14: Pilling a dog who won't accept food

with some butter or oil, then grasp the animal's muzzle from the top with one hand, and hold its head up toward the ceiling. With the other hand, grasp the pill or capsule with the thumb and forefinger and force the lower jaw open with two fingers (see Illustration 14, opposite). Lop the pill gently into the dog's mouth toward the back of the throat, and then push it in with a finger. Close the dog's mouth and stroke its throat while holding the jaw closed to make the dog swallow.

Eye Medicine

There are basically two different types of eye medicine, both of which can be difficult to administer to dogs. To apply ointment, grasp the dog's head and hold it up so that the upper lid can be lifted and a streak of ointment can be placed directly on the dog's eyeball. Sometimes a helper also needs to hold the lower lid down in order to get the eye open. Or the lower lid can be pulled down, and the ointment placed on the inside of the lower lid. Liq-

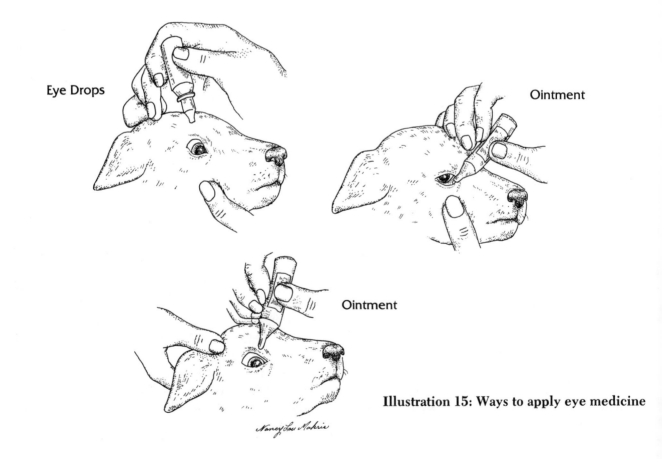

Eye Drops

Ointment

Ointment

Illustration 15: Ways to apply eye medicine

uid eye medicine is a bit easier to apply. Hold the medicine container between thumb and forefinger and rest the palm of this hand flat on top of the dog's head, tipping the head up and back with the other hand. The medicine can then usually be dropped directly into the eye (see Illustration 15, page 166). Alternatively, sit the dog down directly in front of you, hold its head from underneath with one hand, and apply the medicine with the other. Both these methods can be done without assistance with cooperative dogs, but restraint may be needed for less pliable pets.

Ear Medicine

Ear medicine also comes in ointment or liquid form. To apply, grasp the dog's ear flap gently, and thrust the applicator into the ear canal. It must go into the ear canal. Squeeze the required amount of medicine into the ear, pulling the applicator out while still squeezing to lubricate the entire canal. Still grasping the ear flap, massage the ear canal itself to spread the medication up and down its length. Because the dog's ear canal is a cartilage cylinder that goes down the side of the head before going inside, it can be felt from the outside.

Skin Medicines and Injections

Owners often need to apply topical skin medications. These are usually ointments and are easily applied with the fingers. Problems arise when dogs immediately try to lick the medication off. If the animal can be prevented from licking off the ointment for fifteen minutes to a half hour after it has been applied, the medicine will have had a chance to soak in and go to work. If it is impossible to keep a dog from constantly licking a sore spot, an Elizabethan collar, as described before, may be necessary.

Sometimes it is necessary to instill an antiseptic solution into a pocket of infection, such as an abscess. The veterinarian will demonstrate this when necessary.

Injections: In general, the only type of medicine that an owner will be asked to give by

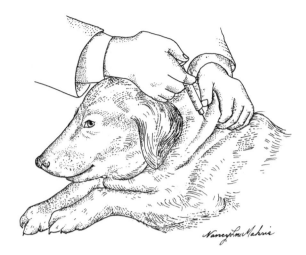

Illustration 16: Giving a dog a subcutaneous injection

injection at home is insulin. Sometimes, antibiotics are also given in this way. The veterinarian will give instructions on how to give a subcutaneous injection, but here is a quick rundown on how it is done. A subcutaneous injection is one that is given beneath the skin. The easiest method is to first find an area of skin that is loose and easy to pick up. We find that for most dogs the least painful areas are over the back of the neck or the shoulder blades. With thumb and index finger, pick up a bit of skin, and with one finger, push in just ahead of the thumb and index finger, creating a dimple, or dent. Place the needle right on this dimple and thrust it in at a slight angle so that it goes beneath the skin. The medicine can then be injected and the needle and syringe withdrawn (see Illustration 16 above).

Medicated Baths: A medicated bath is sometimes necessary for a dog. The least messy way to accomplish this with a large or medium-sized dog is to take the dog into the shower with you. First, put boric or ophthalmic ointment onto the dog's eyes to protect them, and put lamb's wool into its ears. (Note: This works better than cotton as it does not absorb moisture.) Wet the dog down, lather it completely with medicated shampoo so that no area is left untreated, and rinse very thoroughly—at least one or two times more than seems enough. Small dogs can usually be bathed successfully in the kitchen sink or a washbasin. Large dogs can also be bathed in a bathtub, if the shower method is not appealing.

Dipping: This is another procedure that must be done with the animal standing in a shower or bathtub. Again, eyes and ears must be protected. A dipping solution that has been made up in advance according to the veterinarian's instructions is applied with a sponge or washcloth all over the dog. Most dipping solutions are not rinsed off but are left on the skin. Ask the veterinarian for specific instructions.

Soaking: Wounds and various dermatological conditions often require soaking. To soak a dog's feet, the solution is placed in a wide-bottomed container, such as a bucket or bowl (a cup may do for small dogs), and the dog can stand with its foot in it. For other parts of the body, a towel or cloth is soaked in the solution, wrung out, and held gently but firmly against the affected area while the animal stands, sits, or lies down. The cloth may have to be re-wet several times. A helpful hint—while soaking, use an egg timer to be sure that enough time has lapsed.

Care of Bandages and Casts

Owners will rarely if ever be required to change either a bandage or a cast for a dog. Their job is to keep the bandaging clean, dry, and in place and to check for swelling. If an animal is chewing a bandage, the veterinarian should be contacted. A homemade Elizabethan collar may be used as a stop-gap measure until something further can be done at the veterinarian's office. Any swelling or redness requires immediate veterinary attention.

Keeping a bandage or cast dry and clean can be a problem. The easiest way to protect bandaging temporarily against rain or muddy conditions is with a heavy-duty plastic bag cut in squares approximately the size of the bandage and attached over the bandaging with standard adhesive tape. When the dog comes in, the plastic must be removed immediately, otherwise dampness can form underneath it, creating an environment in which bacteria can build up. Waterproof bandages and casts are not practical for dogs because they must be changed every twelve hours to prevent infection.

Dealing with Frustration

It is easy to become very frustrated when dealing with a sick dog for several reasons. First, as we discussed, some dogs are very difficult, or even seemingly impossible, to medicate. Second, busy people can find it hard to spend time performing lengthy procedures such as soaking on a regular basis. But most frustrating of all is the situation in which an owner has religiously followed instructions and bathed, medicated, and/or soaked regularly only to find no improvement in a pet.

It's hard not to take these frustrations out on the animal or on family and friends. Sometimes enlisting the aid of other family members who can share the responsibility for the dog's care can help. Often, however, the best way to deal with any of these problems is to consult the veterinarian who can use her years of experience to view the situation objectively. She will usually be able to suggest a new approach to the situation or prescribe a different kind or form of medication that may work better.

Encyclopedia
of Diseases of Dogs,
Their Treatment and Prevention

I. Infectious and Contagious Diseases of Dogs,
Michael S. Garvey, DVM

II. Diseases and Disorders of Dogs:
Symptoms, Diagnosis, Treatment, Prognosis

Aural Diseases and Disorders: Karen A. Helton, DVM

Autoimmune and Blood Diseases and Disorders:
Connie E. Leifer, DVM, and Robert E. Matus, DVM

Cardiac Diseases: Philip R. Fox, DVM

Dermatologic Diseases and Disorders: Karen A. Helton, DVM

Endocrine Diseases: Mark E. Peterson, DVM

Gastrointestinal Diseases and Disorders: Dennis A. Zawie, DVM

Musculoskeletal Diseases and Disorders: David T. Matthiesen, DVM

Neurologic Diseases and Disorders: Joseph M. Carrillo, DVM

Oncology: Connie E. Leifer, DVM, and Robert E. Matus, DVM

Ophthalmic Diseases and Disorders: Stephen L. Gross, VMD

Renal Diseases and Disorders: Richard C. Scott, DVM

Reproductive Disorders: Kathleen E. Noone, VMD

Respiratory Diseases and Disorders: Kathleen E. Noone, VMD

It still comes as a surprise to some people, even dog owners, that dogs are subject to most of the same diseases and illnesses that humans are. Probably one reason for this surprise is that until less than fifty years ago, there were few veterinarians who specialized in specific canine illnesses. In our parents' and grandparents' day, dogs simply died of "old age" rather than of cancer or heart or kidney disease.

Unfortunately, dogs also suffer from a number of genetic diseases and disorders to which humans are not subject. In an effort to develop specific physical traits, dog breeders may also unwittingly foster physical weaknesses by mating animals with undetected recessive genes containing faults. The resulting puppies will then have a predisposition toward these faults. Readers will find references to the predispositions of certain breeds of dogs toward specific physical problems or disorders in this chapter. Prospective dog owners should bear this in mind and research carefully before deciding on a particular breed, or even a particular physical type of dog. Once you have made the decision to buy a certain breed of dog, research carefully the specific ancestry, or "line," to rule out as far as possible predispositions toward problems associated with the breed. Knowing about the possibility of these kinds of problems can also help a dog owner to recognize a problem early, should one occur.

Chapter 5 may help prevent dog owners from contributing further to these kinds of problems through casual breeding of pets. Genetically induced disorders can occur in any part of a dog's body, but we find that they tend to surface most often in the eyes and in the skeletal and respiratory systems. Details about some of these problems can be found under the appropriate listings in the last section of this chapter.

Infectious and Contagious Diseases of Dogs

There are a number of canine diseases that can be transmitted from animal to animal via direct contact with an infected animal or with its feces, urine, or saliva. Others are transmitted by airborne viruses, and still others need an intermediate host, such as an insect or parasite, to be taken from one animal to another.

An infectious disease is caused when a disease-producing organism—a bacterium, fungus, virus, protazoan, or parasite—invades a dog's body. A contagious disease is an infectious disease that can be transmitted from one dog to another. All contagious diseases are infectious diseases, but not all infectious diseases are contagious. As a general rule, viral diseases are highly contagious, while bacterial diseases have a much smaller chance of being contagious.

Today, proper immunization can almost entirely prevent most canine infectious viral diseases. Most other infectious diseases can be treated if prompt medical attention is provided. Some parasitic diseases can be avoided with preventive medicine, which the veterinarian usually gives puppies and dogs automatically following an appropriate schedule. (See Chapter 3.) A brief rundown of these diseases follows. We will start with those against which dogs are now routinely immunized.

Canine Distemper

Once the principal killer of puppies, the incidence of this disease has been greatly reduced in this country by appropriate immunization. However, so-called temporary shots often given by breeders and pet stores may not be adequate protection against this highly contagious virus, which is spread by contact with an infected animal. The incubation period of distemper after exposure is anywhere from a few days to two weeks. Signs of distemper are diarrhea, listlessness, fever, "cold" symptoms. In a few days, these symptoms usually progress to a heavier nose and eye discharge, a cough, and shaking or trembling. Neurologic disorders such as seizures, confusion, and spasmodic twitching or jerking may develop. There is no direct effective treatment against the virus itself. Treatment, including antibiotics and intravenous fluids, is provided to support the patient, to prevent secondary bacterial infection, and to help the dog combat the disease. The prognosis varies widely, depending on the severity of the disease and on early recognition and therapy.

Canine Parvovirus

This is a highly contagious infectious viral disease of sudden onset, which can attack dogs of any age and swept the country in epidemic proportions in the late 1970s. It is spread primarily via contact with the feces of an infected dog. The virus can also be carried on the shoes and clothing of people. The incubation period of the disease is three to twelve days. Signs of parvovirus are severe gastrointestinal distress, usually vomiting and bloody diarrhea, accompanied by fever and obvious illness and listlessness. Symptoms are generally sudden but may be preceded by a loss of appetite. Because parvovirus is a viral disease, antibiotics are not directly effective against the infection. They are a standard part of therapy, however, as secondary bacterial infections usually occur. Intravenous fluids, withholding of food and water, intestinal protectants, and symptomatic treatments are also part of the supportive treatment. Success of treatment is dependent on early diagnosis, since death can occur within two to four days after onset. Prevention: In addition to the appropriate immunization, which is now available, the virus causing the disease can be destroyed by an appropriate solution of Clorox or other chlorine bleach (following manufacturer's mixing instructions), which should be used to clean kennels and other areas where dogs congregate.

Heartworm

This is a parasitic disease prevented by proper testing and medication (see Diseases and Disorders of Dogs). Although it is not contagious in the usual sense, it goes through an intermediate host, in this case the mosquito, which ingests the larvae from an infected dog and deposits them in another animal. Heartworm testing and prevention should also be part of every dog's annual routine.

Infectious Canine Hepatitis

This viral disease is rarely seen anymore, because dogs are routinely vaccinated against it. It can sometimes, however, affect young puppies who have not as yet been immunized. Signs can mirror those of canine distemper and range from very mild to severe and acute. The disease primarily affects the tonsils, kidneys, and liver (see Liver Disease in the Diseases and Disorders part of this chapter). Treatment, after confirmation of the disease by blood tests, consists of hospitalization and supportive treatment. The prognosis is very poor in young puppies.

Leptospirosis

This is a bacterial disease that is caused by leptospira bacteria and can lead to kidney failure and liver disease in the dog. Many animal species, including cattle, pigs, sheep, rats, and dogs, harbor leptospira. The disease is spread by direct contact with the bacterial organisms shed in the urine. Signs of leptospirosis include fever, depression, lack of appetite, jaundice, vomiting, and muscle pain. An animal with leptospirosis can be extremely sick and may also show signs of uremia (see Diseases and Disorders of Dogs). Treatment consists of fluids and specific antibiotics, including penicillin and streptomycin or penicillin and another antibiotic similar to streptomycin or tetracycline. The prognosis for a dog with the disease is guarded, and it can be fatal. Prevention is attempted by use of a bacterin (a bacterial vaccine). However, a bacterin does not work as well as a viral vaccine for prevention in many cases. Veterinarians may or may not include leptospirosis in their canine immunization programs, depending on geographic location, incidence of the disease, and personal preference.

Parasitic Diseases

Among these diseases are various intestinal parasites, such as worms, and parasites that affect the skin, such as fleas, ticks, mites, and lice (see Diseases and Disorders of Dogs). These diseases can usually be prevented by strict attention to cleanliness, both of the dog and its environment, and by immediate control once initial signs of infestation appear.

Rabies

This viral disease has an unusually long incubation period—anywhere up to several months—which can make it particularly difficult to isolate. It is a fatal disease, transmitted primarily by a bite from an infected animal (see also the Emergencies section). Initial symptoms of rabies are personality changes, causing an animal to behave in uncharacteristic ways, followed either by paralysis of the mouth and throat or by viciousness and frenzy. Prevention by vaccine is essential for all dogs and always part of a regular immunization series. Periodic booster shots are always recommended.

Tracheobronchitis, or "Kennel Cough"

This is an infectious tracheal and bronchial condition, which can be caused by the combination of a virus (parainfluenza) and a bacterium (Bordetella). The name "kennel cough" developed because the disease usually affects dogs after they have been boarded or kenneled and is attributed to the increased risk of exposure and often poor ventilation. Stress is thought to be a contributing factor, along with close proximity to other dogs. The incubation period is anywhere from five to seven days after exposure, so symptoms may not appear until after the dog has been taken home. The primary symptom is a dry, hacking cough, which is exacerbated by pressure on the windpipe, such as a tightly pulled collar or vigorous exercise. It is usually self-limiting, but if the cough persists or the dog is uncomfortable, it can be treated with appropriate antibiotics. Immunization with parainfluenza vaccine (CPI) one or two weeks before boarding affords the best protection.

Canine Illnesses
That Can Be Transmitted to People

This brings us to the subject of *zoonoses*, or infectious diseases of animals (in this case, dogs) that can be transmitted to people. A few of the infectious canine diseases can infect people, and, given the close proximity in which owners and their dogs usually live, it is surprising that this crossover doesn't occur more often. In fact, the incidence of zoonoses is relatively small. Veterinarians, kennel owners, dog groomers, and other people who work and live in close daily contact with a number of dogs have no higher degree of the illnesses or diseases that also occur in dogs than the general population does.

When a dog and a person in the same household have the same disease, it is usually assumed that the dog infected the person. There is a lot of evidence these days that in many cases the reverse is true.

A very common question asked of veterinarians is "Can my dog catch my cold?" The answer is "No." Common viruses of humans are not contagious to dogs and vice-versa. This becomes confusing because the disease may look the same and sometimes even share the same name. For example, people can develop infectious hepatitis and there is an infectious canine hepatitis, but these are different viruses and neither infects the other species.

Rabies is the most dreaded zoonotic disease because it is deadly to humans. This is why canine vaccinations are so important for the health of the dog and the peace of mind of the owner. Visceral larval migrans is a rare disease of children caused by immature forms of the dog roundworm. The best prevention for this problem is to make sure that dogs' stools are periodically checked and that canine roundworms are treated promptly. Transmission occurs by ingestion of contaminated dog fecal material; thus, children should be kept away from areas containing dog feces.

Dogs are sometimes blamed for transmitting diseases to humans that could not possibly be transmitted by the dog. A prime example is toxoplasmosis. While dogs can be infected with this protozoal organism, they cannot pass the infection along to people or to other animals. Pinworms, which children sometimes pick up at school, are not carried by dogs—just other children. Head lice, another parasite associated with school children, is not a dog-transmitted problem.

If a dog is properly immunized and it and its living quarters are kept clean, the chances of a human catching a disease from his pet are very slim.

Diseases and Disorders of Dogs:
Symptoms, Diagnosis, Treatment, Prognosis

NOTE: Capitalized words within entries are cross-referenced and have an entry of their own.

See Glossary 2 for definitions of various diagnostic tests and procedures referred to throughout this section.

A

ACANTHOSIS NIGRICANS: This is a skin condition in which hyperpigmentation (darkening) of the skin occurs, usually in the dog's axillary region (the armpits), which may or may not be itchy. It is seen frequently in dachshunds and is often confused with chronic skin changes secondary to allergies. Treatment is often palliative, consisting of topical cortisone therapy.

ACRAL LICK GRANULOMAS: This skin condition is caused by the dog's constant licking of a localized area, usually on a leg or foot. The cause of this disorder is unknown. It is occasionally secondary to arthritic joint pain. Boredom is frequently incriminated. It is a common condition of Doberman pinschers. Many treatments have been attempted; none of them are 100 percent effective. We are now using acupuncture in an attempt to treat this disorder and are having variable success.

ACTINIC DERMATITIS, or NASAL SOLAR DERMATITIS: This condition is often confused with dicoid lupus erythematosus (DLE), an AUTOIMMUNE SKIN DISEASE, and occurs most frequently in collies and German shepherds. The pigmented skin areas, usually the planum nasale (nose), loses pigment and can show some crustiness. The condition is known to be aggravated by the sun. Dogs with this condition should be protected from the sun, or sunblock lotion (SPF 15) can be applied to affected areas. Owners who notice this condition should have a dog examined by a veterinarian for a definitive diagnosis.

ACUTE RENAL FAILURE (ARF): ARF can be the result of any disease or agent that abruptly causes kidney damage and ultimately UREMIA. Causes of ARF include toxins such as mercury, lead, arsenic, and ethylene glycol (antifreeze); solvents such as carbon tetrachloride; dehydration as a result of severe loss of body water from diarrhea, vomiting, or lack of adequate intake; and infectious agents such as LEPTOSPIROSIS and acute bacterial PYLONEPHRITIS. Clinical signs are similar to those of UREMIA but are very acute and very abrupt in onset. Treatment consists of parenteral fluids, antibiotics, and supportive care. Prognosis for ARF is guarded; however, with prompt therapy, a dog can recover. RENAL FAILURE can also become chronic.

ADDISON'S DISEASE: Named after Sir Thomas Addison who described this disease in people in the mid-1800s, Addison's disease was first described in the dog in 1953. This ENDOCRINE DISEASE occurs when the adrenal cortex fails to manufacture sufficient cortisone (cortisol) and aldosterone, a condition known as hypoadrenocorticism. Without cortisone and aldosterone, the electrolytes in the blood (sodium, chloride, potassium, and calcium) get out of the proper proportions in relationship to each other, and the dog becomes very ill. Symptoms include loss of appetite, weakness, and vomiting. The disease can be diagnosed by a blood test. There is no breed predilection for Addison's disease but it is a young female dogs' disease; 70 percent of the victims are females with an average age of five years. The disease is easy to treat by replacing the deficient hormones with synthetic analogs taken in pill form, and the prognosis for a properly treated dog is good.

AGALACTIA: *See* Chapter 5.

ALBUMINURIA: *See* PROTEINURIA.

ALLERGIC SKIN DISEASES: There are a number of allergic skin diseases to which dogs are prone. All of them produce severe pruritus (itching). Dogs with allergic skin diseases are usually "face rubbers, foot lickers and/or armpit scratchers." Among the kinds of allergic skin diseases that dogs are susceptible to are:
Atopic Dermatitis: These skin conditions are caused by inhaled allergens; the itching gets progressively worse as the dog gets older. They can be seasonal and/or nonseasonal. Atopic dermatitis is treated with cortisone and/or intradermal skin testing to identify the allergen so a hyposensitization process in which the allergen is made into a vaccine can be begun. The latter process is only performed in a few of the larger veterinary institutions, such as The AMC.
Allergic Contact Dermatitis: *See* CONTACT DERMATITIS.
Food Allergies: These allergies are nonseasonal. They are not always associated with the addition of a new food; a dog can suddenly become allergic to a food that it has eaten for years. Food allergies are sometimes treated with cortisone, although they may not be as responsive to it as atopic dermatitis. Diet testing is usually performed to determine the particular food to which a dog is allergic.
Insect Hypersensitivity: Flea-bite allergic dermatitis is not as common as is usually thought. Often, the condition is simply flea-bite dermatitis, rather than an allergic reaction, and the rash is the result of bites, not an allergy. If there is a hypersensitivity, or allergic reaction, it is usually treated with rigorous flea control, with or without the addition of oral cortisone.
Drug Eruptions: Drug eruption can mimic virtually any dermatosis. This rare condition is usually pruritic (itchy) and often poorly responsive to steroid therapy. Diagnosis often involves discontinuing the offending medication and observing clinical recovery. Therapy includes discontinuing the drug, avoiding chemically related drugs, and systemic topical and systemic medications.

AMYLOID GLOMERULONEPHRITIS (AMYLOIDOSIS): This is a RENAL (KIDNEY) DISEASE that is caused by the abnormal formation of amyloid, which deposits in the glomerulus after the normal filtration action of the kidneys and which causes damage. All the glomeruli are involved. (*See* RENAL DISEASES AND DISORDERS for definitions of the parts of the kidneys.) The cause of amyloid formation is unknown. The signs of this disease are similar to those of GLOMERULONEPHRITIS (GN). There is no current treatment that is efficacious, and the prognosis is poor.

ANAL SAC (GLAND) IMPACTION: There are two sacs on either side of a dog's anus in which secretions accumulate. Usually, these secretions are released as a result of pressure when a dog defecates. Occasionally, this automatic emptying doesn't occur, and the sacs will become impacted, or full of matter, and will have to be manually emptied before they become infected, which may lead to abscessing. In general, owners should not attempt to perform this, as improper emptying can force the matter deeper. Signs of anal sac impaction are scooting along the ground and excessive licking. If the anal sacs, or glands, cause frequent problems, they can be surgically removed.

ANEMIA: Anemia is a condition in which there are too few red blood cells present in a dog's bloodstream to carry enough oxygen throughout its body. It is characterized by shortness of breath, weakness, and lethargy. It can be caused by a number of factors, including severe infestations of INTESTINAL PARASITES, skin parasites such as fleas, and HEARTWORM DISEASE. It can also be the result of a systemic problem such as RENAL (KIDNEY) DISEASE. Anemia is diagnosed by means of a blood test and is treated symptomatically.

APLASTIC ANEMIA: This is a condition of generalized bone-marrow suppression. It is characterized by neutropenia (low white-blood-cell count), thrombocytopenia (low platelet count), and anemia (low red-blood-cell count). A dog may show signs of bleeding tendencies related to the thrombocytopenia, infections caused by the neutropenia, or lethargy and pale mucous membranes because of anemia. Aplastic anemia may be caused by a malignancy, AUTOIMMUNE DISEASE, may be induced by estrogens or other drugs, or the cause may be unknown. Therapy is supportive and symptomatic, involving blood transfusions and attempts to stimulate normal bone-marrow function with several drugs.

ARTHRITIS: *See* DEGENERATIVE ARTHRITIS, IDIOPATHIC IMMUNE-MEDIATED ARTHRITIS, INFECTIOUS BACTERIAL ARTHRITIS, RHEUMATOID ARTHRITIS, and SYSTEMIC LUPUS ERYTHEMATOSUS ARTHRITIS.

ATAXIA: This is a term that means lack of coordination. Sensory ataxia is the inability of the body to sense position of its limbs in space. This position-sense loss is termed a *conscious proprioception deficit.* Motor ataxia is seen with lesions in the cerebellum, vestibular apparatus, or spinal cord. Ataxia is clinically manifested by a tendency to cross the limbs so that they interfere with one another, to walk on the dorsal (top) surface of the paw, to abduct the limbs (move them away from the center of the body), and/or to appear hypermetric (an overmeasurement in the gait response, observed as greater movements of the limbs than normal). *See* BALANCE DISORDERS for methods of diagnosis and treatment of vestibular and cerebellar ataxia. (*See* DEGENERATIVE MYELOPATHY and INTERVERTEBRAL DISC DISEASE as examples of spinal motor ataxia.)

AURAL DISEASES AND DISORDERS: Problems with dogs' ears are usually confined to the ear flap, or pinna, and the ear canal. Middle-ear problems, affecting balance, are considered to be NEUROLOGIC DISORDERS. Many canine ear problems develop because of the anatomy of dogs' ears (*see* Illustration 17, below). The dog's ear canal starts off vertically and then makes a horizontal turn, forming an angle in which fluid and debris can become trapped and creating a stagnant environment for the growth of bacteria. Because of this angle, dogs' ear canals can only adequately be examined with an otoscope. Dogs who have pendulous, floppy ear flaps, or pinnas, are prone to suffering damage to their ear flaps, such as EAR FISSURES. In addition, flop ears can prevent air circulation, promoting bacterial

Illustration 17: The dog's ear, showing the angle formed at the juncture of the vertical and horizontal canals

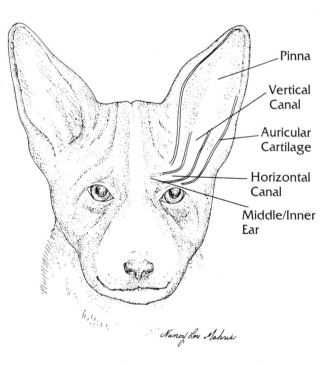

Pinna

Vertical Canal

Auricular Cartilage

Horizontal Canal

Middle/Inner Ear

Nancy Lou Mahrie

growth. Hairy-eared dogs like cocker spaniels, Irish setters, and poodles often develop hair plugs that can seal off the opening of the ear canal, creating an environment suitable for bacterial growth.

Canine ear problems can result in hair loss, such as PINNA ALOPECIA, or in death of skin tissue as a result of an infection of the ear margins (EAR MARGIN DERMATOSIS). Inhaled allergens, or atopy, can also lead to canine ear problems—see OTITIS EXTERNA. Some AUTOIMMUNE DISEASES can affect dogs' ears, attacking the tissue and causing it to become crusty. Usually these lesions are nonitchy and nonpainful. In addition to EAR MITES, parasites such as the spinous ear tick, found in some parts of the country, like to attack dogs' ears; and many outdoors dogs with erect ears are bothered in warm weather by stable flies (FLY-BITE DERMATITIS) that bite their ears until the pinna bleeds and becomes infected. This can be handled with soothing ointments and repellants.

Almost every canine ear problem will manifest itself in the same way. The dog will shake its head, scratch, and rub against the floor and furnishings. Excessive agitation of the pinna can damage it and lead to AURAL HEMATOMA. In severe cases, there may be tenderness at the jawline. Owners may become aware of this if they take the dog's head in their hands or pull on a collar. Many ear problems, however, go undetected until they become chronic. In general, with ear disease, we talk about controlling rather than curing the problem.

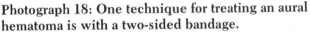

Photograph 18: One technique for treating an aural hematoma is with a two-sided bandage.

Although it is hard to cause damage to a dog's eardrum while cleaning the ear, owners should be careful not to clean out an animal's ear too vigorously with a cotton swab. In addition to the possibility of causing trauma to the ear, this method of cleaning will simply impact any foreign material and wax down into the ear canal. The best method of cleaning out a dog's ear is to flush it with warm otic solutions, which can be mixed with medication if desired. A syringe or plastic bottle with dropper top can be used, or a water pic with gentle water pressure works very well. Of course, owners should always consult with their veterinarian before putting anything in a dog's ear. *See also* DEAFNESS and SCARCOPTIC MANGE (SCABIES).

AURAL HEMATOMA: This is a blood-filled swelling in the pinna of a dog's ear that causes the ear flap to become distended. An aural hematoma usually has an underlying cause; that is, something causes an irritation of the pinna or canal (e.g., allergic OTITIS EXTERNA, etc.), and the animal reacts by vigorously shaking its head, which can cause a blood vessel in the pinna to rupture. Treatment of a hematoma consists of surgical removal and placing the ear flap in a two-sided bandage (*see* Photograph 18, page 178), or suturing it through and through for several weeks to prevent the vessels from refilling and encourage the formation of scar tissue. In addition, the predisposing cause must be identified to prevent recurrence.

Photograph 19: Dr. Karen A. Helton examining a dog's outer ear

AUTOIMMUNE DISEASES: An autoimmune disease is one in which the body is attacking itself in one of a number of ways: by the formation of antibodies against tissue or body organs; by the formation of antigen-antibody complexes that may attack different tissues and organs; or by the direct attack of the immune-defense cells themselves (cellular attack). The causes of autoimmune diseases are not known but are closely related to the causes of cancer in that there is a probably paradoxical failure of the body's immune system, or a general imbalance in the autoimmune defense system, which can have a genetic, viral, or environmental basis or be caused by a combination of any of these. These influences can bring about changes in the cellular components allowing the normally inhibited antibody formation to proceed at an enhanced rate. Autoimmune diseases are diagnosed by the use of blood tests for specific antibodies, and in the case of SYSTEMIC LUPUS ERYTHEMATOSUS and the PEMPHIGUS GROUP, appropriate biopsies of affected organs such as the skin, kidneys, and joints. In general, autoimmune diseases are treatable and controllable but not curable. Canine autoimmune diseases include AUTOIMMUNE-HEMOLYTIC ANEMIA, IMMUNE-MEDIATED THROMBOCYTOPENIA, SYSTEMIC LUPUS ERYTHEMATOSUS, RHEUMATOID ARTHRITIS, and the PEMPHIGUS GROUP.

AUTOIMMUNE HEMOLYTIC ANEMIA: This is a disease in which a dog's body is destroying its own red blood cells, resulting in anemia. Symptoms include lethargy, possibly dark-colored urine, and pale mucous membranes. It is diagnosed by means of a specialized blood test called the Coomb's test. Initial therapy consists of administering immunosuppressive corticosteroids and a blood transfusion if the anemia is severe. If the dog is nonresponsive to corticosteroids, other immunosuppressive medications or a splenectomy may be suggested. The prognosis is generally fair, with a more optimistic prognosis given if there is a marked response to initial steroid therapy.

AUTOIMMUNE SKIN DISEASES: There are a number of skin diseases caused by an autoimmune condition. All look very similar clinically and can require similar therapy, yet they involve differing prognoses; therefore, a correct diagnosis is essential in treating these diseases. In many of these diseases, there is crusting, heavy scales on the skin, nail bed involvement, and lesions on or in the mouth. Autoimmune skin diseases include a number of different conditions, such as the PEMPHIGUS GROUP, SYSTEMIC LUPUS ERYTHEMATOSUS, and dicoid lupus erythematosus, which is limited to the nose. *See also* ACTINIC DERMATITIS.

B

BACTERIAL DISEASES/INFECTIONS OF THE SKIN: Canine bacterial skin infections, or pyodermas, are divided into three categories: those that affect only the surface of the skin including the skin folds; those that are superficial, involving the upper layers of the skin; and deep bacterial infections.

Surface Pyodermas: Surface pyodermas are often referred to as "hot spots." The underlying cause of these infections is varied, ranging from parasites and trauma such as a scrape or burn to poor grooming, in which mats of hair prevent the circulation of air and provide a moist environment for bacterial growth. Surface infections can occur anywhere on a dog's body. Treatment consists of discovering and treating the underlying cause and using topical astringents, shampoos, antiseptics, etc., to clear up the dermatologic condition.

Skin fold pyodermas: These surface infections occur in a dog's skin folds, where overlapping skin prevents air circulation and promotes bacterial growth. It commonly occurs in the lip folds of cocker and springer spaniels and setters, in the vulvar folds of obese dogs, in the facial folds of brachycephalic breeds, and in the tail folds of screw-tailed breeds, such as Boston terriers and English bulldogs. Treatment is aimed at drying up the area in addition to topical medication.

Superficial Pyodermas: IMPETIGO, seen in four- to twelve-week-old puppies as pustules in the groin and armpit regions, is caused by unsanitary conditions. FOLLICULITIS is a very common skin infection seen in short-haired breeds. Bacteria proliferates in the hair follicles with variable itchiness. It can be either primary or secondary, when it is caused by another condition such as parasites, allergies, or a systemic imbalance or disorder. Folliculitis may have predisposing causes, such as the parasite demodex canis (*see* PARASITIC DISEASES OF THE SKIN), or an immune deficiency.

Interdigital pyoderma: This has the same predisposing causes as above and is seen commonly in heavy breeds of dogs such as the bull mastiff.

Perianal pyoderma: This infection may involve the anal sacs and may result in perianal fistulas. It is seen often in German shepherds.

Deep Pyodermas: There are several categories of deep pyodermas, which tend to be harder to clear up than surface pyodermas and are apt to become chronic. These infections usually require rigorous therapy with antibiotics and topical antibacterial shampoo. They may involve scarring.

Juvenile pyoderma: This infection of unknown origin occurs in puppies less than four months old and has a facial distribution with abscesses, ulcers, fistulous tracts, and facial distortion. The lymph nodes can also be affected.

Dry pyoderma: This affects puppies four to nine months old and is of unknown cause. It appears as tightly adhered scales on the face, extremities, and pressure points. Doberman pinschers are commonly affected.

BALANCE DISORDERS: The maintenance of balance and coordinated movement is mediated by a dog's central nervous system. Balance disorders are usually the result of VESTIBULAR and/or CEREBELLAR disease. *Vestibular* refers to the part of the nervous system that orients most animals to their surroundings. The vestibular system maintains equilibrium by channeling information to the appropriate brain divisions, resulting in smoothly coordinated movement.

Information regarding head position is "sensed" by structures in the inner ear (vestibular system). This information is then conveyed by a nerve (vestibular/cochlear) to the brain, whereupon information regarding linear, angular, acceleratory, and declaratory movement is relayed to other parts of the brain, resulting in balanced movement. The coordination of movement occurs in the cerebellum. The cerebellum "smoothes out" movement. Thus, abnormalities of the cerebellum may evoke uncoordinated movement, and disease of the vestibular system results in imbalance.

Vestibular disease is very common. Signs include head tilts, falling, rolling, veering, stumbling, tripping, rapid eye movements, and disorientation. In addition, facial paralysis, uneven eye pupil size, unilateral head muscle atrophy, and weakness may be observed. Onset is usually sudden, and the earliest signs may be nausea and vomiting. When facial paralysis is present, drooling and apparent eating difficulty may also be observed. Diagnosis is by means of a neurologic examination to determine where a disturbance has occurred along the complex interconnected pathway for balance or coordinated movement.

When the disturbance is outside the substance of the nervous sytem, it is called a peripheral disturbance. Peripheral disturbances most commonly seen in dogs can be associated with an outer-ear infection (OTITIS EXTERNA) or an inflammation of the inner or middle ear. Disturbances that are inside the substance of the nervous system, or central, include infections, vascular insults (strokes), tumors, thiamine deficiencies, congenital abnormalities, and trauma. Treatment of a central process will include a complete neurologic workup, which may be preceded by a medicine trial. When the disturbance is suspected to be peripheral, medication alone may be prescribed. Prognosis for balance disorders varies. Most peripheral diseases improve progressively in anywhere from one to six weeks. In all neurologic diseases, follow-up consultation with a veterinarian is extremely important. *See also* ATAXIA.

BLADDER TUMORS: *See* UROGENITAL TUMORS.

BLINDNESS: Blindness in the dog can be caused by a number of different factors, ranging from trauma to disease and genetic malformation. Many of these diseases and disorders are described in these pages. Dogs are very good at adjusting to gradual visual impairment. A dog who is blind in one eye, for instance, almost always behaves just like a perfectly normal dog. Even a dog who suddenly goes completely blind will do very well after a brief period of adjustment to the environment and will use other senses to adapt. The only exception to this is very old dogs who also have some hearing loss. They may take longer to adjust. Since even completely blind dogs function well in familiar surroundings, an owner is sometimes unaware of a pet's sight loss until the pet is taken into a new environment.

BONE TUMORS: Primary bone tumors are uncommon, but not rare. They usually occur on the leg in older large breed dogs and are manifested by a progressive lameness associated with swelling of the leg. They are extremely painful. The three most common bone tumors found in dogs are osteogenic sarcoma, chondrosarcoma, and synovial cell sarcoma. A bone tumor may often be confirmed with a high degree of correlation by X-ray examination, with a biopsy to confirm the diagnosis. Osteogenic sarcoma, the most common type of canine bone tumor, often spreads to other parts of the body, most commonly the lung, and this is the ultimate cause of death. Surgical amputation is the treatment of choice, and the prognosis is guarded. In the case of osteogenic sarcoma, amputation is often followed by chemotherapy. Other types of bone tumors, which are rare in the dog, can be confirmed by biopsy.

BRONCHIAL DISEASE: Bronchial disease in dogs is usually characterized by a chronic cough, and because it is often accompanied by TRACHEAL DISEASE, it can be difficult to differentiate between the two. The cause of bronchial disease can also be hard to determine. It can be caused by a bronchial tumor; by an allergy; or, most often, by an infection such as TRACHEOBRONCHITIS. Bronchial tumors, which are rare, can sometimes be removed surgically if they are localized in one lung lobe. Allergies and infections are treated medically with appropriate drugs. Because bronchial disease can be very difficult to diagnose, we always perform a complete medical workup on a dog who has a chronic cough.

BRUCELLOSIS: This is a rare venereal disease seen in male and female dogs, which can be transmitted to humans. In many "carrier" dogs there is no outward sign of the disease, while other animals may have a slight discharge or swelling in lymph nodes or testicles. In advanced cases, there may be a lot of pain in the spine. Because the disease is spread mainly through sexual contact, both dogs and bitches who are going to be bred should always have an antibody test, or Brucella-titer, a blood test that shows whether or not the animal has been exposed to the disease. If this test is positive, an additional blood test must be done to determine whether or not the animal is actually infected with brucellosis. Brucellosis can cause orchitis, which is inflammation within the testicles; epididymitis, which is inflammation of the epididymus; and sterility. If the disease is transmitted to a bitch it can result in reproductive failure. It can also spread to the bones causing a lot of pain and arthritis. There is currently no treatment that totally eliminates brucellosis. Antibiotics are sometimes used, but the disease tends to recur. Castration or an ovariohysterectomy is always necessary to prevent spread of the disease.

C

CANCER: *See* ONCOLOGY.

CANINE DISTEMPER: *See* Infectious and Contagious Diseases.

CANINE PARVOVIRUS: *See* Infectious and Contagious Diseases.

CARDIAC DISEASES: Cardiac diseases in dogs fall into several catagories: CONGENITAL HEART DISEASE results from abnormal embryologic development, and clinical signs are often obvious during puppyhood. Acquired Heart Diseases are more common and most frequently involve the heart valves (VALVULAR HEART DISEASES). Valvular heart disease commonly affects small breeds (although any breed can be affected), and clinical signs are more prevalent during adulthood. Acquired disorders of the heart muscle are termed CARDIOMYOPATHIES, usually affecting large and giant breeds. HEARTWORM DISEASE is caused by a mosquito-transmitted parasite infecting dogs that have not had preventative medication. Other cardiac disease processes may occasionally occur.

Signs of heart failure are similar no matter what the particular inciting cause. Any dog who has shortness of breath, persistent coughing, breathing difficulty, or progressive lethargy should be suspected of having cardiac disease. No time should be wasted in contacting a veterinarian. Untreated cardiac disease may eventually result in CONGESTIVE HEART FAILURE.

The first step in diagnosis of heart disease is a thorough general physical examination by a veterinarian. This is begun by evaluation of the heart and lungs with a stethoscope. An electrocardiogram (EKG) and a chest X ray may be performed to obtain more information if needed. More advanced diagnostic techniques are reserved for unusual circumstances.

Treatment depends on the nature and severity of the problem. With early detection, the majority of canine cardiac patients can be treated. A good prognosis for an improved, quality life is often attainable. Surgery may be needed in some cases of CONGENITAL HEART DISEASE in order to avoid CONGESTIVE HEART FAILURE. See also COMPLETE HEART BLOCK, ENLARGED HEART, HEART MURMUR.

CARDIOMYOPATHY: These are CARDIAC DISEASES that affect large and giant breed dogs—those weighing more than fifty to sixty pounds. An acquired heart disease that usually affects young to middle-aged males, cardiomyopathy causes the heart muscle either to become dilated, flabby, and weak or to become thickened and stiff. It will eventually lead to CONGESTIVE HEART FAILURE.

CATARACTS: Any opacification or clouding of the normally clear lens of the eye is called a cataract. Almost all dogs with DIABETES MELLI-

TUS will develop cataracts eventually because of an abnormally high concentration of glucose bathing the lens. This leads to a biochemical reaction within the lens, resulting in a clouding of the tissue. A cataract can be anything from a microscopic dot on the lens to complete opacification. A cataract can progress in size very, very slowly or extremely fast. The only way for a veterinarian to predict the rate of progression is by examining a dog at regular intervals.

Cataract surgery is a great deal more difficult in dogs than it is in humans. Dogs' lenses are very much bigger than humans'; therefore a cataract is also larger and more difficult to remove. In addition, dogs' eyes are very sensitive to surgical intervention and become badly inflamed. This can result in eventual scarring in the eye and BLINDNESS. For these reasons, cataract surgery is usually reserved for animals who are totally blind in both eyes. Small cataracts do not require surgery. Owners who are contemplating cataract surgery should make sure that the dog has a very thorough medical workup to ascertain that it is a good risk for anesthesia. In addition, a complete evaluation of the tissues of the eye behind the lens itself should be performed to be certain that the retina and optic nerve are still functioning properly.

CEREBELLAR DISEASE: *See* BALANCE DISORDERS.

CHERRY EYE: This is a condition in which the gland of the third eyelid has prolapsed out of its normal position and appears as a very swollen red structure on the inside, nose edge, of the eye. It generally occurs in animals between two and eight months old and is most commonly seen in American cocker spaniels, Boston terriers, English bulldogs, and Lhasa apsos. It is not known why this happens. The treatment of choice is to place the gland back into its normal position using a topical anesthetic. It will occasionally remain in place. If not, successful surgical techniques have been developed to keep the gland in position. Formerly, this tissue was often cut off. We feel that this treatment is contraindicated. Since the gland makes a significant portion of the liquid tears, removal can predispose the animal to develop a dry eye situation at a future date.

CHRONIC INTERSTITIAL NEPHRITIS (CIN)—CHRONIC KIDNEY FAILURE: CIN is a condition in which chronic kidney disease has led to severely damaged kidneys, with the result that the normal nephrons are largely replaced by scar tissue. This is not a specific kidney disease but the end-stage of many different kidney diseases including PYELONEPHRITIS, GLOMERULONEPHRITIS, and HYDRONEPHROSIS. Clinical signs are those of UREMIA, and treatment consists of supportive care.

COLITIS: Colitis is a general term meaning inflammation of the colon. It is characterized by tenesmus, or straining to defecate; by mucoid, bloody diarrhea; and by an increased frequency of daily bowel movements. The most common cause of colitis in dogs is INTESTINAL PARASITES, such as hookworms or whipworms. It can also be the result of a number of nonspecific causes or of an ulcerated colon. Treatment includes worming, antibiotics and other antiinflammatory medications, and dietary therapy in the form of additional roughage and bulkier-type foods to stimulate the colon and aid in the absorption of water in order to add form to the stools. Occasionally, bone splinters can lodge in the colon, causing so much pain when the dog has a bowel movement that it becomes constipated and must be hospitalized so that the bone fragments and hardened feces can be removed.

COLOR MUTANT ALOPECIA: This is a hereditary skin disease occurring in dogs with fawn-colored, or blue coats, such as the blue Doberman pinscher, dachshund, whippet, Irish setter, and Great Dane. There is a slowly progressive sparse haircoat that begins to appear at less than one year of age and may be followed by other bacterial FOLLICULITIS. There is no treatment for this condition; however, it is not dangerous to the dog and should not cause discomfort.

COMA: *See* STATES OF CONSCIOUSNESS.

COMPLETE HEART BLOCK: The heart has a series of electrical connections through which an electric impulse is initiated and conducted. This impulse then follows a set pattern that innervates different parts of the heart to contract, or beat, in a given sequence. Sometimes this sequence can be interrupted by disease, causing the heart not to contract, or beat, as it should. In this situation, the heart rhythm may become dangerously slow. In a few cases, Pacemaker implantation can be used successfully. A dog must be thoroughly assessed by a veterinarian to determine if it is a suitable candidate for this therapy.

CONGENITAL HEART DISEASE (a disease or abnormality existing at birth): There are several common congenital heart diseases in dogs. It is important for prospective dog owners to be aware of the possibility of congenital heart disease when they get a puppy. Immediately have a new puppy evaluated for this disorder by a veterinarian in the manner described under CARDIAC DISEASES. Breeders will often allow substitution of another puppy for one who is found to have a HEART MURMUR, but this can become a very difficult thing for the owner to do, even after only a few days of ownership. It's best to have the pup examined right away, before you become attached to it. Any puppy who is not thriving, fails to gain weight, breathes heavily, or tires easily should be suspected of having HEART DISEASE. A persistent cough is also a possible sign of heart disease, although respiratory infections and disorders can produce the same clinical signs. (*See* TRACHEAL DISEASE.) The prognosis for a healthy life for a dog with congenital heart disease varies tremendously depending on the nature and severity of the problem. While many dogs with congenital heart disease can live normal lives to maturity, others will not survive. A complete assessment by a veterinarian is the only way to determine the cause, extent, and proper therapy for heart disease.

Sometimes, a HEART MURMUR will not be detected in puppyhood and will only be discovered during a routine examination after the dog is mature. If the dog is over three years of age and has been able to lead a normal life, the condition causing the HEART MURMUR may not be serious enough to require therapy—or may be managed medically when and if problems arise. Each case is different, however, and must be individually evaluated by a veterinarian.

CONGESTIVE HEART FAILURE: This is the end result of any CARDIAC DISORDER—congenital, valvular, heart muscle, or of HEARTWORM DISEASE—in which the heart fails to pump enough blood. Symptoms usually include one or more of the following: fatigue, coughing, exercise intolerance, weight loss, rapid and difficult breathing, and sometimes abdominal distention. There is often effusion (fluid buildup) in the abdomen and thoracic cavity. Edema (or fluid buildup) in the lungs themselves is also possible. Fluid in the lungs or chest is suspected when rapid breathing is observed. The dog's head and neck will often be extended in this situation, and it will appear troubled and distressed as it gropes for air. *This is a serious emergency.* Treatment must be individualized for each dog and may consist of drugs such as diuretics and digitalis. Prognosis is often favorable. *See also* the Emergencies section.

CONJUNCTIVITIS: This is a very common problem with dogs. The mucous membrane tissue, or conjunctiva, adjacent to the cornea becomes irritated. This tissue produces mucus, which helps to keep the tear film on the cornea, and it also secretes material to help fight bacteria on the eye surface. A number of different things can irritate the conjunctiva and cause conjunctivitis: foreign bodies such as dust or dirt; a viral disease that causes dryness such as CANINE DISTEMPER; and bacteria growing in the eye at an abnormal rate. Treatment varies, depending on the cause. In some cases conjunctivitis can be chronic, but even then it can usually be kept under control.

CONTACT DERMATITIS: There are two kinds of contact dermatitis, allergic contact dermatitis (ACD) and irritant contact dermatitis (ICD), which are very difficult to differentiate. Both conditions are manifested by severe itching, and often there is a rash on the ventral (stomach) area. Allergic contact dermatitis is a rare, variably pruritic dermatitis, usually affecting sparsely haired skin in "contact" areas. It may be seasonal or nonseasonal, depending on the allergen. Irritant contact dermatitis is clinically similar to ACD, yet the mechanism of action is different. Contact dermatitis is diagnosed by means of isolation and provocative exposure (e.g., trial and error) and treated accordingly.

CORNEAL TRAUMA: Cat scratches and other kinds of eye wounds are very common dog problems. Because any eye injury can be serious, even seemingly minor eye injuries need immediate veterinary attention. Superficial scratches will usually heal on their own with the use of antibiotic ointment or drops to prevent secondary infection. If an eye laceration goes through the cornea, however, it usually must be treated surgically—stitches will be placed using very fine suture material. Sometimes a graft of tissue is put over the defect to make sure that it is sealed. After surgery, the eye must be watched very carefully for signs of infection or inflammation within the globe. *See also* the Emergencies section.

COXOFEMORAL LUXATION: Luxation or dislocation of the coxofemoral joint (hip) as a result of trauma is more common in dogs between ten and twelve months of age. Younger dogs usually sustain a fracture through the growth plate of the femur as a result of the same type of trauma that causes dislocation in older animals. Diagnosis is based on orthopedic examination and confirmed by radiographs of the hip joint. Generally, an attempt is made to correct the luxation by manipulation of the joint and limb under general anesthesia. Once the luxation is corrected, the leg is placed in a special bandage (ehmer sling) for ten to fourteen days. Surgical correction is indicated when the luxation cannot be corrected with external manipulation, a fragment of bone is present within the hip joint, the conformation of the hip joint is poor, or ARTHRITIS was already present in the hip joint prior to injury.

CRANIAL CRUCIATE LIGAMENT RUP-TURE: This is one of the more common orthopedic injuries in the dog and is a major cause of DEGENERATIVE ARTHRITIS of the stifle (knee) joint. The cranial cruciate ligament is a major ligament within the stifle joint, helping stabilize the joint. Rupture of this ligament results in instability of the stifle joint. Basically two types of dogs are prone to this injury: middle- to older-aged obese dogs with poorly developed musculature, for whom a minor amount of trauma to the knee can result in injury to the cruciate ligament, and active, athletic dogs who rupture the cruciate ligament through major traumatic injury. Injury to the cartilage within the stifle joint can occur secondarily because of the resulting instability. Clinical signs relate to pain in the knee joint with varying degrees of lameness present. Diagnosis is based on orthopedic examination and occasionally radiographs. Treatment is generally limited to surgical stabilization of the knee joint. Prognosis is dependent on the size and activity level of the dog, success of the surgery, the degree of ARTHRITIS already present, and whether one or both knees are involved.

CRANIOMANDIBULAR OSTEOPATHY: This is a bone disease characterized by a bony proliferation involving the mandible (jaw) and surrounding skull bones. The disease is primarily seen in Scottish terriers, West Highland white terriers, and Cairn terriers. Occasionally, boxers, Great Danes, Doberman pinschers, and Labrador retrievers are also affected. Onset of the disease usually occurs when a dog is between four and eleven months of age. Signs include swelling of the jaw, drooling, inability to open the mouth, and pain on manipulation of the mouth. Radiographs are required to confirm the diagnosis. The cause of the disease is unknown. Treatment is symptomatic, and most dogs can be made comfortable with steroids or aspirin. The disease is generally self-limiting. Many animals may continue to have impaired mouth function but are usually capable of eating.

CUSHING'S SYNDROME: The most common ENDOCRINE DISEASE occurring in dogs, Cushing's syndrome, discovered by Dr. Harvey Cushing in 1932, is the result of an overproduction of cortisol by the adrenal cortex, or hyperadrenocorticism. In 85 percent of cases, it develops because the pituitary gland produces too much adrenocorticotropic hormone (ACTH) causing an adrenal gland enlargement. This is known as pituitary-dependent Cushing's disease. Adrenal gland tumors account for only 15 percent of dogs with Cushing's syndrome. In both cases, the resulting symptoms are increased appetite, thirst, and urination; lethargy; muscle weakness; abdominal distention; mild to severe hair loss; and absence of estrous cycles or testicular atrophy. This disease is usually found in middle- to old-aged dogs, and it affects both sexes equally. All breeds may be affected, but there is a breed predilection for the disease among poodles, dachshunds, Boston terriers, and boxers. Blood tests are used to diagnose Cushing's syndrome, and the cause of the disease determines the treatment used. If an adrenal tumor is the cause, it should be surgically removed. If the disease is pituitary-dependent, it can be managed with medication. The prognosis for a dog who is properly treated for Cushing's syndrome is fair to good. When the disease is left untreated, death usually occurs within two years of onset.

CUTANEOUS ASTHENIA (EHLER-DANLOS SYNDROME): This disease is characterized by multiple lacerations and sagging of skin with minimal trauma observed. It is due to a hereditary abnormality of the connective tissue of the skin that occurs most often in Springer spaniels and boxers. If the skin is sutured, it usually rips again. There is nothing that can be done for dogs with this condition.

CYSTITIS: This is a bacterial infection of the urinary bladder, which almost always ascends from the lower urinary tract. Clinical signs include accidents in the house, straining to urinate, desire to go outdoors often to urinate, and blood in the urine. The same clinical signs can occur when URINARY TRACT STONES are present.

If stones have lodged in the urethra for one or two days, the symptoms may begin to include those of UREMIA. Treatment of cystitis is with appropriate antibiotics, as advised by the veterinarian. If treatment fails or cystitis returns, then further tests should be performed. The prognosis for recovery from cystitis is good.

D

DEAFNESS: There is no clinical test for canine deafness, and owners, generally, are the best judges of deafness in a dog. Many dogs' hearing diminishes or fails with age. There is no treatment for hearing loss in dogs.

DEFICIENCY OF TEAR PRODUCTION: Also called Dry Eye, a deficiency of tear production is a very common canine eye problem. There are two glands that are responsible for the watery part of tears: the gland of the third eyelid and the lacrimal gland. A number of different situations can cause damage to these glands, resulting in decreased tear production. These include certain viral diseases and some drugs used to control diarrhea and urinary infections. Evidence has accumulated recently pointing to the possibility that an AUTOIMMUNE DISEASE, in which the body's own defense system is turned against itself, can be a cause of tear gland damage. Tear deficiency can lead to gradual haziness of the cornea, and an acute loss of tears can result in an ULCERATED CORNEA. Treatment involves attempting to remove any toxic influence to the glands, such as drugs being used to treat other problems; trying to stimulate remaining gland(s) to produce more tears; and providing artificial lubricants to keep the cornea as moist as possible. In extreme situations where none of the above remedies is possible or effective, two of the dog's eight salivary gland ducts can be surgically transplanted from the mouth to the eyes, beneath the facial skin. Thus, when the dog salivates, the eye is kept somewhat moist. Although there may be some attendant problems caused by the different nature of the lubricating material, this procedure is preferable to allowing the eye to become completely dry.

DEGENERATIVE ARTHRITIS: This is a degeneration of cartilage in older dogs. It is the result of wear and tear that comes with aging. Fissures and erosion initially develop in the articular cartilage, and this leads to inflammation and associated joint pain. Degenerative arthritis also develops from a predisposing injury or disease such as FRAGMENTED MEDIAL CORONOID PROCESS (FCP), PATELLAR LUXATION, or HIP DYSPLASIA. Clinical signs include pain when the joint is moved, lameness, mild to moderate joint swelling, stiffness, and joint crepitation (grating, crackling). Diagnosis is based on orthopedic examination and radiographs. Treatment is aimed at relieving pain with painkilling drugs such as aspirin. Infrequently, surgery is indicated, depending on the location of the arthritis and the number of joints involved.

DEGENERATIVE MYELOPATHY: This is a neurologic disease that occurs primarily in aging German shepherds. It is characterized by a slowly progressive rear-limb weakness and ATAXIA. Postural (proprioception) reactions are poorly performed by the rear legs, resulting in paw-dragging and crossing of the hind legs. There is often disuse atrophy of the muscles in the dog's rear quarters. The cause is unknown, although a degeneration of the spinal cord is observed histopathologically. Dogs with this condition are not in pain. There is no therapy. Near complete paralysis occurs over months to years. (*See* spinal/motor ATAXIA.)

DELAYED UNION, and NONUNION: Delayed union refers to a fracture that has not healed in the usual time expected for that particular type of fracture and the age of the patient. Nonunion refers to a fracture in which all evidence of bone healing at the fracture site has stopped and motion and instability are present at the fracture site. The most common causes for delayed union and nonunion are inadequate immobilization of the fracture site for a sufficient period of time, inadequate alignment of the fracture ends, damage to the blood supply to the fracture site, or infection in the fracture site. Treatment of delayed union involves maintaining the existing fixation of the fracture site for an extended period of time until healing occurs, or, if necessary, surgical intervention to stabilize and realign the fracture ends. Nonunions are treated surgically by applying rigid internal stabilization to the fracture site (i.e., metal bone plates).

DENTAL DISEASE: *See* Chapter 3, Chapter 7, NASAL DISEASE, and ORAL TUMORS.

DEPRESSION: *See* STATES OF CONSCIOUSNESS.

DERMATOLOGIC DISEASES AND DISORDERS: Dogs are subject to a number of skin diseases and disorders and can suffer from almost all of the conditions that humans can have, including cysts and tumors (*see* HISTIOCYTOMAS, MAST CELL TUMORS, MELANOMAS, SKIN TUMORS, SEBACIOUS GLAND ADENOMAS). Skin problems can be very difficult to diagnose and to treat for two primary reasons. First, the skin has only a limited number of pathologic responses to disease or irritation, making it very hard for a clinician to determine which of hundreds of possibilities a particular condition may be. Second, with skin conditions there may be a primary as well as a secondary problem. In other words, some underlying disease or disorder may be causing a secondary skin problem. Often, skin problems are treated superficially with ointments or salves, etc., without regard for the actual cause of the condition. This may afford some relief, but generally the primary condition that is causing the skin problem must be found and treated before any real success is possible. Treatment should always be under a veterinarian's care, because over-the-counter remedies are often not effective. Skin disorders can be of allergic, bacterial, endocrine, parasitic, irritant, fungal, hereditary, autoimmune, immune-mediated, and unknown origins. ALLERGIC SKIN DISEASES, PARASITIC DISEASES OF THE SKIN, CONTACT DERMATITIS, and most BACTERIAL DISEASES/INFECTIONS OF THE SKIN are accompanied by extreme pruritus, or itchiness, while the ENDOCRINE-RELATED SKIN DISORDERS and FUNGAL DISEASES OF THE SKIN may or may not be. In addition to attacking the skin surface itself, bacteria can affect the hair follicles, causing FOLLICULITIS. Most of the hereditary skin diseases, such as

ACANTHOSIS NIGRICANS, COLOR MUTANT ALOPECIA, CUTANEOUS ASTHENIA, NODULAR PANNICULITIS, and ZINC-RESPONSIVE DERMATITIS, appear when a dog is very young—often under one year of age. Diagnosis of skin diseases is varied but usually includes a skin scraping and bacterial/fungal culture, blood tests, and a complete medical workup to determine underlying factors. *See also* ACRAL LICK GRANULOMAS, ACTINIC DERMATITIS, ANAL SAC IMPACTION, AUTOIMMUNE SKIN DISEASES, CONTACT DERMATITIS, IMPETIGO, IMMUNE-MEDIATED SKIN DISEASES, SCHNAUZER COMEDO SYNDROME, SEBORRHEIC SKIN DISEASE.

DERMOID: This is a congenital canine eye abnormality that has a very distinctive appearance. A piece of skinlike material with hairs growing out of it is imbedded in the otherwise crystal-clear cornea. These hairs can often remain on the cornea for a long time without causing problems, but as they elongate they will irritate the eye and may cause ulceration. A dermoid can be successfully removed with superficial surgery, which may leave a small scar.

DETACHED RETINA: The retinal tissue of the eye gets its nutrition from the vessels within it and from the choroidal blood circulation just beneath it. Sometimes the retina becomes detached from its nutrient base because of fluid accumulating between the choroid and the retina. If this occurs and is allowed to persist BLINDNESS ensues. A detached retina can be the result of a birth defect in which a dog is born with an improperly formed retina. This is common in English springer spaniels and sometimes Labrador retrievers. It can also be caused by a virus infection such as CANINE DISTEMPER or a tumor in the eye. Treatment depends on the cause and severity of the detachment. If there is a small area of detachment caused perhaps by inflammation, reducing the inflammation with medication will lead to reattachment in that area. If the detachment covers a very large area, little can be done about it in the ordinary private veterinary practice. Lasar therapy is possible to reattach a dog's retina, but it can only be performed in conjunction with a human hospital at an institution such as The Animal Medical Center or a university veterinary clinic.

DIABETES MELLITUS: This ENDOCRINE DISEASE results from a deficiency in the production of the hormone insulin by the pancreas. Insulin facilitates the entry of blood glucose into tissue cells. When there is a lack of insulin, the glucose is unable to move into tissue cells and builds up in the bloodstream. When blood-glucose levels rise to a certain point, the glucose begins to "spill" into the urine; at the same time, the body attempts to compensate for the lack of glucose-produced energy by utilizing stored fats and proteins. This leads to a number of symptoms, including weight loss, weakness, and excessive hunger, thirst, and urination. If the disorder is left untreated, strongly acidic ketone bodies accumulate in the blood as a byproduct of fat metabolism in the liver. The result is called acidosis and can produce extreme weakness, loss of appetite, vomiting, coma, and eventual death.

The cause of diabetes in most dogs is unknown, but many dogs develop the disease in conjunction with a number of other conditions, including CUSHING'S SYNDROME. The disease occurs most frequently in older dogs and is more common among unspayed females. There is a high occurrence among poodles. "Juvenile-onset" diabetes does occur, although rarely, and there seems to be a breed predilection for this type of diabetes among keeshonds and golden retrievers. Diagnosis for both types is made with blood and urine tests. Dietary control alone is almost never successful in dogs, and the disease is therefore treated with insulin injections in all but a few isolated cases. Successful treatment of canine diabetes mellitus requires owners who are able, and willing, to test a dog's urine and to administer injections daily. The two most serious complications that can occur in insulin-treated diabetic dogs are HYPOGLYCEMIA, or low-blood-sugar attacks, and CATARACT formation.

DIARRHEA: *See* GASTROINTESTINAL DISEASES AND DISORDERS.

DIGESTIVE SYSTEM TUMORS: Cancers such as carcinoma involving the stomach, small intestine, and large intestine do occur in the dog. Clinical signs include one or more of the following: vomiting, diarrhea, weight loss, blood in the stool. Diagnosis is confirmed by X ray, dye studies of the intestinal tract, or endoscopy—a visualization of the GI tract through an endoscope, which is commonly performed on human patients. The therapy of choice is surgery when appropriate. Other tumors of internal organs associated with the digestive system can develop in the liver and pancreas. Primary tumors of the liver, though infrequent, may be amenable to surgical therapy if diagnosis is early. Pancreatic cancer, unfortunately, is a disease in which successful therapy is not often possible. One tumor of the pancreas, however, is more commonly associated with the endocrine system. In this case a small part of the affected pancreas can often be surgically removed and a long-term remission of the disease can be provided. This type of cancer, referred to as an insulinoma, is most commonly associated with persistent low blood sugar, or HYPOGLYCEMIA.

DIOCTOPHYMA RENALE: This parasitic worm is only encountered in some parts of the United States. It destroys the kidneys by direct invasion of the renal tissue. Usually, only one kidney is involved, more commonly the right. Clinical signs include HEMATURIA and occasionally lethargy and low-grade back pain. Treatment consists of surgical removal of the parasite, and the prognosis is fair to good if only one kidney is involved.

DISTEMPER: *See* Infectious and Contagious Diseases.

DRY EYES: *See* DEFICIENCY OF TEAR PRODUCTION.

DYSMETRIA: This NEUROLOGIC DISORDER is an inability to regulate the rate, range, and force of movement, which causes the ataxic gait observed in CEREBELLAR DISEASE. Dysmetria usually appears as a hypermetria, or overmeasurement in the gait response, resulting in a greater movement of the limbs than normal in all motion ranges. This clinically resembles goose-stepping. (*See also* CEREBELLAR DISEASE, ATAXIA, BALANCE DISORDERS)

DYSTOCIA: Difficult birth. *See* Chapter 5.

E

EAR FISSURES: This condition affects dachshunds and other dogs with pendulous ears. Fissures, or triangular tears, develop in the ear flap edges. The cause of these tears is not known. These tears can be as big as three centimeters wide, and the ears can become extremely tender and sore. There is no effective cure for these fissures. As treatment, the edges of the ears can be trimmed and the skin sewn over the cartilage flap, but many times they retear. Tying the ears on top of the head may protect them, but if the damage is already too severe, the ears are surgically shortened to excise the affected portions completely.

EAR MARGIN DERMATOSIS, or SEBORRHEA OF THE EAR MARGINS: This condition affects dachshunds and other pendulous-eared breeds of dog and can range from mild to very severe. In a mild case, greasy plugs of wax are seen along the margins of the ears. When the disease is more severe, there can be ulceration and necrotic (dead tissue) areas that develop on the ear margins causing permanent deformities and "scalloped ears." This disease is not curable but can be controlled by washing the ear flaps with an antiseptic shampoo twice a week to dissolve the waxy, sebaceous gland secretion that collects on the margins.

EAR MITES (Otodectes Cyanotis): Ear mites are more common in cats than dogs, but dogs are sensitive to them. Ear mites are very difficult to see with the naked eye but may appear as small white specks on a background of reddish brown exudite in the ear canal opening. There is occasionally some redness and irritation of the canal and pinna. Diagnosis is made by microscopic examination of material swabbed from the ear; it will reveal tiny white mites crawling in reddish brown or blackish waste material. Treatment consists of solutions applied in the ear two or three times daily for two to three weeks.

EARS, DISEASES AND DISORDERS: *See* AURAL DISEASES AND DISORDERS.

ECLAMPSIA: Also called HYPOCALCEMIA. *See* Chapter 5 and the Emergencies section.

ECTOPIC PREGNANCY: *See* Chapter 5.

ECTOPIC URETER: This is a birth defect in which the entrance to the urethra is in an abnormal location, causing urine to flow into the urethra of males and females or the vagina in the female instead of into the dog's bladder. Ectopic ureters can occur on one or both sides. Most dogs affected by ectopic ureters have continuous URINARY INCONTINENCE. This condition can also be associated with HYDRONEPHROSIS and URINARY TRACT INFECTIONS. Treatment is surgical. The ureter is placed so that it enters the bladder normally, and the prognosis is fair to good in most cases.

EHLER-DANLOS SYNDROME: *See* CUTANEOUS ASTHENIA.

ENDOCRINE DISEASES: The endocrine glands, located in various places throughout a dog's body (*see* Illustration 18, page 191), are the manufacturers of hormones, which, when released, travel in the bloodstream throughout the body to reach another gland or part of the body. These hormones, sometimes called the chemical messengers of the body, regulate body functions in numerous ways. Because there is a tremendous amount of interaction between hormones, it is often difficult to isolate them. The tables that follow summarize the endocrine system. Table 13, page 192, lists the endocrine glands, the hormones they secrete, and the function of these hormones. Table 14, page 193, shows the disorders resulting from endocrine gland malfunctions.
Thyroid gland: Located under a dog's chin, this gland makes two main hormones, T4 and T3. The most common problem associated

with the thyroid gland is underproduction, resulting in HYPOTHYROIDISM. Hyperthyroidism, or an overproduction of these hormones, is very rare in the dog. When it does occur, it is always the result of thyroid cancer and, although it can sometimes be successfully treated with radiation and/or chemotherapy, often the dog is already too ill for treatment to be appropriate.

Parathyroid glands: There are four parathyroid glands, which lie in the soft tissue around the thyroid gland in a dog's neck and secrete parathyroid hormone, which is important in the regulation of blood calcium. A deficiency of this hormone, or hypoparathyroidism, causes the blood calcium to drop and a dog to go into a condition called tetany in which the muscles twitch and spasm the way they do in an epileptic seizure. This condition is quite rare. A tumor on a parathyroid gland will cause hyper-parathyroidism in which the blood calcium will go up and settle in the kidneys, causing the animal to go into KIDNEY FAILURE. Symptoms are all of the classic ones of kidney disease.

Adrenal glands: Two adrenal glands are located at the front of each kidney. They are divided into two parts, similar to a plum or peach—the inner part corresponding to the pit, the outer to the flesh of the fruit. Each part makes different hormones. The outer part, or adrenal cortex, manufactures cortisol/cortisone and aldosterone. Too much cortisone, or hyperadrenocortisism, results in CUSHING'S SYNDROME. A deficiency of cortisone and aldosterone, or hypoadrenocortisism, is called ADDISON'S DISEASE. Both of these diseases are quite common in the dog and are described in detail in separate listings.

Illustration 18: Location of the dog's endocrine glands

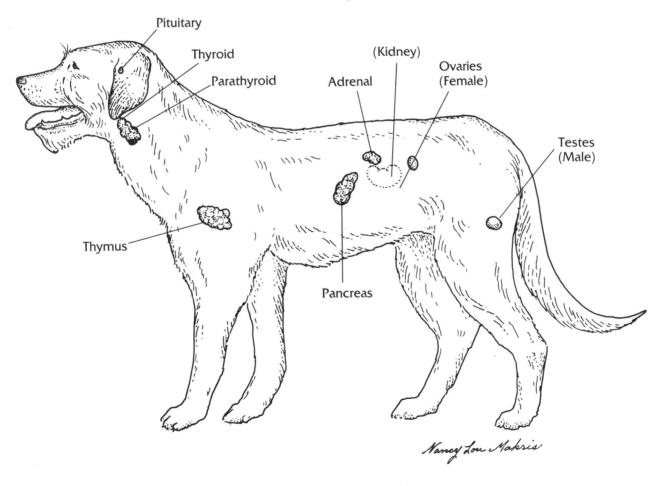

Nancy Lou Makris

TABLE 13

THE DOG'S ENDOCRINE SYSTEM

Endocrine Glands	Hormone(s)	Function
Pituitary	Adrenocorticotropic Hormone (ACTH)	Promotes growth and secretion of adrenal cortex
	Thyroid Stimulating Hormone (TSH)	Promotes growth and secretion of thyroid
	Follicular Stimulating Hormone (FSH)	Promotes growth of ovarian follicle (female) and spermatogenesis (male)
	Luteinizing Hormone (LH)	Promotes ovulation (female) and testosterone secretion (male)
	Prolactin	Promotes milk secretion from mammary gland
	Growth Hormone (GH)	Promotes growth in young dogs; elevates blood glucose
Thyroid	Thyroxine (T4), Triiodothyronine (T3)	Increase metabolic rate; necessary for hair growth
Parathyroid	Parathyroid Hormone	Increases blood calcium
Adrenal Cortex	Cortisol	Elevates blood sugar; increases protein and fat breakdown; necessary for stress
	Aldosterone	Controls sodium, chloride, and potassium balance
Adrenal Medulla	Epinephrine (Adrenaline)	Elevates blood glucose; increases blood pressure and cardiac output
Pancreas	Insulin	Promotes glucose transport from blood cells
Gonads	Estrogen, Progesterone	Necessary for fertility (females)
	Testosterone	Necessary for fertility (males)

The inner part of the adrenal gland is called the adrenal medulla; it produces adrenaline, or epinephrine. A deficiency of adrenaline won't cause any signs. Too much adrenaline can be produced by a very rare tumor called a pheochromocytoma, which will cause a dog to develop a rapid heartbeat, become nervous and sweaty, and run a mild fever.

Pancreas: This gland serves two distinct functions. One part of the pancreas is an endocrine gland; the other is an exocrine gland that releases digestive enzymes into the small intestine to help in the absorption of food. The endocrine part of the pancreas makes many hormones, the most important of which is insulin. Not enough insulin will result in DIABE-

TABLE 14

ENDOCRINE DISORDERS OF DOGS

Endocrine Gland	Malfunction	Disorder(s) Caused
Pituitary	*Deficiency* of ACTH	Addison's Disease
	Excess of ACTH	Cushing's Syndrome
	Deficiency of TSH cells	Hypothyroidism
	Deficiency of GH in young dogs	Dwarfism
	Excess of GH in older, unspayed females	Acromegaly
Thyroid	*Deficiency* of T3 and T4	Hypothyroidism
	Excess of T3 and T4 (very rare)	Hyperthyroidism
Parathyroid	*Deficiency* of parathyroid hormone	Hypoparathyroidism
	Excess of parathyroid hormone	Hyperparathyroidism
Adrenal Cortex	*Excess* of cortisol	Cushing's Syndrome
	Deficiency of cortisol and aldosterone	Addison's Disease
Adrenal Medulla	*Excess* of adrenaline (very rare)	Pheochromocytoma
Pancreas	*Deficiency* of insulin	Diabetes Mellitus
	Excess of insulin	Hypoglycemia
Gonads	*Deficiency* of estrogen and progesterone in females and of testosterone in males	Infertility

TES MELLITUS. An overproduction of insulin can be caused by a tumor of the pancreas, a condition that usually occurs in older large-breed dogs. Signs of this disorder are similar to those found in HYPOGLYCEMIA. In dogs, these tumors, called insulinomas, are almost always malignant, but in many cases they can be removed with a resulting remission of clinical signs for up to one or two years before a recurrence of the tumor occurs. This cancer can often spread to the liver, making it impossible to remove the tumor, but even then it can be treated with drugs. In both instances, the dog can be kept alive and feeling pretty good for some time. *See also* PANCREATITIS and PANCREATIC INSUFFICIENCY.

Gonads: These include both testicles in males and ovaries in females. In the male, the testicles make testosterone, which is necessary for fertility. If there is a deficiency, the sperm count goes down and the dog is no longer fertile. A deficiency of testosterone is very common in older males and presents no clinical problems other than a lack of fertility—just as in a castrated, or neutered, dog. The same pattern holds true for bitches—a deficiency of estrogen or progesterone brought about by lack of production of the gonads or by surgical spaying simply prevents an estrous or heat cycle, and renders the animal incapable of mating. Excesses of either testosterone or estrogen are very rare. In females an excess occasionally occurs because of a tumor of the ovaries. A TESTICULAR CANCER usually makes female hormones, causing a male dog to act more like a female, in extreme cases even attracting other males.

Pituitary gland: Located at the base of the brain, the pituitary is known as the "master gland" because it controls and regulates the function of many of the other glands through the action of its six major types of hormones. Adrenocorticotrophic hormone (ACTH) is released from the pituitary and regulates the adrenal cortex, which manufactures cortisone. A deficiency of this hormone is very unusual, but if there were one, the signs would be similar to those of ADDISON'S DISEASE. An excess will cause the most common type of CUSHING'S SYNDROME. Thyroid stimulating hormone, or TSH, stimulates the thyroid gland to make T4 and T3. An excess or deficiency of TSH has not been very well defined, but occasionally a tumor on the pituitary can destroy the TSH-producing cells, resulting in an underactive thyroid gland. The growth hormone, or GH, does just what it says—stimulates growth. A deficiency of this hormone in a young dog will result in a dwarf, which happens very rarely. A tumor of the GH-producing cells has never been recorded; however, we do see a condition in older, unspayed female dogs where too much progesterone and estrogen can stimulate GH cell hyperplasia, or the production of too many GH cells, forcing GH levels to go up and causing acromegaly, a condition in which the bones and tissues in an adult animal want to grow but don't have room. The result is a thickening of bones and skin, which causes wide spaces between teeth and enlarged internal organs.

Other hormones secreted by the pituitary gland are follicular stimulating hormone, or FSH, and luteinizing hormone, or LH, both of which are important in stimulating ovaries and testicles. Excesses or lacks of these hormones are rare and don't seem to cause any clinical problems. The pituitary gland also secretes prolactin, which is very important in milk secretion in the lactating bitch.

Basically, most overproduction of a hormone, known as *hyper-*, is caused by a tumor or tumors of one of the endocrine glands. Underproduction of a hormone resulting in a deficiency, or *hypo-*, is usually of unknown cause, or idiopathic. There is some evidence that hormone deficiencies are caused by an AUTOIMMUNE DISEASE, in which the body attacks its own endocrine system for unknown reasons. In general, ENDOCRINE DISEASES of the dog are treatable either by removal of the tumor or tumors causing hyper-conditions or by medications that replace missing hormones in the case of hypo-conditions, and the prognosis is good for recovery or at least for the dog's leading a normal life. Left untreated, most ENDOCRINE DISEASES will cause death in a dog within a period of one to two years. Diagnosis of these diseases is most often made by means of a combination of clinical signs and blood tests. *See also* ADDISON'S DISEASE, CUSHING'S SYNDROME, DIABETES MELLITUS, GLANDS, HYPOGLYCEMIA, HYPOTHYROIDISM.

ENDOCRINE-RELATED SKIN DISORDERS: There are a large number of skin disorders that are related to endocrine gland malfunctions. Generally, these conditions are not itchy but manifest themselves in other ways. Treatment, of course, consists of treating the underlying ENDOCRINE DISEASE *(see above)*.

A dog with hypothyroidism will have a slowly progressing alopecia, or hair loss, in a symmetrical pattern on both sides of the trunk, accompanied by a lusterless coat.

When a dog has CUSHING'S SYNDROME, its coat will thin progressively, there may be blackheads on its belly caused by the plugging of the hair follicles, and calcium deposits may appear within the skin.

A pituitary deficiency, resulting in a dwarf, may also lead to a sparse coat and hair loss. This condition is rare in the dog.

There are two dermatologic conditions that can affect female dogs with an ovarian imbalance. The first affects older, unspayed bitches, who may develop hyperpigmentation, or darkening of the skin, with variable hair loss in the posterior aspect of the body, or perivulvar region. Spaying is therapeutic. The second condition occurs in middle-aged and older bitches who were spayed very early and maintain an immature haircoat, which becomes progressively more sparse. In this case, estrogen therapy is used.

The male feminizing syndrome, discussed above in ENDOCROCRINE DISEASES and in TESTICULAR CANCER, will also cause hyperpigmentation (darkening skin) on the flanks and genital area.

Male dogs are also subject to a sertoli cell tumor, which occurs in adult males with UNDESCENDED TESTICLES (usually cryptorchid animals, with only one testicle retained). There is hair loss and hyperpigmentation of the posterior thigh. See also TESTICULAR CANCER.

Growth hormone–responsive dermatosis occurs mostly in keeshonds, chow chows, Pomeranians, and poodles. There are multifocal areas of hair loss and marked hyperpigmentation of the neck, trunk, and genital areas. This is diagnosed by what we call an exclusion diagnosis or by eliminating all other possibilities. A diagnosis is occasionally made by means of a skin biopsy. There is currently no cure for this condition.

A seminoma (testicular tumor) occurs in dogs over seven years of age and may cause hair loss. (See TESTICULAR TUMORS.)

ENDOMETRITIS: The endometrium is the glandular, secretory portion of the uterus, and endometritis implies inflammation of the endometrium. Symptoms can be a vaginal discharge, fever, and signs similar to a PYOMETRA, except that radiographically the uterus is not greatly enlarged. Treatment depends on severity and may include antibiotics and/or an ovariohysterectomy.

ENLARGED HEART: A dog's heart can gradually become enlarged as the result of any congenital or acquired HEART DISEASE. If untreated, CONGESTIVE HEART FAILURE may result.

ENTERITIS: Although this inflammatory disease of the small intestine is characterized by large volumes of watery, brown diarrhea, the frequency of bowel movements is usually not increased. Most often, the cause of enteritis is a viral disease such as parvovirus (see Infectious Diseases); but it can also be caused by INTESTINAL PARASITES, bacterial infections, and other nonspecific inflammatory diseases of unknown etiology. Treatment for enteritis depends on the underlying cause and will primarily be directed at reducing inflammation and treating the diarrhea, depending on its severity. See GASTROINTESTINAL DISEASES AND DISORDERS for treatment of diarrhea.

EPILEPSY (SEIZURE DISORDERS, ictus, "fit"): Seizures and seizurelike disorders are common entities in veterinary medicine. The term seizure refers to an involuntary paroxysmal disturbance in the normal function of the brain. Seizures may result from a variety of causes, which include infections, vascular accidents (strokes), neoplasias, posttraumatic and congenital involvement of the brain. In some instances, HYPOGLYCEMIA, LIVER DISEASE, and RENAL (KIDNEY) FAILURE may precipitate a seizure. A common classification of seizures experienced by young dogs is termed idiopathic (of unknown cause) since no other clinical signs are detected following a detailed neurologic evaluation.

A variety of types of seizures exist. The most common is a generalized grand mal seizure, which consists of an aura, prodrome, ictus, postictus, and interictus. The aura is the time prior to the seizure during which the dog can sense its onset. Restlessness, anxiety, affectionate behavior, a "blank" expression, or other behavioral changes may be noticed by an owner. The prodrome follows the aura as the dog becomes still and loses consciousness. During the ictal event there is a sudden increase in muscle tone followed by rhythmic contractions. Stiffening and running movements of the legs, chomping, and facial twitching are often seen. Urination, defecation, hypersalivation, and eye pupil changes may also be present. This phase can last from thirty seconds to three minutes but often seems longer to an apprehensive owner. During the postictal period, which follows the event, a dog may exhibit blindness, ATAXIA, confusion, depression, and fatigue, or any other kind of behavioral change. This phase can last minutes, hours, or days. It's important to note that the length of the ictus and postictus do not necessarily have a relationship to the severity of the seizure cause. In the interictal period, which follows, the dog is normal. If there is persistent behavioral change, gait disturbance, or visual problems, the veterinarian will be alerted to a nonidiopathic cause.

Partial or focal seizures may occur independently from or concurrently with grand mal seizures. Partial seizures are usually very short (five to fifteen seconds) but will often occur more frequently than grand mal seizures (two to twenty in an hour). An incomplete collapse may also be seen.

First steps in diagnosis consist of a thorough history and routine physical examination of the dog, including an attempt to characterize and localize the problem. Frequently, a neurologic examination is also performed. The decision as to when neurodiagnostic tests should be performed varies depending on history and clinical findings. Symptomatic therapy with anticonvulsants is frequently prescribed on a "trial" basis, because medications, dosages, and routes of administration depend on the individual dog's needs and change suddenly. Owners must work closely with the veterinarian by observing their pets carefully and keeping a log of each seizure event. Large-breed dogs often have seizures in clusters, with anywhere from two to twenty seizures occurring in a twenty-four-hour period. Characterization of each phase is very useful for the veterinarian. (See Appendix for the possible side effects of anticonvulsants.) Two emergency situations may occur in regard to seizures: prolonged status-epilepticus and sequence clustering— see the Emergencies section for how to proceed should these events occur.

ESOPHAGITIS: Problems with the esophagus, or "swallowing tube," of the dog are very common. Especially in younger dogs, bones and other swallowed objects can become lodged in the esophagus. Here at The AMC we often use an endoscopy to visualize the problem and remove the object. When this is not available, surgery may be required. The most common swallowed object is a bone, which can be pushed down into the stomach where it will usually be broken down by gastric acids and intestinal enzymes (see COLITIS). This, of course, should not be attempted with anything that will not be broken down in the stomach and intestines. The ingestion of a strong acid or alkali can also cause severe inflammation of the esophagus and stomach (see GASTRITIS and the Emergencies section). When the inflammation is extensive, scar tissue will form in the esophagus, creating strictures that prevent normal passage of food into the stomach with resulting regurgitation. For esophageal or stomach irritation, antacid-type medications such as Maalox are often soothing. Esophageal damage can also be caused by thermal burns, the result of a dog swallowing something very hot such as a baked potato or hamburger right off the grill. There is also a congenital esophageal disorder called PERSISTENT RIGHT AORTIC ARCH.

EYE DISEASES AND DISORDERS: See OPHTHALMIC DISEASES AND DISORDERS.

EYE INJURY: See CORNEAL TRAUMA.

EYE OUT OF SOCKET: This is an emergency problem requiring immediate veterinary attention. It is frequently seen in prominent-eyed breeds of dogs such as Boston terriers, English bulldogs, Lhasa apsos, Pekingese, pugs, and Shih-Tzus. Because these dogs' eyes are in a very shallow orbit and have extremely wide open lids, it takes very little for the globe of the eye to be forced out beyond the lids. First aid is to keep the cornea as moist as possible with cool cloth compresses and ophthalmic ointment (see also the Emergencies section). Treatment consists of surgically replacing the globe behind the eyelid and stitching the eyelid closed until the hemorrhaging and swelling that usually occur have subsided, and the globe has returned to its normal position. Vision is almost always lost, so in general the best that can be done is to save the globe. Sometimes there is an abnormal sideways deviation of the globe after surgery, but this will eventually correct itself.

F

FACIAL PARALYSIS: Diseases that interfere with the facial nerves produce a change in a dog's facial expression, such as an asymmetrical drooping of the ears and lips and an inability to blink an eye on the affected side. Facial nerve paralysis can be caused by infection, trauma, and neoplasia. A middle-ear infection is the most common cause of this problem, which may be accompanied by VESTIBULAR (inner ear) signs. To find the neuroanatomic cause of facial paralysis, have the dog given a complete neurologic examination.

FALSE PREGNANCY: *See* Chapter 5.

FAMILIAL AND CONGENITAL RENAL DISEASES: These are conditions in which the kidneys fail to develop and mature normally, resulting in small kidneys in which normal tissue is replaced by scar tissue. There are several degrees of this failure to develop properly: complete failure, or renal aplasia, and partial failure, or renal hypoplasia. When this type of disease is encountered in an individual dog without any history of former disease in any family member or predecessors, the disease is congenital. When it occurs repeatedly in a family of dogs with predecessors or family members affected, then the disease is inherited or familial.

Familial renal disease is also known as renal dysplasia and renal cortical hypoplasia, and all the familial renal diseases affect both kidneys. Breeds with a predisposition toward familial renal diseases include cocker spaniels, Alaskan malamutes, Norwegian elkhounds, Samoyeds, Doberman pinschers, Lhasa apsos, Shih Tzus, standard poodles, and basenjis. A puppy with familial renal disease will show signs of increased water intake and urine volume early in life. There is often a progression to depression, loss of appetite, vomiting, anemia, and other symptoms of UREMIA before one year of age. In rare cases, this progression of symptoms does not occur, and a dog will continue to demonstrate increased water consumption and urine volume while other symptoms of UREMIA vary in severity.

All breeds are susceptible to congenital renal disease, but these "birth defects" are rare. Specific congenital renal diseases that can occur include renal hypoplasia, renal aplasia, and polycystic renal disease. These diseases can affect one or both kidneys. When renal aplasia involves both kidneys, a puppy will die before or very shortly after birth, but if renal aplasia or hypoplasia involves only one kidney, clinical symptoms can be entirely lacking throughout life. When renal hypoplasia or polycystic renal disease involves both kidneys, then clinical signs are identical to those of familial renal disease.

Therapy for these diseases largely involves treatment of uremic symptoms, general supportive care, and parenteral fluid therapy. These treatments are not curative, and most (but not all) dogs with familial or congenital renal disease involving both kidneys die at an early age.

When congenital renal disease involves only one kidney the prognosis is good, and no treatment is needed unless the good kidney becomes involved in a second, unrelated disease.

FLEAS: *See* PARASITIC SKIN DISEASES.

FLY-BITE DERMATITIS: *See* AURAL DISEASES AND DISORDERS.

FOLLICULITIS: *See* BACTERIAL DISEASES/INFECTIONS OF THE SKIN.

FRACTURES: A fracture is a complete or incomplete break in the continuity of bone. Fractures are most commonly caused by a traumatic injury such as a fall or car accident. Infrequently, a fracture can result from a disease that causes destruction or weakening of bone, such as BONE TUMORS, or nutritional diseases affecting the bone. There are a number of different types of fractures:

Closed fracture: The fracture does not communicate to the outside environment. In other words, the skin is intact.

Open, or compound, fracture: The fracture site communicates to the outside environment. These fractures can be contaminated or infected, which may complicate fracture healing.

Green-stick fracture: One side of the bone is broken, and the other is bent. This type of fracture usually occurs in young dogs.

Comminuted fracture: Splintering or fragmentation of bone is present.

Avulsion fracture: A fragment of bone that is normally at the site of insertion of a muscle or tendon is detached following an abnormal, forceful pull.

Physeal fracture: The fracture occurs through the growth plate in a young dog.

Clinical signs of a fracture may include pain or localized tenderness, local swelling, crepitus (crackling, grating) at the fracture site, inability to use the limb, and deformity of the limb. Radiographs are necessary to determine the type and precise location of the fracture. Treatment of a fracture should first be directed at possible injury to other parts of the dog's body, such as abdominal or chest injuries. Fracture repair is divided into conservative management, using casts or splints, and surgical repair utilizing metal plates, pins, or wires. The location and type of fracture, degree of instability, age and size of the dog, and economic limitations of the owner will dictate the type of repair utilized. Prognosis depends on the type of fracture, associated joint injury incurred, whether the fracture is contaminated or infected initially, and if the optimum means of repair was utilized based on the type of fracture and assessment of the patient. See also DELAYED UNION, and NONUNION. For handling of a dog with a suspected fracture, *see* the Emergencies section.

FRAGMENTED MEDIAL CORONOID PROCESS (FCP): This is a fragmentation of a portion of one of the forearm bones (ulna) where it articulates with other leg bones at the elbow of the dog. This condition is usually seen between the ages of five and nine months and is common in retrievers and rottweilers, although several other large breeds can also be affected. Signs are foreleg lameness or stiffness, which is worsened by exercise and is often noticeable immediately after resting. The condition can be accompanied by OSTEOCHONDRITIS DISSECANS (OCD) of the medial humeral condyle (the articular surface of the humerus). Diagnosis of both conditions is based on orthopedic examination, radiographs and, occasionally, surgical exploration. Treatment is by surgical removal of the fragmented coronoid process and, if also present, removal of the OCD cartilage flap. Prognosis is dependent on early diagnosis and surgical removal of the FCP and on the degree of DEGENERATIVE ARTHRITIS that develops.

FUNGAL DISEASES OF THE SKIN: An important point to make about canine fungal diseases is "if it looks like a fungus, it probably isn't." Canine fungal diseases and skin lesions generally bear no resemblance to those that occur in humans, although they are contagious to humans and to other animals. They are treated with oral antifungal medication as well as topical therapy, and because of potential contagion and reinfection, environmental control is very important.

There are three types of Dermatophytes (fungi) that affect dogs: microsporum canis, which is commonly contracted from cats; microsporum gypseum, which is a common soil contaminant; and trichophyton mentagrophytes, which is carried by rodents.

Subcutaneous mycoses (fungal infections beneath the skin) are rare and cause draining nodules.

Zygomycosis is a fungal infection caused by exposure to water and soil and affects the extremities and base of the tail. It is rare.

Mycetomas cause chronic draining lesions on the feet and legs, with granules in the exudate. Aspergillosus begins with respiratory signs and may later appear as subcutaneous lesions in the nasal cavity, progressing to deep ulcers. Systemic mycoses (internal fungal infections) can cause skin lesions as well. In some parts of the country, chronic respiratory diseases often precede skin lesions. Diagnosis must be made by means of seriologic tests.

G

GASTRITIS: This is a nonspecific term meaning inflammation of the stomach. It is a very common problem in canine medicine and occurs primarily when a dog ingests something irritating or caustic such as plant material, garbage, etc. Vomiting is the hallmark of gastritis, which usually clears up after routine therapy. *See* GASTROENTERITIS.

GASTROENTERITIS: This is a more severe inflammation of the stomach and intestines than GASTRITIS and is characterized by vomiting and diarrhea. In routine cases, treatment consists of an antiemetic or antidiarrheal injection, followed by oral antispasmodic medication, which is usually given for three to five days at home. *See* GASTROINTESTINAL DISEASES AND DISORDERS for a feeding routine after vomiting/diarrhea.

GASTROINTESTINAL (GI) DISEASES AND DISORDERS: Most of the problems that occur in the dog's digestive tract are inflammations, which can be caused by the ingestion of foreign bodies or substances; infections, either viral or bacterial; INTESTINAL PARASITES; systemic disorders; cancers, or DIGESTIVE SYSTEM TUMORS; and congenital abnormalities, such as PANCREATIC INSUFFICIENCY, PERSISTENT RIGHT AORTIC ARCH, and sometimes portocaval anomalies, causing HEPATIC ENCEPHALOPATHY. Poor diet and obesity can also lead to PANCREATITIS. GI problems in the dog are almost always characterized by vomiting or diarrhea or a combination of both, but sometimes nonspecific anorexia, or appetite loss, and an attendant weight loss is the only symptom of disease. When any of these symptoms persist, we must suspect something potentially serious.

Vomiting: This is a nonspecific sign of the GI tract that doesn't necessarily mean that a dog has a primary GI disorder, although it is usually related to a problem in this area. It can also be a symptom of systemic disease, such as DI-ABETES MELLITUS, KIDNEY DISEASE, LIVER DISEASE, or an electrolyte disturbance. In young puppies it can indicate an infectious disease such as parvovirus, INTESTINAL PARASITES, or the presence of foreign bodies or substances in the GI tract. Vomiting is often accompanied by drooling and/or salivating, and the dog is in obvious discomfort. Owners often mistake regurgitation for vomiting. Regurgitation usually occurs almost immediately after eating. The food is not digested and often comes up in a long tube-shaped form. Regurgitation is not accompanied by retching or abdominal contractions, and the animal is not uncomfortable. Persistent regurgitation implies esophageal disease.

Diarrhea: Diarrhea can also be the result of a number of different problems, systemic and other. It can take several forms and generally, when it is very frequent, mucoid (with mucous) and bloody, it can be assumed to be from the colon; when it is voluminous but of normal frequency with no blood or mucous, it is probably from higher up in the digestive tract.

Most dogs tolerate vomiting and diarrhea well. If a dog seems happy and continues to have an appetite, the attack will probably be self-limiting and an owner can afford to treat the dog at home, as described below. If, however, vomiting/diarrhea doesn't clear up in twenty-four hours, or an animal is feverish, depressed, lethargic, and obviously ill or in pain, professional help should be sought immediately. This is an emergency and could be the sign of an infectious disease, such as parvovirus, or of GASTRIC DILATATION/TORSION COMPLEX ("Bloat")—*see* the Emergencies section.

Treatment of routine vomiting and/or diarrhea usually consists of withholding food for twelve to twenty-four hours, and if vomiting is severe, water is also withheld for a period of time. This is done because if a dog continues to vomit when water is given, it is losing body fluids and electrolytes in addition to the water, and this can lead to dehydration and electrolyte imbalance. After a period of time, a few ice cubes can be given to the dog, and then water can be increased gradually as long as it is being held down. At the same time, Kaopectate or Pepto-Bismol remedies, given according to the veterinarian's instructions, will calm the dog's stomach and help to stop the diarrhea. After twenty-four hours, bland food can be started. Whole-grain rice, combined with chicken or chopped meat that has been boiled to remove the fat, is digestible and binding. Strained baby food is also recommended for a dog recovering from a GI disorder.

If a vomiting/diarrhea attack has been more severe, a veterinarian will often give the dog an antiemetic or antidiarrheal injection followed by antispasmodic/antibacterial medication.

In cases where a GI disorder does not respond to treatment, the veterinarian may perform further tests such as abdominal X rays or a barium series to determine the problem. *See also* COLITIS, ENTERITIS, ESOPHAGITIS, GASTRITIS, and GASTROENTERITIS.

GLANDS: The word *glands* is used correctly in reference to the endocrine glands, which secrete hormones and are located throughout a dog's body. However, sometimes *glands* is also used incorrectly to refer to the lymph nodes, which are also located throughout a dog's body. The term is often used, in particular, when referring to the lymph nodes that are located directly under the jaws and ears—as in "swollen glands." Swollen glands are commonly caused by a systemic infection, or LYMPHOSARCOMA.

GLAUCOMA: Glaucoma is a general term that refers to increased pressure within the eye. It is seen in dogs only occasionally, but when it does occur it is an emergency situation. It happens when the fluid, or aqueous humor, which is constantly manufactured, circulated through the eye, and drained out, fails to drain properly because of scarring or inflammation of the drainage area. This area, known as the iridocorneal angle, extends 360 degrees around the circumference of the eye. Sometimes LENS LUXATION can block the proper flow of fluid in the eye. When the fluid does not drain, pressure builds up within the eye. With an acute rise in interocular pressure, damage can be done to the optic nerve within twelve to eighteen hours, irreparably harming vision. Symp-

toms of glaucoma are extreme discomfort, squinting, red eyes, widely dilated pupils, and a hazy blue cast to the cornea. There are a number of surgical and medical techniques used in dealing with glaucoma. All of these treatments consist basically of trying to reduce pressure as quickly as possible, before damage is done. If treatment is unsuccessful and vision is lost, pain very often remains, and further treatment may be necessary to make the dog comfortable.

GLOMERULONEPHRITIS (GN): This kidney disease damages the glomerulus. The glomerulus supplies blood to the tubule that comprises the rest of the nephron (*see* RENAL DISEASES AND DISORDERS for a description of parts of the kidneys). Damage to the glomerulus ultimately leads to damage of the tubule and the entire nephron. GN affects virtually all of the glomeruli when it occurs and involves both kidneys. The cause of GN is not clear, but it is related to exposure to an antigen that is foreign to the body and that causes the body's immune system to produce an antibody. In GN, the antibody and antigen combine to form soluble complexes that circulate in the blood, and when they are filtered by the glomeruli, they damage the kidneys. If there is an ongoing exposure to an antigen, and antibody production continues, GN persists and worsens until severe kidney damage occurs. If the production of antibodies ceases because exposure to the antigen stops, GN can stabilize or resolve. The antigens that can cause GN are rarely identified. When they are identified, some can be removed (e.g., tumors, PYOMETRA, HEARTWORM DISEASE). More often, they are systemic disease states such as SYSTEMIC LUPUS, extensive tumors, etc., and cannot be removed.

Clinical symptoms of GN may include fluid in the body tissues (edema) and body cavities. This is the result of glomerular damage that brings about loss of albumin (protein), which is necessary to hold fluid in the blood vascular compartment. When low-blood-albumin concentration occurs, it will result in loss of water from the blood to the tissues, causing edema. This is not an invariable clinical sign of GN, however. Other signs include those of UREMIA, since damage occurs to all of the nephrons.

Treatment consists of diuretics, or water pills, when edema is present. Otherwise it involves supportive care, parenteral fluids, and antibiotics. Specific therapy aims at suppressing the production of antibody and/or removal of antigen(s) when possible. The prognosis is guarded.

GROWTH PLATE DISORDERS: Conformational abnormalities of the limbs can result from damage to the growth plate of immature dogs. Growth plate disorders can result from trauma in dogs generally three to six-and-a-half months of age, and they usually involve the bones of the forelimb (the radius and ulna). Damage to the growth plate of one bone results in cessation of growth of that particular leg bone, while the other leg bone continues to grow, resulting in limb deformities, joint damage, or a shortened limb. Surgical treatment is often required. Prognosis depends on the age and breed of the dog, the particular growth plate involved, and the degree of deformity present at the time of diagnosis.

H

HEART DISEASE: *See* CARDIAC DISEASE.

HEART MURMUR: Heart murmurs may commonly accompany many heart diseases in dogs. Therapy is not directed at the murmur per se but rather at the underlying cause of the murmur when this cause warrants treatment.

HEARTWORM DISEASE: This acquired CARDIAC DISEASE in dogs is transmitted from an infected animal to a healthy one through the bite of a mosquito. When an infected dog is bitten, the mosquito ingests some of the immature larve present in the infected animal's bloodstream. These are then deposited into another dog's skin. The infective larvae then develop and, after several changes, find their way through the bloodstream to the dog's heart and lungs. Eventually, they will cause severe changes in the right side of the heart resulting in an ENLARGED HEART, CONGESTIVE HEART FAILURE, lung abnormalities, and eventual death. Owners can easily prevent this disease with a small amount of time, effort, and expense (*see below*).

Symptoms are essentially those of other CARDIAC DISEASES, including coughing, lethargy, loss of appetite, and general signs that a dog is not thriving. Diagnosis is made by a blood test that is given yearly in most parts of the country —more often where mosquitoes are found year-round. Prevention: Once it has been ascertained that a dog is uninfected, there is a commercial medication in pill or liquid form that is given daily before, during, and beyond the mosquito season. This medication will prevent the dog from contracting the disease if bitten by an infected mosquito. In areas that have a year-round mosquito season, the preventive measures may differ. A local veterinarian will know how best to protect a dog. It is important to note that a blood test to determine that a dog is not already infected is essential before giving heartworm-preventive medication as the dog can be made very sick otherwise.

If a bood test indicates that the dog is infected, treatment is necessary. Most often, a dog is given controlled doses of intravenous medication to kill the worms. This treatment may sometimes cause a dog to become sick. Careful monitoring of the animal throughout the period when the medication is being given and for some time afterward is essential. The prognosis for a dog treated for heartworm disease depends on the severity of the infestation and on how much damage has already been done to the heart and lungs, but it is generally good.

HEMANGIOSARCOMAS: Hemangiosarcomas are malignancies arising from the blood-vascular system, most often caused by the abnormal proliferation of blood vessel walls. They are generally associated with older large-breed dogs, most particularly the German shepherd and shepherd mixes, and most commonly involve the spleen. Symptoms include acute weakness, abdominal distention, and an associated anemia. These tumors are prone to rupture and cause blood loss as a result of hemorrhage (*see* the Emergencies section). Surgery is the treatment of choice; however, the prognosis must be extremely guarded, as this is a highly malignant tumor. In diagnosing this condition, exploratory surgery and biopsy are recommended because a hematoma, or blood clot, of the spleen may resemble and imitate a hemangiosarcoma. If this is the case, surgical removal of the spleen would cure the dog.

HEMATOPOIETIC TUMORS: These are liquid tumors of the blood-forming elements, such as LEUKEMIA and LYMPHOSARCOMA. See also ONCOLOGY.

HEMATURIA: This is a condition in which there are an abnormally large number of red blood cells present in the urine. The causes of hematuria can be infections such as CYSTITIS, PYLONEPHRITIS, URINARY TRACT STONES; tumors anywhere from the kidneys to the urethra; and trauma. In rare cases, the cause can be HYDRONEPHROSIS, with or without stones; RENAL CYSTS; and DIOCTOPHYMA RENALE. Other clinical signs that may be present are straining to urinate (STRANGURIA); an urge to go out to urinate often (POLLAKIURIA); inability to pass urine; and blood in the urine. If hematuria is suspected, the veterinarian should be consulted for tests and treatment.

HEMOPHILIA: Hemophilia is a hereditary blood-clotting disorder caused by the deficiency of a needed clotting factor. This condition most often occurs in purebred dogs, although mixed-breed dogs may be affected. The clinical signs are influenced by several factors including the severity of the deficiency, the size of the dog, and the degree of organ impairment induced by hemorrhage. Large, frisky breeds may bleed into their joints. There may be bleeding from the mouth, which is usually noticed when the dog is teething; bruising; or bleeding from the gastrointestinal or urinary tract. Specialized blood tests include factor analysis and coagulation (clotting) studies. The lifelong treatment of hemophiliacs can be quite difficult in the case of severe deficiencies. Because this is a hereditary condition, these animals should not be used for breeding. Animals who carry the hemophiliac trait but who themselves are not clinically affected can be detected by the use of blood tests and should also be prevented from breeding.

HEPATIC ENCEPHALOPATHY: Liver failure. *See* LIVER DISEASE.

HEPATITIS, INFECTIOUS CANINE: *See* Chapter 6.

HIP DYSPLASIA: This is a developmental disease recognized in most breeds of dogs. It tends to occur in larger fast-growing breeds. Several causes for the disease are known, including genetic, environmental, and dietary factors. Several anomalies are identified radiographically or pathologically: joint looseness (laxity), shallow joints, dislocation of the hips, erosion of the articular cartilage, remodeling of the bony surfaces of the joint, and secondary degenerative joint disease. There are marked differences in the severity of clinical signs, the age of onset at which signs appear, the rate of disease progression, and the degree of pain and associated lameness.

Joint looseness is one of the earlier signs of hip dysplasia. Often changes in the normal gait of the dog are seen before limping or stiffness of the hind legs is seen. Young dogs with loose hips may develop episodes of lameness, particularly after strenuous exercise. With time, DEGENERATIVE ARTHRITIS develops in the hips, causing additional pain and discomfort. Treatment is mainly symptomatic and varies with the stage of the disease. In early stages of the disease there can be laxity and looseness in the hip joints, associated with pain and minimal DEGENERATIVE ARTHRITIS. Rest, exercise restriction, and analgesic drugs (aspirin, for instance) may be adequate at this time. As DEGENERATIVE ARTHRITIS develops and becomes more severe, anti-inflammatory drugs, such as steroids and other analgesic-type drugs, may be required. Several different surgical procedures may improve this condition.

HISTIOCYTOMAS: These skin tumors usually occur in young dogs. Most often they are self-limiting and benign and regress spontaneously with time or are cured by surgery. Because of their appearance, they may frequently be misdiagnosed as a malignant form of skin cancer, which occurs more often in older dogs.

HOOKWORM DERMATITIS: *See* PARASITIC DISEASES OF THE SKIN and INTESTINAL PARASITES.

HORNER'S SYNDROME: This syndrome occurs when the sympathetic nervous system is disrupted along its neuroanatomical route. The classic signs of this disorder include a smaller eye pupil on the side involved, protrusion of the third eyelid, a retraction of the eye globe, and a drooping of the upper eyelid. Common causes of this disorder include injury to the high thoracic spinal cord, avulsions (ripping) of the nerve plexus of the front legs, and a middle-ear inflammation. Diagnosis and treatment depend on the neuroanatomical location of the injured pathway of the sympathetic nervous system.

HYDROCEPHALUS: *See* Chapter 6.

HYDRONEPHROSIS: This is a KIDNEY DISEASE resulting from obstruction to urine outflow anywhere in the ureter. More rarely, obstruction of the urethra can eventually lead to hydronephrosis. Common causes include URINARY TRACT STONES, tumors in and outside of the urinary tract, trauma, bleeding with blood-clot formation in the urinary tract, and congenital anomalies involving the urinary tract that cause obstruction. There are often no signs, but when infection is present, with or without stones, symptoms can include those of CYSTITIS. Intermittent blood in the urine can also occur without other signs being present.

Treatment aims at relieving urinary tract obstruction if possible. If one kidney is severely damaged, it can be surgically removed as long as the other kidney is normal and/or is capable of sustaining adequate renal function. The prognosis varies. It is guarded when both kidneys are involved, but when only one kidney is involved and the cause of hydronephrosis can be corrected, the prognosis is fair to good.

HYPERTROPHIC OSTEOARTHROPATHY: This is a bone disease resulting in proliferation of new bone along the shaft of bones of the front or rear legs. Signs include lameness, reluctance to move, and swelling of the limbs. Most victims are middle aged or older. The disease is generally associated with neoplasia (cancer) or an infection in the chest cavity. Radiographs are required to diagnose the disease. Treatment is aimed at curing the chest disease if possible. The prognosis is dependent on the type of chest disease and is generally poor.

HYPERTROPHIC OSTEODYSTROPHY (HOD): This is a bone disease affecting the metaphysis (the area of bone adjacent to the growth plate) of young, large or giant-breed dogs. The cause and cure remain unknown. Affected dogs have mild to moderate swelling of the ends of the radius and ulna or tibia. Signs include limping, fever, depression, and loss of appetite. The age of onset is generally three to seven months. The disease is diagnosed by physical examination and radiographs. Treatment is directed at controlling fever and reducing pain. Most dogs show a spontaneous recovery, but in severe cases, permanent bone deformities may result.

HYPOCALCEMIA: Also called ECLAMPSIA. *See* Chapter 5.

HYPOGLYCEMIA (Low Blood Sugar): Hypoglycemia in dogs is almost always caused by one of two ENDOCRINE DISEASE factors: a tumor of the pancreas resulting in an overproduction of insulin, which produces the same symptoms as low blood sugar, or a complication arising in an insulin-treated diabetic dog. Symptoms are always neurologic, because the brain requires a constant supply of blood sugar. Signs usually include weakness and seizures; the dog may also have an increased appetite. Because of the seizures, this condition is frequently misdiagnosed as EPILEPSY. Treatment is dependent on the cause. If the cause is a tumor, it can be removed; in the case of a diabetic dog, the veterinarian will have to adjust the insulin dosage. *See also* the Emergencies section.

HYPOTHYROIDISM: This is a fairly common ENDOCRINE DISEASE, the result of an underproduction of T4 and T3 by the thyroid gland. It can appear in any age dog but is more common in young to middle-aged animals. There is a breed predilection toward this disease among Doberman pinschers, Great Danes, golden retrievers, and Irish setters.

Symptoms of the disease vary but usually include lethargy, fatigue, and increased somnolence. Most dogs also slow down mentally, becoming less alert and excitable. Some dogs gain weight, but others remain at their normal weight or lose. Hypothyroidism can also produce skin and coat changes including scaling, a dry, sparse coat, and sometimes a dark pigmentation of the skin. Some dogs lose a great deal of hair, especially over the neck, hind thighs, flanks, and abdomen. Others develop thickened skin folds over their faces and foreheads. Diagnosis of the disease is made by blood test, in addition to clinical observation. Hypothyroidism in dogs is treated with daily oral medication that replaces the missing hormone. Once the disease is treated, the prognosis is excellent, and the dog's life span should be normal.

I

IDIOPATHIC IMMUNE-MEDIATED ARTHRITIS: This is a common arthritis disorder caused by an immune-mediated phenomenon. Antibody complexes in the dog's circulation are either deposited or formed within the joint, causing reaction in the joint lining and fluid production. The precise cause of the immunologic basis for the disease is unknown. Signs include fever, depression, loss of appetite, lameness, general limb stiffness, and swelling of the joints. Diagnosis is based on orthopedic examination, radiology, and blood tests. The disease has to be differentiated from INFECTIOUS, RHEUMATOID, and SYSTEMIC LUPUS ERYTHEMATOSUS ARTHRITIS. Treatment involves the use of steroids, alone or in combination with immunosuppressive drugs. Prognosis is generally good, although recurrences commonly occur after drug therapy has been discontinued.

IMMUNE-MEDIATED SKIN DISEASES: There are a number of immune disorders that affect dogs' skin. They are relatively uncommon and difficult to diagnose, yet owners should be aware of them. Several of these diseases are currently under study. These diseases are dermatitis herpetiformes, toxic epiermal microlosis (TEN), drug eruptions, epidermolysis bullosa dermatomyositis (seen most often in collies and Shetland sheep dogs), and subcorneal pustular dermatosis (SPD).

IMMUNE-MEDIATED THROMBOCYTOPENIA (IMT), or low platelets: This condition is caused by antibody destruction of the dog's platelets, a component of the blood necessary for normal blood clotting. In some cases, IMT may be associated with, or traced to, recent vaccinations and/or drug therapy. Signs of this disease include pale mucous membranes, bruises, bleeding from the nose or urinary tract, or possibly bloody diarrhea. Diagnosis is made by means of blood tests, bone marrow aspiration, and a special platelet antibody test. Like AUTOIMMUNE HEMOLYTIC ANEMIA, IMT is initially treated with corticosteroids. Blood transfusions are sometimes necessary if the problem is severe. The prognosis is variable, but in many cases long-term control is possible.

IMPETIGO: *See* BACTERIAL DISEASES/INFECTIONS OF THE SKIN.

INFECTIOUS BACTERIAL ARTHRITIS: This condition results from the presence of bacteria within a joint. Bacteria may gain entrance into a joint by a penetrating injury (e.g., a bite wound); from bacterial septicemias, in which bacteria within the bloodstream are carried into the joint; and as a complication of joint surgery. Signs include a painful joint, swelling of the joint, lameness, fever, and depression.

Diagnosis is made by orthopedic examination and aspiration of joint fluid via a sterile needle, followed by microscopic examination and culture of the fluid for confirmation of the specific type of bacteria. Radiographs may demonstrate the degree of joint damage and help establish a diagnosis. Treatment with appropriate antibiotics for several weeks is necessary. Surgical therapy may be indicated to drain and flush the joint and assess the amount of damage caused by the infection. Complications of infectious arthritis include spread of the infection into adjacent bones (i.e., OSTEOMYELITIS, fusion or ankylosis of the joint, and secondary DEGENERATIVE ARTHRITIS). Prognosis is dependent on the number of joints infected, how quickly and effectively the joint infections are treated, the amount of damage to the joint caused by the infection, the particular joint involved, and the dog's size and activity level.

INFECTIOUS CANINE HEPATITIS: *See* LIVER DISEASE and Infectious and Contagious Diseases.

INFERTILITY: *See* Chapter 5.

INFRASPINATUS MUSCLE FIBROTIC CONTRACTURE: This is a condition causing shoulder lameness in hunting or working dogs because the muscle has been replaced with scar tissue. This occurs as a result of trauma causing a partial rupture of the infraspinatus muscle (one of the major supportive muscles of the shoulder joint, which also flexes the joint normally). Diagnosis is based on orthopedic examination. Treatment consists of surgically cutting the tendon of insertion of the infraspinatus muscle. The prognosis is good.

INTERVERTEBRAL DISC DISEASE: Intervertebral disc protrusion/extrusion occurs in all breeds of dogs but is most common in the chondrodystrophic breeds, such as dachshunds and Pekingese. It also has a high incidence in miniature poodles, beagles, and cocker spaniels. It may occur in these breeds as a result of early spontaneous degeneration of disc material and usually develops at less than two years of age.

A majority of intervertebral disc protrusions occur in the high back or low neck. The signs caused by extruded disc material vary from pain without other neurologic signs to mild or severe limb weakness and ATAXIA. A complete neurologic examination is essential. In general, the more function that is lost to the limbs, the more severe the spinal cord compression caused by a "slipped disc." Proprioception is lost first, followed by motor dysfunction and sensory loss, which may range from mild to severe. Complete loss of proprioception, motor function, and sensation to the limbs suggests near complete or complete loss of normal spinal cord functions. The prognosis is poor in these instances. Many gradations exist. A veterinarian or veterinary neurologist should be consulted prior to making any medical or surgical decision about treating a dog with this disorder.

INTESTINAL PARASITES: Intestinal parasites are the most common cause of diarrhea in the dog. Diagnosis is usually made by microscopic examination of a stool sample. Sometimes a blood count is also performed to help confirm diagnosis. Because some dogs can have perfectly normal stools while harboring parasites, a yearly stool-sample analysis should be part of every dog's health routine. Although there are some anthelmintics (deworming medications) on the market, it is best to let the veterinarian decide on the type of medication to use and the method of deworming the dog.

Roundworms (Ascarids): These are the most common canine parasites. They lodge in the small intestine and are usually not a problem for older dogs. They are, however, generally present in newborn puppies, who have been infected by their mothers (*see* Chapter 5). Although humans can get roundworms by ingesting their eggs, the worm can only complete its life cycle in the dog and will only grow into the larval stage in people. Cases have been reported of the larvae migrating into human tissue and causing problems, but this is very rare.

Hookworms (Ancylostoma): Also a very common intestinal parasite, which lodges in the dog's small intestine, hookworms are associated with vomiting and diarrhea—in severe cases, bloody diarrhea. Occasionally, a heavy hookworm infestation in a young pup can result in ANEMIA and other complications. (See HOOKWORM DERMATITIS.)

Whipworms (Trichuris vulpis): These parasites usually reside in the dog's cecum (the junction of the small and large intestine) and, because they cause inflammation in the lower part of the GI tract, their symptoms may mirror those of COLITIS. Signs may vary, however. Whipworms can be very difficult to diagnose, as the eggs often don't show up in a stool sample. Therefore, veterinarians often treat a dog for whipworms when clinical signs are present, and the final diagnosis is based on the animal's response to treatment.

Roundworms, hookworms, and whipworms are all nematodes, which have a direct life cycle in which the eggs that are ingested by a dog hatch, develop into larvae, and then into adult worms in the dog's body.

Tapeworms (Cestodes): Unlike the above parasites, tapeworms must go through an intermediate host in order for growth and larvae forms to develop. In the dog, the most common host is the flea, which ingests the eggs and hosts the larvae. The dog then ingests the flea, with its resident tapeworm. Therefore, flea control is essential when treating a dog for tapeworms, or the animal will reinfest itself. Tapeworms usually do not cause any clinical signs, although diarrhea may be present, and they are virtually impossible to detect by microscopic examination. They are visible to owners as little grains, or "packets," resembling rice, which are seen around the dog's rectum or in its stools. The worms may tickle, and a dog with tapeworms will often rub its rear end along the ground, mimicking ANAL GLAND IMPACTION.

Puppies are also prone to contracting protazoan parasites. Coccidia and Giardia, both parasites of the small intestine, can cause watery diarrhea. Coccidia as a rule is strictly a puppy parasite, which can get into the pup via the mother or through the environment. Giardia is usually environmental in origin and can also infest adult dogs. It is often endemic in wildlife around ponds or lakes, where it gets into the water and is then ingested by dogs who drink. Giardia is transferable to and from humans. Coccidia is usually treated with sulfas,

and Giardia with Flagyl, or metronidazole.

IRIS ATROPHY: An older dog may have a loss of muscle tone in the sphincter of the irises of the eyes, resulting in an inability to close the pupil in bright light and causing the dog to squint. This is not a significant visual problem, although the loss of pupillary movement can be quite upsetting to owners.

K

KENNEL COUGH: *See* TRACHEOBRONCHITIS.

KIDNEY DISEASES AND DISORDERS: *See* RENAL DISEASES AND DISORDERS.

KIDNEY FAILURE: *See* RENAL FAILURE.

L

LARYNGEAL DISEASE: Signs or symptoms of problems in the larynx, or "voice box," of the dog include phonational changes, or hoarseness of the voice, and difficulty breathing, particularly during inspiration (breathing in). This is because the larynx is located at the beginning of the trachea; so if there's a problem with the larynx, the intake of air can be compromised. Many puppies born with severe congenital problems of the larynx simply will not survive. Invasive laryngeal tumors are not very amenable to surgical excision because of their location. Problems of postoperative aspiration of food particles can occur if the surgery is extensive. Edema, or swelling of the larynx, can occur when there has been excessive barking or panting; most often it is associated with a dog who has been closed in a hot car. Treatment consists of cooling the dog down and treating him for heatstroke, which will usually reduce the swelling. Laryngeal paralysis, in which the larynx is paralysed in a closed position, will produce a very weak, hoarse bark and will cause the animal to breath very stridulously. This condition can be congenital and commonly occurs in Bouvier des Flandres and sled dogs. It is also often an acquired disorder in large-breed, older, long-nosed dogs. Treatment of this disorder is surgical removal of part of the paralyzed tissue so the laryngeal opening is enlarged. Laryngeal collapse is usually the final event in the brachycephalic syndrome. It is caused by a combination of STENOTIC NARES, SOFT PALATE DISORDERS, and other abnormalities of the nasal and pharyngeal passageways that have put so much wear and tear on the larynx that it eventually collapses.

LEGG-CALVE PERTHES DISEASE (Aseptic necrosis): This is a noninfectious necrosis of the head and neck of the femur (top end of the leg bone leading into the hip joint). The cause of the necrosis is not precisely known. The bone of the femoral head and neck dies and is gradually resorbed, resulting in collapse of bone and deformation of the hip joint. The condition leads to degenerative changes in the hip and to the development of ARTHRITIS. Clinical signs include lameness and pain associated with the hip joint. Small breeds and terriers are most susceptible to this disease. Age of onset is usually five to nine months. Radiographs are required to confirm the diagnosis. Surgical treatment is recommended. With surgical correction, the prognosis is generally good.

LENS LUXATION: The lens of a dog's eye is held in place by fine little fibers, which can become weak and torn with age, allowing the lens to move around inside the eye abnormally. This is known as lens luxation. If the lens stays in the posterior part of the eye, it is not a major problem. If, however, it moves to the forward part of the eye it can block the flow of fluid within the eye and lead to GLAUCOMA.

LENTICULAR SCLEROSIS (NUCLEAR SCLEROSIS): This is a universal condition of all dogs over eight to ten years of age, in which the lenses of the eyes take on a hazy appearance. It is a result of the natural growth of the lens, which adds layers like an onion all through life and becomes more and more densely packed as a dog ages. It is a normal age change and does not affect vision.

LEPTOSPIROSIS: *See* Infectious and Contagious Diseases.

LEUKEMIA: Leukemia exists in dogs as in humans in two forms, acute and chronic. Acute leukemia is a rapid-onset process in which general symptoms range in severity from simple fatigue to overt bleeding and hemorrhage from the body. The most common leukemia seen in dogs is acute lymphoid leukemia, which may occur in either young dogs or older animals. This is because it has what are called "bi-peaked-phases," just as it does in humans. Diagnosis is made by the use of blood tests and a specialized bone-marrow examination. Chemotherapy is the treatment of choice, and prognosis is guarded.

Chronic leukemia in the dog exists in several cell lines of the blood-forming elements, and the prognosis with very moderate therapy is extremely good. Sometimes, however, a "blast crisis," which resembles acute leukemia, may occur. This may happen months to years following the original diagnosis, and treatment and prognosis will then be the same as for acute leukemia. Diagnosis is made by blood tests and bone-marrow examination, as above, in order to differentiate between chronic and acute leukemia. Symptoms resemble those of acute leukemia but are usually much less severe and may often go unnoticed for long periods of time before diagnosis is sought for persistent nonspecific signs of moderate illness.

LICE: *See* PARASITIC DISEASES OF THE SKIN.

LIVER DISEASE: Liver disease in dogs is often very nonspecific. As in humans, liver disease in dogs is characterized by icterus, or jaundice, and ascites, or abdominal distention, caused by fluid accumulation in the abdominal cavity, and is often accompanied by other signs such as vomiting, diarrhea, and loss of appetite. Because the liver has an enormous regenerative capacity, liver disease may progress for a long time with no clinical signs at all, until it reaches a critical point. If there is inflammation of the liver cells it is called a hepatitis, but if the inflammation is in conjunction with the bile ducts or gallbladder, it is called a cholangitis.

Dogs do suffer from cirrhosis of the liver. Its cause is essentially unknown, except that there has been some kind of chronic inflammatory liver disease, which has resulted in destruction of the normal tissues and the formation of scar tissue.

Because dogs are now routinely vaccinated against it, we rarely see INFECTIOUS CANINE HEPATITIS any more, except occasionally in very young dogs who have not yet been immunized. Sometimes we see a condition known as HEPATIC ENCEPHALOPATHY, in which the liver completely fails to eliminate toxic products from the body. In young dogs, this can be a congenital problem, which causes the blood from the intestines to bypass the liver, where it would normally go to be detoxified, and instead go directly into the general circulation. The toxins in the blood will then immediately cause the dog to lapse into a coma or go into a seizure, especially after eating a meal high in meat proteins. Dietary therapy is important in these cases, with dairy proteins being substituted for meat and meat-type proteins, which are high in toxic products.

LUNG CANCER: There are two types of lung cancer seen in dogs: primary lung cancer and secondary lung cancer, which has metastasized from another part of the body, such as the mammary glands. A diagnosis is made by X ray and a specialized biopsy. Coughing may be the only symptom of canine lung cancer. Surgery is the treatment of choice for primary lung cancer. Treatment for cancer that has spread from other parts of the body depends on the specific diagnosis, and chemotherapy is the treatment of choice. In most cases, chemotherapy will not cure the disease but it may provide prolonged, useful, good-quality life by slowing down the rate of disease progression.

LYMPHOSARCOMA: Lymphosarcoma is a disease of the lymphoid tissue of the body. It is considered a treatable but not curable disease. It is similar to non-Hodgkins lymphoma in humans. Signs can be vague and range from swollen lymph nodes, listlessness, weakness, and general lack of energy to extreme illness. Sometimes the first sign may be creamy infiltration in a dog's eye. Diagnosis is most often made by a combination of blood tests, radiographic examination, and, finally, biopsy of one of the affected lymph nodes and/or a bone-marrow exam. With combination chemotherapy, the prognosis is good for extended, long-term survival. Lymphosarcoma is a relatively common malignancy in the dog, occurring with an incidence of twenty-four cases for each one-hundred thousand of the population at risk.

M

MALIGNANT TUMORS: *See* ONCOLOGY.

MAMMARY GLAND CANCER: After skin cancers, mammary gland tumors, or mammary gland adenocarcinomas, are the most common malignancy seen in dogs. They generally occur in older unspayed female dogs, and 35–50 percent of canine mammary gland masses are malignant. Owners should know that the incidence of breast cancer is greatly reduced if a bitch is spayed before her third heat cycle.

A mass or swelling may be the only sign of a mammary tumor. Here at The AMC, surgery is the treatment of choice when a mass is found. A biopsy and X rays are recommended to ascertain malignancy and possible spreading. When there is evidence that the cancer has spread, chemotherapy is also used. Because there is a 40 percent incidence of hormonal receptors associated with mammary gland cancer in the dog, we also routinely recommend that an ovariohysterectomy, or "spay" operation, be done at the same time if the dog is a good surgical risk and will not be compromised by an additional procedure. When a malignancy hasn't spread, long-term survival may be achieved by surgery alone, but this depends on the specific degree of malignancy as determined by the biopsy.

MAST CELL TUMORS: Mast cell tumor occur with some frequency in older dogs. There is a predisposition toward these tumors among boxers and Boston terriers. Mast cell tumors usually appear on extremities and external body walls. Documentation of malignancy requires a biopsy, and whenever possible, surgical removal is the immediate therapy of choice. Prognosis depends on the degree of malignancy, which is determined by a biopsy. Approximately 50 percent of these tumors may be curable by surgical removal alone. The more malignant types as determined by biopsy may also require chemotherapy or radiation therapy, as in most cases these tumors tend to recur and may spread to other parts of the body.

There is a second form of mast cell tumors, systemic mastocytosis, in which there is an invasion of the blood-forming organs of the body such as the bone marrow and the spleen. In this case, prognosis must be extremely guarded, and chemotherapy is indicated.

MASTITIS: *See* Chapter 5.

MELANOMAS: Malignant melanomas tend to occur most frequently in dark-pigmented dogs. They are most common in the mouth, but melanomas may also occur on the digits and on the scrotum of male dogs. In the dog, melanomas are highly malignant, but with early surgical intervention, the rate of spread may be altered to allow for a longer, good-quality life. *See* ORAL TUMORS, SKIN CANCER, and ONCOLOGY.

METRITIS: *See* Chapter 5.

MITES: *See* PARASITIC DISEASES OF THE SKIN.

MUSCULOSKELETAL DISEASES AND DISORDERS: The dog's musculoskeletal system contains essentially the same parts as a human's (*see* Illustration 19, below), with the exception that its front legs must carry half of

Illustration 19: The dog's skeletal system

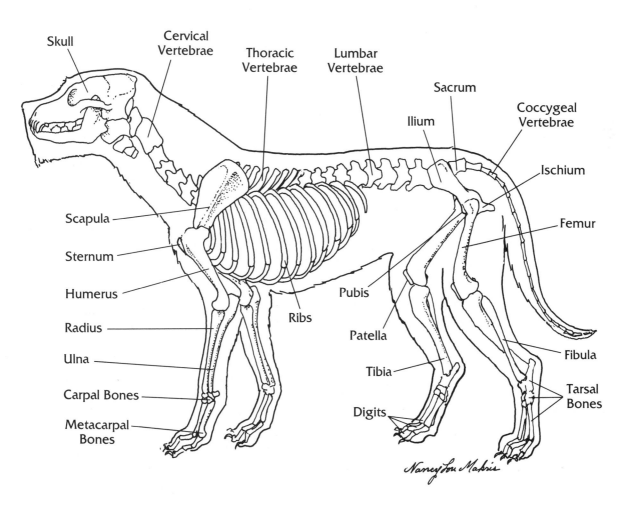

its body weight. The bones of the skeleton provide support and also serve to protect the internal organs. When bones join together to form a joint, there is a protective layer of cartilage on each bone end, or head, to prevent friction. Most of the dog's joints are hinged, except for the shoulder and hip joints, which fit together like a ball and socket. Ligaments and tendons hold bones together and joints in place, and the muscles cause them to move. Diseases and disorders can occur in any part of the dog's musculoskeletal system.

Problems have a number of different origins. Trauma, or injury, can occur to the bones themselves and cause FRACTURES; they can also occur to the ligaments, as in CRANIAL CRUCIATE LIGAMENT RUPTURE, and to the muscles (INFRASPINATUS MUSCLE FIBROTIC CONTRACTURE). Dislocation of a joint can occur as a result of trauma, as in PATELLAR LUXATIONS, a dislocation of the knee cap. Disease can cause inflammation of the bones. PANOSTEITIS is an inflammatory disease while bacterial infection, such as that causing INFECTIOUS BACTERIAL ARTHRITIS, can affect the joints. There can also be congenital malformations of joints, such as HIP DYSPLASIA. Owners should know that indiscriminate supplementation with minerals may cause severe skeletal problems in young dogs, especially the large breeds. The wear and tear of use over the years, exacerbated by injury or disease, can cause an older dog to develop degenerative joint disorders such as DEGENERATIVE ARTHRITIS. Signs of musculoskeletal problems are varied but usually include one or more of the following: lameness, stiffness, swelling, and joint crepitation (grinding, grating). Symptoms may be confined to one area of the dog's body, or there can be multiple involvement of many joints. Diagnosis is generally made via orthopedic examination and X rays, with other specific tests, such as fluid aspiration and blood tests, as required. Treatment varies widely, depending on the particular disease and degree of involvement. *See also* COXOFEMORAL LUXATION, CRANIOMANDIBULAR OSTEOPATHY, DELAYED UNION AND NONUNION, FRAGMENTED MEDIAL CORONOID PROCESS, GROWTH PLATE DISORDERS, HYPERTROPHIC OSTEOARTHROPATHY, HYPERTROPHIC OSTEODYSTROPHY, IDIOPATHIC IMMUNE-MEDIATED ARTHRITIS, LEGG-CALVÉ PERTHES DISEASE, OSTEOCHONDRITIS DISSICANS, OSTEOMYELITIS, RHEUMATOID ARTHRITIS, SYSTEMIC LUPUS ERYTHEMATOSUS ARTHRITIS, and UNUNITED ANCONEAL PROCESS.

MYASTHENIA GRAVIS (MG): This disease is characterized by episodic weakness associated with exercise. A dog's stride may be shortened, followed by collapse in the hind legs, or all four limbs. The PARESIS may involve facial nerves as well as spinal nerves. Inability to blink both eyes is most commonly observed along with generalized muscle weakness. Additionally, there may be a change in bark, respiratory difficulty, and vomiting. The vomiting is due to a megaesophagus (abnormal/enlarged esophagus). MG can be either congenital or acquired. Springer spaniels, Jack Russell terriers, and fox terriers have been reported to have congenital MG. It is an immunopathologic disease in which antibodies are produced against receptors in the muscle junction. Diagnosis is made through the use of a test dose of a medicine called edrophonium chloride given intravenously. An immediate short-lived (three- to eight-minute) response is observed. Long-term treatment requires a longer-acting medicine and corticosteriods.

MYOSITIS: This is a condition in which the skeletal muscles become inflamed. Viruses, bacteria, fungi, protozoal organisms, immune-mediated diseases, and coccidian parasitism have been variably implicated as causative agents. Signs of this disease are a stiff gait and malaise. Upon examination, dogs with this disease are found to have a stilted gait, palpable muscle pain, muscle atrophy, and, occasionally, fever. Myopathies (muscle diseases) may affect a particular body part (masticatory myositis/myopathy) or be generalized (polymyositis). There are various laboratory tests used for diagnosis. A definitive diagnosis can be made by electrodiagnostics (electromyogram—EMG) and muscle biopsy. The technique of muscle biopsy and analysis is very specialized, and a veterinarian should be well versed in these techniques.

Masticatory myositis is characterized by bilateral involvement of the muscles that control chewing, either causing pain when the mouth is opened or an inability to open the mouth fully. It is common among German shepherds. An immunopathologic etiology is suspected. When generalized, a coccidian organism (toxoplasmosis) has been most frequently described as the causative agent. Many other muscle disorders exist, some of which are hereditary.

N

NASAL CANCER: The most common tumor in a dog's nose is a nasal carcinoma, which is usually diagnosed by the use of a surgical biopsy and X rays of the nose. Signs of nasal cancer include sneezing, nosebleeds, and a chronic nasal discharge, usually from only one nostril in the beginning, but later it may be from both. In advanced cases there will be facial deformity or swelling. Chronic rhinitis symptoms can mirror the early signs of nasal cancer, but, in our opinion, testing should always be done for cancer when the above symptoms are present because early diagnosis increases the possibility of a remission of cancer of the nose. Nasal carcinoma may be highly responsive to radiation therapy when X rays show no bone invasion. If the cancer has spread to the bone, radical surgery may be necessary. It will be followed by radiation therapy to attempt to slow recurrence.

NASAL DISEASE: The clinical signs of nasal disease include a discharge that can range from clear to purulent and mucoid, with or without blood streaks; nosebleeds; frequent sneezing; congestion; pawing at or rubbing the face; and, in extreme cases of NASAL CANCER, or tumors, facial deformity.

Nasal disease can be caused by a number of different factors. Congenital defects of the nose occur commonly in brachycephalic, or flat-faced, dogs such as Pekingese, pugs, and Boston terriers, who may be born with STENOTIC NARES in which the outside opening of the nose is much too narrow. This condition may

lead to problems in the upper respiratory passage. Cleft palates (see SOFT PALATE DISORDERS), another congenital disorder, can also lead to a nasal discharge because the nasal cavity and oral cavity are connected. These congenital disorders are corrected surgically once a puppy is old enough to withstand surgery. A nasal discharge can also be caused by DENTAL DISEASE. An abscessed tooth in the back of the mouth can cause a dog to have a nasal discharge. In this instance, extraction of the tooth and long-term antibiotic therapy will usually clear up the problem. Infections, either bacterial or fungal, are also causes of nasal discharge. A history of exposure and immunization may be helpful in diagnosing an infection, and treatment depends on the disease. Long-term, or chronic, infections can be very stubborn and hard to control. A series of tests to evaluate the nasal passage may be required.

NASAL SOLAR DERMATITIS: *See* ACTINIC DERMATITIS.

NEUROLOGIC DERMATITIS: The most common form this disorder takes is flank sucking, which results in a bare patch of skin with no hair growth. Commonly, Doberman pinschers are afflicted with this problem. It is treated with medications such as phenobarbital.

NEUROLOGIC DISEASES AND DISORDERS: The dog's nervous system may be roughly divided into five gross structures: the cerebrum, the brain stem, the cerebellum, the spinal cord, and the peripheral nerves/muscles. To understand diseases and disorders that may affect a dog's nervous system, it is necessary to define these subdivisions.
Cerebral Cortex: This part of the brain is composed of four parts: frontal lobes, parietal lobes, occipital lobes, and temporal lobes. Each lobe has a particular function. For example, the frontal lobes are associated with intellect, behavior, and fine motor abilities. The parietal lobes process sensory information such as pain, touch, and position sense. The temporal lobes are responsible for complex behavior and hearing. And the occipital lobes are associated with vision. The entire cerebro-cor-

tical function is complex and integrated. Injury to the brain may cause abnormalities in one or more of these functions. Common signs include seizures, behavior change, loss of intellect, gait abnormalities, sensation difficulties, altered consciousness, and visual loss.

Brain Stem: This part of the brain is also subdivided. Twelve nerves exit from the brain stem and innervate muscles of the face, mouth, and glands of the head. Within the brain stem lie a complex series of tracts that communicate information to or from the cerebral cortex to the nerves of the limbs and internal organs, by way of the spinal cord. Dysfunction resulting from injury to the nerves that leave the brain stem depends on the particular nerve involved. For example, if cranial nerve two is damaged, vision is impaired; if cranial nerve seven is injured, facial paralysis may ensue; if cranial nerve eight (vestibular portion) is affected, balance difficulties may occur. In short, depending on the particular function of each set of cranial (brain stem) nerves, abnormalities will be reflected by a loss of that function. Lesions of the brain-stem substance create a host of abnormal signs, including head tilts, spontaneous eye movements, coma, severe gait disturbance, abnormal respiration, and abnormal heart rhythms.

Cerebellum: This part of the brain coordinates and "smoothes out" movement. Injury to the cerebellum may cause loss of balance, or jerky, uncoordinated body and limb function. Typically, dogs will have a "drunken" gait and will high-step their legs. A tremor will develop, which worsens when an animal is attempting to do something, and it will alter its stance by placing its legs far apart. The CANINE DISTEMPER virus commonly shows itself as a cerebellar disorder. Many breeds of dogs also have a congenital or early-acquired form of cerebellar disease. These may be hereditary or can result from metabolic abnormalities.

Spinal Cord: The spinal cord extends from the brain stem outside the skull and is encased by the vertebral column. The spinal cord has ascending (to the brain) and descending (from the brain) pathways. The ascending pathways convey the perception of pain and conscious and unconscious position sense. Descending pathways include those that posture the animal against gravity and initiate movement.

Peripheral Nerves: Information leaves the spinal cord by way of spinal nerves that are known as ventral roots (descending). Information also enters the spinal cord by spinal nerves known as dorsal roots (ascending). In this manner, the body and limbs are constantly kept in touch with the environment or the appropriate reactions resulting from the environment. The peripheral nerves generally carry this input/output. For example, input would go to the brain, and output would be received by a muscle.

Muscle/Neuromuscular Functions: These represent the final common pathways of descending information. There are different types of muscles that are innervated by different parts of the nervous system. The complexity of this system is beyond the scope of this book. *See* ATAXIA, BALANCE DISORDERS, VESTIBULAR AND/OR CEREBELLAR DISEASES, DEGENERATIVE MYELOPATHY, DYSMETRIA, EPILEPSY, FACIAL PARALYSIS, HORNER'S SYNDROME, INTERVERTEBRAL DISC DISEASE, MYASTHENIA GRAVIS, MYOSITIS, PARALYSIS, PARESIS, PERIPHERAL NEUROPATHY, PLEGIA, RADIAL NERVE PARALYSIS, TOXICITY.

NODULAR PANNICULITIS: This skin disease has an acute onset at less than six months of age of nodules, which may or may not rupture, discharging an oily brown fluid. There is sometimes fever and/or anorexia as well. This disease is often mistaken for abscesses and treated with antibiotics, but it is actually an inflammation of the fat layer of the skin (subcutaneous tissue) and responds well to steroid treatment.

NUCLEAR SCLEROSIS: *See* LENTICULAR SCLEROSIS.

O

OCULAR TUMORS: There are several types of tumors that are fairly common in and around dogs' eyes. Most frequently seen is one involving the glands that line the eyelid, known as the miebomian glands. These glands secrete an oily material that helps to make up the tears and helps to keep them from evaporating too quickly. As a dog gets older, these glands can develop very small growths, which will appear at first as small nodules on the eyelid or on the margin of the eyelid. These growths can often extend onto the conjunctival surface under the eyelid. They are almost always benign, do not spread, and tend to grow slowly. If they are not causing any irritation to the eye, they can be left alone; but if they get large and irritate the dog's eye or begin to bleed, they should be removed surgically. If surgery is performed, it is very important that it be done carefully so as not to deform the eyelid.

Other tumors that can involve the dog's eyes are squamous cell carcinomas, or tumors that occur in the conjunctiva of the eye, and MELANOMAS, which are the most common intraocular tumors seen in the dog. These melanomas, or dark-pigmented malignant tumors, usually appear in the iris or the scleral body of the eye. In dogs these tumors hardly ever metastasize (spread) within the body. However, although they may start small, they can gradually enlarge to a point where they can obstruct the function of the eye, leading to a DETACHED RETINA or GLAUCOMA. If a melanoma becomes large enough, removal of the eye is indicated.

There are other conditions, such as LYMPHOSARCOMA, where tumors involving the dog's entire body can eventually invade the eye as well. Other tumors, such as tumors of the uterus, mammary glands, or thyroid, have also been known to spread to the eye. *See also* ONCOLOGY.

ONCOLOGY (The Study of Tumors): The incidence of cancer in dogs is approximately the same as in humans. There are two basic types of canine tumors: liquid or HEMATOPOIETIC TUMORS, such as LEUKEMIA and LYMPHOSARCOMA, which involve blood-forming elements; and solid tumors, or masses, which may be external or internal (involving organs within the body).

There is no known single cause for cancer, either in dogs or in humans. There are environmental influences, such as diet or radiation. There are also familial or genetic predispositions toward cancer and infectious or viral causes of cancer. Today, the most commonly held unifying theory of cancer is related to the oncogene; this theory is that basically there is a combination cause in which certain genetic predispositions are influenced by environment or infection to cause either a malignant growth or LEUKEMIA.

An older, yet still widely held, theory about cancer is that of the failure of immuno-surveillance. This theory holds that all living bodies have mutant or abnormal cells that arise either intermittently or continuously, and that a normally functioning immune system recognizes these cells as abnormal and destroys them as they are formed. Cancer would then result from one of two causes: (1) Escape from immuno-surveillance, as in the case of tumors that are not detected as abnormal because they are in a "sanctuary" such as the eye or the central nervous system of the body and are therefore not exposed to the system and not recognized as abnormal until they are big enough to cause problems; or (2) the immune system does recognize the abnormal cells yet fails to function properly or to mount a response of significant magnitude to destroy these abnormal cells and allows the cancer to grow. This theory is controversial.

To unify the two theories: Immune system failure could be an aftermath rather than a forerunner. The activation of the oncogene could cause an immune system failure that would then cause cancer.

As to the frequency of types of cancer in dogs: SKIN TUMORS occur most frequently, followed by MAMMARY GLAND CANCER in females and HEMATOPOIETIC TUMORS. Giant breeds of dogs are prone to BONE TUMORS, while highly pigmented dogs, such as Scotties, black Labrador retrievers, black poodles, black cocker spaniels, and Kerry blue terriers are susceptible to MELANOMAS of the mouth and skin. MAST CELL TUMORS are often seen in boxers and Boston terriers, and HEMANGIOSARCOMAS seem to occur more often in German shepherds. In general, however, all dogs can develop cancer in all parts of the body. Other types of canine tumors covered in this section are DIGESTIVE SYSTEM TUMORS, HISTIOCYTOMAS, LUNG CANCER, ORAL TUMORS, PERIANAL ADENOMAS, SEBACEOUS

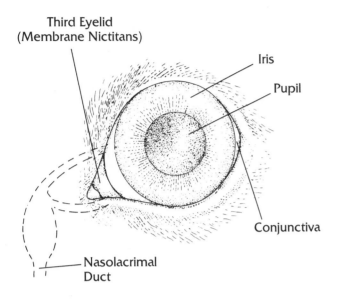

Third Eyelid
(Membrane Nictitans)

Iris

Pupil

Conjunctiva

Nasolacrimal
Duct

Illustration 20: The dog's external eye

GLAND ADENOMAS, TESTICULAR CANCER, TRANS-
MISSIBLE VENEREAL TUMORS, and UROGENITAL
TUMORS.

**OPHTHALMIC DISEASES AND DISOR-
DERS:** Unfortunately, the negative results of
too much inbreeding show up very dramati-
cally in the eye of the dog, and many of the
diseases and disorders of the eye to which
purebred dogs are prone can be attributed, in
part, to inbreeding. Because of the small gene
pool that is the result of this inbreeding, a
number of recessive-type inherited ocular abnormalities, which don't occur in mixed breed
animals, are often seen in purebred dogs. *See*
Illustrations 20 and 21, page 214, for diagrams
of the canine eye.

Specifically, many breeds are developed to
have eyelids and eyelashes that do not perform
their functions properly. Dogs with protruber-
ant eyes, such as the Boston terrier, English
bulldog, Lhasa apso, Pekingese, and pug, are
prey to a great many eye problems and diseases. Because their eyes are not set deeply
into their sockets, they are very prone to damage such as CORNEAL TRAUMA and EYE OUT OF
THE SOCKET. In the normal dog eye, the cornea

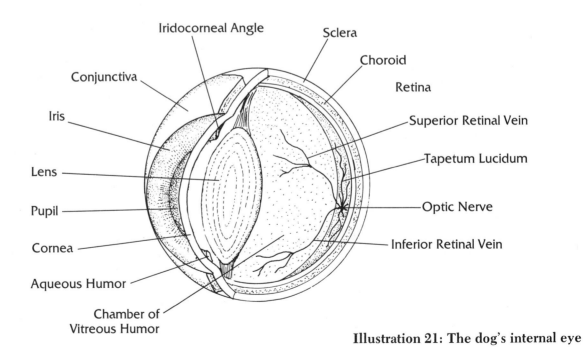

Iridocorneal Angle

Sclera

Choroid

Retina

Conjunctiva

Iris

Lens

Pupil

Cornea

Aqueous Humor

Chamber of
Vitreous Humor

Superior Retinal Vein

Tapetum Lucidum

Optic Nerve

Inferior Retinal Vein

Illustration 21: The dog's internal eye

is lubricated and washed off by tears from two tear glands. These tears are constantly distributed over the surface of the eye by the action of the eyelids. In the case of protruding eyes, the lids cannot perform this important function, and the cornea can dry out and be damaged (*see* DEFICIENCY OF TEAR PRODUCTION). The cornea can also be irritated when eyelashes are too close to the eye and rub the eyeball. This is particularly common in small breeds.

The cornea responds to abnormal situations in several ways. It can become scarred with pigment, and it can be invaded with blood vessels. This is not always desirable, because although scarring helps the eye withstand the dryness, some of the clarity of the cornea is sacrificed in the process. This can eventually affect the dog's vision. The cornea will also react to insult by ulcerating (ULCERATED CORNEA), which is a common problem with small breeds of dog who have very exposed eyes. Even if no acute condition occurs, older dogs (especially the breeds mentioned above) may often require artificial lubrication of the cornea to slow down the scarring process after a lifetime of chronic dryness or cornea irritation. Other genetic corneal problems are PANNUS and DERMOID.

A common canine birth defect is that of abnormally developed areas in the retina, often seen in English springer spaniels and occasionally in Labrador retrievers. This birth defect can remain static for an animal's entire life, causing no problems, but it can also lead to a DETACHED RETINA. Viruses can also affect the retina, leading to inflammation and scarring of the tissue. CANINE DISTEMPER is one of the most common. Probably the most frequent retinal problem seen in dogs is retinal degeneration. This term covers a number of different eye diseases that are usually lumped under the heading of PROGRESSIVE RETINAL ATROPHY. Although it can occur in any breed, this problem is most commonly due to a genetic abnormality in cocker spaniels, collies, Irish setters, Norwegian elkhounds, poodles, and schnauzers.

An eye tissue in which problems frequently arise is the lens, a densely proteinous tissue that acts inside the eye, behind the iris, to focus beams of light entering the eye to form an image on the retina in the back of the eye. The lens of a dog's eye is a great deal larger than that of a human eye and is held in place by very, very fine fibers around its entire circumference. Problems affecting the lens of a dog's eye are CATARACTS, LENS LUXATION, and LENTICULAR SCLEROSIS.

The optic nerve head is a tissue that is also located in the back of the eye. It is the aggregation of the retinal nerves, which come together and form into the optic nerve. Congenital abnormalities are sometimes seen in the optic nerve. One is a nerve that is too small and improperly formed. Another infrequent congenital problem is a pit in the nerve, called OPTIC NERVE COLOBOMAS, seen most often in collies. Viruses sometimes attack the optic nerve, mainly the CANINE DISTEMPER virus, killing the tissue and causing BLINDNESS. Inflammation of the optic nerve, called OPTIC NEURITIS, can also occur.

Just behind the iris of the eye, there are cells that produce fluid, or aqueous humor, which nourishes the iris, lens, and cornea. Normally, this fluid is drained out in an area known as the iridocorneal angle. Should this drainage area become damaged, fluid and pressure can build up in the eye, leading to GLAUCOMA.

OCULAR TUMORS are fairly common in dogs, and tumors from other parts of a dog's body have been known to spread to the eyes.

A dog's eyes are also good mirrors of general bodily condition. Changes throughout a dog's body, brought about by disease, are often reflected in the eyes. For example, the first noticible sign of LYMPHOSARCOMA may be a creamy infiltration in the anterior chamber of the dog's eye. Signs of some infectious diseases that affect the entire body can be seen first in the eyes, too. LEPTOSPIROSIS, BRUCELLOSIS, and toxoplasmosis may sometimes be initially detected through changes in the clarity of the aqueous humor and inflammation of the retina.

See also CHERRY EYE, CONJUNCTIVITIS, IRIS ATROPHY, OVERFLOW OF TEARS, and RED EYES.

OPTIC NERVE COLOBOMAS: An infrequent congenital abnormality most often occuring in collies, this is a condition in which there is a large pit in the head of the optic nerve tissue, which can lead to severe visual problems and sometimes to a DETACHED RETINA. In mild cases there may be no noticeable visual problems. When severe BLINDNESS occurs, there is no treatment to improve the condition.

OPTIC NEURITIS: This is an inflammation of the optic nerve, which, if allowed to persist, will lead to BLINDNESS in a short time. Outward signs are an acute onset of blindness and widely dilated pupils that are not responsive to light. If this condition is treated appropriately within the first few days, many dogs regain useful vision.

ORAL PAPILLOMATOSIS: *See* Chapter 6.

ORAL TUMORS: Canine oral malignant tumors account for about 8 percent of all malignancies seen in the dog. Masses in the mouth may be either benign or malignant. Diagnosis can only be made by means of a biopsy, which should be made whenever a mass of any kind is surgically removed from a dog's body. A common benign fibroma mass often seen in the dog's mouth is an epulis. Surgical removal will often clear up this condition; however, the tumor may recur, at which time repeat surgery is advised. These tumors are radiosensitive, but it is usually not necessary to use X-ray treatment.

Malignant MELANOMAS, fibrosarcomas, and squamous cell carcinomas are the three kinds of malignant oral tumors most commonly seen in dogs. Fibrosarcomas and squamous cell carcinomas are often confined to a local area and may respond to treatment if discovered early in the course of the disease. Malignant melanomas, on the other hand, have a high propensity to spread throughout the body, usually to the lungs and regional lymph nodes. A differentiation can only be made through a biopsy of the removed tissue. Treatment consists of surgical removal of the mass; ancillary therapies, depending on spread, include radiation, chemotherapy, and radical surgery. Prognosis for remission or "cure" depends on the type of cancer and especially on early recognition and

diagnosis, which, unfortunately, is rare in dogs. Signs of oral tumors are inability to eat, bad breath, bleeding or discharge from the mouth and, of course, visible masses.

OSTEOCHONDRITIS DISSICANS (OCD): This is a defect in the normal development for the articular (joint) cartilage and underlying bone surface. Both transient and permanent lameness can occur. The lesion develops most commonly in the shoulder joint (head of the humerus). The stifle (knee) and hock (ankle) joints can similarly be involved. The condition is most common in large to giant breeds. Diagnosis is by orthopedic examination and radiographs. Treatment is often by surgical exploration of the joint; removal of the cartilage flap is required. The prognosis depends on the joint involved and the degree of secondary DEGENERATIVE ARTHRITIS.

OSTEOMYELITIS: This is an infection of bone that may be caused by several different types of bacteria or fungi. Introduction of the bacterial or fungal agent can occur via the bloodstream after a direct injury such as a bite wound or gunshot injury or during surgical repair of a fractured bone. Diagnosis is based on history, physical examination, blood tests, and radiographs. Treatment depends on the acuteness or chronicity of the infection. Generally, chronic osteomyelitis cases must be treated surgically to remove dead and infected bone, promote drainage, and retrieve an accurate culture (an uncontaminated specimen) from the infected area. Appropriate antibiotics or antifungal drugs are used in most cases for osteomyelitis. Prognosis depends on the severity and chronicity of the infection, the amount of bone infected, and the type of bacteria or fungi causing the infection.

OTITIS EXTERNA: This is a general term meaning inflammation or infection of the epithelium of the external ear canal. It can be acute or chronic and is very common in flop-eared dogs, whose ear pinna hangs over the canal opening, restricting air movement and therefore promoting infection and bacterial growth. Primary bacterial ear infections are rare in the dog. Usually, bacterial ear infections are secondary or caused by something else in the environment.

Causes of otitis externa are varied. There can be something in the ear that sets up an irritation, such as water in the ear canal, which because of the conformation of a dog's ear tends to stay in the canal and promote a yeast infection, similar to "swimmer's ear" in people. Plant awns (foxtails) can become stuck in a dog's ear canal and have to be removed. Tumors, or polyps, can form in the ear canal. They can cause irritation and a secondary bacterial infection. These growths can be detected with an otoscope and are removed surgically and a biopsy performed. Long-haired dogs like poodles can develop hair-filled otic canals or hair plugs in the inner portion of the ear canal, which trap moisture and can lead to bacterial growth and infection. This hair must be plucked out by a groomer or veterinarian. EAR MITES can also cause a great deal of ear irritation.

Atopy, or an allergic reaction to inhaled allergens, is very common in dogs and can lead to inflammation of the ear caused by an increased production of cerumen (ear wax). The pinna and its base are usually all that is affected, even though it often appears that the canal opening is closed. The only way to clear up the allergic otitis externa is to identify the source of the allergy.

Skin problems can also spread to the ears. Seborrhea, a generalized term that includes many abnormal skin conditions, can cause purulent exudate in the ear. This condition often affects cocker spaniels. It is treated with medicated shampoo to control the seborrhea and light medication to flush out the ear. Mycotic, or fungal, infections cause a musty odor and a caseous gray discharge. Treatment is with a fungicidal solution. SCARCOPTIC MANGE can affect the ears, as can demodecosis (demodectic mange). This is strictly a disease that affects an individual animal and is not contagious to other animals or people. It is potentially related to a deficiency in the animal's immune system. AUTOIMMUNE DISEASE can cause the ears to become crusty.

Owners who overtreat by using ear medications on dogs for long periods of time can kill off the normal bacteria/flora and set up an environment in which overgrowth of bacteria resistant to the medication can occur.

When otitis externa conditions fail to respond to normal therapy and become chronic, there are several surgical procedures that can help to cure the symptoms by draining the area. In one, the lateral wall of the ear canal is removed so that drainage can occur from the horizontal canal. In another type of surgery, the vertical ear canal is removed altogether, and an opening is made so that the horizontal canal can drain outside. While these procedures can help to relieve chronic otitis, they do not cure the underlying problem, which must still be dealt with.

OVERFLOW OF TEARS: This condition manifests itself as large reddish streaks on either side of the nose. It need not mean that a dog has too many tears but simply that there are too many tears for the drainage system to handle properly. The stain appears reddish because of a chemical reaction that takes place when normal tears sit on the fur. If the tear drainage system is improperly formed or obstructed, surgical correction may improve the tear overflow, but removal of the tear-producing ducts may lead to a dry-eye condition. Overflow is a far better condition for a dog to have than eyes that are too dry.

P

PANCREATIC INSUFFICIENCY (Maldigestion): This disease is thought to be hereditary in the German shepherd but may exist in other breeds as well. It is characterized by chronic diarrhea, a ravenous appetite, and weight loss. In this disease, the pancreas atrophies, so that it does not produce enough digestive enzymes. Thus, water is drawn into the undigested food particles in the intestinal tract, causing diarrhea. Weight loss occurs because food nutrients are not made available to the dog's body, and the animal's ravenous appetite is its body's natural reaction to malnutrition. This disease can be treated very successfully with pancreatic enzyme replacement.

PANCREATITIS: Pancreatitis, or inflammation of the pancreas, is most commonly seen in obese middle-aged female dogs. Clinical signs may vary from mild appetite loss and occasional vomiting to severe gastrointestinal upsets, including bloody diarrhea and, eventually, severe shock. Because dietary fat is a very potent stimulator of pancreatic enzymes, the disease can be associated with the regular ingestion of high-fat foods. The inflammation itself is an autodigestive process in which the pancreatic enzymes that are released actually digest the pancreas itself, thereby perpetuating the inflammation. Therapy involves hospitalization, during which the dog is kept off food for a long period while being supported by intravenous fluids and antibiotics. The aim of this therapy is to decrease the pancreatic enzyme flow. This is followed by dietary therapy, in which the dog is given a reduced intake of low-fat foods along with moderate exercise to reduce weight. Chronic pancreatitis is a common cause of DIABETES MELLITUS in older dogs, while the more severe, acute form of pancreatitis can result in severe shock and death.

PANNUS: An eye disorder seen mostly in German shepherds and German shepherd crosses, this is an ingrowth of blood vessels into the cornea, appearing to the naked eye as hazy reddish tissue on the surface of the cornea. Although incurable, pannus can be controlled very well with medication. Left untreated, it can lead to BLINDNESS.

PANOSTEITIS: This is a self-limiting inflammatory disease of the long bones that occurs in immature large-breed dogs. It is characterized by a sudden onset of limping unrelated to trauma. The lameness may suddenly resolve, only to recur in a different limb. Radiographs are generally required to confirm the diagnosis. The cause of this disease is unknown. Treatment is symptomatic, and pain-relieving drugs are used. The prognosis is generally good; however, episodes of shifting leg lameness may continue for many months.

PARALYSIS: *See* PLEGIA.

PARAPARESIS: Weakness of the hind limbs. *See* PARESIS.

PARASITIC DISEASES OF THE SKIN: External parasites are a very common cause of skin problems in the dog. Some of these parasites are contagious to humans and other animals and may also serve as potential carriers of other diseases (*see* INTESTINAL PARASITES). Control is extremely important for both the dog and its environment. A veterinarian is the best source of parasite-control shampoos, powders, dips, etc., that will work in a specific geographical area. Over-the-counter preparations are usually not strong enough and are not designed to work in a particular location.

Fleas (ctenocephalides canis): Fleas can cause varying amounts of pruritis (itching) and sometimes produce an allergic reaction in a dog. Fleas are not always visible. The place to look for fleas is on top of the back at the base of the tail. (*See also* Chapter 3.)

Mites: There are several different types of mites that affect dogs. Sarcoptes scabies can cause crusting of the ear margins, elbows, etc. Cheyletiella yasiguri is a mite that is usually seen in puppies and appears as dandruff along the spine. These mites may or may not cause itching in the pup, but they are very contagious to people. Demodex canis lives in the hair follicles and can cause itching, especially if there is infection present. Otodectes cyanotis, or EAR MITES, are discussed in a separate entry.

Ticks: Ticks may cause crustiness and redness at the site of attachment after they fall off of the dog. If they remain on the dog, the female tick will become engorged with blood and will swell, appearing light gray in color. To remove an attached tick, grasp it with tweezers as close to the dog's skin as possible. Tick dips are the only effective way to rid a dog of severe infestation. (*See also* Chapter 3.)

Lice: Lice are not common in dogs. If present, they can be found in thickly haired areas and should be treated with a special dip, or shampoo.

Chiggers (trombiculiasis): These insects are present in some parts of the country and can affect dogs. They should be removed manually.

Flies: Flies can affect dogs' ears with FLY-BITE DERMATITIS. *See* AURAL DISEASES AND DISORDERS.

Dogs with hookworms (*see* INTESTINAL PARASITES) may, in rare cases, get HOOKWORM DERMATITIS, which appears clinically as itchy feet, infection of the nail beds, and thickened foot pads. If these symptoms should appear, the dog should be tested for hookworms.

PARESIS: This is a disturbance in the mechanism for initiating voluntary motor function that causes weakness or paralysis, depending on the severity of the lesion. The severity of paresis increases as the location of the lesion descends in the upper motor neuron to involve more of the pathways. (*See* NEUROLOGIC DISEASES AND DISORDERS.) PARAPARESIS is a weakness of the hind limbs, and TETRAPARESIS is a weakness of all four limbs.

PARVOVIRUS: *See* Infectious and Contagious Diseases.

PATELLAR LUXATIONS: Luxation, or dislocation of the knee cap (patella), can be congenitally or traumatically induced. The luxation is classified as either medial (displacement of the patella out of its normal femoral groove to the inner aspect of the leg), or lateral (displacement to the outer aspect of the leg). Congenital medial luxations often take place in toy breeds of dogs, while congenital lateral luxations occur more commonly in large and giant breeds. Trauma-induced luxations can be either medial or lateral and are seen in every breed. Clinical signs vary according to the degree of luxation. Some dogs may be in intermittent pain and occasionally limp on a rear leg, while others have a persistent, severe lameness. Diagnosis is made by orthopedic examination. Treatment is determined by the severity of the luxation and resulting lameness. Surgery is the primary means of treatment when indicated. Prognosis depends on the severity of the luxation, the breed of dog, and the particular surgical technique used.

PEMPHIGUS GROUP: This is a collective term for certain autoimmune skin diseases in which the body forms antibodies that are directed against specific layers of the skin. This disease complex may take many forms and may cause a variety of skin problems. Diagnosis is achieved by biopsy of the affected skin area and special tests for appropriate antibodies. As in other AUTOIMMUNE DISEASES, treatment initially involves corticosteroids and other immunosuppressive drugs. Cure is rare, but control may be achieved with appropriate medication.

PERIANAL ADENOMAS: These benign tumors of small glands of the anus are usually seen in male dogs. Because there is a less frequently seen malignant counterpart, which occurs more often in females and castrated males, a biopsy must always be performed after a tumor is removed. Perianal adenomas appear as raised lumps or bumps on one or both sides of the rectum and can be painful. Because they are dependent on testosterone, we always recommend castration when we surgically remove the growth.

PERIPHERAL NEUROPATHY: This refers to any disorder of the lower motor neuron system that involves the spinal roots, spinal nerves, peripheral nerves, or neuromuscular junction. Diseases of the spinal roots and peripheral nerves include inflammation (polyneuritis), neoplasia (neurofibroma), trauma (root avulsion, FRACTURES), and ischemia (aortic thromboembolism). Diseases of the neuromuscular junction include MYASTHENIA GRAVIS, botulism, and tick paralysis. Clinical signs include PARESIS (paralysis of one or more limbs), voice change, eye-blink difficulty, megaesophagus, and respiratory difficulty. Treatment varies with the cause and severity of the case.

PERSISTENT RIGHT AORTIC ARCH: This congenital disorder of the esophagus becomes evident when a puppy is weaned from milk to solid food, which he regurgitates. It is due to an abnormal formation of the vasculature of the aorta that leaves the heart at the right, rather than the left side, constricting the esophagus so that solid food cannot pass into the stomach. Surgery is the only treatment, and it must be performed early in life, before the esophagus loses its tone, or the dog will never be able to swallow properly.

PHARYNGEAL DISEASE: The pharynx is actually the back of the mouth, where a sore throat is generally felt. Signs associated with pharyngeal disease are usually related to eating or drinking; a dog will gag, choke, have difficulty swallowing, or make a noise (gulp) when swallowing. In addition, a gurgling or rasping noise can sometimes be heard when a dog swallows. Problems associated with the pharynx include an overlong SOFT PALATE, TONSILLITIS, cysts or masses, and, in rare cases, tonsilar neoplasia, or cancer.

PINNA ALOPECIA: Pinna alopecia is hair loss of the pinna (ear flap). The majority of cases are hereditary, or congenital, and occur in dachshunds, who begin to lose hair on their ear flaps when they are less than one year old, slowly progressing to complete baldness at eight or nine years of age. This hereditary type of alopecia is irreversible. Hair loss on the ear flap can also be due to CONTACT DERMATITIS, which may be the result of chronic use of neomycin or steroid ointments for minor irritation of the ear. Hormone-related dermatosis, or a low estrogen level, can cause ear-flap hair loss, as can seborrhea of the ear flap. Another form of pinna alopecia is a variant seen only in poodles, who will suddenly lose tufts of hair from their ears over a period of several months only to have the hair grow back later on. Diagnosis must be based on history, physical examination, skin scraping, and other specific tests performed by the veterinarian.

PLEGIA: *Plegia* is a suffix meaning paralysis. Motor plegia is the complete absence of purposeful movement. Sensory plegia is the complete absence of deep pain sensation.

PNEUMONIA: Pneumonia in the dog can be the consequence of a severe viral or bacterial infection, or it can be due to the aspiration of food into the lungs, either after a dog has vomited or because of swallowing disorders in which food is inhaled. Signs include fever, lethargy, loss of appetite, weight loss, and a cough. Treatment is with the long-term use of antibiotics, even well past apparent cure. Dogs who have had pneumonia may be predisposed to a recurrence of the disease. Severe pneumonia can be an emergency. (*See* the Emergencies section.)

POLLAKIURIA, or FREQUENCY OF URINATION: This is a condition in which a dog needs to urinate more often than normally, with small amounts of urine passed each time. It often occurs when there is a urinary tract infection caused by bacteria or when the urinary tract is obstructed.

POLYDIPSIA: The ingestion of more than normal amounts of water. Normal daily water intake for a dog is one pint per ten pounds of body weight. Overdrinking can occur with RENAL FAILURE that is either acute or chronic, DIABETES MELLITUS, diabetes insipidus, CUSHING'S SYNDROME, PYOMETRA, HYPERTHYROIDISM, primary polydipsia, ECLAMPSIA, and gastric tumors.

POLYURIA: The output of larger than normal amounts of urine. This almost invariably occurs with POLYDIPSIA.

PROGRESSIVE RETINAL ATROPHY: This is a umbrella term under which a number of different degenerative retinal diseases are lumped. The most common retinal problem seen in dogs, it can affect all breeds, but most often appears in American cocker spaniels, collies, Irish setters, Norwegian elkhounds, poodles, and schnauzers. One of two things can occur: Either the photoreceptor cells in the retina are improperly formed at birth, or they do not hold up as well as they should and degenerate with age. We often see the latter condition with poodles who begin to lose vision as they get older. The most common initial sign is night blindness. This is because the disease seems to first affect the rod photoreceptors, which are used mostly in dim light. Retinal atrophy is often a problem that develops gradually and is only noticed when a dog is taken from its normal environment. There is no known treatment for this disease, which can eventually lead to irreversible BLINDNESS.

PROSTATITIS: The male dog's prostate gland is under hormonal control, and the chronic stimulation of the gland by hormones can lead to prostatic cysts, or prostatitis, especially in older dogs. These cysts can become infected and form prostatic abscesses. A sign of prostatitis is blood dripping from the tip of the penis and also blood in the urine. These abscesses need to be drained, which entails opening up the abdominal wall, breaking down the abscesses, and placing drains from the abscesses to the outside of the body, so that the pus and purulent material can be drained outside. Simultaneously, the animal is castrated. *See also* UROGENITAL TUMORS.

PROTEINURIA, or ALBUMINURIA: This is the abnormal presence of albumin (albuminuria) and other abnormal proteins (proteinuria) in the urine. This condition is detected by routine urine dipsticks, or by twenty-four-hour urine collections. Diseases that cause proteinuria include GLOMERULONEPHRITIS, AMYLOID GLOMERULONEPHRITIS (massive proteinuria), ACUTE RENAL FAILURE (mild proteinuria), and URINARY TRACT INFECTIONS (very mild and transient). Proteinuria can also occur with fever after excercise. Treatment consists of appropriate therapy for the causative condition or disease.

PYELONEPHRITIS: This is an infection of the kidney(s) by bacterial organisms. One or both kidneys can become infected in a dog having pyelonephritis. Clinical signs are the same as those of CYSTITIS at some time in the pyelonephritis, but often there are no symptoms of note until the clinical signs of UREMIA appear, when both kidneys are in an advanced state of infection. The disease can occur with or without URINARY TRACT STONES and with or without HYDRONEPHROSIS. Treatment aims at eradicating infection with appropriate antibiotics as directed by the veterinarian. If both kidneys are involved and clinical signs of UREMIA are present, then treatment includes supportive care, fluids, and appropriate antibiotics. The prognosis varies, depending on the presence or absence of UREMIA, HYDRONEPHROSIS, URINARY TRACT STONES, etc.

PYOMETRA: Pyometra is a collection of inflammatory material and fluid within the uterus that is functionally considered an abscess and can only occur in unspayed females. The toxins from the bacteria and pus cells are what makes the dog sick. Pyometras most commonly occur two to three weeks after a heat cycle, and symptoms are loss of appetite, vomiting, diarrhea, depression, possible fever, and often increased thirst and urination. Pyometras can take two forms: The cervix may remain closed, and the pus accumulates within the uterus; or the cervix opens, and a very purulent, occasionally bloody, and sometimes malodorous discharge appears from the vagina. Diagnosis is based on history, examination, and radiographic confirmation. In cases of open pyometra, drainage through the vagina aids in diagnosis. Treatment is surgical removal of the uterus, and the prognosis is good for otherwise healthy dogs. Exceptions are those dogs who have suffered from toxic kidney changes caused by released toxins, or in those cases where the uterus has ruptured as a result of weakened walls or severe distention, releasing pus into the dog's abdomen. *Pyometra is a surgical emergency.* Other methods of treatment, not generally available, include hormonal treatment and drainage through the cervix.

PYURIA: This is the presence of abnormally high numbers of white blood cells in the urine. It frequently occurs with HEMATURIA (which can occur without pyuria). The causes of pyuria are bacterial infections of the urinary tract (UTI). Signs of pyuria can include straining to urinate and an urge to go out to urinate often, and an inability to pass urine is also possible. If signs of pyuria are observed, a veterinarian should be consulted.

R

RABIES: *See* Infectious and Contagious Diseases.

RADIAL NERVE PARALYSIS: Radial nerve paralysis is commonly caused by injury. In distal radial nerve paralysis, the wrist (carpus) and digits do not extend properly, causing knuckling of the paw on its dorsal surface. There is a reduced sensibility to pain of the forelimbs and the back part of the paw, but the limb can support weight. This injury often follows a FRACTURE of the distal humerus. In proximal radial paralysis, the limb cannot support weight and collapses toward the rear of the paw. The limb is often carried off the ground with the elbow flexed. There is loss of perceived sensation (analgesia) of the forelimb and rear part of the paw.

RED EYES: Red eyes are caused by constant eye irritation, which can be due to any number of OPHTHALMIC DISEASES AND DISORDERS, many of which are described here. Sometimes, however, dogs have red eyes simply because of an abnormally shaped eyelid. This is especially true of dogs with normally droopy lower eyelids such as the Basset hound, in which the droop of the eyelids exposes the pink inside tissue (conjunctiva). Often, older dogs' lower eyelids will sag, or droop, too. If a dog is not uncomfortable, and the exposed tissue remains pinkish rather than deep red, there is probably no cause for concern.

RENAL CYSTS: These fluid-filled, encapsulated cysts in the kidney can be solitary or multiple, large or small to tiny, and they can involve one or both kidneys. When multiple and small, the disease is called polycystic renal disease—*see* FAMILIAL AND CONGENITAL RENAL DISEASES. The cause of renal cysts is unknown, unless they appear in conjunction with RENAL TUMORS. In that setting, the tumors obstruct the outflow of urine and produce the cysts. Signs are often absent, unless both kidneys are involved. Treatment is at the discretion of the veterinarian. Prognosis is variable.

RENAL DISEASES AND DISORDERS (KIDNEY DISEASES AND DISORDERS): Like humans, dogs have two kidneys, located in the abdomen, which act as filters for waste materials in the bloodstream, eliminating toxins from the blood. The kidneys also regulate the dog's body-fluid composition and volume and aid in the production of certain hormones, which in turn regulate the production of red blood cells and assist in the formation of bones. The nephron is the functional unit of the kidney. The dog has approximately a million nephrons, each of which consists of a glomerulus that filters blood and a tubule that modifies the filtrate formed by the glomerulus. The glomerulus is a tuft of tiny blood vessels (capillaries) that filters blood to begin the production of urine. The fluid resulting from this filtration is called glomerular filtrate. The tubule is the part of the nephron that modifies the fluid that was produced by the filtration of blood. Urine is transported from the kidney to the urinary bladder via the ureters. It is then stored in the urinary bladder, which contracts to empty itself of urine when full. The urine travels through the urethra to the outside, via the vagina in females and the penis in males. Male dogs also have a prostate gland located outside the urethra and connected by tiny tubes to the urethra. If only one kidney is damaged or rendered incompetent by virtue of disease, bacterial infection, trauma, or congenital malformation, the remaining kidney is usually able to take over and perform the necessary renal functions entirely as long as it is healthy. However, if both kidneys become incompetent, an animal will suffer from RENAL FAILURE, and UREMIA will occur.

Kidney damage can occur from birth (*see* FAMILIAL AND CONGENITAL RENAL DISEASES, ECTOPIC URETER, and HYDRONEPHROSIS). It can also result from bacterial urinary tract infections, such as PYELONEPHRITIS, or from invasion of the kidneys by an outside parasite (DIOCTOPHYMA RENALE) or LEPTOSPIROSIS. The kidneys can also become damaged by kidney stones, RENAL CYSTS, and RENAL TUMORS. Kidney diseases can be of unknown origin, such as AMYLOID GLOMERULONEPHRITIS and most forms of GLOMERULONEPHRITIS. Signs of kidney disease vary, depending on the severity of the disorder and the degree of kidney involvement. When only one kidney is affected, clinical signs may be entirely absent or extremely mild. Virtually all of the signs such as HEMATURIA, POLLAKIURIA, POLYDIPSIA, POLYURIA, PYURIA, STRANGURIA, etc., which are listed in this section, are possible, but they may not necessarily be present. There are a number of tests and studies available to veterinarians to help them diagnose kidney disease (*see* Glossary). Treatment of kidney diseases varies widely, depending on the severity of the disease and the amount of kidney damage already sustained by a dog, but it almost always includes parenteral fluids (fluids given intravenously) and supportive care. Depending on the disease, antibiotics and diet may also be used as therapy. The prognosis for a dog with kidney disease also varies widely. *See also* CHRONIC INTERSTITIAL NEPHRITIS, CYSTITIS, PROTEINURIA, and URINARY TRACT TRAUMA.

RENAL FAILURE (KIDNEY FAILURE): This is a disease state that occurs when the kidneys have been damaged. It can be abrupt (ACUTE RENAL FAILURE) or come on slowly (CHRONIC KIDNEY FAILURE). In both cases, UREMIA will be the end result.

RENAL TUMORS (KIDNEY TUMORS): Tumors, or cancer, can arise in the kidneys themselves (primary renal tumors) or spread from other organs to the kidneys (secondary, or metastatic renal tumors). Frequently, renal tumors exhibit no clinical symptoms, but symptoms can include HEMATURIA (blood in the urine) and ANEMIA if the tumor bleeds a lot. Once the diagnosis is certain, treatment is the surgical removal of the involved kidney. But if both kidneys are affected, there is little that can be done therapeutically. In either case, the prognosis is guarded.

REPRODUCTIVE DISORDERS: In the female dog, the one thing that will stop reproductive system disorders in their tracks is an early ovariohysterectomy. Reproductive disorders of the female dog such as ENDOMETRITIS

and PYOMETRA are generally uterine, although there are some rare ovarian tumors, and all these problems can be totally avoided by an early spay.

In the male, UNDESCENDED TESTICLES, TESTICULAR TUMORS, and PROSTATITIS are the most common reproductive disorders. Again, castration is preventative.

Reproductive system disorders relating to breeding and birth, such as infertility, mastitis, etc., are discussed in detail in Chapter 5. BRUCELLOSIS, an infectious disease spread mainly through sexual contact, is discussed in this section.

RESPIRATORY DISEASES AND DISORDERS: The respiratory tract of a dog consists of the nose, pharynx, larynx, trachea, bronchi, and lungs. Each of these separate areas can become infected, diseased, or can suffer from congenital disorders; and in each case symptoms and treatment will vary. In general, abnormal breathing, excessive sneezing, hoarseness, and coughing are all signs of some kind of respiratory disorder. Foreign bodies can become wedged in a dog's throat, or pharynx, and the animal may have to be anesthetized in order to remove them. (*See* ESOPHAGITIS.) Congential disorders of the respiratory tract include STENOTIC NARES, SOFT PALATE DISORDERS, LARYNGEAL PARALYSIS, and a predisposition toward tracheal collapse (*see* TRACHEAL DISEASE). A dog that has had a traumatic chest injury, such as a fall from a height or being hit by a car, should always be suspected of having contused lungs or of having a rib that has punctured a lung. For more about how this should be treated, *see* Emergencies section. *See also* BRONCHIAL DISEASE, LUNG CANCER, NASAL CANCER, NASAL DISEASE, PHARYNGEAL DISEASE, PNEUMONIA, TONSILLITIS, and TRACHEOBRONCHITIS.

RHEUMATOID ARTHRITIS: This is a deforming, painful joint disease producing multiple joint swelling and lameness in dogs. It can resemble SYSTEMIC LUPUS ERYTHEMATOSUS, except that it is generally seen in older dogs. If it has progressed far enough, X rays will show the bony changes that are generally characteristic of rheumatoid arthritis. There is also a blood test for the presence of rheumatoid factors. Occasionally, a biopsy of the joint capsule is performed. Treatment is supportive and often directed at pain relief, as it is for people. At The AMC we recommend an initial use of corticosteroids and perhaps other immunosuppressive drugs and pain relievers such as aspirin. With proper management, it is possible to alleviate the pain and lameness and slow down the inevitable process of bone change, but in most instances the disease is not considered curable.

S

SCABIES: *See* SCARCOPTIC MANGE.

SCARCOPTIC MANGE: Scarcoptic mange, or SCABIES, commonly affects dogs' ears and elbows, causing severely crusty, itchy skin. On the ear, the pinna, or ear flap, is usually affected, rather than the ear canal. This type of mange is contagious to people and other dogs via contact. Scarcoptic mange is diagnosed by microscopic examination of a skin scraping. It is treated with special antiparasitic dips.

SCHNAUZER COMEDO SYNDROME: This is a skin disease affecting miniature schnauzers. It is characterized by a persistent dorsal eruptive dermatitis consisting of small nodules that can erupt all over the body. Treatment is with a special medicated shampoo.

SEBACEOUS GLAND ADENOMAS: Sebaceous gland adenomas, sometimes called cysts, are benign tumors of the oil-forming glands of the skin. They may be multiple and often occur in older dogs.

SEBORRHEIC SKIN DISEASES: Seborrhea is an umbrella term connoting an abnormal skin condition, and 90 percent of so-called seborrheas are secondary to other skin problems, such as allergies or bacterial infections. There are two types of seborrhea: seborrhea sica, or dry seborrhea, and seborrhea oleosa, or oily seborrhea. True seborrheas include SCHNAUZER COMEDO SYNDROME, TAIL GLAND HYPERPLASIA, and EAR MARGIN DERMATOSIS.

SEIZURE DISORDERS: *See* EPILEPSY.

SEMICOMA: *See* STATES OF CONSCIOUSNESS.

SKIN DISEASES AND DISORDERS: *See* DERMATOLOGIC DISEASES AND DISORDERS.

SKIN TUMORS: Tumors of the skin are frequently seen in dogs. The treatment of choice for canine skin tumors is surgical removal, followed by a biopsy to ascertain whether or not the growth is cancerous.

Young dogs are prone to benign skin tumors called HISTOCYTOMAS.

SLIPPED SPINAL OR NECK DISCS: *See* INTERVERTEBRAL DISC DISEASES.

SOFT PALATE DISORDERS: Cleft palates and overlong soft palates are both congenital disorders seen in the dog, most commonly the brachycephalic, or flat-faced breeds. A puppy born with a cleft palate will pass milk out of its nose when nursing. The problem is corrected surgically as soon as the pup is old enough, but tube feeding is required to support the pup prior to surgery. The primary sign of an overlong soft palate is excessive snoring and snorting. This problem can be corrected surgically if severe enough but is left alone if the palate is only mildly elongated.

STATES OF CONSCIOUSNESS: The ascending reticular activating system (ARAS) functions to "arouse" the cerebral cortex and awaken the brain to consciousness. Disturbances of consciousness can result from lesions in the ARAS. Depression occurs when a dog responds slowly or inappropriately to verbal stimuli. Stupor or semicoma implies that a dog is unresponsive except to vigorous and repeated stimuli that may necessarily be painful. Coma means complete unresponsiveness to repeated noxious stimulation.

STENOTIC NARES: *See* NASAL DISEASES.

STRANGURIA: This is the symptom of straining to urinate, which can occur with a bacterial urinary tract infection or when the urethra is blocked as a result of URINARY TRACT STONES, TUMORS, or a birth defect (the latter condition is rare). Stranguria may or may not be accompanied by an increased frequency of urination (POLLAKIURIA), PYURIA, or HEMATURIA. Consult a veterinarian if stranguria is observed.

STUPOR: *See* STATES OF CONSCIOUSNESS.

SYSTEMIC LUPUS ERYTHEMATOSUS: Lupus is mainly a disease of young to middle-aged dogs (two to five years of age) and seems to be more common in females than males. There may be a predisposition toward the disease among Shetland sheepdogs and German shepherds. With dogs, the most common signs of lupus are fever, lameness, and multiple joint swellings (*see* SYSTEMIC LUPUS ERYTHEMATOSUS ARTHRITIS), skin lesions (*see* AUTOIMMUNE SKIN DISEASES), and lethargy. Lupus is diagnosed by means of special immunologic tests for the presence of specific antibodies and also through a biopsy of affected organs.

While it is not considered curable, it is treatable, but the treatment of choice varies, depending in part on the organ system involved. Here at The AMC, we recommend immuno-suppressive therapy with corticosteroids and possibly other drugs if the disease is aggressive and active, along with supportive care. When the disease is more benign and not causing potential life-threatening illness, we may recommend less intensive supportive general care.

SYSTEMIC LUPUS ERYTHEMATOSUS ARTHRITIS: This is an arthritis that often involves multiple joints and is one of several conditions associated with SYSTEMIC LUPUS ERYTHEMATOSUS. Diagnosis is based on orthopedic examination, blood tests, radiographs, and microscopic examination of aspirated joint fluid. Treatment with immunosuppressive drugs such as corticosteroids is required. With proper drug therapy, the disease can usually be controlled.

T

TAIL GLAND HYPERPLASIA: This skin disease, which causes recurrent or persistent alopecia (hair loss) over the tail gland area, is usually seen in males and is common in German shepherds. It is thought to occur when nearby females are in heat, as this causes the gland to increase its secretions.

TEAR PRODUCTION PROBLEMS: *See* DEFICIENCY OF TEAR PRODUCTION and OVERFLOW OF TEARS.

TESTICULAR CANCER: Basically, there are three forms of testicular cancer in dogs: seminomas, interstitial cell tumors, and sertoli cell tumors. Unlike in man, seminomas in the dog are commonly benign. Sertoli cell tumors may be associated with estrogen production and may cause anemia and feminization (*see* ENDOCRINE DISEASE and ENDOCRINE-RELATED SKIN DISORDERS). Castration and biopsy are the therapies of choice. A physical examination of a male dog should include careful palpation of the scrotum and testicles.

TETRAPARESIS: Weakness in all four limbs. *See* PARESIS.

TICKS: *See* PARASITIC SKIN DISEASES.

TONSILLITIS: Tonsillitis in the dog is rarely a problem in and of itself but is usually a reflection of a problem in another area of the dog's respiratory tract, which must be diagnosed and treated. Tonsillar tumors or cancers are rare in the dog. *See also* PHARYNGEAL DISEASE.

TOXICITY: Common causes of toxicity that produce neurologic signs in the dog are lead and drug ingestion. Lead toxicity may cause a wide range of medical difficulties; however, the nervous system may be indirectly affected. Delirium and SEIZURES are most commonly seen. Drug intoxications (Valium, amphetamines, and marijuana) are not infrequent. Depending on the particular drug ingested, a wide range of neurologic signs may appear. *See* the Emergencies section.

TRACHEAL DISEASE: A dog with tracheal disease, or tracheitis (inflammation of the trachea), will always cough or honk. Irritation of the trachea can occur when a dog has a respiratory infection, such as TRACHEOBRONCHITIS ("kennel cough") or canine distemper, has inhaled smoke, or is coughing frequently because of bronchial disease. In general, these disorders are treated medically. Compression of the trachea can be caused by a tumor or an ENLARGED (failing) HEART. Heart disease can be treated medically. Depending on the tumor type, either surgery or chemotherapy may be indicated.

A congenital tracheal problem associated with small-breed dogs, such as Yorkshire terriers and toy poodles, is a predisposition toward tracheal collapse. This is a condition in which there is insufficient rigidity in the tracheal rings that serve to keep the tracheal tube open. The rings flatten, and the tube collapses inward, narrowing or closing the opening through which air must pass. This condition can be present at birth or can develop over time with wear and tear. Sometimes there can be a congenital condition in which the entire trachea is incompletely developed at birth. This condition can be diagnosed by means of external palpation, X rays, dye studies, and tracheoscopy. In general, little can be done when there is complete tracheal collapse, although surgery has been performed at some large universities.

TRACHEOBRONCHITIS: *See* Infectious and Contagious Diseases.

TRANSMISSIBLE VENEREAL TUMORS: These malignancies of the mucous membrane are spread by direct sexual contact. They are usually on the vagina, vulva, and penis but can also develop on a dog's mouth or nose because of licking. They are visible as masses on the male's penis and on the outside of the female's genitalia. There may also be vaginal bleeding. These tumors are apt to recur after surgery, so

the treatment of choice is radiation therapy and/or chemotherapy. Even when a venereal tumor has spread to the uterus or lymph nodes, it is responsive to chemotherapy. Owners who want to breed their pets should check both dogs carefully for signs of a venereal tumor.

TUMORS: *See* ONCOLOGY.

TUMORS, EYE: *See* OCULAR TUMORS.

TUMORS, URINARY TRACT: *See* RENAL TUMORS, UROGENITAL TUMORS.

U

ULCERATED CORNEA: Cornea ulceration is a very common canine problem, especially among small breeds with very exposed eyes. The top (epithelial) layer of the cornea is approximately ten layers thick, and along with the flushing action of tears, serves to protect the eye. If this layer of cells has been weakened or damaged because of constant dryness, any insult or injury to the deeper tissues of the eye such as a foreign body, cat or dog scratch, etc., can quickly cause the eye to become infected. As bacteria grow, they can enter the inner layer of the cornea, or stroma, and literally begin to eat this layer away. At worst, so much of the thickness of the cornea will be lost that the innermost corneal layer will be pushed outward by the normal pressure within the eye, and appear as a small bubble on the surface of the eye. *This is a serious emergency* and underlines the importance of having any eye injury seen by a veterinarian as soon as possible. Even the deepest ulcerations or lacerations can frequently be helped with intensive medication or surgery.

UNDESCENDED TESTICLES: If two testicles are not found in a male dog's scrotum, they usually are located either within the groin area or are within the abdominal cavity. Retained testicles have a predisposition toward tumor formation. Some of the tumors are of little consequence, but others can become malignant

—*see* TESTICULAR CANCER, ENDOCRINE DISORDERS, and ENDOCRINE-RELATED SKIN DISORDERS. Treatment of choice for a male with a retained testicle is first to run a white-blood-cell count, red-blood-cell count, and platelet count to determine if there is any bone-marrow suppression. If the blood counts are normal, the testicles are removed surgically. If the blood tests indicate bone-marrow suppression, the animal must be transfused with whole blood during the operation, and the prognosis is guarded.

UNUNITED ANCONEAL PROCESS: This is a condition found primarily in large-breed dogs, especially the German shepherd. It is a failure of the ossification center, or growth plate, of the anconeal process of the ulna to close or fuse completely by five months of age. Instability and detachment cause inflammation within one or both elbow joint(s), eventually leading to DEGENERATIVE ARTHRITIS. Signs are usually not apparent before a dog is six to eight months old and may initially consist of a slight limp in the foreleg. Joint swelling, crepitus (grinding, grating) of the elbow joint, and lameness become noticeable as the animal gets older. Diagnosis is based on symptoms, age, breed, and radiographs of the elbow joint. Treatment is usually early surgical removal of the anconeal process. Prognosis depends on the degree of DEGENERATIVE ARTHRITIS that develops.

UREMIA: This is a constellation of abnormalities in body-fluid composition and volume that are caused by both acute and chronic RENAL FAILURE. Typical signs of uremia include increased water intake (POLYDIPSIA), increased urine volume (POLYURIA), lack of appetite, vomiting, depression, lethargy, and ANEMIA. These symptoms will vary in severity depending on the degree of kidney damage.

URINARY INCONTINENCE: Urinary incontinence is the loss of urine in any unaccustomed or undesirable area. Sometimes this only occurs when a dog barks or coughs. Most urinary incontinence is involuntary and can be due to a number of very different causes, including a congenital defect, such as an ECTOPIC URETER; a neurologic disorder or spinal disease; and, most commonly, the loss of sex-steroid hormones after an ovariohysterectomy or castration operation. Sometimes urinary incontinence is not of physical origin but is the result of a behavior problem, such as submissive or excitement urination, sexual marking, or poor initial housetraining (*see* Chapter 8 for more about these problems). In many instances, it can be very difficult to ascertain the cause of urinary incontinence. If the cause is determined to be physical, treatment will depend on the specific condition and may include drugs to control the abnormality. In the case of a deficiency of sex-steroid hormones, treatment is usually successful.

URINARY TRACT STONES: Canine urinary tract stones develop most commonly in the bladder but can be in any part of the urinary tract. They can occur alone or in more than one place at the same time and, in addition to the bladder, can be in one or both kidneys, in the urethra after they pass from the bladder, and in the ureter after passing from the kidney(s). There are several types of stones in dogs. The most common type of stone is triple phosphate, with fewer reports of struvite, urate, cystine, ammonium biurate, and oxalate stones. Most rarely, canine stones are composed of silica.

The cause of urinary tract stones is unknown, but urinary tract infections, impedence of urine outflow, hereditary factors, and diet are all known influences. Clinical signs of stones include HEMATURIA, PYURIA, obstruction of the urethra, straining to urinate (STRANGURIA), frequent urination (POLLAKIURIA), and ultimately UREMIA if the obstruction is complete.

Treatment aims at increasing urine volume via increased water intake and controlling bacterial infection if it is present. Dietary management and urine acidification may also form part of the treatment. Dietary management to dissolve known struvite stones can be attempted along with efforts to control infection, but dietary management for other than struvite stones has not been proved efficacious. In general, because it is difficult to determine which kind of stone is present, surgical removal is recommended and should be followed by stone analysis. Drugs aimed at preventing specific kinds of stones can only be prescribed after stone analysis has been performed.

URINARY TRACT TRAUMA: Urinary tract trauma can occur as the result of a number of accidents, including being hit by an automobile or bicycle or a fall from a height. A sign of a problem after a known accident can be blood in the urine (HEMATURIA). If blood clots have formed in the urinary tract, obstruction is possible, causing straining to urinate (STRANGURIA) and/or inability to urinate. Ultimately, signs of UREMIA will appear if the obstruction involves the urethra or both kidneys. Treatment aims at supportive care, parenteral fluids, antibiotics, and removal of any obstructions.

UROGENITAL TUMORS: The most common identified urogenital tumor in dogs is cancer of the bladder. The most common symptom is unrelenting CYSTITIS and/or HEMATURIA, which is not responsive to appropriate medical therapy. Dye studies of the urinary tract and bladder should be performed, followed by surgical exploration and biopsy to confirm disease.

In the male, prostatic cancer may be more common than primary bladder cancer. It usually occurs in intact males and must be differentiated from the benign conditions of prostatic hyperplasia, the acute infectious disease PROSTATITIS, and prostatic abscesses. This is done by means of a surgical biopsy. Signs are similar to those of CYSTITIS, including bloody urine (HEMATURIA) and straining to urinate (STRANGURIA).

Other primary tumors of the urogenital system can involve the kidneys and urethra and the vulva and vagina. *See also* RENAL TUMORS, TESTICULAR CANCER, and TRANSMISSIBLE VENEREAL TUMORS.

UTERINE INERTIA: *See* Chapter 5.

UTERINE TORSION: *See* Chapter 5.

V

VALVULAR HEART DISEASE: Abnormality of the heart valves, or valvular heart disease, is the most frequently seen acquired CARDIAC DISEASE among older dogs. It is especially common among the smaller breeds. Normal heart valves oppose each other and direct the flow of blood through the heart and vessels in a specific direction. Sometimes the valves become damaged and no longer meet properly. This allows the blood to flow in a reverse direction, causing a progressively ENLARGED HEART. This puts more and more strain on the heart and can eventually lead to CONGESTIVE HEART FAILURE, depending on the severity of the valvular abnormalities.

Symptoms similar to those of other types of CARDIAC DISEASE usually become evident in severe cases. Owners will notice that a dog displays weakness, shortness of breath or rapid breathing, becomes easily tired, and may start to cough with any excitement or exercise. If valvular heart disease is suspected, it is an *emergency situation*, requiring immediate medical attention. Treatment, either with controlled exercise/diet and medication or with surgery, depends on the extent and severity of the disease. Successful treatment usually offers a good prognosis for a good-quality life.

VESTIBULAR AND/OR CEREBELLAR DISEASE: *See* BALANCE DISORDERS.

VOMITING: *See* GASTROINTESTINAL DISEASES AND DISORDERS.

VON WILLEBRAND'S DISEASE: This hereditary bleeding disorder is particularly prevalent in Doberman pinschers. Signs are excessive bleeding in pups when they are teething and when they sustain ear or tail traumas. Occasionally adults also show abnormal bleeding. The disease is diagnosed by means of a special blood test. Treatment is primarily supportive.

W

WARFARIN POISONING: Accidental ingestion of warfarin or similar chemicals commonly found in rat poisons can cause serious bleeding problems in dogs. The poison interferes with vitamin K and the production of several blood-clotting factors. Clinical signs may be varied and include ANEMIA, pale mucous membranes, nosebleeds, difficulty breathing, gastrointestinal or urinary bleeding, and bruising. In most cases, the problem can be controlled with vitamin K injections, blood transfusions, and prevention of further exposure to the poison. *See also* the Emergencies section.

WATERY EYES: *See* OVERFLOW OF TEARS.

WORMS: *See* INTESTINAL PARASITES.

Z

ZINC-RESPONSIVE DERMATOSIS: There are two syndromes associated with this disorder, both of which are successfully treated with zinc, given orally, for the remainder of a dog's life. They commonly affect Siberian huskies and malamutes. Onset of one type occurs at one year of age or older and consists of crustiness and scaliness around the facial area. The second variety affects puppies with multiple hyperkeratotic (excessively scaly) plaques and fissures of the foot pads.

About The
Animal Medical Center

The Animal Medical Center is known worldwide for its pioneering approach to pet care and veterinary medicine. *Town and Country* magazine recently called it the world's best hospital, animal or human. In any event, it is the hospital where New Yorkers from all walks of life take their sick or injured pets. Even at midnight, there is likely to be a steady stream of pet owners bringing everything from dogs and cats of all descriptions to birds, reptiles, and other exotic animals to The AMC for treatment.

The AMC had its beginning in 1910 as a clinic to treat the pets and work animals of the poor people living on New York's Lower East Side. Founded by the New York Women's League for Animals under the leadership of Ellin Prince Speyer, the clinic treated 6,000 animals in its first year. In 1914, with the help of a donation from James Speyer, the Ellin Prince Speyer Hospital for Animals was founded at 350 Lafayette Street. In 1955 the Speyer Hospital received a large grant from the estate of Alfred H. Caspary to build the Institute of Veterinary Research adjacent to the hospital. Several years later, with the help of another grant from the Caspary estate, the Speyer Hospital and the Institute of Veterinary Research were combined in a new building at 510 East 62nd Street, in the Rockefeller University/New York Hospital/Cornell Medical Center area, enabling the facility to be in close proximity to other medical institutions.

Providing High-Quality Services
For Sick Animals

The first aim of The AMC, laid down in its Charter, "to establish high quality medical, surgical, laboratory, and nursing services for sick animals," has been well met. Over seventy veterinarians with specialties in a wide range of fields from dermatology to radiology, assisted by a devoted staff of trained paramedical personnel, treat more than 60,000 patients

231

a year. Support systems such as a pharmacy, medical library, and computer system for the storage of clinical data help to make the Center's operations run smoothly. The Center never closes. It is open twenty-four hours a day, 365 days a year, and provides the only full-service veterinary emergency operation in the New York metropolitan area during the hours of 5:00 P.M. to 8:00 A.M. Nearly 15,000 emergency cases are handled by The AMC annually.

In addition to treating individual pets, The AMC's Dr. Philip Fox (a contributor to this book) has provided veterinary care for the New York Police Department's Bomb Squad dogs for the past five years, and he has recently been asked to add the new Canine Unit of the NYPD to his patient roster.

To Improve the Quality of Care Through Study

The second aim set down in The AMC's Charter is "to study animal diseases with the object of improving the quality of care for animals." Its unique location in the midst of a densely populated pet-owning area and large caseload make it possible for The AMC to carry out all research into new methods of diagnosis and treatment by observing and treating naturally occurring disease and performing clinical and comparative studies. The AMC does not support any research programs in which diseases are artificially induced. Currently, AMC research programs include investigations into improved methods of treatment of cancer and of cardiovascular, ophthalmologic, and kidney diseases. The AMC's Donaldson-Atwood Cancer Clinic, for example, works closely with the Memorial Sloan-Kettering Cancer Center in developing innovative therapies for treating cancer.

New equipment to help increase diagnostic capabilities is often acquired. Recently, for example, The AMC purchased a portable X-ray machine that enables an animal to be X-rayed during surgery without having to be transported to the Radiology Department. New specialty areas such as veterinary dentistry are currently being developed.

AMC staff members regularly receive grants that enable them to further their research into particular areas of veterinary medicine, and many are the recipients of awards recognizing their work.

Postgraduate Teaching

The third aim set down in The AMC's Charter is "to develop postgraduate teaching facilities for veterinarians." Each year between twenty and twenty-five veterinarians, graduates of veterinary medical colleges in the United States and abroad, join The AMC as interns to further their training. Competition is stiff to be accepted for the Center's postgraduate training —there are a great many more people applying than can be accepted. Following a year of rigorous training, these interns may continue their training at The AMC as medical or surgical residents. After residency, some veterinarians join the staff of The AMC, while others go on to private practice or return to veterinary medical colleges to teach. Many AMC graduates are internationally known for their work.

In addition, The AMC runs a continuing education program for its staff veterinarians and area practitioners. Lectures and workshops covering a wide range of veterinary specialties are covered.

Other educational programs for veterinarians and veterinary medical college students are also offered, often in cooperation with organizations such as the American Animal Hospital Association (AAHA) and the American Veterinary Medical Association (AVMA).

One Step Further

In addition to providing the best possible medical care for pets and furthering the development of even better animal medical care through research and the training of veterinarians, The AMC goes one step further. It also ministers to pet owners and other animal lovers.

Since 1982, The AMC has had a full-time clinical social worker on the staff. Susan Phillips Cohen is the Director of Counseling and the chairperson of The AMC Institute for the Human/Companion Animal Bond. She works with pet owners to help them to understand and cope with their grief and bewilderment at a pet's death or sudden illness and to aid them in making difficult decisions about hospitalization, surgery, and euthanasia. She also runs workshops and self-help groups for bereaved pet owners. In 1983 two social-work interns joined the Center's Human/Companion Animal Bond program personnel. In addition, The AMC's Pet Outreach Program, in which volunteers bring cats and dogs to visit the residents of nursing homes, mental institutions, senior citizen centers, and hospices, has met with tremendous success.

Another unique AMC program, The Animal Behavior Therapy Clinic (ABTC), was established in 1978. Under the directorship of Dr. Peter L. Borchelt, the ABTC is dedicated to the diagnosis and treatment of behavior problems in pet animals. Seminars and courses for pet owners on various aspects of pet behavior are also given on a regular basis.

The AMC is always striving to find ways to make pet ownership more viable for people. A recently innovated program, The AMC's Surviving Pet Maintenance and Placement Program, for instance, is designed to take the worry out of what will happen to a pet if an owner is no longer able to care for it. Designed specifically to meet the needs of older pet owners, the program assures that a pet will be well cared for for the rest of its normal life should its owner become ill or die.

The Human Element

None of these impressive facts and programs would combine to work as well as they do to fulfill The AMC's primary aim to provide high-quality care for sick animals if it weren't for the people involved.

In my year of visiting The AMC at all hours of the day and evening to interview veterinarians and collect material for this book, I saw The AMC staff at work. I saw a lot of pats, kind words, and tender, loving care for the animals. I saw a veterinarian carrying one of her patients (a large dog) upstairs in the elevator in her arms to have a consultation with another doctor. Doctors interrupted interviews to answer pages and attend to patients. In short, the dedication, enthusiasm, energy, concern, and responsibility of all the people at The AMC, coupled with their professional ability, combine to make The Animal Medical Center a very special place.

Spring 1985   Elizabeth Randolph

APPENDIX

Medications

David P. Aucoin, DVM

Throughout this book, we refer to various medications or drugs that veterinarians may prescribe to treat, prevent, and control disease in dogs; relieve pain or discomfort; and sedate or tranquilize dogs so that they can be treated or operated on. These medications or drugs may be used by a veterinarian during the course of treatment or may be sent home with an owner to give the dog as directed. In Chapter 12, we offer detailed instructions on how to give various forms of medicine to a dog.

Owners should always be sure to get the generic name of any medication that is used in treating a dog, whether it is used in the doctor's office or at home. There are several reasons why it is very important to know exactly what kind of medicine (rather than a brand name) an animal has been given: in case another doctor is seen in the future, in case of successful treatment with a particular medication, and in case of an idiosyncratic reaction (individual hypersensitivity) to a specific drug. Because there are often many different brands of a drug, a brand name alone may often be extremely difficult to identify. It is particularly important for an owner to remember to obtain this information if a dog is treated in an emergency clinic by a doctor other than its regular veterinarian, so that the dog's own doctor can be told what the dog has been given. Having said that, it is interesting to note that some drugs, such as Valium, are always referred to by brand, or trade, name and never by generic name.

Common sense is important when it comes to medicating a dog. If an animal seems to be having a bad reaction to a medicine, an owner should not be afraid to stop giving it. There is no medication that is so important that an animal will suffer irreparable harm if a dose or two is missed until the doctor can be consulted. The veterinarian should also be consulted if a medication isn't having the desired effect. Under no circumstances should owners take it upon themselves to increase the dosage of any medicine.

Household Drugs

As a general rule, no drugs should ever be given to a dog without a veterinarian's advice. There are many household drugs intended for human use that should not be used for dogs. Some are much too strong—human laxatives, for instance. Others, such as allergy medications and cold remedies, are usually combination medicines and contain a variety of drugs in a formula designed specifically for people, which dogs can't handle.

Although they are not as toxic for dogs as they are for cats, products that contain acetaminophen such as Tylenol analgesic and other "aspirin substitutes"

235

should not be given to dogs at home. These medications are not totally aspirin substitutes, because they are not anti-inflammatory and will not help a dog with arthritis pain.

In an emergency, or until the doctor can be reached, the following household drugs can be used with impunity for dogs:

Aspirin: Aspirin can be safely used to reduce both fever and pain in dogs. It is especially effective against arthritic pain. Because dogs require fairly heavy doses of aspirin, it is best to use a buffered product (Bufferin, Ascriptin) to avoid stomach irritation. For arthritis, one-half aspirin tablet three times a day for dogs up to twenty pounds, and one tablet for those twenty to forty pounds; for fever reduction, one-quarter aspirin tablet three times a day for small dogs, and one-half tablet for dogs up to forty pounds.

Kaopectate: For simple diarrhea, which is not accompanied by vomiting or other signs of illness (*see* "Gastrointestinal Diseases and Disorders" in the Encyclopedia), one cc (approx. 16 drops) of Kaopectate diarrhea remedy per ten pounds every four hours is usually effective for dogs. As we discussed in Chapter 12, a syringe is the easiest and most accurate way of giving a dog liquid medication.

Hydrogen Peroxide: Giving a dog enough hydrogen peroxide to make it throw up is a relatively harmless way to induce vomiting if the dog is known to have eaten something noncorrosive, such as human medications, antifreeze, or rat poison. Vomiting should never be induced if a dog is known or suspected of having eaten anything corrosive, such as gasoline or oil products (usually the distinctive smell will indicate this) or anything with a lye base, such as drain cleaner. More about poisons in the Emergencies section. An overdose of hydrogen peroxide will not do any permanent damage to a dog; it will simply make the dog very sick to its stomach.

Tranquilizers and Anesthetics

The methods of giving general anesthetics, preoperative testing, and postoperative care are discussed in detail in Chapters 4, 7, and 12. Owners should realize, however, that even if only local anesthetics are to be used for simple procedures (which is rare), dogs almost always need to be tranquilized in order to be worked on. A dog will probably have been given a combination of one or more sedatives or tranquilizers, which it will metabolize according to its own system, the amount of sedative given, etc. Here at The AMC, we routinely keep dogs in the hospital until they have completely regained consciousness after anesthetic. In some situations—an emergency clinic, for example—a dog may be released while still not entirely out of the anesthetic or tranquilizer. In these cases, the dog may be very dopey and thrash around and vocalize while coming out of the anesthetic. These are perfectly normal reactions. As we mentioned above, it is important for the owner to find out the name of the tranquilizer given in case of a bad reaction and for the information of the regular doctor.

Medications Used in Veterinary Medicine

It is also important for a dog owner to realize that almost all of the drugs used in veterinary medicine have an equivalent in human medications and are probably available in human pharmacies. The only difference is in a particular species' reaction to, and metabolization of, a specific medication and in FDA approval of the drug for a given species of animal. Thus, there is no great mystery surrounding veterinary medications, and they can usually be found listed in any standard reference pertaining to human medicines. Below is a list of some of the medications most commonly used in canine veterinary medicine and side effects that may/can occur when these medicines are used, so that dog owners will know what to expect and can ask intelligent questions of their veterinarians.

Some Medications Often Used for Dogs, by Type—
Their Generic Names, with Simplified Pronunciations,
Most Common Trade Names, and Side Effects.

NOTE: Dosages are purposely omitted, as they vary widely.

In general, unless instructed otherwise by a veterinarian, all medications should be given with food. The most common side effect of almost any medication in dogs is gastrointestinal upset, including appetite loss, diarrhea, and vomiting. Some medications also cause dopiness or hyperactivity. If any of these side effects is excessive, or if a dog is exhibiting symptoms that it was not showing prior to being medicated, owners should stop the medication and check back with the veterinarian. Barring this, all medications should be continued up to the full amount prescribed, even after the dog seems better.

ALLERGY MEDICATIONS:
Side effects: Increased water consumption, urination, appetite. With long-term (greater than two months) use, pot belly, haircoat thinning, and slow hair regrowth.
Contraindications: Severity of any of the above.
Metrevet (mét ra vet)
Temeril-P (tém er ill)

ANTIBIOTICS: Used to kill bacteria.
Side effects: Loose stool or diarrhea and/or vomiting.
Contraindications: Excessive severity or duration of any or all of the above.
Ampicillin (am pi síll in). Trade names: Omnipen, Princillin
Amoxicillin (a mox i síll in)
CephaLexin (sef a léx in). Trade name: Keflex
Cephalothin (sef á loe thin). Trade name: Keflin
Chloramphenicol (clor am fenicol)
Erythromycin (er ith roe mýe sin)
Gentamicin (jen ta mýe sin)
Lincomycin (lin koe mýe sin)
Metronidazole (me troe ní da sole). Also used for worming. Trade name: Flagyl
Neomycin (nee oh mýe sin). Trade name: Biosol
Penicillin G (pen i síll in)
Sulfadiazine/trimethoprim (sol fa dýe a zeen/trye meth oh prim) Trade names: D. Trim, Tribrissin
Sulfadimethoxine (sul fa dye meth ox een). Trade name: Bactrovet
Sulfisoxazole (sul fi sox a zole). Trade name: Gantrasin

Tetracycline (tet ra sýe kleen). Trade name: Panmycin
Ticarcillan (tye kar síll in)

ANTICONSTIPATION MEDICATIONS:
Side effects/contraindications: Diarrhea
Bisacodyl (bis a kóe dill). Trade name: Dulcolax

ANTICONVULSANT MEDICATIONS:
Side effects: Expect increased water consumption, urination, and appetite. Also, dog will be very sedated for one to two weeks, after which sedation will wear off.
Contraindications: Inform veterinarian if dog is not initially sedated.
Phenobarbital (fee noe bar bi tal). Also used as a tranquilizer.
Phenytoin (fen i toe in)
Phenytoin with Phenobarbital
Primidone (prím a don). Trade name: Mylepsin

ANTIDIARRHEA MEDICATIONS:
Side effects/contraindications: Constipation
CMP (Corrective Mixture of Paregoric)
Diathal (dýe a thall)

ANTIFUNGAL MEDICATIONS:
Side effects/contraindications: Vomiting/diarrhea
Griseofulvin (gri see oh fúl vin). Trade name: Fulvicin

ANTIHEARTWORM MEDICATIONS:
Side effects/contraindications: Vomiting, diarrhea, anorexia
Diethylcarbamazine Citrate (dye eth il kar bam a zeen). Trade name: Dirocide

ANTI-INFLAMMATORY MEDICATIONS:
Side effects: Gastrointestinal upsets
Aspirin. Use only buffered aspirin; for example, Bufferin or Ascriptin.
Phenylbutazone (fen ill byóo ta zone)
Steroids. *See* separate listing.

ANTIMITE MEDICATIONS:
Side effects: No major side effects.
Amitraz (a mi traz). Trade name: Mitaban
Cerumite (sir yóu mite)

BRONCHODILATORS: Used for breathing difficulty, coughs, asthma.
Side effects/contraindications: Gastrointestinal upset. Can cause dogs to become "hyper"—tense, excitable, hopped-up.
Aminophyline (am in off i lin)
Isoproterenol Elixer (eye soe proe teŕ e nole)
Oxtriphylline (ox trýe filin). Same drug as Theophylline.
Quibron (kwíb ron)

HEART DISEASE MEDICATIONS, including Diuretics:
NOTE: Dosage will vary as disease progresses.
Side effects/contraindications: These are all very potent drugs and may cause severe side effects. If owners see any of these side effects, they should never give more medication and should always stop and consult with the veterinarian. Side effects can include anorexia, vomiting, diarrhea, lethargy, and weakness as a result of lowered blood pressure. When diuretics are given, owners should expect increased water intake and urination.
Captopril (kaṕ toe prill). Trade name: Capoten
Digoxin (di joẋ in). Trade names: Cardoxin, Lanoxin
Hydralazine (hye drál a zeen). Trade name: Apresoline
Procainamide (proe kane á mide). Trade name: Pronestyl
Propranolol (proe prań oh lole). Trade name: Inderal
Quinidine (kwín i deen)
Diuretic: Furosemide (fur oĥ se mide). Trade name: Lasix

HORMONES: Used to treat endocrine-system imbalance disorders.
Side effects: No major side effects.
Diethylstilbesterol (dye eth il stil beśs trole)—used for urinary incontinence.
Levothroxine (lee voe thye roẋ een)—replacement therapy for hypothyroidism.
Oxytocin (ox i tóe sin)—used for whelping/milk production problems. Trade name: Pitocin
Stanozolol (stan oĥ zoe lole). Trade name: Winstrol
Testosterone (tess tośs ter own)

SHAMPOO:
Benzoyl Peroxide (beń zoe ill). Trade name: Oxydex

STEROIDS: Used as antiinflammatory agents.
Side effects: Increased water consumption, urination, food consumption. With long-term (more than two months) usage, will cause a pot belly and haircoat loss.
Contraindications: Severity of any of the above.
Dexamethasone (dex a meth a sone). Trade name: Azium
Hydrocortisone (hye droe koŕ ti sone). Trade name: Topiderm
Prednisone (préd ni sone). Trade name: Meticorten
Triamcinalone (trye am siń oh lone). Trade name: Vetalog

TRANQUILIZERS (Sedatives, antianxiety medications):
Side effects: There is a great deal of variation from dog to dog on how long these various medications last. Owners must determine their own dogs' tolerances and tell the veterinarian. If a dog is knocked out for more than eight to ten hours, it is too much; but if a dog is given a lot of medication and is still lively, the medicine needs changing. Most tranquilizers are short-acting, with a two- to four-hour effect. Valium is not a good tranquilizer for dogs because it is metabolized too fast.
Acepromazine (a se próe ma zeen)
Diazepam (dye aẋ e pam). Trade name: Valium
Phenobarbital

ULCER/ANTIVOMITING MEDICATIONS:
Side effects: No major side effects.
Aluminum Hydroxide. Trade name: AmphoGel
Cimetidine (sye meť ideen). Trade name: Tagamet
Prochlorperazine (proe klor peŕ a zeen). Trade name: Compazine

WORMING AGENTS:
Side effects: These agents are no longer purgative but very parasite-specific and should cause no side effects. Possible side effects are vomiting and diarrhea.
Dichlorvos (dye kloŕ voss). Trade name: Task
Mebendazole (me beń da zole). Trade name: Telmintic
Metronidazole. *See* Antibiotics.
Piperazine (pí per a zeen)
Praziquantel (pray zi kwoń tel). Trade name: Droncit
Pyrantal Pamoate (pi rań tel páy o mate). Trade name: Nemex
Thenium Closylate (theń ee um klóe si late). Trade name: Canopar

Some Terms Commonly Used in Veterinary Medicine

Abdominal: Pertaining to the belly cavity containing the stomach, intestines, liver, kidneys, urinary bladder, uterus, etc.

Abscess: A collection of pus anywhere in the body, usually surrounded by inflamed, damaged tissue.

Acquired disease/disorder: A condition that develops after birth, as opposed to one that is present at birth (congenital).

Acute: Of sudden or rapid onset, as opposed to chronic.

Adreno-: Pertaining to the adrenal gland.

Alopecia: Hair loss.

Analgesia: Loss of sensation of pain.

Anasarca: Fluid in limbs or under the skin.

Arthro-: Pertaining to joints.

Atopy: An allergic reaction to inhaled allergens that usually appears as a skin problem.

Aural: Pertaining to the ear.

Autoimmune disease: A disease in which the body destroys its own tissues.

Benign: A tumor or growth that is not malignant (cancerous).

Bitch: A female dog.

Brachycephalic breeds: Breeds of dogs with short noses and pushed-in faces (e.g., pug).

Carcinoma: A cancer that arises in the epithelium, the tissue that lines the skin and internal organs of the body.

Cardio-: Pertaining to the heart.

Cardiology: The study of the diseases, functions, and structures of the heart.

Castration: Neutering of a male dog by surgical removal of the testicles.

Chronic: A condition that continues or recurs and often lasts a long time, as opposed to one that is acute.

Clinical signs: Overt symptoms or signs, visible to the naked eye.

Coagulation: Clotting, as blood.

Congenital: A condition or disease present at birth; it may surface later in life. It is not necessarily hereditary.

Cyst: An abnormal sac filled with liquid.

Dam: The mother of a litter of puppies.

Dermatology: The study of diseases of the skin and their diagnosis and treatment.

Edema: Abnormal collection of fluid in tissue spaces (*see* Anasarca).

Encephalo-: Pertaining to the brain.

Endocrinology: The study of the endocrine glands and the hormones they secrete.

Entero-: Pertaining to the intestines.

Estrus: The regularly occurring "heat" period of a bitch. (Estrous: "heat" cycle)

Fibroma: A nonmalignant tumor of connective tissue.

Gastro-: Pertaining to the stomach.

Gastroenterology: The study of diseases of the stomach, intestines, liver, and pancreas.

Hematoma: A blood-filled swelling; blood clot outside the blood vessels.

Hepato-: Pertaining to the liver.

Hereditary: A disease or condition present at birth that can be traced back to ancestors/parents. It can surface later in life.

Hyper-: An overproduction, as in hyperthyroidism.

Hyperplasia: Enlargement.

Hypo-: A deficiency or underproduction, as in hypothyroidism.

Hypoxia: A deficiency of oxygen in the tissues.

Idiopathic: Of unknown cause.

Incubation period: The time between infection and the onset of disease symptoms.

-itis: Inflammation of, as in pancreatitis.

Malignancy/malignant: Term(s) used to describe a cancer that can spread (metastasize) to other parts of the body.

Metastasize: Spread to other parts of the body, as a cancer.

Metro-: Pertaining to the uterus.

Mycosis: A disease caused by a fungus.

Myo-: Pertaining to the muscles.

Neonatals: Newborns.

Neoplasia: Abnormal cell growth; tumor or cancer.

Nephro-: Pertaining to the kidneys.

Nephrology: Study of disorders of the kidneys.

Neuro-: Pertaining to the nervous system.

Neurology: The study of diseases, functions, and structures of the nervous system.

-ology: A term meaning "the study of."

Oncology: The study of tumors.

-opathy: Disease or dysfunction of, as in cardiomyopathy.

Ophthalmo-: Pertaining to the eye.

Ophthalmology: The study of diseases, functions, and structures of the eye.

Orthopedics: The study of bones and joints.

-osis: A diseased condition, as in hydronephrosis.

Otic: Relating to the ear.

Oto-: Pertaining to the ear.

Ovariohysterectomy (OHE, "spay"): The neutering of a female dog by surgical removal of the ovaries and uterus.

Pancreat-: Pertaining to the pancreas.

Perianal: Beside or around the anus.

Perineum: Region between the anus and the urethral opening.

Pneumo-: Pertaining to the lungs.

Pruritis: Itching.

Pulmono-: Pertaining to the lungs.

Pyo-: Pus in, as in pyometra.

Renal: Relating to the kidneys.

Sarcoma: Malignant tumor of the cells that make up the body tissues.

Thoracic: Pertaining to the chest cavity, which contains the heart, lungs, and major blood vessels.

Toxic: Poisonous.

Trauma: A sudden physical injury or wound; a shock.

Uremia: Buildup of poisons in the bloodstream as a result of kidney failure.

Some Tests, Procedures, and Equipment Used in Diagnosing and Treating Canine Diseases and Disorders

Acupuncture: A traditional Chinese healing system in which symptoms are relieved by the use of thin metal needles inserted at specific points.

Aspiration: The process of removing fluid or other matter from any part of the body using a fine sterile needle and syringe.

Barium series: GI diagnostic tests in which a dog is usually made to fast for twenty-four hours, given a white chalklike liquid (barium), and then X-rayed. The white barium will highlight any abnormalities or stoppages in the GI tract.

Biochemical profile (SMA-20): A series of blood tests evaluating the function of internal organs such as the liver and kidneys.

Biopsy: Examination by a pathologist of a piece of tissue that has been removed surgically to confirm a diagnosis of a condition or disease process. This is not confined to the diagnosis of a malignant cancer.

Blood tests: A diagnostic tool used in a number of canine illnesses. A small amount of blood is removed and tested for various components; e.g., CBC (complete blood count), platelet count, RBC (red-blood-cell count), WBC (white-blood-cell count), etc.

Blood transfusion: The placement of whole blood or plasma directly into a dog's vein via a catheter.

Blood Urea Nitrogen (BUN): A blood test of kidney function. The normal in the dog is 10–20 Mg%.

Bone-marrow aspiration: The removal of a small amount of bone marrow for evaluation under a microscope (*see* Aspiration).

Bronchoscopy: The process of examining the trachea and bronchi and/or removing tissue or foreign bodies using a special instrument (bronchoscope).

Brucella titer: A blood test for brucellosis.

Casts: The formal element in the urine that is created when proteinaceous material in the urine is compressed in the nephrons (*see* in the Encyclopedia, "Renal Diseases and Disorders") to form a "cast" of the tubule that it forms in. A few granular casts in the urine are normal.

Catheter: A flexible tube used to remove or insert fluids.

Catheterization: The process wherein a urinary catheter is passed up the urethra to enter the bladder. Catheterization is done with sterile equipment. It is sometimes needed to relieve obstructions of the urethra. It may also be done to obtain a urine sample for diagnosis or to monitor urine output.

Chemotherapy: The treatment of disease with chemicals given orally or by injection.

Coagulation studies: Studies of the clotting ability of the blood.

Complete Blood Count (CBC): Blood test to inspect white and red blood cells and their status.

Coomb's test: A specialized blood test to determine autoimmune hemolytic anemia.

Creatinine: A blood test of kidney function in the dog. Normal is less than 1.2 Mg%.

Culture: Process by which specimens collected from a patient and incubated in a laboratory medium are examined for bacterial or fungal growth.

Cystocentesis: A procedure wherein a urine sample is obtained by aspiration of urine directly out of the bladder (*see* Aspiration).

Cystogram: An X-ray study that directly evaluates the size and contour of the urinary bladder. Air is injected by a urinary catheter into the urinary bladder, and a small amount of contrast material (opaque to X rays) is injected. The study is usually performed under sedation.

Cystoscopy: The examination of the bladder using an instrument (cystoscope) inserted into the bladder via the urethra.

Cytology: The study of the function and structure of cells by microscopic examination, as in vaginal cytology.

Dietary therapy: Control of diet or food intake as a tool for treating various diseases.

Diuretics: Medications that increase the output of urine.

Dye studies: The injection of a dye into a part of the body prior to taking X rays in order to highlight abnormalities, etc.

Electrocardiogram (EKG): Heart-function evaluation using an electrocardiograph, an instrument which records the electric currents traversing the heart.

Electroencephalogram (EEG): Brain-function evaluation using an electroencephalograph, which records the electrical activity occurring in the brain.

Endoscopy: Visualization of the gastrointestinal tract by use of a special instrument (endoscope).

Exclusion diagnosis: The process of making a diagnosis by ruling out everything else that could cause the problem.

IM: An injection given intramuscularly.

Intravenous fluids: Fluids given via a catheter directly into a vein.

Intravenous pyelogram (IVP): An X-ray study to evaluate the size, contour, and function of the kidneys and ureters. The urinary bladder is also evaluated by this study.

IV: An injection given intravenously.

Otoscope: An instrument used to examine a dog's ears.

Palpation: Examination of a part of the body with the hands and fingers.

Parenteral fluids: Fluids not given orally; given either subcutaneously (SQ) or intravenously (IV).

PO: Medicines given orally (per os).

Radiation therapy: Treatment using X rays.

Radical surgery: Surgery aimed at removing all traces of a disease or growth.

Radiograph: An X ray.

Skin scrapings: The removal of thin layers of skin for microscopic study.

SMA-20: Biochemical profile.

Speculum: An instrument used to hold open a body cavity, such as the vagina, nostril, etc., for examination.

Spinal tap: The removal of fluid from around the spinal cord by aspiration.

Stool sample: The collection of feces for microscopic examination in order to identify intestinal parasites in the dog.

Subcutaneous (SQ): Giving anything, such as fluids or medications, beneath the skin.

Tracheoscopy: An examination or visualization of the trachea using a tracheoscope.

Urethrogram: An X-ray study that directly evaluates the size and contour of the urethra. The bladder is filled with sterile fluids, and a contrast is injected into the urethra through a catheter placed in the very end of the urethra to outline the urethra. The study is usually done under sedation.

Urinanalysis (Urinalysis): A test of kidney function that examines the composition of urine chemicals and the concentration of solutes, cellular elements, and formed elements (casts).

Vaginal swab/culture: A collection of matter from the vagina on a swab for microscopic examination and/or culture.

X-ray examination: Examination of skeleton or internal organs by the use of radiographs—negative prints that reveal abnormalities inside the body.

Bibliography

INTRODUCTION

Books:

THE AKC'S WORLD OF THE PURE-BRED DOG, edited by Duncan Barnes and the staff of the AKC. New York: Howell Book House Inc., 1983.

THE COMPLETE DOG BOOK, Official Publication of the American Kennel Club. New York: Howell Book House Inc., 1979.

THE RIGHT DOG FOR YOU, Daniel G. Tortora, Ph.D. New York: Simon & Schuster, 1980.

THE ROGER CARAS DOG BOOK, A Guide to Purebred Dogs, Roger Caras. New York: Holt, Rinehart & Winston, 1980.

SIMON AND SCHUSTER'S GUIDE TO DOGS, Gino Pugnetti. Edited by Elizabeth Meriwether Schuler. New York: Simon & Schuster, 1980.

Alpine Publications
1901 South Garfield Street
Loveland, CO 80537
Books on many breeds, including West Highland white terriers, Lhasa apsos, bearded collies, collies, and Shelties.

Breed Clubs:

American Kennel Club (AKC)
51 Madison Avenue
New York, NY 10010
Free information on breeds, breeders, choosing dogs.

Cavalier King Charles Spaniel Club, USA
c/o Mr. John Gammon
Shiloh-Canan Road
Palmyra, TN 37142
Free information on breeders in the U.S.

Jack Russell Terrier Club of America
c/o Mrs. Hardin Crawford III
P.O. Box 365, Long Run
Far Hills, NJ 07931
Free information on breeders in the U.S.

United Kennel Club (UKC)
100 E. Kilgore
Kalamazoo, MI 49001
Free information on breeds and breeders that are not included in AKC listings.

CHAPTER 3: KEEPING YOUR DOG HEALTHY

Books About Natural Foods/Cooking for a Dog:

DOG AND CAT GOOD FOOD BOOK, Terri McGinnis, DVM. San Francisco: Taylor and Ng, 1977.

DR. PITCAIRN'S COMPLETE GUIDE TO NATURAL HEALTH FOR DOGS AND CATS, Richard C. Pitcairn, DMV, Ph.D., and Susan Hubble Pitcairn. Emmaus, PA: Rodale Press, 1982.

THE HEALTHY CAT AND DOG COOK BOOK, Joan Harper. Chicago: Soodik Printing Co., 1975.

KEEPING YOUR PET HEALTHY THE NATURAL WAY, Pat Lazarus. Indianapolis/New York: The Bobbs-Merrill Company Inc., 1983.

Natural Pet Food Manufacturers:

"Cornucopia"
Veterinary Nutritional Associates, Ltd.
229 Wall Street
Huntington, NY 11743

The Iams Company
Box 855
Lewisburg, OH 45338

Foods of Nature Pet Food
Jones Manufacturing Company
P.O. Box 1515
Covina, CA 91722

CHAPTER 8: CANINE BEHAVIOR

Doctoral-Level Animal Behaviorists and Veterinarians with Animal Behavior Training Who Specialize in Pet Behavior Problems (listed by state):

CALIFORNIA
Ian Dunbar, Ph.D.
Animal Behavior Clinic
San Francisco SPCA
2500 16th Street
San Francisco, CA 94103

Benjamin C. Hart, DVM, Ph.D.
Lynette A. Hart, Ph.D.
Behavioral Service
Veterinary Medical Teaching Hospital
University of California at Davis
Davis, CA 95616

Richard H. Polsky, Ph.D.
Animal Behavior Counseling Service
11251 Greenlawn Avenue
Culver City, CA 90230

COLORADO
Philip N. Lehner, Ph.D.
Suzanne Arguello, MS
Animal Behavior Associates, Inc.
P.O. Box 8473
Fort Collins, CO 80525

Stephen W. Horn, Ph.D.
Consultants in Animal Behavior
55 Hoyt Street
Lakewood, CO 80226

FLORIDA
Walter F. Burghardt, Jr., DVM, Ph.D.
Behavior Clinic for Animals
447 South Federal Highway
Deerfield Beach, FL 33441

GEORGIA
Sharon Crowell-Davis, DVM, Ph.D.
Teaching Hospital
College of Veterinary Medicine
University of Georgia
Athens, GA 30602

John C. Wright, Ph.D.
P.O. Box 180 MU
Macon, GA 31207

INDIANA
Eric Klinghammer, Ph.D.
Animal Behavior Advisory Service
Battle Ground, IN 47920

MARYLAND
Ginger Hamilton, Ph.D.
Consultants in Animal Psychology
1508 Vivian Court
Silver Springs, MD 20902

MICHIGAN
Eli Barlia, Ph.D.
Hunters Creek Animal Behavior Clinic
P.O. Box 10
Metamora, MI 48455

NEW JERSEY
Perry Frantzman, MBA, Ph.D.
Animal Training and Behavior Center
58 Kinderkamack Road
Emerson, NJ 07630

Joseph G. Griswold, Ph.D.
Dog's Best Friend
Behavior Information Service
P.O. Box 315
Wyckoff, NJ 07481

Daniel J. Tortora, Ph.D.
RemBehCon, Inc.
Pine Hill Kennels
547 West Saddle River Road
Upper Saddle River, NJ 07481

NEW YORK
Peter L. Borchelt, Ph.D.
Animal Behavior Clinic
The Animal Medical Center
510 East 62nd Street
New York, NY 10021

Animal Behavior Consultants, Inc.
108-25 63rd Road
Forest Hills, NY 11375

Kathryn A. Houpt, VMD, Ph.D.
Animal Behavior Clinic
New York State College of Veterinary Medicine
Cornell University
Ithaca, NY 14853

NORTH CAROLINA
Margaret Sery Young, Ph.D.
Donna S. Brown, Ph.D.
School of Veterinary Medicine
North Carolina State University
Raleigh, NC 27606

OHIO
Robert M. Andrysco, Ph.D.
P.O. Box 12410
Columbus, OH 43212

David Hothersall, Ph.D.
David Tuber, Ph.D.
Animal Behavior Associates
1853 Kenny Road
Columbus, OH 43220

PENNSYLVANIA
Victoria L. Voith, DVM, Ph.D.
Animal Behavior Clinic
School of Veterinary Medicine
University of Pennsylvania
Philadelphia, PA 19104

CHAPTER 9: DOGS AS COMPANIONS

Traveling with a Dog:

Pet Express, members Independent Pet and Transportation Association (IPATA)
Pet-relocation experts. Pamphlets on shipping a dog by air domestic/international. Shipping service, flight reservations, boarding, etc.
Write to: Pet Express, P.O. Box 40160, San Francisco, CA 94140

The ASPCA Animalport
24-hour service, 365 days a year. In-transit services. Shipping, pickups, boarding, transfers, veterinary service.
Air Cargo Center, Building 189
Kennedy International Airport
Jamaica, NY 11430
(718) 656-6042

"Touring with Towser"
A guide to 2,000 independent hotels and motels and 4,000 chain locations that will accept dogs. Addresses and telephone numbers included.
Send $1.25 to: Gaines TWT, P.O. Box 8172, Kankakee, IL 60902

"Traveling with Your Pet"
Travel tips and regulations for 177 nations/dependencies and the U.S., plus special tips on containers, etc.
Send $4.00 to: ASPCA Education Dept., 441 East 92nd Street, New York, NY 10028

CHAPTER 10: WHEN A DOG DIES

Books Specifically About the Death of a Pet:

BRISTLE FACE, Zachary Ball. New York: Holiday House Inc., 1962.

CHARLOTTE'S WEB, E. B. White. New York: Harper & Row, 1952. For adults and children, a charming book about a friendship that transcends death.

PET LOSS, Herbert A. Nieburg and Arlene Fischer. New York: Harper & Row, 1982. A guide for adults and older children on dealing with the loss of a pet.

THE TENTH GOOD THING ABOUT BARNEY, Judith Viorst. New York: Atheneum, 1971. How to say good-bye to a departed pet. Simple enough for young children, but effective for anyone.

General Books on Death:

These books have proved helpful to many pet owners, even though not specifically about the death of a dog.

EXPLAINING DEATH TO CHILDREN, Earl Grollman. Boston: Beacon Press, 1967. The advice of specialists from many fields.

ON DEATH AND DYING, Elisabeth Kübler-Ross. New York: Macmillan Publishing Co., Inc., 1969.

HOW TO SURVIVE THE LOSS OF A LOVE, Melba Colgrove, Harold Bloomfield, and Peter McWilliams. New York: Bantam Books Inc., 1977.

THE BEREAVED PARENT, Harriet Sarnoff Schiff. New York: Penguin Books, 1978.

WHEN BAD THINGS HAPPEN TO GOOD PEOPLE, Harold S. Kushner. New York: Schocken Books, 1981.

Index

Note: Photographs and illustrations are designated by *; figures and tables by †.